D1009706

CANCÚN & COZUMEL

GARY CHANDLER & LIZA PRADO

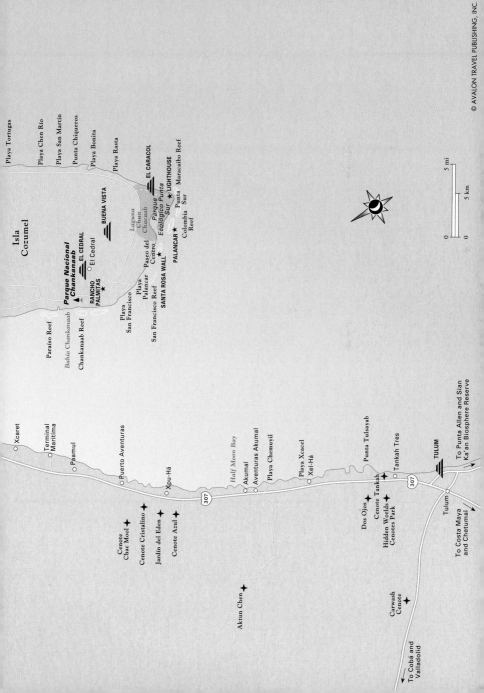

Isla Cozumel

Playa Tortugas
Playa Chen Río
Playa San Martín
Punta Chiqueros
Playa Bonita
Playa Rasta

Parque Nacional Chankanaab

EL CEDRAL
BUENA VISTA
EL CARACOL

El Cedral

Laguna Chan Chaacab

Parque Ecológico Punta Sur
LIGHTHOUSE
Punta Maracaibo Reef
PALANCAR
Colombia Sur Reef

Paseo del Centro
SANTA ROSA WALL

Paraíso Reef
Bahía Chankanaab
Chankanaab Reef
RANCHO PALMITAS

Playa Palancar
Playa San Francisco
San Francisco Reef

Xcaret
Terminal Marítima
Páamul
Puerto Aventuras
Xpu-Há

Half Moon Bay
Akumal
Aventuras Akumal
Playa Chemuyil
Playa Xcacel
Xel-Há

Cenote Chac Mool
Cenote Cristalino
Jardín del Edén
Cenote Azul

Aktun Chen

Punta Tulsayab
Tankah Tres

Dos Ojos
Cenote Tankah
Hidden Worlds Cenotes Park

TULUM

Tulum

To Punta Allen and Sian Ka'an Biosphere Reserve

307

Carwash Cenote

To Costa Maya and Chetumal

To Cobá and Valladolid

0   5 mi
0   5 km

© AVALON TRAVEL PUBLISHING, INC.

DISCOVER
CANCÚN AND COZUMEL

Cancún and Cozumel are places that deserve –
and defy – the many descriptions given to them. Cancún is one of
the most well-known vacation destinations in the world. The name
alone evokes images of endless white-sand beaches, broad turquoise
seas, manicured golf courses, and raucous nightclubs. For scuba
divers, Isla Cozumel is no less mythical, conjuring up dreams of a
pristine coral reef, abundant sealife, and perfect dive after perfect
dive. And the secret is definitely out on the coast stretching south
of Cancún: Known as the Riviera Maya, it includes postcard-perfect
destinations, like Tulum and Playa del Carmen, alongside numerous
family-friendly and eco-minded attractions.

So, how was Cancún? It's a question you definitely will get and
one you might delight in answering. Even before you go it's easy (and
a little fun, to be honest) to imagine how you'll respond: "I spent every

Beaches stretch for miles along Cancún's Zona Hotelera.

day by the pool with a margarita in one hand and a novel in the other, overlooking the most beautiful beach I've ever seen." Or "I went on some incredible dives, took my daughter to an amazing eco-park to swim with dolphins, and ate at a different restaurant every night." Or "I partied until dawn, went skydiving with my buddies, and spent the rest of the time working on my tan." If you're headed to Cancún or Cozumel for any of those reasons, you won't be disappointed.

The region also has a reputation for gaudy commercialism, and nowhere more so than Cancún's Zona Hotelera, which some say is more American than Mexican. Sure enough, you may well hear English more than Spanish, eat at more American chain restaurants than local eateries, and find ATMs that issue greenbacks instead of Mexico's multicolored pesos.

The fact that parts of Cancún and Cozumel are "Americanized"

Divers and snorkelers have been drawn to Cozumel's reefs for decades.

is impossible to deny. But beachgoers and pooh-poohers alike may be surprised to learn that both cities – and the whole region – have rich cultural sides too. Right in Cancún's hotel zone are two small Maya ruins and a terrific folk art museum – one of the best in the region, in fact. And just minutes away is the city's vibrant downtown area, where you can sip an Australian shiraz at a classy wine bar, listen to great live music, and eat tacos in a leafy park without another tourist in sight.

You can spend a whole month in Cancún, taking Spanish classes and living with a local family; Isla Mujeres also has a Spanish school and Playa del Carmen has four. On Isla Cozumel, just beyond its well-touristed shopping zone, is a friendly island community, where old men play dominoes in the late afternoon breeze and kids play *fútbol* in the street. There are large parts of Cozumel that have no roads or power lines, where you can walk for miles along a deserted beach and hear nothing but the birds and the surf.

Inland from Cancún, the city of Valladolid has beautiful colonial architecture, including an impressive church and convent. It also

The one-of-a-kind winged figures at Ek' Balam are well worth a visit.

has a dramatic history, having played a key role in two of Mexico's seminal conflicts, the Mexican Revolution and the Caste War.

Equally unexpected are the variety of natural and ecological attractions in the area, beyond the beautiful beaches and vibrant coral reef. The Riviera Maya is home to the world's longest underground river system, and snorkeling and diving in the caverns is truly an otherworldly experience. There are numerous places for bird-watching, best of all in the Sian Ka'an Biosphere Reserve, a huge expanse of mangrove forests, shallow bays, and freshwater lagoons just south of Tulum. Sian Ka'an is also a world-class fly-fishing destination, as are the bays and channels farther south near the border of Belize; In the open sea, you can hook into any of a dozen different sport fish, including dorado and blue marlin. North of Cancún, Isla Holbox also has mangroves for kayaking, fishing, and bird-watching, but it is better known as a place to snorkel with whale sharks, harmless giants that congregate just off the island's shore for several months every year. At Cobá archaeological site, you can climb the second-highest Maya pyramid,

Far from the bustle of Cancún, you'll find unassuming homes like this one in sleepy fishing villages along the Costa Maya.

and see parrots and toucans, *and* mountain bike through forested paths, all in the same visit.

So what sort of trip will it be? Sunbathing by the pool, diving the cenotes (freshwater sinkholes) and coral reefs, snorkeling with whale sharks, fishing for snook, bird-watching in Sian Ka'an, perusing the museums, or exploring the Maya ruins? Hopefully, you'll do a little of each. Cancún, Cozumel, and the Riviera Maya are places that most people have particular expectations about. Our hope in writing this guidebook is that it will help you meet those expectations and, perhaps more important, show you a side of the Mexican Caribbean that you may not have imagined. That has certainly been our experience, and the reason why we keep returning.

Some of the country's finest hand weaving is sold throughout the region.

Playa Tankah

docks, Isla Mujeres

sea turtles

Contents

MAP
CONTENTS

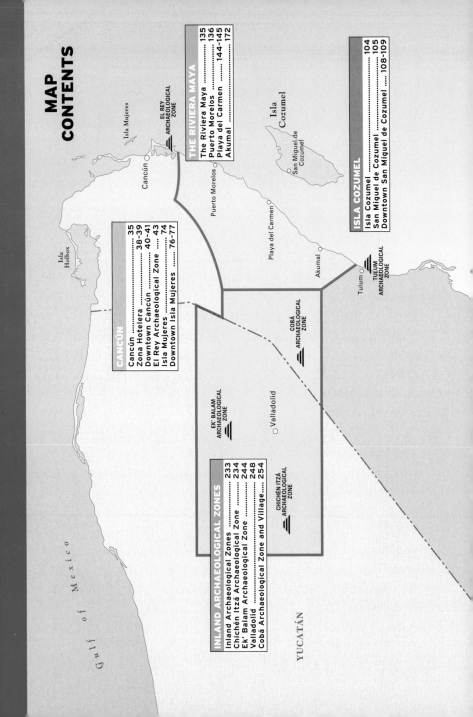

Isla Mujeres

Cancún

EL REY
ARCHAEOLOGICAL
ZONE

Puerto Morelos

Playa del Carmen

Isla
Cozumel

San Miguel de
Cozumel

Akumal

Tulum

TULUM
ARCHAEOLOGICAL
ZONE

Isla
Holbox

EK' BALAM
ARCHAEOLOGICAL
ZONE

Valladolid

COBÁ
ARCHAEOLOGICAL
ZONE

CHICHÉN ITZÁ
ARCHAEOLOGICAL
ZONE

YUCATÁN

Gulf of Mexico

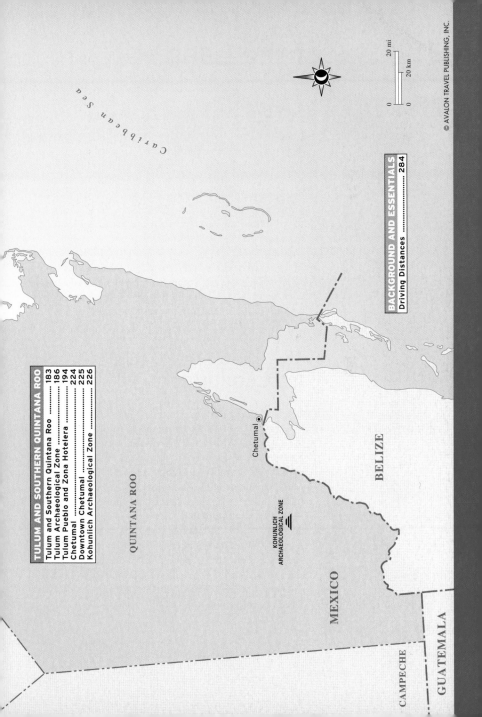

Caribbean Sea

QUINTANA ROO

Chetumal

MEXICO

BELIZE

KOHUNLICH
ARCHAEOLOGICAL ZONE

CAMPECHE

GUATEMALA

20 mi

20 km

© AVALON TRAVEL PUBLISHING, INC.

The Lay of the Land

CANCÚN

Cancún has two parts: the Zona Hotelera (Hotel Zone) and downtown. The **Zona Hotelera** has Cancún's top resorts and nightclubs, and miles of spectacular beaches. It's also quite commercialized—come here for maximum R&R and partying. Cancún's **downtown** area has a surprisingly rich cultural scene, including jazz bars and bohemian cafés. The hotels and restaurants are cheaper, and the beaches are an easy bus or cab ride away.

Isla Mujeres is a long thin island just offshore from Cancún. Everything is mellower here—the people, the nightlife, even the waves. Many come just for the day, but good hotels and a small-town ambiance make it a tempting place to linger for awhile.

Even smaller is **Isla Holbox,** which has sand roads and no cars. The beaches aren't glorious, but the tranquility and isolation more than make up for it.

ISLA COZUMEL

Mexico's largest island and a half-hour ferry ride from Playa del Carmen, Isla Cozumel is a **diving** and **snorkeling** wonderland, with a pristine coral reef and crystal-clear water. With over a hundred dive shops, and an equal number of excellent dive and snorkel sites, it attracts underwater enthusiasts from around the world. But there's more to do than dive: Cozumel has two **eco-parks,** several beach clubs, plus a tournament golf course and world-class **kiteboarding.** Cozumel was an important religious pilgrimage site for the ancient Mayas and there's a fascinating ruin, **El Cedral,** in the middle of the island; on the island's undeveloped eastern side are little-visited beaches with soft sand and dramatic surf. The island's main town has plenty of taxis and car and moped rental agencies, making it easy to explore this diverse island.

THE RIVIERA MAYA

The Riviera Maya is the 130-kilometer-long (80.8 miles) coastal area between Cancún and Tulum. Its biggest city, **Playa del Carmen,** has hotels of all categories, plus great restaurants and shopping, and an active nightlife. However, with a more laid-back atmosphere and fewer large resorts, Playa del Carmen is no Cancún. **Puerto Morelos** and **Akumal** are smaller, but still have ATMs, Internet, and many appealing places to sleep and eat. Along the coast are various private developments, from mega-resorts to modest hotels clustered around a small beach.

The Riviera Maya's best public **beaches** are at Playa del Carmen, Akumal, and **Xpu-Há.** There is terrific snorkeling and diving, not only on the coral reef offshore but in numerous **cenotes** (freshwater sinkholes) that line the inland areas.

Highway 307 runs the length of the Riviera Maya, and can be explored by frequent buses and shuttles, taxi, or rental car.

TULUM AND SOUTHERN QUINTANA ROO

At the southern end of the Riviera Maya, Tulum is famous for its stunning beaches and bungalow-style accommodations. A nearby **Maya ruin** of the same name is perched on a bluff, with a dramatic view of the Caribbean (and a beach of its own). For many, Tulum is Mexico's Caribbean at its best.

Southern Quintana Roo is the least-developed stretch on this coastline. Just south of Tulum, the **Sian Ka'an Biosphere Reserve** is a huge nature reserve with bays, lagoons, and tangled mangrove islands that are not only beautiful but ideal for birding and fly-fishing. Farther south, the isolated area known as the **Costa Maya,** has two small towns with appealingly isolated bed-and-breakfasts and a rather incongruous cruise ship port. **Laguna Bacalar** is a lovely freshwater lagoon a short distance from **Chetumal,** the busy state capital and gateway to Belize.

INLAND ARCHAEOLOGICAL ZONES

The Maya ruins of Chichén Itzá, Ek' Balam, and Cobá are all within easy reach of Cancún and the Riviera Maya.

Chichén Itzá is by far the biggest and most recognizable. Tours to Chichén Itzá leave from Cancún daily, or you can easily visit the site on your own by bus or rental car.

Ek' Balam is a much smaller site, but the home of one of the best-preserved stucco friezes yet uncovered. It is just outside of a tiny indigenous village of the same name.

Cobá's main pyramid is the second highest in the Maya world. The site is nestled in a thick forest near several lagoons—the bird life here is as impressive as the structures themselves.

All three sites can be reached as a day trip from Cancún, albeit a long one. Alternatively, each site has one or more nearby hotels, and the colonial city of **Valladolid** is centrally located and quite charming.

Planning Your Trip

Deciding to visit Cancún, Cozumel, or the Riviera Maya is one thing, and planning your trip is something else altogether. The fact is, for some people a week is all the time they want or need to relax and get a tan, and they would get antsy with any more. For others, a week is barely enough time to settle into the rhythm of a place, let alone do and see everything it has to offer. And of course, the length of any trip or vacation is most often determined by totally separate criteria, like how much time off work you have, how much you care to spend, when the kids have to start soccer camp, etc.

El Castillo, Chichén Itzá

Five to seven days is a good place to start, and the length of time most people come. It's enough to see and do a little of everything: a couple days of pure R&R on the beach or by the pool, a day or two for low-key outings like a beach day at Isla Mujeres or snorkeling on the Riviera Maya, and at least one somewhat more involved excursion, like visiting a Maya ruin, spending the day at an eco-park, or booking a deep-sea fishing trip. With this amount of time, you probably won't switch hotels.

With 10 to 14 days, you can see much more of the region and are sure not to feel rushed. You'll also have time to switch hotels and explore different areas. Of course, dedicate plenty of time—three to five days—of doing not much of anything, whether on the beach or poolside. Definitely take a few days for half-day and full-day excursions, like visiting other beaches, a snorkel trip on the reef, and checking out the eco-parks. After a week, consider switching hotels—if you're in a resort, look for a smaller hotel to spend the balance of your time, if you're on the mainland, take the a ferry to one of the islands for a few days. You also will have time to consider renting a car and taking a multi-day trip inland, or up to Isla Holbox. At least three Maya ruins are within easy reach of Cancún, and with a car you'll appreciate all the more being able to arrive early or stay late.

WHEN TO GO

No matter what you plan to do, you probably wouldn't be coming to the Caribbean if you didn't want good weather, and the likelihood of warm days and cloudless skies is one of the main considerations for most travelers. Many people are genuinely surprised to discover that Cancún and the Riviera Maya have distinct seasons, including several months during which heavy rain and cloud cover are common, and even hurricanes are possible.

Equally important is how much money you're able and willing to spend. The price of many things, especially accommodations, varies dramatically depending on the month and day you visit. Not surprisingly, the best deals are offered when the weather is least reliable. But that doesn't mean you have to trade good weather for reasonable prices; if you're able to visit during the months just before or after the busy season, you have an excellent chance of enjoying good weather and off-peak prices.

Yet another consideration is that some activities can only be done during certain times of the year, like bird-watching or snorkeling with whale sharks. Finally, be mindful of holiday and vacation periods, especially Christmas, Spring Break, July and August (when most of Europe is on vacation) and *Semana Santa* (Holy Week), the week before Easter, and the main vacation period in Mexico. Prices can skyrocket, along with the number of tourists, both foreign and Mexican. That said, if partying is high on your priority list, there is no better time to visit.

So when is the best time to go, all things considered? For most independent, guidebook-toting travelers, the best time to visit Cancún and the Riviera Maya is from mid-January until the beginning of May. The winter rains definitely will have passed (they're supposed to end in November, but can stretch into the new year) yet the summer humidity and high temperatures, which start in May and peak in June and July, have yet to set in. You may get the occasional *norte* (rainy cold fronts from the north) but that's simply the luck of the draw. This period does include Spring Break and *Semana Santa* (the best or worst time to come, depending on your point of view), but otherwise crowds are thinner and prices lower compared to the Christmas and summer periods. September and October see even fewer tourists and lower prices, but that's because it's the heart of hurricane season; the weather is generally rainier and more overcast, even if a big storm doesn't hit. Unfortunately, traveling between January and May means you'll miss the whale sharks In Isla Holbox, which migrate there June–September. If seeing them is a priority, try visiting in July; June is risky as the sharks may come late, August is busy with European travelers, and September may have bad weather.

The first two weeks of December are another pocket of relatively reliable weather, reasonable prices, and relatively light visitation. But expect prices to jump on December 15, like clockwork.

WHAT TO TAKE

Cancún, Cozumel, and Playa del Carmen all have modern stores, supermarkets, and malls, so you don't have to be concerned about not being able to find the basics, and then some. However, this being a vacation destination, prices can be exorbitant, especially on items that shop owners know you can't do without. Sunscreen, bug repellant, billed hats, and bathing suits are the most notable examples—if you think they're pricey at home, the hotel gift shop will leave you floored (and broke!). Cancún and Playa del Carmen have Wal-Marts now, which means somewhat lower prices and better selection than before. It's still best to bring those items from home, however, and a little more than you think you'll need.

A few other items to remember when you're packing: an extra set of contacts or glasses in case the ones you have get lost, broken, or washed away while swimming or snorkeling. Bring a supply of your preferred birth control, condoms, and feminine products—all are readily available in the region (and Mexico in general) but you may have trouble finding the brands you typically use. Same goes for any prescription medications; many people, especially seniors, come to Mexico partly to take advantage of much lower prices on many pharmaceuticals, but you should always bring enough for your whole trip in case what you're looking for isn't available. Also, pharmacists in Mexico receive far less formal training (if any) than elsewhere; be sure you know the exact ingredient and dosage you require, and always double-check that you are getting the correct amount. A travel clock is useful, too, as many hotels don't have reliable wake-up call systems.

Finally, if you plan on visiting the ruins, a good pair of shoes—or at least Teva-style sandals—are essential. Never climb the ruins in flip-flops. The vast majority of accidents and injuries that occur at archaeological sites are from people slipping and falling.

Explore Cancún and Cozumel

THE BEST OF CANCÚN AND THE RIVIERA MAYA

Cancún and the Riviera Maya have many different faces and facets. No trip to Mexico's Caribbean coast would be complete without beaches—this tour gives you plenty of time to enjoy the sand and surf. Below the surface of the water is a whole other world waiting to be explored, and this itinerary also covers that, whether you're a snorkeler or a diver. And just a short distance inland, are charming colonial cities and fascinating Maya ruins, reachable as a day trip or overnight excursion.

Day 1

Arrive in **Cancún.** If you're staying in the Zona Hotelera, head to the beach or the pool after you check in. If you're staying downtown, you can either hop on a bus to the beach or stroll around **Parque las Palapas.**

Day 2

Spend the day on the beach or by the pool. In the Zona Hotelera, you're just steps away from both, complete with lounge chairs and food service. If you need a break from the midday heat, take a quick trip to **La Casa de Arte Popular Mexicano,** a great folk art museum located right in the Zona Hotelera. Those staying downtown can take a bus to one of the public beach areas—**Playa Delfines** has a bus stop right in front and a Maya ruin across the boulevard when you need a change of scenery.

Day 3

Spend a day exploring the **Riviera Maya.** If you've rented a car, you'll be able to visit a couple different places and stop for lunch along the way. By taxi or bus, pick a place with a beach, food, and shopping all relatively nearby, like Playa del Carmen or Akumal. If you like snorkeling, there are plenty of options: **Puerto Morelos, Hidden Worlds,** and **Laguna Yal-Ku** are all great options. Stop for dinner in Playa del Carmen or Puerto Morelos.

Day 4

Leave early to get to the Maya ruins of **Chichén Itzá** before the crowds do. Chichén Itzá is a biggie, and can easily take up a whole day. Or plan to spend just the morning there and have lunch in the charming colonial city of **Valladolid.** From Valladolid, you can go swimming in nearby cenotes, or visit **Ek' Balam,** a much smaller ruin. Both Valladolid and Ek' Balam have good

Ek' Balam

lodging options, if you want to turn this into an overnight trip.

Day 5

Spend this day on either **Isla Mujeres** or **Isla Cozumel.** Both islands are easy to reach by ferry. Divers can plan on enjoying a tank or two, especially at Cozumel. If you prefer snorkeling, trips can be booked at dive shops or on the ferry pier of either island. Definitely think about renting a car or golf cart, too, which allows you time and flexibility to explore beyond the central areas.

Day 6

Spend your last full day on the beach or by the pool again. It's been a busy week!

THE BEST OF ISLA COZUMEL

Isla Cozumel is Mexico's largest island, with much to offer the curious traveler, from Maya ruins to deserted beaches. Of course, Cozumel's claim to fame is its diving and snorkeling, and this tour allots plenty of bubble time. If you prefer to stay on dry land, there is still plenty for you to do and see in Cozumel, though you may find a week to be too much time. No problem—plan on taking the ferry to Playa del Carmen to explore the mainland for a day or two. Borrow a few tips from the *Best of Cancún and the Riviera Maya* itinerary when planning that portion of your trip.

Day 1

Fly straight to **Cozumel.** There are numerous daily flights, including a few non-stops from the United States. This saves you the time and expense of taking a bus or taxi to Playa del Carmen, then a ferry across to Cozumel. Spend the evening strolling around the central park.

formations will whet your underwater appetite, while the shallow profile and mild current will give you a chance to sharpen your buoyancy and finning technique for more challenging dives to come.

Day 4

Take another day for underwater exploration. Talk to your dive guide about Cozumel's myriad dive and snorkel sites, as they can offer very different experiences. If you like drift dives, **Santa Rosa Wall** is hard to beat; for photographers, be sure to check out the dramatic scenery at **Paso de Cedral;** and if you want to up your chances of seeing large animals like sharks and rays, don't miss **Maracaibo.**

Day 5

Rent a car and spend a day exploring the island. Start with breakfast at **Museo de la Isla de Cozumel,** followed by a look at the excellent displays there. Then head to **San Gervasio** archaeological zone, in the middle of the island. Continue on to Cozumel's surprisingly undeveloped east side, where you can enjoy lunch on a deserted beach while watching the waves crash ashore. Plan on returning to town in time for a **night dive,** an incredible experience regardless if this is the 1st or 101st night dive you've been on.

Day 6

Spend the day at one of Cozumel's **eco-parks,** either **Punta Sur** or **Chankanaab,** or take another day to relax on the beach or by the pool. If you're tempted to dive, remember that you need at least 24 hours between your last dive and your flight home—plan accordingly.

Day 2

Spend a day on the **beach** or by the pool. A few of Cozumel's hotels have beaches—the **Intercontinental** has the best of the bunch—otherwise head to a beach club south of town. Some are boisterous, others ideal for quiet relaxation—you're sure to find one that best suits your style. In the evening, spend some time choosing a dive shop, and book a couple days' worth of diving or snorkeling.

Day 3

Revel in Isla Cozumel's richest resource: its marine park and pristine coral reef. **Palancar Reef,** on the island's southwest side, is a good place for your first tank or two. With five sites in one (and suitable for both snorkeling and diving), Palancar's stunning coral

A BEACH LOVER'S GUIDE

If you love beaches, you have come to the right place. But not all beaches were created equal, so we've listed the best beaches in each respective area. Remember that in Mexico all beaches are open to the public (except for ones used by the military). Hotels will often "claim" a section of beach by setting out guest-only beach chairs. However, you are free to lay out your towel and umbrella wherever there's space.

Cancún

Cancún's beaches are in the Zona Hotelera, and are famous for their deep powdery white sand. There are numerous public access points so those staying elsewhere don't have to pass through hotels to get to the beach. Be aware that the surf can be quite heavy.

Playa Chac-Mool is centrally located, and has parasailing and other beach activities. The high-rise hotels behind it cast cooling shadows over the beach in the afternoon.

Playa Delfines is at the southern end of the strip, and the only one not backed by hotels. It has the largest waves of Cancún's beaches—you may even see a few surfers—and there's a small Maya ruin just across the road.

Playa Marlin is near Plaza Kukulcán mall, which has numerous restaurants, shops, and even a bowling alley if you need a break from the sun.

Isla Mujeres

Isla Mujeres's best beaches are located at the northern tip of the island. Unlike Cancún, the beaches here have virtually no surf, making them ideal for families traveling with small children.

Playa Norte has soft white sand and water so shallow and calm you have to wade out nearly 100 meters (328 feet) before it's deep enough to swim. Beach gear can be rented, and there are several oceanfront restaurants.

Playa El Faro is around the corner from Playa Norte and is also quite nice. Larger and nearer to the ferry pier than Playa Norte, it can get crowded with day-trippers from Cancún.

Playa Delfines

Isla Cozumel

Cozumel is better known for its diving than its beaches, but there are a few spots where you can catch some rays. The island's west side has calm seas and several public beach clubs, while the east side has scenic unmanicured beaches and heavy surf.

Playa Palancar is the most low-key of the west-side beaches, with a well-maintained beach area and a restaurant serving tasty meals.

Playa San Francisco is another fine west-side beach, with two large beach clubs. Good if you want a bit more action than the scene at Playa Palancar.

Playa Chen Río is one of several beaches on the east side, but the only one protected from the waves so you can swim. It can get crowded on weekends, but is quite long and a quiet spot always can be found. A lone restaurant serves overpriced meals—do like the locals do and bring a packed lunch.

Isla Holbox

Isla Holbox's **main beach** stretches for several kilometers, and is backed by a low coastal forest and a few bungalow-style hotels. Wind and sand plants make the beach itself only so-so—and the water is more emerald green than the clear blue found elsewhere—but the isolation and peacefulness can't be beat.

Riviera Maya

If you're staying at a resort in the Riviera Maya, you're likely to have a great patch of sand just steps away. But there are plenty of great ones accessible to all travelers.

In Playa del Carmen, **Playa Tukán** is a long swath of blond sand with medium surf. Though increasingly squeezed by resort developments, there's still plenty of free space to set up your own beach blanket. Several beach clubs rent chairs and umbrellas, and offer meal service and even small swimming pools.

South of Playa del Carmen, **Xpu-Há** is easy to miss, but rewards those who find it with a huge white sand beach and mellow surf. There

are fewer services here than elsewhere—and fewer people too—but a couple hotels and restaurants make Xpu-Há a great beach getaway.

Farther south, the town of **Akumal** has a long curving public beach with great snorkeling. Hotel guests can use beach chairs; others should bring a towel and umbrella of their own.

Tulum and Southern Quintana Roo

Many people consider Tulum's beaches to be the best of Mexico's Caribbean coast. It's hard to disagree with white sand, gentle azure surf, and a backing of palm trees and bungalow-style hotels. Southern Quintana Roo doesn't have much to offer the hardcore beachgoer, though the fishing, kayaking, snorkeling, and diving are all stellar.

Tulum's **northern beaches** are easier to reach if you're not staying at one of the hotels, with several public access points and affordable restaurants and beach clubs.

Tulum's **southern beaches** are truly stunning, plucked right from a postcard. Hotel guests have easy access, though non-guests can park beyond the "mini-village" area and walk down the shore. Bring your own supplies, as the beaches here are wonderfully isolated.

Isla Holbox beach

UNDER THE SEA

For all its terrestrial wonders, the Yucatán Peninsula's underwater treasures are no less compelling, including the world's longest underground river system, the second-longest coral reef, and the Western Hemisphere's largest coral atoll. Isla Cozumel, fringed by pristine coral reefs and remarkably clear water, is one of the world's top diving and snorkeling destinations, while Isla Holbox is a favorite feeding ground of manta rays and huge (but harmless) whale sharks. But you need not leave the mainland to appreciate the Yucatán's underwater realm—eerily beautiful cenotes and healthy coral reefs all along the Caribbean coast offer fantastic views and unforgettable experiences and can be enjoyed either on an organized tour or on your own.

Day 1

Arrive in Cancún's International Airport and take a bus or taxi to **Playa del Carmen.** Spend the afternoon at **Playa Tukán**—the white sand and turquoise water will be a welcome sight after hours on a plane. If you don't have your own snorkeling equipment, arrange an extended rental at any of the dive shops in town. You'll want to book a car rental too. Have dinner at one of the eateries along Quinta Avenida.

Day 2

Explore the Riviera Maya—there's great snorkeling on the reefs at **Puerto Morelos,** in the lagoon at **Akumal,** and in the caverns at **Hidden Worlds.** Divers can sign up for a cavern dive at Hidden Worlds, or at any of the shops in Tulum, where underground diving is the specialty.

Day 3

Go cenote-hopping in your rental car. Great options for snorkelers and divers are **Cenote Tankah** in Tankah Tres, **Cenote Azul** and **Cristalina** (both on Highway 307 across from Xpu-Há), and the string of cenotes just west of Tulum on the road to Cobá, including **Car Wash, Kolimba/Kin-Ha, Cenote Grande,** and **Calavera Cenote.**

Day 4

Take the ferry to **Isla Cozumel.** Arrange a snorkeling trip or a set of dives for the next two days. Spend the rest of the day at a beach club

south of town or check out the small town of **San Miguel.**

Day 5

Go on a snorkel or dive trip. Ask to take a break or stop for your surface interval at **Playa Palancar.**

Day 6

Go on another snorkel or dive trip in the morning. **Parque Nacional Chankanaab**

Cozumel ferries

Xcalak beach

and **Parque Ecológico Punta Sur** both offer snorkeling. In the evening, take the ferry back to Playa del Carmen, return the snorkel equipment, and check out the nightlife on **Quinta Avenida.**

Day 7

Head south to **Mahahual** or **Xcalak,** two small towns near the Belize border with fantastic snorkeling and diving right from the shore. Xcalak is the best jumping-off point for **Chinchorro Bank,** a spectacular coral atoll, two-hours away by boat.

Day 8

Spend this day snorkeling from the shore or taking a dive trip, either on the reef or at **Chinchorro.**

Day 9

Head back to **Playa del Carmen** or **Cancún.** Be sure to enjoy your last afternoon on one of its beautiful beaches. Remember, you shouldn't dive for at least 24 hours before flying.

A 10-DAY ECO-ADVENTURE

Lazing on a beach or by the pool is all right, but some travelers crave a little more action. The Riviera Maya has plenty to offer active travelers, including scuba diving, kiteboarding, fly-fishing, kayaking, and bird-watching. This tour is a workout for the eyes, too, taking you to some of the peninsula's most stunning (and little-visited) natural areas, from deserted shores to tangled mangrove forests to limestone caverns filled with the clearest, bluest water you've ever seen. This 10-day tour includes an excursion to Isla Holbox, a windswept island north of Cancún where the Caribbean and the Gulf of Mexico meet. This portion of the tour is best done during whale shark season (June–September); during the rest of the year, you can spend your time on Holbox perfecting your kiteboarding and windsurfing skills, or simply omit the Holbox excursion by flying home on Day 7.

Day 1

Arrive at the airport and head to **Playa del Carmen.** Once you've settled into your hotel, head immediately to the beach—why waste any time? Besides, the afternoon sun is great. In the evening, arrange a diving or snorkeling excursion in Cozumel for the following day.

kel at **Car Wash, Kolimba/Kin-Ha, Cenote Grande,** and **Calavera Cenote** (all just west of Tulum on the road to Cobá). Check into your hotel and relax. In the evening, arrange a kayaking or bird-watching tour in **Sian Ka'an Biosphere Reserve** for the next day, or set up a fly-fishing trip instead.

Day 5

Spend most of the day exploring Sian Ka'an or fishing its waters. When you get back, relax on one of Tulum's white sand beaches—no shame in that!

Day 6

Head back to Playa del Carmen. Along the way, stop at **Hidden Worlds** to try cavern diving or do a little snorkeling at **Casa Cenote** (in Tankah Tres) if you prefer to have the sun on your back. For a real high, take a scenic flight or try skydiving over the Riviera—both can be arranged in Playa del Carmen.

Day 7

Wake up early to drive to Chiquilá. Leave your car in one of the guarded lots and take the ferry to **Isla Holbox**—look for dol-

Day 2

Spend the morning exploring the waters around **Cozumel.** If you have time, check out the **Museo de la Isla de Cozumel**—it has excellent exhibits on the island's wildlife and coral reefs. Head back to Playa del Carmen and spend the late afternoon on the beach. Before dinner, arrange a car rental for the rest of your vacation.

Day 3

Pick up your rental in the morning and head to **Puerto Morelos** for a couple hours of snorkeling. Have lunch at one of the excellent restaurants in town. Do some snorkeling of a different sort in one of the nearby cenotes, including **Jardín del Eden** or **Cristalina** (across from Xpu-Ha). In the evening, window-shop or bar hop on **Quinta Avenida.**

Day 4

Pack up the car and head south toward **Tulum.** On the way there, take a slight detour to snor-

snorkeling

Tulum beach

phins swimming alongside the boat as you cross the channel. Check into a hotel and arrange a tour to go snorkeling with whale sharks the next morning. Spend the rest of the afternoon wandering through the village or beachcombing.

Day 8

Go **snorkeling with whale sharks.** Afterward, spend the afternoon on the beach, or arrange for an evening **kayak tour of** **the mangroves,** where there's great bird-watching.

Day 9

Take the ferry back to Chiquilá and drive back to **Playa del Carmen.** Check into your hotel and return the rental car. Spend the rest of your day on the beach.

Day 10

Fly home.

ROMANTIC GETAWAY TO TULUM

Although a number of places in and around Cancún have the makings of a romantic getaway—picturesque beaches, elegant restaurants, relaxing spas, and cozy accommodations—we picked our favorite for this itinerary: Tulum. The beaches are spectacular, and the cabaña-style hotels exude a quiet romantic charm like nowhere else. Many offer professional massages, facials, and other treatments, while others specialize in gourmet dining.

Day 1

Fly into Cancún, and make your way by bus or taxi straight to **Tulum.** Settle into your beachside bungalow, complete with a hanging bed, mosquito net, and candles. If you want something a little more upscale, consider staying in a suite in one of the chic high-end hotels. Spend the remainder of the day on the beach. Before heading to dinner, book a **couples massage** for the next day at the oceanside spa **Ana y José.**

Day 2

Visit the **Tulum ruins** in the morning before the crowds arrive. Bring your swimsuits to enjoy the small beach there. Afterward, walk or drive to **Playa Paraíso,** just south of the ruins. Eat lunch at the excellent restaurant there and enjoy the rustic windswept beach. Don't forget to go to your massages!

Day 3

Choose between taking an organized ecotour in the **Sian Ka'an Biosphere Reserve, cenote hopping** (four cenotes on the road to Cobá are just minutes away), or just beach-combing on **Tulum's southern beaches.** If you are at a high-end hotel, book a **beachside dinner** for two—complete with candles, flowers, and a personalized menu—before starting your day. If you're looking for something a little more impromptu, consider heading to **Mezzanine** or **Diamante K** for drinks, followed by dinner at **Posada Margherita.**

Day 4

Have breakfast brought to your room and enjoy lingering over it. Spend your last full day on the beach, for maximum relaxation.

Tulum ruins

CANCÚN

Cancún is a big, beautiful, contradictory place. For many people, it is the ultimate vacation destination, with five-star hotels, white sand, impossibly blue waters, and a nightlife that never stops. Others dismiss Cancún as "inauthentic," a place where you can spend a week and never speak Spanish, never convert your dollars into pesos, and never eat at a restaurant you don't recognize from malls back home.

Both perspectives are true, but one-sided. It's hard not to cringe at those loud tourists who don't bother to explore—or even care about—any part of Mexico beyond their beach chairs. Yet those who pooh-pooh Cancún are also selling the city short. Cancún makes no apologies for being a mega-destination, for bending over backward to please travelers, no matter how obtuse. At the same time, Cancún is a working, breathing city with a fascinating history and plenty of "real" Mexican culture: a charming central plaza, friendly hardworking residents, and quesadilla stands you wish you could resist.

Why not take advantage of both sides of Cancún? The beaches and nightclubs will blow your mind—don't miss them! But be sure not to miss out on Cancún's more subtle side, from live music in a bohemian downtown café to munching on corn on the cob sold from a cart on the street.

And when you need to, just get away. A 15-minute ferry ride delivers you to the slow-paced island of Isla Mujeres, a sliver of sand surrounded by breathtaking blue waters. Farther north and even more mellow is Isla Holbox; no cars, no banks, no post office, it's a world away from Cancún, yet reachable in a morning.

© LIZA PRADO

HIGHLIGHTS

((Zona Hotelera Beaches: With deep white sand and impossibly blue water that extends for miles, it's no wonder Cancún's beaches are considered some of the best in the world (page 36).

((La Casa de Arte Popular Mexicano: A small museum with a truly amazing collection of Mexican folk art from around the country (page 43).

((Playa Norte: While away the day on Isla Mujeres' best beach, where soft white sand is gently lapped by a waveless azure sea (page 75).

((Isla Contoy: Go snorkeling, hiking, and bird-watching on a day trip from Isla Mujeres to this protected island preserve (page 78).

((Whale Shark Feeding Grounds: Snorkel alongside the world's biggest fish – up to 9 meters (30 feet) long and weighing in at 10 tons – when they congregate off Isla Holbox June-September (page 94).

LOOK FOR ((TO FIND RECOMMENDED SIGHTS, ACTIVITIES, DINING, AND LODGING.

PLANNING YOUR TIME

A week will do just fine in Cancún, time enough to get your tan on, plus take a day trip or two, like visiting Isla Mujeres or one of the nearby Maya ruins. Ten days gives you time to explore deeper and farther, turning a day trip to Isla Mujeres or the Maya ruins into an overnighter, or venturing north to the remote island of Isla Holbox. Isla Mujeres and Isla Holbox are quite small but wonderfully relaxing; if either is your main destination, budget three or four days to experience them fully, but don't be surprised if you end up staying longer.

Cancún, Isla Mujeres, and Isla Holbox can all be reached and navigated by bus, ferry, taxi, and on foot—no need to rent a car. Same for destinations along the Riviera Maya, although

a car will help you maximize your time there. You should definitely consider getting a rental car, however, to see the Maya ruins near Cancún. Being able to arrive early and visit some of the smaller ruins makes an inland excursion significantly more rewarding.

HISTORY

Cancún is a new city in a new state. In the 1960s, the Mexican government set out to create the next Acapulco; in 1967 a data-crunching computer selected a small, swampy Caribbean island ringed with sparkling white sand as the country's most promising tourist town. The area was a backwater—not even a state yet. Nevertheless, thousands of mangroves were torn out to make room for an international

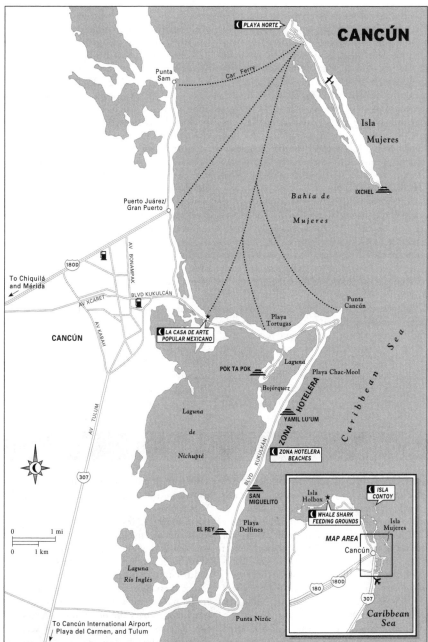

CANCÚN

PLAYA NORTE

Punta Sam

Car Ferry

Isla Mujeres

✝

IXCHEL

Bahía de

Mujeres

Puerto Juárez/
Gran Puerto

AV BONAMPAK

1800

To Chiquilá
and Mérida

AV XCARET

BLVD KUKULCÁN

Punta Cancún

AV KABAH

CANCÚN

LA CASA DE ARTE
POPULAR MEXICANO

Playa Tortugas

Laguna

POK TA POK

Bojórquez

Playa Chac-Mool

Caribbean Sea

ZONA HOTELERA

Laguna

de

Nichupté

YAMIL LU'UM

AV TULUM

ZONA HOTELERA
BEACHES

BLVD KUKULCÁN

307

SAN
MIGUELITO

0   1 mi

0   1 km

EL REY

Playa
Delfines

Laguna
Río Inglés

Punta Nizúc

To Cancún International Airport,
Playa del Carmen, and Tulum

ISLA
CONTOY

Isla
Holbox

WHALE SHARK
FEEDING GROUNDS

Isla
Mujeres

MAP AREA

Cancún

180   1800

307

Caribbean
Sea

© AVALON TRAVEL PUBLISHING, INC.

beach destination, with new infrastructure, electrical plants, purified tap water, and paved avenues lined with trees. A nearby fishing village was expanded to house workers for the new hotels—it is now downtown Cancún and serves much the same purpose. Cancún was officially "opened" in 1974, the same year the territory was elevated to statehood. (The state was named after army general Andrés Quintana Roo, and is pronounced "keen-TA-nah Roh".) Today, it is one of the top beach destinations in the world.

ORIENTATION

Cancún's Zona Hotelera lies on a large narrow island in the shape of a number "7." The southern foot of the "7" is called Punta Nizúc—a few hotels and clubs are there. The bend or corner of the "7" is Punta Cancún—this is the heart of the Zona Hotelera and is crowded with hotels, restaurants, and most of the nightclubs and malls. Between Punta Nizúc and Punta Cancún is the island's long (13 kilometers/ eight miles) "leg," lined with high-end hotels and resorts on the ocean side, and restaurants, clubs, and some water-sport agencies on the other. (The latter overlook Laguna Nichupté, the lagoon formed between the island and the mainland.) Boulevard Kukulcán is the island's busy main drag—it runs the entire length and

care should be taken whenever crossing it as cars and buses race by without seeming to notice the tourists in the crosswalks. Boulevard Kukulcán is marked off by kilometers and most addresses in the Zona Hotelera include a kilometer number (e.g., Boulevard Kukulcán Km. 5.5). There are spectacular beaches up and down the island. Public buses run the length of Boulevard Kukulcán and into downtown Cancún all day and well into the night. Service is cheap and frequent.

Downtown Cancún is on the mainland, near the northwestern tip of the "7." It is divided into various *super manzanas* (square blocks) and most addresses include the particular *super manzana* (e.g., S.M. 4) along with the street name and number. Avenida Tulum is downtown's main throughway. Boulevard Kukulcán intersects Avenida Tulum (and turns into Avenida Cobá) just south of the downtown center—look for a roundabout with huge shells and starfish stood on end. Cancún's bus terminal is a few blocks north of there, at the intersection of Avenida Tulum and Avenida Uxmal. West of Avenida Tulum is a large park (Parque Las Palapas) and beyond that Avenida Yaxchilán. Most of downtown Cancún's hotels, restaurants, and music venues are on or around Parque Las Palapas and Avenida Yaxchilán, primarily in Super Manzanas (S.M.) 22–25.

Sights

◖ ZONA HOTELERA BEACHES

The beaches in Cancún are among the most spectacular in the world. You see postcards of them and you think they must be digitally enhanced—the sand could not be *so* white or the sea *so* aquamarine. But a combination of clear Caribbean water, a shallow sandy seafloor, and a high bright sun make for incredible colors. At high noon, even the postcards don't compare to the living picture show that is Cancún's coastline.

There is a notion that the high-rise hotels have monopolized Cancún's best beaches.

This is only partly true. While most hotels *do* front prime real estate, all beach areas in Mexico are public (except for those used by the military). Hotels cannot, by law, prohibit you or anyone else from lying out on your towel and enjoying the sun and water. Many high-end hotels subvert this by making it difficult or uncomfortable for non-guests to use their beaches: very few maintain exterior paths and others spread guest-only beach chairs over the best parts. (In the hotels' defense, they do a good job of keeping their areas clear of trash and seaweed, which can mar otherwise beautiful beaches.) If your hotel has a nice beach area, you're all set. If not, you can just walk through a hotel lobby to the beach—as a foreigner you are very unlikely to be stopped. (The real shame is that hotel employees seem much more apt to nab locals doing the same thing.) But even that is unnecessary if you don't mind a little extra walking. The city maintains several public access points, marked with large white signs along Boulevard Kukulcán. The area right around the access point is often crowded, but you can walk 100 meters (328 feet) or so to less crowded areas. Also, some fantastic beaches (Playa Delfines, especially) are totally hotel-free and have a refreshing mix of both Mexican and foreign beachgoers.

Be aware that the surf along the Zona Hotelera's long east-facing leg can be heavy. You should pay attention to the colored flags on the beach: green is Safe, yellow is Caution, red is Closed. There are lifeguards near all public access points, but instances of drowning (and near-drowning) do occur occasionally. The beaches along the short north-facing leg are much calmer. For really calm waters head to Isla Mujeres, where the water can be waist deep more than 75 meters (246 feet) from shore. The Laguna Nichupté is not recommended for swimming because of pollution and crocodiles.

Playa Caracol

Playa Caracol (Blvd. Kukulcán Km. 8.5) has a small stretch of beach right at the public access point, but it's not too pleasant and often very crowded. The beach is much better just east of there, in front of the Fiesta Americana Coral Beach. Unfortunately, it's difficult to access without cutting through the hotel.

Playa Chac-Mool

Playa Chac-Mool (Blvd. Kukulcán Km. 10) is the beach you see from Forum by the Sea mall. The beach and water are a bit rocky right at the access point, but wide and beautiful just a few hundred meters south, in front of the Hotel Sierra and Hyatt Cancún Caribe. There

is parasailing here, and the hotels cast afternoon shadows on the beach, in case you forgot your umbrella.

The beach club **Playa Cabana** (tel. 998/848-8380 ext. 113, www.playacabana .com, 10 A.M.–6 P.M. daily, US$10) also is here. Tahiti-esque in style—dark wood cabañas have billowing curtains, queen-size beach loungers, and incredible views of the turquoise sea just a few feet away (US$20 extra). There's a DJ who spins cool tunes, a split-level infinity pool, plus a full bar and restaurant. It's definitely a scene. But then again, it's in the heart of the Zona Hotelera—kind of goes with the territory.

Playa Marlín

Playa Marlín (Blvd. Kukulcán Km. 12.5) is a wide and clean beach. There is parking and Plaza Kukulcán, with a bowling alley and restaurants, is nearby. The public access here is unappealing, through an unused parking lot and past the gutted shell of a former beach club—a victim of Hurricane Wilma. But if

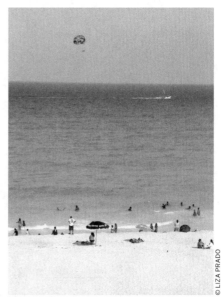

© LIZA PRADO

Playa Delfines is a popular beach for both locals and travelers.

To Isla Mujeres

DETAIL

Punta Cancún
PALOMA BONITA ▼
FIESTA AMERICANA ▼
GRAND CORAL BEACH
DREAMS CANCÚN HOTEL ●
DELI-MART ■
PLAYA CARACOL PIER ■
CONVENTION CENTER ■
BULLDOG CAFÉ ▼
EL MORTERO ▼
THE CITY ▼
COCOBONGO ▼
FORUM BY THE SEA ■
CONDOMINIOS CARISA Y PALMA ●
HOTEL GIRASOL ●
100% NATURAL ▼
9km
FARMACIA DEL AHORRO ■
DADY'O ▼
DADY ROCK ▼
PLAZA CARACOL ■
HOTEL RIU PALACE ■
LAS AMÉRICAS ■
PLAYA CARACOL
FLEA MARKET ■
CORAL NEGRO
SEÑOR FROG'S ▼

C a r i b b e a n

Playa Marlin
RITZ-CARLTON ▼
PUERTO MADERO ▼

☐ ZONA HOTELERA BEACHES

Playa Ballenas
CASA MAGNA MARRIOTT CANCÚN RESORT ●
GRAND MELIÁ CANCÚN ●
LA DOLCE VITA ■
AQUA WORLD ■
SAN MIGUELITO ▲
OASIS CANCÚN ●
LAGUNA GRILL ▼
OMNI CANCÚN HOTEL & VILLAS ●
HILTON CANCÚN BEACH AND GOLF RESORT ●

KUKULCÁN BLVD

Playa Delfines

HILTON CANCÚN GOLF CLUB
EL REY ▲
18km

L a g u n a   d e   N i c h u p t é

HOTEL & MARINA EL MANGLAR ●
WESTIN RESORT & SPA ●
20km
CLUB MED CANCÚN ●

Punta Nizúc

Nizuc Channel

L a g u n a   R í o   I n g l é s

→ To Wet 'n Wild, International Airport, and Playa del Carmen

0   1 mi
0   1 km

© AVALON TRAVEL PUBLISHING, INC.

CANCÚN

DOWNTOWN CANCÚN

MEXICA HOSTEL ●

HOTEL PUNTA ALLEN ●

PUNTA NICCHEHABI   ROSAS
LOS ARCOS ▼
LA PARRILLA ▼
                                    ROSAS
LA TABERNA
YAXCHILÁN ▼
HOTEL MARGARITAS ●

100% NATURAL ▼

HOTEL XBALAMQUÉ/
EL PABÍLO ●

PASTELERÍA ▼
ITALIANA

PERICOS ▼

POST
OFFICE ■

Mercado 28/
Plaza Bonita

TAE KWON DO 28 AND ■
FITNESS CENTER

PESCADO ▼
CON LIMÓN

RESTAURANTE
TAJ MAJAL
▼

PALETERÍA
MONARCA ▼

CHABAL

CHABAL

PIÑA

LOS GIRASOLES ●

Plaza Las
Avenidas

0   100 yds

0   100 m

To Baseball
Stadium

To Casa de la
Cultura de Cancún

CANCÚN

© AVALON TRAVEL PUBLISHING, INC.

© LIZA PRADO

Maya ruins and high-rise hotels stand side-by-side in the Zona Hotelera.

you can ignore that, the beach itself is as glorious as everywhere else.

Playa Ballenas

Playa Ballenas (Blvd. Kukulcán Km. 14.5) is yet another wide and gorgeous beach. A kiosk right near the entrance rents personal watercraft and boogie boards and offers parasailing and banana boats. As at other beaches, walk a little way in either direction to get away from the crowds. There is no food or drink service here. Parking is at the entrance.

Playa Delfines

Playa Delfines (Blvd. Kukulcán Km. 17.5) is our favorite, if we had to pick. The access path is on a bluff, affording a panoramic view of the beach and water, unobstructed by hotels. There's a mix of tourists and local families, and you may see surfers. (The waves can be strong here—take care swimming.) The beach is also just across the road from Ruínas El Rey, which makes a nice side trip. There is no food or drink service here. Parking is at the entrance.

ARCHAEOLOGICAL ZONES

Cancún has two archaeological sites, both in the Zona Hotelera. Both are minor compared to the big sites spread throughout the Yucatán Peninsula, but they are still worth visiting and can be easily combined with a day at the beach.

El Rey Archaeological Zone

Just across from Playa Delfines, Ruínas El Rey (Blvd. Kukulcán Km. 17.5, 8 A.M.–5 P.M. daily, US$3, use of video camera US$3) consist of several platforms, two plazas, and a small temple and pyramid, all arranged along an ancient 500-meter (1,640-foot) roadway. The ruins get their name (Ruins of the King) from a skeleton found during excavation and believed to be that of a king. The ruins date from the late Postclassic period (A.D. 1200–1400); various plaques give explanations in English, Spanish, and Maya. One curious note—the ruins are home to literally hundreds of iguanas, some quite beefy, which make a visit here all the more interesting.

CANCÚN

EL REY ARCHAEOLOGICAL ZONE

STRUCTURE 7

To Entrance

STRUCTURE 1

STRUCTURE 2

STRUCTURE 5

STRUCTURE 3

STRUCTURE 4

SCALE NOT AVAILABLE

© AVALON TRAVEL PUBLISHING, INC.

Yamil Lu'um Archaeological Zone

Lodged between the Westin Laguna Mar and the Park Royal Pirámides, Yamil Lu'um (Blvd. Kukulcán Km. 12.5, free) consists of two small temples that were built between A.D. 1200 and 1550: the **Templo del Alacrán** (Temple of the Scorpion), owing its name to the remains of a scorpion sculpture on one of its walls, and the **Templo de la Huella** (Temple of the Handprint), named so because of a handprint in the stucco. Unfortunately, neither the scorpion sculpture nor the handprint is visible these days. The ruins are well above the beach on Cancún's highest point, suggesting that the two small temples were used as watchtowers, lighthouses, and navigational aids. To see the ruins, go to the concierge at either the Westin or the Park Royal Pirámides and ask if you can walk through to the site. If you are refused, head to Playa Marlín—at the very least, you can see them from afar.

◖ LA CASA DE ARTE POPULAR MEXICANO

If you have any doubts about the genius of Mexican art, put them permanently to rest at La Casa de Arte Popular Mexicano (El Embarcadero, Blvd. Kukulcán Km. 4, tel. 998/849-4332, 9 A.M.–7 P.M. Mon.–Fri. and 11 A.M.–7 P.M. Sat.–Sun, US$5). This small museum brims with folk art from around Mexico, including fantastic masks, intricate nativity scenes, and truly remarkable *árboles de vida* (trees of life)—large hand-painted clay pieces that defy description. If there's a flaw, it's that the curators try to display too much, and the smallish space can feel cluttered. Fortunately, a free audio tour, available in English or Spanish, literally guides you step-by-step through the museum, while explaining the techniques and stories behind many of the pieces. Surprisingly little-known, even here in Cancún, this is one of the most comprehensive displays of its kind in the country.

PARQUE LAS PALAPAS

Parque Las Palapas is a classic Mexican plaza—complete with shade trees, quesadilla stands, and little girls running around in frilly dresses and big sneakers. It's the place where locals come to take a break from the heat, to gossip with their friends, and to listen to the local teenagers playing their guitars. On weekends, artisans set up tables to sell their creations and the merry-go-round across the street lights up.

At the corners of Parque Las Palapas are two smaller parks also worth checking out. **Parque**

Los Artesanos is a young bohemian hangout, with disaffected young artists who fill the small park with their bongo drum jam sessions, and on weekend evenings, with their beautiful handmade clothes, jewelry, and art. **Jardín del Arte** is a space reserved for art expositions (artwork is displayed under a series of stationary white umbrellas) and concerts on its small stage. Some of downtown's best restaurants and hotels are situated here or on nearby Avenida Yaxchilán as well.

The park could certainly use some renovation: First the band shell's huge *palapa* roof burned down, then Hurricane Wilma damaged the already aging sidewalks and common squares. Oddly, the city seems in no hurry to make the needed repairs, and the park has lost some of its former charm and ambiance. It's still worth a visit, and with any luck Parque Las Palapas will be back in shape when you do.

SCENIC VIEWS

In case you got stuck with the aisle seat on your flight here, **La Torre Escénica** (Scenic Tower, El Embarcadero, Blvd. Kukulcán Km. 4, 9 A.M.–10 P.M. daily, US$9) is an 80-meter (262.5-foot) tower with a rotating passenger cabin, affording a good 10-minute view of this part of the coastline. Audio description is available in Spanish, English, German, and French.

Entertainment and Events

Cancún is justly famous for its nightlife, with a dozen or more world-class clubs throbbing with music of all sorts and filled with revelers of all ages and nationalities every single night of the week. The partying is especially manic during spring break, summer, Christmas, and New Year's Eve. The city also offers a good mix of small music venues, theaters and cultural centers, bars, and cinemas.

LIVE MUSIC

As the name suggests, **Hard Rock Cafe** (Forum by the Sea mall, Blvd. Kukulcán Km. 9, tel.

998/881-2020, 11 A.M.–2 A.M. daily) is the place to go for live rock. Bands play at 10 P.M. every night except Sunday when the tunes start at 9 P.M.

For soft jazz, head to **Cassis Jazz Bar** (Hyatt Cancún Caribe Resort, Blvd. Kukulcán Km. 10.5, 998/884-7800 ext. 7270) a chic lounge bar where musicians serenade guests from 6 P.M.–1 A.M. every night.

A lively jazz and blues joint, **Roots Jazz Club** (Tulipanes 26, tel. 998/884-2437, 6 P.M.–1 A.M. Tues.–Sat.) is arguably the best music venue in town. Get there early for a quality dinner and—almost more importantly—a seat near the small stage. Music starts at around 10 P.M. and a US$3–5 cover may apply.

El Pabilo (Hotel Xbalamqué, Av. Yaxchilán 31, tel. 998/892-4553, 8 A.M.–midnight daily, free) is a small artsy café with great live music Monday–Saturday. Music featured includes *bohemia cubana,* fusion jazz, classical guitar, and flamenco. Shows start at 9 P.M.

At the corner of Parque Las Palapas, **El Rincón del Vino** (Alcatraces 29, tel. 998/898-3187, 6 P.M.–1 A.M. Mon.–Sat.) is a lively wine bar that carries labels from all over the world, including Mexico, Chile, South Africa, Italy, Spain, and the United States (US$5–7/glass). The friendly staff can provide recommendations, and a short menu of baguettes, salads, and tapas help keep you thirsty. Live music, usually a guitar soloist, begins at 9:30 P.M. every night but Sunday and Monday.

For bongo drum jam sessions, wandering guitarists, and other street musicians, head to **Parque Las Palapas** on weekend evenings where you're likely to catch one or all of these performers.

PERFORMING ARTS

Teatro Cancún (El Embarcadero, Blvd. Kukulcán Km. 4, 998/849-5580, ticket office on ground level open 11 A.M.–7 P.M. Mon.–Sat., cash only) stages shows by a variety of performers, from dance schools to professional musicians, several times a year. The theater is large and has some interesting murals, though overall it's a bit auditorium-like. Ticket prices vary depending on the event, but range US$10–25.

For *ballet folklórico* (traditional dances from around Mexico) head to **La Joya** restaurant at the Fiesta Americana Coral Beach for colorful live performances (7:30 P.M. Tue., Thu., Fri., and Sat., US$5).

Casa de la Cultura de Cancún (Av. Yaxchilán s/n, S.M. 21, 998/884-8364, casaculturacancun@prodigy.net.mx) is a state-funded institute that offers an incredible gamut of artistic workshops, performances, and expositions (free–US$3.50). While the institute has an ever-changing schedule, which often includes dance, dramatic, and visual art presentations, some events are fixed: Monday is movie night, with films falling into a monthly theme (8 P.M., US$2); Tuesday is open-mike night, when artists are invited to share their poetic, musical, and story-telling talents (8 P.M.); on Thursdays a live concert—varying from folk to classical—is presented (8:30 P.M., US$5); and Saturday mornings are dedicated to children in what is called "Sábados de Minicultura" with offerings including puppet shows, educational movies, and theater (no admission fee). Be sure to call for weekly listings, as the calendar is packed with programming.

DISCOTHEQUES AND BARS

Most of Cancún's biggest, most popular nightclubs are near the Forum by the Sea mall in the **Zona Hotelera,** with a few a bit farther afield. Each club has a different "on" night—Monday is Dady-O, Tuesday is Fat Tuesday, etc. These don't seem to change much, but definitely ask around before buying your tickets. Dress code is casual but don't wear flip-flops, Tevas, or bathing suits (unless, of course, it's Speedo Night).

Some hotels organize clubbing trips—this may seem lame, but it can mean priority admission, reserved tables inside, and a shuttle there (but typically not back). And the organizers head to the same nightly hotspots you're probably looking for anyway. **Downtown** venues are definitely on the quieter side, lacking the bells and whistles you'll find in the Zona Hotelera.

BULLFIGHTS

If you're curious about bullfighting, head to Cancún's **Plaza de Toros** (Av. Bonampak at Sayíl, tel. 998/884-8372, US$33, children under 6 free) where every Wednesday at 3:30 P.M. you can get a glimpse of what makes this sport so popular in Latin America. Cancún's bullfights differ from traditional *corridas* (runnings) in that only four bulls are fought (versus five or six) and a mini-*charrería* (rodeo) and a *ballet folklórico* performance are also

PARTYING IN CANCÚN

Travelers flock to Cancún as much for its vibrant nightlife as for its white sand beaches. Hands down, it's the hottest – and some say, wildest – scene on the Riviera.

ZONA HOTELERA

Dady-O (Blvd. Kukulcán Km 9.5, tel. 998/883-1626, www.dadyo.com.mx, 10 P.M.-6 A.M. nightly, US$16 cover, US$37 with open bar and entrance to both Dady-O and Dady Rock) is, well, the daddy of Cancún's nightclubs, with seven different "environments," including CO_2 blasts, laser shows, and theme parties on several different levels.

Next door, **Dady Rock** (Blvd. Kukulcán Km 9.5, tel. 998/883-1626, 6 P.M.-4 A.M. nightly, US$16 cover, US$37 with open bar and entrance to both Dady-O and Dady Rock) is technically a restaurant and bar – there is no dance floor – but popular rock music, sometimes live, has partiers dancing every place possible, including on the bar. Dady Rock also hosts some contests: "Hot Male," "Hot Legs," "Wet Body," etc. (Gary was the runner-up – again – in the "Hot Legs" contest.)

Bulldog Cafè (Blvd. Kukulcán Km 9.5, tel. 998/848-9850, www.bulldogcafe.com, 10 P.M.-6 A.M. daily high season, Fri.-Sat. only in low season, US$20 cover, US$40 with open bar high season, US$30 low season), features hip-hop, rock, and Latin dance music. Friday and Saturday are the big nights. Five enormous bars and a private VIP lounge with a whirlpool tub are the highlights.

The City (Blvd. Kukulcán Km 9, tel. 998/848-8380, www.thecitycancun.com, 10 A.M.-6 P.M. daily, beach club US$10, 10 P.M.-5 A.M. daily, nightclub US$30 cover with open bar, no cover Mon.-Tues., women drink free Wed. and Sun.) is a mega-club with a total capacity of 15,000. During the day, you can hang out at its beach club, **Playa Cabaña,** with its split-level infinity pool, queen-size lounge chairs, and DJed tunes (see *Playa Chac-Mool*). At night, party inside, with your eyes on the cinema-size screen, and under what's claimed to be the biggest disco ball in the world (it's pretty big). Be sure to break loose on the movable dance floor, which travels from the third floor to the center of the club below.

CocoBongo (Blvd. Kukulcán Km. 9, tel. 998/883-5061, www.cocobongo.com.mx,

---

held. Because of this, you won't see bullfighting aficionados here—which changes the experience dramatically—but it's a good cultural sampler. Tickets are available at the box office or through most travel agencies in Cancún.

PROFESSIONAL BASEBALL

Baseball is huge in Mexico, particularly in the north, where you'll see as many baseball diamonds as you will soccer fields. While still not having the pull in the Yucatán as it does elsewhere, it is a sport on the rise. The local team **Los Langosteros** (The Lobstermen) are one of the 18 teams that make up Mexico's professional baseball league, the Liga Mexicana de Beisbol. You can catch a game from the beginning of March through the end of June at the **Estadio Beto Avilá** (Avenida Xcaret s/n, behind Wal-Mart, US$2–7), which was remodeled in 2007.

FESTIVALS

Held annually since 1991, the **Cancún Jazz Festival** is a weeklong event held in mid- to late May, drawing top jazz musicians from around the world. This is a huge crowd-drawing event so be sure to reserve tickets early. Prices and venues vary—ask your hotel concierge or call the city's tourist information office for details.

CINEMA

Cancun has several major movie theaters, all offering the latest American and Mexican releases. Make sure you see *subtitulada* after the listed titles unless, of course, you want to hear Arnold Schwarzenegger dubbed. Also, if you can, go on a Wednesday, when most movie theaters throughout the country feature discounted ticket prices.

Cinemark (La Isla Shopping Village, 2nd

US$40 with open bar, US$45 Fri.-Sat., 10 P.M.-4 A.M. daily) is a spectacular club featuring live rock and salsa bands, flying acrobats, and rotating impersonator shows of The Mask, Beetle Juice, Madonna, and Spiderman. Not only will you see them on stage, but you'll also find them on the bar and swinging in the air. Movie clips are also projected onto huge high-tech screens.

Old standbys **Carlos'n Charlie's** (Forum by the Sea mall, Blvd. Kukulcán Km. 9, tel. 998/883-1862) and **Señor Frog's** (Blvd. Kukulcán Km. 9.5, tel. 998/883-3454) both open at noon for meals and stay open until 2 A.M. for drinking, dancing, and general mayhem.

If you're looking for a sports bar, a popular one is **Champions** (Marriott Casa Magna, Blvd. Kukulcán Km. 14.5, tel. 998/881-2000, 5 P.M.-2 A.M. daily). It's got 40 screens, including a giant wide-screen TV, which play nonstop live sports. A few pool tables and a DJ also add to the mix.

DOWNTOWN CANCÚN

Located inside Plaza Las Américas, **Mambo-café** (Av. Tulum at Av. Sayil, tel. 998/887-7891, www.mambocafe.com.mx, 10 P.M.-4 A.M. Wed.-Sun., cover US$4-5, free some nights) is one of the hottest spots in the downtown Cancún scene. Popular with locals and expats, you'll be assured of spinning to the sounds of salsa, *cumbia*, and merengue.

La Taberna Yaxchilán (Av. Yaxchilán 23, tel. 998/887-5433, 1 P.M.-6 A.M. daily) is a game-themed bar with pool tables, darts, dominoes, cards, backgammon, chess...more games than you probably saw at your last sleepover. Excellent two-for-one drink specials typically run 6 P.M.-9 P.M. and again 2 A.M.-4 A.M. The only real downside of the place is the cloud of cigarette smoke – prepare to inhale lots of it whether you're puffing or not.

Across the street, **Los Arcos** (Av. Yaxchilán 57, 10 A.M.-3 A.M. daily) doesn't do much business as a restaurant – La Parilla a few doors down is better – but it gets packed at night with a young mix of locals and tourists. At last check, national beers were two-for-one all day and night.

Fl., Blvd. Kukulcán Km. 12.5, tel. 998/883-5604, US$4.50 general, US$3 matinee, US$2 Wed.) has five screens showing fairly recent Hollywood films, plus a Mexican or Latin American option now and again.

In Plaza Las Américas, **Cinépolis** (Av. Tulum at Av. Sayil, 1st Fl., tel. 998/884-0403, US$4.50 general, US$3-4 matinee, US$2 Wed.) is a popular choice among locals.

Upstairs, treat yourself to a first-class movie experience at **Cinépolis VIP** (Plaza Las Américas, Av. Tulum at Av. Sayil, 2nd Fl., tel. 998/884-4056, US$7 general, US$5-6 matinee, US$5 Wed.). Inside you'll find overstuffed leather seats with extra leg room, side tables for your munchies, and waiters who will bring you sushi, crepes, gourmet baguettes, cappuccinos, cocktails and—oh, yeah—buttered popcorn too.

Shopping

With five major malls, several smaller ones, and hundreds of independent shops, you can buy just about anything in Cancún. The malls are large, modern, and busy, with name-brand clothes, jewelry and watches, movies, arcades, bowling, aquariums, and a full range of restaurants. The malls also have T-shirts, souvenirs, and handicrafts, but you may find better prices at **Flea Market Coral Negro** (Zona Hotelera, across from Forum by the Sea, 8 A.M.–midnight daily) or **Mercado Ki-Huic** (downtown, Av. Tulum at Av. Cobá, 9 A.M.–9 P.M. Mon.–Sat., 10 A.M.–8 P.M. Sun.), both easy to reach by bus or on foot. There are many more shops north of Ki-Huic on Avenida Tulum (the other side of the street is best) and a couple of open-air markets are nearby. Most mall and independent shops accept credit cards, but plan on paying in cash at the markets.

OPEN-AIR MARKETS

Mercado 28 (Av. Sunyaxchen at Av. Xel-Ha, 9 A.M.– 8 P.M. daily) is a large open-air market featuring a wide variety of Mexican handicrafts: ceramics from Tonalá, silver from Taxco, hammocks from Mérida, *alebrijes* (wooden creatures) from Oaxaca, hand-woven shirts from Chiapas. You'll also find a fair share of T-shirts, key chains, coconut monkeys, and women offering to braid your hair. Basically, you'll find a little of everything. If you're hungry, head toward the center of the complex, where a handful of restaurants offer traditional Mexican fare.

On weekend evenings, stroll through **Parque Las Palapas** and **Parque Los Artesanos,** both great spots to pick up local handicrafts, Chiapanecan clothing, bohemian jewelry, and art.

Since 2001, the **Concurso Municipal de Artesanías,** a city-wide handicraft competition, has been held annually the first week in November in Cancún's Palacio Municipal. In addition to showcasing the city's best artisans, many participants also sell their work just in front of the building. Look for the large white tents—and the crowds—on Avenida Tulum.

ARTESANÍA

Next to Mercado 28, **Plaza Bonita** (Av. Sunyaxchen at Av. Xel-Ha, 9 A.M.–8 P.M. daily) is a multileveled shopping center built to look like a colonial village—bright courtyards, fountains, greenery, and all. Items are a little more expensive than those found in the market next door, but the quality is almost always better.

In the Zona Hotelera, the gift shop at **La Casa de Arte Popular Mexicano** (El Embarcadero, Blvd. Kukulcán Km. 4, tel. 998/849-4332, 9 A.M.–7 P.M. Mon.–Fri. and 11 A.M.–7 P.M. Sat.–Sun,) has a quality—and pricey—selection of authentic Mexican folk art from around the country. If you can get past the price tag, the challenge becomes getting the stuff home in one piece!

BOOKSTORES

For a serious bookstore, head to Alma Libre books in Puerto Morelos (see *Riviera Maya* chapter), which has 20,000 titles in numerous languages. In Cancún, your best bet is **Librería La Surtida** (Av. Tulum directly across from Palacio Municipal, tel. 998/887-1428, 9 A.M.–10 P.M. daily) which has one shelf of English-language guidebooks to the Yucatán Peninsula, Central America and Cuba, plus a number of maps and Spanish phrasebooks. The prices are jaw-dropping—US$35–50!—but the store does a decent job of stocking at least one copy of the most relevant titles. You can also get a copy of *USA Today* for the bargain price of US$3.50.

MALLS

Plaza Caracol (Blvd. Kukulcán Km. 8.5, tel. 998/883-1038, www.caracolplaza.com, 8 A.M.–10 P.M. daily) is a modern mall with narrow, winding corridors that somehow never lead you out, kind of like a Vegas casino without the gambling. Shops mostly sell clothing and kitschy souvenirs and the main food court fails to inspire. At best, it's an option on a rainy day.

Forum by the Sea (Blvd. Kukulcán Km. 9, tel. 998/883-4425, www.forumbythesea.com .mx, 10 A.M.–11:30 P.M. daily) is a doughnut-shaped building with its three floors opening onto the airy main lobby. The stores offer mid- to high-end goods varying from nice T-shirts to expensive jewelry. The best reason to come, however, is the spectacular view of the Caribbean from the third-floor balcony, which has tables and chairs set up for food court customers. The view is so good, you almost forget you're in a mall.

La Isla Shopping Village (Blvd. Kukulcán Km. 12.5, tel. 998/883-5025, www.laislacancun .com.mx, 9 A.M.–8 P.M. daily) is the most pleasant of the Zona Hotelera malls, and the only one set outdoors. Arranged around an artificial river, it has wide airy passageways and plenty of genuinely good shops and restaurants. There

are also the popular Interactive Aquarium and a five-screen movie theater.

Plaza Kukulcán (Blvd. Kukulcán Km. 12.5, just past La Destilería, tel. 998/885-2200, www.kukulcanplaza.com, 9 A.M.–10 P.M. daily) underwent extensive renovation in 2005 and is now anchored by Maraf Jewelry and a handful of upscale shops dubbed "Luxury Avenue." Some usual suspects can also be found here, including Señor Frog's, Sunglass Island, MixUp music store, and a Sergio Bustamante gallery. Ruth's Chris Steak House is on the 1st floor and an innovative bar/bowling alley is on the 2nd floor.

You don't have to go to the Zona Hotelera for your mall fix. **Plaza Las Américas** (Av. Tulum at Av. Sayil, tel. 998/887-4839, 9 A.M.–midnight daily) stretches almost a block and includes dozens of mid- to upscale shops, a discotheque, and two movie theaters. Unlike the Zona Hotelera, here you'll be among mostly Mexican shoppers.

Sports and Recreation

While relaxing by the pool or on the beach is more than enough sports and recreation for many of Cancún's visitors—and who can blame them?—there *are* a number of options for those looking for a bit more action. From golf and fishing to scuba diving and kiteboarding (and a whole bunch of things in between), Cancún has something for everyone.

BEACH ACTIVITIES

Parasailing (*paracaídas* in Spanish) is that classic beach thrill ride in which you don a parachute and are pulled behind a boat to a dizzying height. If you do it only once, do it in Cancún for views of the endless white beaches and impossibly turquoise sea. You can choose a traditional one-person ride (with takeoff from the shore) or a two-person ride, in which you sit in a small raft and take off from the boat or the water. Price and duration are fairly uniform: US$45–55 per person for a 10- to

12-minute ride. Look for independent operators at most public beaches, especially **Playa Ballenas** (Blvd. Kukulcán Km. 14.5, Cancún Palace Hotel), **Playa Chac-Mool** (Blvd. Kukulcán Km. 10, near the Hotel Sierra), and **Playa Delfines** (Blvd. Kukulcán Km. 17.5, near the Hilton) roughly 10 A.M.–6 P.M. daily. Or sign up at friendly **Solo Buceo** or **Aqua World** (Blvd. Kukulcán Km. 15.2, tel. 998/848-8300, www.aquaworld.com.mx), both of which offer many other activities as well.

Personal watercraft (aka wave runners) are rented at various places along the beach, including all the same places that offer parasailing. Prices are US$50 for 30 minutes or US$90 for an hour; one or two people can ride at a time. **Banana boats** (those big yellow rafts pulled behind a motorboat) are somewhat less common but are definitely available at Playa Ballenas. The cost there is US$20 per person for a 20-minute ride.

SNORKELING AND SCUBA DIVING

For experienced snorkelers and divers, Cancún proper is less interesting than Isla Mujeres and doesn't even compare to Cozumel. Cancún's sandy seafloor simply doesn't have the coral and rock formations that make for great underwater excursions. Where there are large reefs, as at Punta Nizúc, neglect and heavy boat traffic have left much of the coral dead. If you're aching for a fix, there are a few good sites, including a ship intentionally sunk 24 meters (80 feet) down. Most local shops also offer diving and snorkeling trips to Cozumel and the cenotes—inland freshwater sinkholes south of Cancún offering superb cavern and cave diving.

For the best **open-water snorkeling,** talk to a scuba diving shop. All those listed here offer guided snorkeling trips, and are invariably better than the ubiquitous "jungle trips" hawked around Cancún, even for beginners. For something different altogether, arrange a **cenote snorkeling** trip. The water is unbelievably clear and swimming through and among the cave formations is otherworldly. Perhaps the best introduction to cenotes is at Hidden Worlds Cenote Park, which offers several guided trips daily through its own cenote system just north of Tulum.

For **diving,** a number of shops offer fun dives as well as certification courses at all levels. Again, the diving in Cancún is okay for a quick fix on a tight schedule, but you'll find better conditions and smaller groups just about anywhere else on the Riviera Maya or Isla Cozumel.

Solo Buceo (Dreams Cancún Hotel, Blvd. Kukulkán Km. 9.5, tel. 998/883-3979, www .solobuceo.com, 9 A.M.–4:30 P.M. daily) is a friendly shop at the Dreams Cancún hotel with a strong reputation for service, and where most dives are led by instructors rather than dive masters. Two-tank reef dives run US$70, while two-tank Cozumel or cenote trips cost US$145, including lunch; prices include all gear except a wetsuit (US$10, recommended for cenote trips). Open-water certification classes (US$370, 2–4 days) can also be arranged. Despite its name, Solo Buceo offers more than "only diving," including snorkeling, parasailing, and Hobie Cat rides.

Scuba Cancún (Playa Langosta, Blvd. Kukulcán Km. 4.5) tel. 998/849-4736, www .scubacancun.com.mx, 7 A.M.–8 P.M. daily) is one of Cancún's oldest dive shops, founded in 1980 and still run by the same family. It offers the standard selection of dives, including one-tank (US$54), two-tank (US$68), night (US$56; Thurs. only), and two-tank cavern and Cozumel dives (US$135, including lunch); all prices include equipment. Snorkel trips are offered in Cancún (2 P.M. daily, US$29) and Cozumel (US$95). This is a popular shop and dives can sometimes get crowded—ask ahead.

Aqua World (Blvd. Kukulcán Km. 15.2, tel. 998/848-8300, www.aquaworld.com.mx) is Cancún's biggest, most commercialized water sports outfit, of which scuba diving is only a small part. Come here if you are looking for activities for the whole family, divers and non-divers alike, all in one spot. Otherwise, head to smaller shops for more personal attention.

Many hotels are affiliated with independent shops that cater exclusively to guests there. Ask your concierge if that's the case at the hotel you're in.

WIND SPORTS

Ikarus Kiteboarding School (tel. 984/803-3490, www.kiteboardmexico.com) is based in Playa del Carmen but opened a new kiteboarding camp at Isla Blanca, a huge saltwater lagoon north of Cancún. Conditions for learning to kiteboard don't get much better than this: steady wind, kilometers of flat water with few boats or other obstacles, and the water's never more than waist deep. Private classes are US$75 an hour, while groups are US$45–55 an hour per person (maximum three to a group). Most first-timers need 3–6 hours of instruction to learn the basics.

Solo Buceo offers one-hour Hobie Cat sailboat trips for US$50 (up to four people).

WATERSKIING, WAKEBOARDING, AND SURFING

Waterski Cancún and Wakeboard (Marina Manglar, Blvd. Kukulcán Km. 20, cell tel. 044-998/874-4816, toll-free USA tel. 800/697-1517, www.waterskicancun.com) has three slalom courses and a number of ski sites at the far southern end of Laguna de Nichupté and the Zona Hotelera, opposite the Sun Palace Resort. Free skiing and wakeboarding cost US$120 an hour, while the slalom course is US$40 for six runs.

The **Asociación de Surf de Quintana Roo** (Quintana Roo Surf Association, Blvd. Kukulcán Km. 13, tel. 998/847-7006, surf-cancunmex@hotmail.com) offers surf classes and rentals and hosts occasional surf competitions. The group has a kiosk on Playa Delfines, which is generally the best surf beach.

SWIMMING WITH DOLPHINS

The **Interactive Aquarium** (Plaza La Isla, Blvd. Kukulcán Km. 12.5, tel. 998/883-0411, toll-free Mex. tel. 800/812-0856, 9 A.M.–7 P.M. daily, adults US$13, children US$10) has a disappointingly small display of fish and other sea creatures, but its main raison d'être are the interactive dolphin and shark exhibits. A 20-minute dolphin show is held daily at 6 and 7 P.M. (free with admission) and definitely makes a visit here more worthwhile. Interactive programs for kids and adults range from petting and swimming with the dolphins (US$66–130) to being "trainer for a day" (US$240); reserve well in advance. You can climb into an acrylic phone booth and be lowered into the aquarium's huge shark tank, and feed bull, brown, and nurse sharks from small slots (US$65 one person, US$100 two, US$120 three; 30 minutes).

Other dolphin interaction programs include those at Cancún's **Wet 'n Wild** (see *Eco- and Water Parks*), Isla Mujeres' **Dolphin Discovery** (tel. 998/877-0875, reservations 998/849-4748, www.dolphindiscovery.com), and the Riviera Maya's **Delphinus** (toll-free Mex. tel. 800/335-3461, www.delphinus.com.mx). Visitors can go to the parks directly but most sign up at their hotels or online.

ECO- AND WATER PARKS

Visitors to Cancún have three major eco-parks to choose from: **Xcaret, Xel-Ha,** and **Parque Garrafón.** Good for both kids and adults, all offer a combination of outdoor activities, including snorkeling and tubing, plus optional add-ons such as dolphin-interaction programs and modified scuba diving. Admission is far from cheap, especially the all-inclusive packages that come with meals and extra activities. Still, each park is unique and interesting in its own way, and many people list a visit as the highlight of their vacation.

Despite the deluge of advertising you'll see downtown and in the Zona Hotelera, none of the three parks is actually in Cancún. Parque Garrafón is the closest, situated on the southern tip of Isla Mujeres. The others are 60–90 minutes south of Cancún, near Playa del Carmen and Tulum. You can buy tickets at the gates, though most people buy them at their hotels or in a travel agency in Cancún so that bus transportation is included in the cost; discounted park tickets also are popular giveaways for taking part in a time-share presentation. For more detailed information about each park, see the *Isla Mujeres* section, the *Riviera Maya* chapter, or the *Tulum and Southern Quintana Roo* chapter.

If you're tired of the hotel pool, check out the **Wet 'n Wild** water park (aka Parque Nizuc, Blvd. Kukulcán Km. 25, tel. 998/881-8000, US$28 Mon.–Sat., US$15 Sun. 10 A.M.–5 P.M. daily). As the name suggests, it offers classics like twisting slippery slides, high-speed water toboggans, and family-size inner tubing—a great way to cool off. The park also has dolphin and sea lion interaction programs (US$70–130 pp) which includes entry to the park. Beware of some hidden charges—inner tubes, lockers, towels—as well as pricey snacks.

SPORT FISHING

More than a dozen species of sport fish ply the waters off Cancún, including blue and white marlin, blackfin tuna, barracuda, dolphin dorado, wahoo, grouper, and more. **Fishing Charters Cancún** (Blvd. Kukulcán Km. 7.5, tel. 998/883-2517, www.fishingcharters.com .mx, 6:30 A.M.–9 P.M. daily) operates a fleet of custom fishing boats, ranging 30–38 feet. Expert anglers can reserve the type and size boat they like and request particular captains; a chart on the website gives peak seasons for 10 species of fish. The boats hold 4–8 people and go out for 4–8 hours; prices range US$385–595 for four hours, and US$585–795 for all day. Individual anglers can sign up for "shared" trips for US$99 pp for four hours or US$115 for six hours. All trips include captain, mates, gear, bait, tackle, drinks, and, in some cases, lunch. Hotel pickup by SUV or boat can be arranged, and the crew will fillet your catch upon return. Reservations required.

Fly-fishing for bonefish, tarpon, snook, and permit is also good in this part of the world. **Villas El Manglar** (Blvd. Kukulcán Km. 19.8, tel. 998/885-1808, www.villasmanglar.com) organizes trips to the shallow waters surrounding Isla Blanca, about 40 minutes away, north of Cancún. The trip costs US$375 for two anglers, runs 5:30 A.M.–4 P.M., and includes equipment, box lunch, and drinks. The hotel will also provide free door-to-door service.

GOLF

With a recent US$6 million face-lift, the **Hilton Cancún Golf Club** (Blvd. Kukulcán Km. 17.5, tel. 998/881-8016, www.hiltoncancun .com) is considered one of the finer courses in the region. This 18-hole par-72 course hugs Laguna Nichupté and boasts Paspalum Sea Isle turf, new landscaping, and even a great view of the Maya ruins El Rey from the 16th hole. Alligators also are rumored to be in one of the water hazards so consider leaving those waterbound balls behind. Green fees are US$199; after 2 P.M. they're US$149. Both rates include a shared golf cart. There's a driving range and putting green to practice all of your strokes. Equipment rental also is available.

The **Cancún Golf Club at Pok-ta-Pok** (Blvd. Kukulcán Km. 7.5, tel. 998/883-1230,

www.cancungolfclub.com) is an 18-hole championship golf course designed by Robert Trent Jones, Jr. The course runs along the Caribbean and the Laguna Nichupté and features its own Maya ruin near the 12th hole, discovered when the course was built. Green fees are US$140 and drop to US$90 after 2 P.M. Rates include a shared golf-cart rental. Clubs and shoes can be rented at the pro shop. Some Zona Hotelera hotels receive discounts—ask your concierge for details.

If you feel like a short round of golf but don't want to shell out the big bucks, there are also two par-3 courses in the Zona Hotelera: **Grand Melia Golf Club** (Blvd. Kukulcán Km. 16.5, tel. 998/881-1100, US$28 green fees) and **Oasis Cancún Golf Club** (Blvd. Kukulcán Km. 16, tel. 998/885-0867, ext. 6277, US$22 green fees). Club rentals are available at both courses too.

If you're willing to travel a bit, you'll find the only Jack Nicklaus course in the region at **Moon Palace Golf & Spa Resort** (Carretera Cancún-Chetumal Km. 340, tel. 998/881-6088, www.palaceresorts.com). Just 15 minutes south of the Zona Hotelera, this resort has three 9-hole courses—each par 36—that make up its impressive 9.9 kilometers (10,798 yards). Green fees are US$260 and include a shared golf cart, snacks, drinks, and a round-trip transfer to the Golf Club. After 2:30 P.M., the green fee drops to US$170 with no perks included. There's also a driving range, a green side bunker, and putting and chipping greens. Club rentals also are available at the pro shop.

TENNIS

Many of the hotels in the Zona Hotelera have their own tennis courts. Most are lit for night play and many are open to nonguests for a fee. Good choices include the **Fiesta Americana Coral Beach** (Blvd. Kukulcán Km. 9.5, tel. 998/881-3200, US$22/hr. indoor clay courts, 7 A.M.–7 P.M. daily, until 9 P.M. Mon.–Fri. high season) and the **Hilton Cancún Beach and Golf Resort** (Retornos Lacandones Km. 17, tel. 998/881-8000, US$20/hr. daytime US$40/hr. after dark). Both have rackets for rent.

JUNGLE TOURS

It sure *looks* as if it would be fun: driving your own personal watercraft or two-person speedboat across the lagoon and through the mangroves to a national marine park where you snorkel with the fishes before returning home. Unfortunately, the rules—Stay in line! Don't go too fast! Don't pass!—keep the boat part pretty predictable and you see very few birds in the mangroves. The snorkeling is also disappointing, with dozens of tourists swarming a dead coral reef that is home to few fish. We don't recommend this sort of trip, but dozens of agencies will gladly take your money (US$55 pp, 2–2.5 hours).

HORSEBACK RIDING

Rancho Loma Bonita (Carretera Cancún-Chetumal, four km/2.5 mi south of Puerto Morelos, tel. 998/887-1708, US$66 adults, US$60 children) is the place to go to ride horses. Tours last two hours and include horseback riding along the beach or into the jungle. Drinks and lunch are included in the rate. Tours start at 9 A.M., noon, and 3 P.M.; there's a free shuttle from Plaza Kukulcán (Blvd. Kukulcán Km. 12.5) at 8 A.M., 10:30 A.M. and 1:30 P.M.—reservations required.

BOWLING AND ARCADES

There's nothing like a couple games of *boliche* (bowling) or *billar* (billiards) in an air-conditioned mall to take the edge off the midday heat and humidity. This one doubles as a bar at night, a unique alternative to Cancún's more frenetic nightlife options. Arcades are in most malls and most are kid-oriented.

This is not your father's bowling alley: **2.02 South** (Plaza Kukulcán, Blvd. Kukulcán Km. 12.5, tel. 998/885-0441, open 11 A.M.–2 A.M. daily) has eight lanes with neon lighting along the medians, several red-carpeted pool tables, a full bar serving every mixed drink imaginable, even a DJ and small dance floor. During the day, kids and adults alike can enjoy bowling (US$6/lane, US$1 shoes) and pool (US$10/hr.), plus a hamburger or half-rack at the Houlihan's-style restaurant.

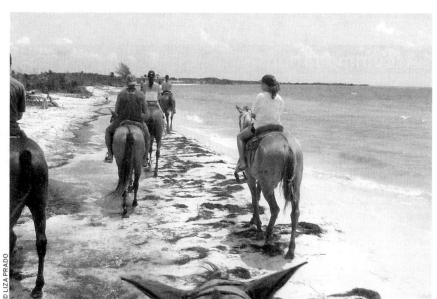

© LIZA PRADO

Horseback riding on deserted beaches is just one of many excursions available.

Above the food court in Plaza Las Américas, **Recórcholis!** (Av. Tulum at Av. Sayil, 11 A.M.–11 P.M. daily) offers a fully loaded kids' zone, with video games, air hockey, skeet ball, and other carnival games. There is also an area reserved for children ages 4–10 that has—among other things—jungle gyms, playhouses, and an arts and crafts section.

BODY WORK

The **Centro Naturista Xbalamqué** (Hotel Xbalamqué, Calle Jazmines near Av. Yaxchilán, tel. 998/887-7853, 9 A.M.–8:30 P.M. Mon.–Fri.) offers a full line of massages (US$36–42), body wraps (US$42), and spiritual treatments like Reiki and crystal therapy (US$36–42) in its downtown location. If you prefer to stay in the Zona Hotelera, most hotels either have their own spa or can arrange for an on-site treatment.

Next to Mercado 28, **Tae Kwon Do 28 and Fitness Center** (Av. Xel-Ha 5, tel. 998/884-6765, 6 A.M.–10 P.M. Mon.–Fri.) offers a wide variety of classes, including yoga, spinning, Pilates, kick boxing, and capoeira. Classes cost US$3 per session, but if you're staying longer than a couple of weeks, ask about the monthly rates.

SPANISH CLASSES

El Bosque del Caribe (Av. Nader 52, tel. 998/884-1065, www.cancunlanguage.com, 7:30 A.M.–2 P.M., and 5–7 P.M. Mon.–Fri.) is Cancún's best Spanish language school, with experienced instructors and individual attention. Group classes never exceed six students, and often have just two or three. Group courses are US$195 a week for 25 hours of class (five hours/day Mon.–Fri. mornings), or US$145 a week for 15 hours. Either can be combined with a four-day open-water diving certification course for US$545 or US$495, respectively. Private classes run US$20 an hour or US$340 for 20 hours a week, and are typically held in the afternoon. A US$100 registration fee includes airport pickup and materials, but you can cut it to just US$20 (for books) if you come directly instead of signing up on the Internet. The school can arrange lodging at a great price, whether at the center itself (US$20/night), at a nearby eight-room student house (US$15/night), or with local families (US$23/night with breakfast). Lodgings can fill up in the summer months, so reserve in advance.

Accommodations

Cancún has scores of hotels, varying from backpacker hostels to ultra-high-end resorts. Price usually dictates where people stay, but definitely consider the type of experience you want as well. The most important decision is whether to stay in the Zona Hotelera or downtown. The Zona Hotelera has spectacular views, easy access to glorious beaches, excellent familiar foods, but not much "authentic" interaction with local people. Expect to pay U.S. prices or higher. Downtown Cancún is culturally rich—offering good hotels, varied culinary treats, bohemian music venues, and a great central park. It's less expensive in almost every way from the Zona Hotelera (hotels, restaurants, telephone, Internet) but staying here means taking a bus to the beach and not having access to hotel pools and beach clubs. Many locals live and shop in this area, and Mexicans generally outnumber tourists.

Hotel rates are lowest in late spring and early fall; they rise in July and August when Mexicans and Europeans typically take long vacations, and from December to April when many Americans travel. Prices often double between December 15 and New Year's Day, and the week before Easter (*Semana Santa*). The Internet is the best place to find a bargain, especially in the Zona Hotelera—there are some amazing deals in the off-season. Package deals are worth investigating too, but be aware of pseudo-perks such as welcome cocktails or "free" excursions. Most of that stuff you can arrange when you arrive for a fraction of the cost. On the other

CANCÚN

hand, car rentals, airport pickup, or a free meal or two can be convenient.

ZONA HOTELERA
Under US$150

Although it doesn't appear to have changed much since the mid-1980s, **Hotel Girasol** (Blvd. Kukulcán Km. 9.3, tel. 998/883-5045, hgirasolcun@hotmail.com, US$100 s/d with a/c, US$116 s/d with a/c and kitchenette) offers clean and comfortable rooms with fantastic views of the Caribbean. The beach in front is spectacular and a well-maintained infinity pool does the trick if you want to relax off the sand. Probably the best aspect about this place is its location—just at the end of the nightclub strip—perfect for partying.

Next door, **Condominios Carisa y Palma** (Blvd. Kukulcán Km. 9.4, tel. 998/883-0287 or U.S./Canada tel. 866/521-1787, www.carisa ypalma.com, US$106 s/d with a/c) rents out private condominiums with fully equipped kitchenettes. Accommodations vary significantly in style but all are clean and have mag-

nificent views of the ocean or the lagoon. Strangely, some condos feature kitchenettes within a few inches of the bed so make sure you look at your room before moving in. A tennis court and large pool also are on-site.

As the name suggests, **Laguna Suites Golf & Spa** (Paseo Pok-Ta-Pok No. 3, tel. 998/891-5252, toll-free U.S. tel. 800/690-8590, www .lagunasuites.com.mx, US$102 s/d with a/c) is located off the strip, on the Laguna de Nichupté. A restful place, it offers simple but modern rooms with tile floors, cable TV, and air-conditioning. There's a small pool with a chic *palapa* lounge in the center of the property. For quality pool and beach time, guests are better off taking the free shuttle to Laguna Suites' sister hotels—Sunset Royal and Sunset Laguna—both just minutes away. Discounts for the Pok-Ta-Pok golf course and spa also are available.

On the lagoon side of the strip, the quiet **Hotel & Marina El Manglar** (Blvd. Kukulcán Km. 19.8, tel. 998/885-1808, www.villasmanglar .com, US$120 s/d with a/c) has spacious and

Wake up to impossibly turquoise waters in the Zona Hotelera.

© LIZA PRADO

nicely appointed rooms. Each one has a king-size bed and two couches that can double as twin beds—perfect for a family with children. There is a well-maintained pool on-site and daily continental breakfast is served under a *palapa*. If you're interested in fly-fishing or diving, ask at the front desk about booking a trip.

US$150-250

Located on a spectacular beach, [Omni Cancún Hotel & Villas (Blvd. Kukulcán Km. 16.2, tel. 998/881-0600, toll-free U.S. tel. 888/444-6664, www.omnihotels.com, US$214-249 s/d with a/c, US$560 suite) has newly renovated rooms, all decorated in a contemporary style with muted colors, marble floors, luxurious linens, and amenities like flat-screen TVs, extra large safes, and minibars. A series of refreshing pools and a mega-Jacuzzi (seating 35) lead to the beach with plenty of *palapa* sunshades. All-inclusive packages are available, though many guests prefer to just eat à la carte at one of the four restaurants and snack bars. Service is top notch—the only downers are the "customer service" agents near the lobby bar who try to rope guests into time-share presentations.

Renovated in 2006, **Casa Magna Marriott Cancun Resort** (Blvd. Kukulcán Km. 14.8, tel. 998/881-2000, toll-free U.S./Canada tel. 800/228-9290, www.marriott.com, US$149-219 s/d with a/c, US$319-339 suite) offers over 400 rooms, all with private terraces, sleek decor, and modern amenities. Guests can choose from five eateries including an Argentinean steak house and a Japanese and Thai restaurant. There's also a full-service spa, two tennis courts with lights, and a gym with separate men's and women's saunas. The main drawback of the hotel is the pool—it's well-maintained but too small; fortunately, it's just steps from the Caribbean, where there's plenty of room to swim. All-inclusive packages are also available.

The **Westin Resort & Spa** (Blvd. Kukulcán Km. 20.2, tel. 998/848-7400, www.westin.com, US$240-289 s/d with a/c) is a minimalist-style hotel with clean lines, square windows, stark white walls, and a splash of color here and there. It's breathtaking. Situated at the southernmost end of the Zona Hotelera, the Westin also is in a prime location—with a beach on the Caribbean, and another on Laguna Nichupté, both lined with *palapas*. There are three impressive pools: two infinity ones ocean-side and one "normal" pool lagoon-side. A full-service spa and two tennis courts also are on-site.

Over US$250

The **Hilton Cancún Beach and Golf Resort** (Blvd. Kukulcán Km. 17, tel. 998/881-8000, www.hilton.com, US$249-299 s/d with a/c, US$319-349 s/d villa) is a classy resort spread luxuriously over 250 acres of land. Cascades encircle the grounds, pools upon pools stretch to the ocean, and seemingly endless windows look out onto the Caribbean and Laguna Nichupté. Rooms range from deluxe standards to ocean front villas. All are decorated similarly in cool blues and whites and feature top-of-the-line amenities. Villas include a light breakfast and a complimentary cocktail hour. Two tennis courts, an 18-hole golf course, a modern gym, and a full-service spa also are open to all guests.

Considered the epitome of luxury, **The Ritz-Carlton** (Blvd. Kukulcán Km.13.9, tel. 998/881-0808, www.ritzcarlton.com, US$459 s/d with a/c, US$679 suite) is unparalleled in its elegance. Fine art, chandeliers, and marble floors greet you the moment the white-gloved porter opens the door for you. Although you may feel like you've entered an ultra-conservative country club, the staff is attentive and friendly, striving to make you feel at home. All 365 rooms have ocean views and balconies and while tastefully appointed, lack the presence that the lobby evokes—it feels like just another high-end hotel room. The two pool areas are nice but unremarkable—the beach, however, is beautifully maintained. The gym is definitely another highlight—kids are even allowed to work out, an unusual plus.

Well located at Punta Cancún, [**Fiesta Americana Grand Coral Beach** (Blvd. Kukulcán Km. 9.5, tel. 998/881-3200, www.fiesta

mericana.com/grand-coralbeach-cancun, US$492–514 s/d junior suites, US$626 s/d Grand Club) is an elegant hotel offering 602 spacious and comfortable suites all with ocean-view balconies. It features a spectacular series of infinity pools, lush and manicured gardens, and views that will leave you breathless. It's set on one of the calmest beaches of the Zona Hotelera, and guests can lounge under one of the many *palapas,* wade into the impossibly clear turquoise water, and enjoy service at one of its five restaurants. Activities such as Spanish lessons, tennis, and free use of a par-72 golf course also are available. Catering to families and older couples, this hotel feels calm and soothing in a sea of rowdy hotels.

All-Inclusive Resorts

The current trend is toward all-inclusive packages, which often include all meals, drinks, activities, taxes, and tips. The deal is a great one if you plan on spending most of your time at your hotel, but if you stay for more than a few days, it can get tiresome.

The adults-only **Blue Bay Getaway and Spa** (Blvd. Kukulcán 3.5, tel. 998/848-7900, www.bluebayscancun.com, US$143–158 pp) is a perfect place for 20- and 30-somethings looking to be in a racy atmosphere. Along with five restaurants to choose from, three pools to play in, and a discotheque and spa on-site, Blue Bay also offers daily games in which losers have to give up most of their clothes, kissing games in which the most outrageous kiss wins, and inventive sexual position games (with swimsuits on, of course). Toplessness also is invited on the premises. The resort itself is basic but nice enough—the rooms are simple, the pools are well maintained, and the stretch of beach, though nowhere near the nicest on the strip, is decent. The biggest complaint? Weak drinks. Ask for them strong.

Hotel Riu Palace Las Americas (Blvd. Kukulcán Km. 8.5, tel. 998/891-4300, www.riu.com, US$197–274 pp) is the most elegant of the three Riu hotels in the Zona Hotelera. A starkly white complex, you'll feel as if you've been transported to a Victorian-age hotel: crys-

tal chandeliers, gilt-framed mirrors, mahogany detailing, bronze statutes, and an enormous stained-glass ceiling. The 368 junior and full suites are not quite as impressive but nice nonetheless; each has a separate sitting area, a minibar that's restocked every day, and amenities that you'd expect from a high-end hotel (e.g., satellite TV, air-conditioning, hair dryer, in-room safe). The biggest complaint guests seem to have with the rooms are the ultra-firm beds—be sure to ask for a foam topper if it's an issue. Outside of the rooms, the beach is narrow but the two infinity pools, endless water activities, six restaurants, and five bars make for many repeat customers.

Occupying the southernmost tip of the Zona Hotelera's long ocean-facing leg, **Club Med Cancún** (Blvd. Kukulcán Km. 20.6, tel. 998/881-8200, toll-free U.S. tel. 888/932-2582, www.clubmed.com, US$685 s, US$830 d, club membership required, US$60/year adult, US$30/year child) has a secluded feel that is rare on the strip. Secluded, however, does not mean boring. A huge variety of activities ranging from sailboarding and water skiing to learning to trapeze to salsa dancing, with instruction if you need it, are included. And if you've got kids, the Mini-club keeps the little ones happy and busy all day long with things like tennis lessons, tie-dying, and performing in variety shows. Two excellent restaurants, a snack bar, and free-flowing drinks assure that all guests are kept full and happy.

DOWNTOWN HOTELS
Under US$25

Opened in 2005, **⟨⟨ Hostal Haina** (Orquídeas 13, tel. 998/898-2081, www.hainahostal.com, US$11 dorm, US$39 s/d with a/c)is the best budget option in town. Dorms are spotless and have bunks with thick mattresses, plenty of fans, and gleaming bathrooms. Private lockers, linens, towels, and soap are included. Private rooms are equally as comfortable but with the added features of mini-split air-conditioning, cable TV, and small fridges. All guests receive a hearty continental breakfast, and have access to a fully equipped Mexican-tile kitchen.

Common lounge areas are welcoming too—a leafy, well-tended garden as well as two TV rooms. All in all, a sure thing.

Mexica Hostel (formerly Mexico Hostel, Palmera 30, 998/887-0191, www.mexicohostels.com.mx, US$10 dorm, US$32.50 d) is the new name of Cancún's longest-running hostel, still the go-to spot for backpackers here. The hostel was bought and renamed by, of all people, the owner of The Weary Traveler in Tulum, and basic features like free hearty breakfasts, a fully equipped kitchen, and storage lockers haven't changed a bit. The hostel's interior is as labyrinthine as ever, with dorm rooms, large and small, all with heavy-duty fans, squeezed into every nook and cranny. That doesn't leave much room for common space, but a bar is being built alongside the rooftop kitchen and dining area. What the hostel doesn't lack—and what keeps travelers coming—is that worldly, outgoing, traveler-friendly ambiance that you just can't get in a hotel.

Run by a friendly family from Veracruz, **The Nest** (Alcatraces at Margaritas, tel. 998/884-8967, mjkglobal@yahoo.com, US$12 dorm, US$14 dorm with a/c, US$37 s/d with a/c) is a remodeled one-story house, offering single-sex and mixed dorms as well as one private room. In the summertime, the dorms with air-conditioning are worth the extra two bucks—your sweat glands will thank you. The Nest also has a huge and well-equipped kitchen, a TV room, wireless Internet access, and laundry service. Lockers and a hearty continental breakfast are included in the rates.

Club Hostel (Orquídeas 7, tel. 998/892-3384, US$11 dorm with a/c, US$23 s/d with shared bathroom and a/c, US$33–37 s/d with a/c) is the perfect name for this hostel, which feels more like a frat house than a guest house: X-box tournaments in the TV room, guys lounging on couches, an empty pool in back, a messy kitchen. The rooms themselves are pretty comfortable though—even the dorms have thick beds, mini-split air-conditioning, and hot water. Everyone gets a continental breakfast during the high season

too. An excellent deal, especially if this feels like home.

Run by a friendly family, **Mayan Hostel** (Margaritas 17, tel. 998/892-0103, www.cancunhostel.com, US$11 dorm, US$35 s/d, US$40 s/d with a/c) offers dorms and private rooms, most with *palapa* roofs and direct access to a leafy rooftop lounge, creating a beachy feel in the middle of downtown Cancún. The accommodations are very clean—dorms have bunks and include sheets and a locker—though bathrooms are showing some wear. A common rooftop kitchen is fully equipped and kept up nicely. Purified water and continental breakfast are included in the rate. English and German spoken.

For a proper hotel, the **Hotel San Carlos** (Cedro 28, tel. 998/884-0602, www.hotelsancarloscancun.com, US$18.50 s, US$28 s with TV, US$32.50 s/d with a/c, US$35 t with fan) offers perfectly adequate rooms, with clean private bathrooms and tiny balconies looking onto the market below. The balconies have flowers—all right, they're fake—and bright paint to cheer up the otherwise aging walls. The beds are a bit hard, and the cheapest rooms have no windows (avoid those if you can) but this isn't a bad option, all in all. Located five blocks north of the bus terminal; an Internet café on the ground level charges US$1 an hour.

US$25-50

A great little hotel on a quiet street, ◖ **Los Girasoles** (Piña 20, tel. 998/887-3990, los-girasolescancun@hotmail.com, US$37 s/d with kitchenette and a/c) offers 18 spotless and colorful rooms with kitchenettes. Rooms are sunny and have wood and ironwork furnishings. Air-conditioning, cable TV, wireless Internet, and friendly service make it an especially pleasant place to stay.

Once a solid option for budget travelers, **Hotel Punta Allen** (Punta Allen 8, tel. 998/884-0225, www.puntaallen.da.ru, US$45 s/d with a/c) is now a hit-or-miss experience. Rooms are basically clean but some are missing toilet seats, have chipping walls, and worn floors. The ones in back, while dark, are better maintained—it's amazing what a coat of paint and new curtains can do to a room. The biggest plus about the place is its location—just half a block from the bar and restaurant scene.

Opening onto a lively pedestrian walkway lined with shops and restaurants, **Hotel Colonial** (Tulipanes 22, tel. 998/884-1535, hotel-colonialcancun@hotmail.com, www.hotelcolonial.com, US$32.50 s/d with fan, US$37 s/d with a/c) is a decent option if every penny counts. The rooms are dark and no frills, but they're clean, have hot water, and the bright bedspreads cheer up the place just a bit. Besides the nightly rate, the location is, without a doubt, its biggest draw.

Next to Chedraui supermarket, **Soberanis Hostal** (Av. Cobá near Av. Tulum, tel. 998/884-4564, www.soberanis.com.mx, US$49 s/d with a/c, US$12 dorm with a/c) offers minimalist-style rooms with sleek wood furnishings and tile floors. All have cable TV, telephone, and security boxes. Four small single-sex dorms are a steal, with two bunk beds apiece, lockers, and private bathrooms. Be sure to ask for a room toward the back of the building as street noise can border on unbearable. Continental breakfast is included in all the rates. A discount is available by showing this guidebook or your ISIC card.

Suites El Patio (Av. Bonampak 51, tel. 998/884-3500, www.cancun-suites.com, US$50 s, US$62 d) is a charming colonial hotel with clean, airy rooms decorated with Mexican tiles and hand-carved wardrobes. Although it's seemingly in the middle of nowhere, the bus headed directly to the Zona Hotelera stops a few blocks from its front door and downtown Cancún is only minutes away by foot. Continental breakfast is served in the lush outdoor patio or in the common room, which has board games, books, and several decks of cards.

US$50-100

Bougainvillea and a gurgling fountain welcome you to the excellent **(Hotel El Rey del Caribe** (Av. Uxmal at Nader, tel. 998/884-2028, www.reycaribe.com, US$53 s, 63 d, most with kitchenette), an eco-friendly hotel two blocks east of the bus terminal. Rooms are clean and comfortable (if a bit plain), but it's the verdant tropical garden with hammocks, pool, and an outdoor dining area with beautiful hardwood flooring that make this such a memorable place—you might even forget for a moment you're in the city. The hotel employs solar heating, rainwater recovery, and organic waste composting. Definitely think about treating yourself to a milk-and-honey massage offered poolside.

Conveniently located kitty-corner to the bus station, **Hotel Kin Mayab** (Av. Tulum 75, tel. 998/884-2999, www.hotelkinmayab.com, US$45–51 s/d with a/c) offers 45 rooms in two buildings. All are clean and air-conditioned, with heavy wood furnishings, stenciled walls, and tile floors. The ones in the main building are a bit bigger and open onto a bright interior courtyard with lots of hanging plants and comfy chairs; the rooms in the adjacent building are set up like a motel, opening directly onto the hotel's T-shaped pool, garden, and *palapa*. Either way, be sure to ask for a room facing away from Avenida Tulum—the street noise can get pretty loud, especially in the early morning.

Located in the heart of downtown, **Hotel Antillano** (Claveles at Av. Tulum, tel. 998/884-1132, www.hotelantillano.com, US$55 s, US$72 d) offers 48 air-conditioned, very 1980s-style rooms. Though all are reasonably comfortable, rooms facing the interior courtyard are much quieter. A well-maintained pool is a bonus, as is the daily continental breakfast. Seniors: be sure to ask for a discount.

The **Hotel Xbalamqué** (Av. Yaxchilán 31, tel. 998/884-0699, www.xbalamque.com, US$60 s/d with a/c, US$80 suite, including light breakfast) goes further than any other to remind you you're in Maya country: imposing replicas of Maya statues and stelae decorate the common areas and complement the impressive mural in the main lobby and many corridors. Rooms are showing their age, but still comfortable and decorated in traditional Mexican decor and tile inlaid floors. In back, a lush pool complete with waterfall makes for a restful escape, and a small spa offers a variety of massages and treatments (guests receive 10 percent off). A bohemian coffeehouse is also on the premises, offering nightly live music. Contrary to some travelers' expectations, the hotel does not have a beach club in the Zona Hotelera, but has half-off passes for The City's beach club.

Over US$100

Directly across from the bus station, **Hotel Plaza Caribe** (Av. Tulum at Av. Uxmal, tel. 998/884-1377, www.hotelplazacaribe.com, US$102 s/d with a/c) offers comfortable, somewhat character-less rooms with air-conditioning, cable TV, and wireless Internet. All open onto two lush court-yards—one with a pool, the other with a play-ground—plus a reliable *palapa*-roofed restaurant. Ultimately, you'll get more bang from your buck elsewhere, but the Plaza Caribe's location can't be beat if you're traveling by bus, especially if you ar-rive late or have an early morning departure.

In the middle of the Yaxchilán strip, **Hotel Margaritas** (Av. Yaxchilán 41, tel. 998/884-9333, ventashic@sybcom.com, US$104 s/d with a/c) offers dated though sunny rooms with bright bedspreads and marble floors. Some are a bit musty, but once you get the air-conditioning running, the smell should diminish. The hotel also offers a pleasant pool and an open-air restau-rant. Well-located for the action downtown.

Food

Cancún has dozens of excellent restaurants. Seafood is the area specialty, but you'll find a full range of options, from Cajun to Japanese, vegetarian to Argentinean steak houses. The finest restaurants are in the Zona Hotelera, mostly along the west side of Boulevard Ku-kulcán or in the high-end hotels. You'll also find several very good restaurants in the malls, believe it or not. Eating out in the Zona Ho-telera is by no means cheap—lobster fetches U.S. prices or higher. The malls have some cheapish eats, mostly fast food such as Subway, McDonald's, and Burger King, and we've in-cluded a few budget restaurants as well. Down-town Cancún, just a short cab or bus ride away, is the place to go for good sit-down restaurants that won't blow your budget, though up-scale diners will find a number of satisfying places to eat there as well.

MEXICAN

This is the category where you will find the widest price range, from upscale restaurants to good cheap eateries.

Zona Hotelera

With great views of the lagoon, especially at sunset, **(La Destilería** (Blvd. Kukulcán Km. 12.5, tel. 998/885-1086, 2 P.M.–11 daily, US$11–25) serves inventive Mexican food, in-cluding cilantro fish fillet, tenderloin medal-lions in chipotle sauce, and shrimp cooked with tequila and lime. Speaking of tequila, the restaurant has more than 150 types of the agave-derived drink and even offers a guided "tequila tour" (5:30 P.M. Mon., Wed., Fri., US$5), with an explanation of tequila brew-ing and an option to order sample tastings (at additional cost). Dinner, appetizers, and drinks can add up to a hefty outlay here, but it's worth the expense. Reservations recommended.

El Mortero (Blvd. Kukulcán Km. 8.9, tel. 998/848-9800, 6–11 P.M. daily, US$18–35) is a replica of an 18th-century hacienda, complete with a fountain on the patio and roving maria-chis. Grilled dishes are the specialty, from huge steaks for two to *camaron al pastor*—literally "shepherd's shrimp," a tasty recipe using red adobo chili that has been adapted from a pe-rennial favorite at roadside taco stands. Served, as it should be, with pineapple slices.

Overlooking Playa Caracol, **Paloma Bonita** (Punta Cancún, Blvd. Kukulcán Km. 8.8, tel. 998/848-7082, 6:30 P.M.–11:30 P.M. Mon.–Sat, noon–11:30 P.M. Sun., US$12–35) is a real find, serving creative Mexican dishes in three lovely dining rooms. Try the quail in rose-petal sauce or pork loin wrapped in banana leaf, seasoned with *achiote* seed, a spice used by the Mayas. There are also a dozen different types of homemade *mole,* a classic Mexican sauce originally made from chocolate and served over chicken, pork, or beef. The restaurant has live music, usually mariachi or marimba, 6:45–10:30 P.M. daily.

Downtown

On the southeast corner of Parque Las Palapas, **Restaurante Los Huaraches de Alcatraces** (Alcatraces 31, tel. 998/884-3918, 8 A.M.– 6:30 P.M. Tues.–Sun., entrées US$3–5) is a nice place for lunch or early dinner. Served cafeteria-style, traditional Mexican dishes, such as garlic-baked fish or chicken in homemade mole, come with a choice of two sides, such as veggies or beans. There are some pre-Hispanic options, too, such as quesadillas made with blue-corn tortillas.

If Disneyland ever created a Mexican Revolution ride, it would surely look like **Pericos** (Av. Yaxchilán 61, tel. 998/884-3152, open noon–midnight daily, US$13–25), one of downtown Cancún's most well-known restaurants. In a huge eating area bedecked in Revolution-era photos and classic Mexican artwork, *bandito* waiters sport headbands and criss-crossed ammo belts, the bar has saddles instead of stools, there are not one but two gift shops, and kids may get a rubber chicken on their plates as a joke. Low-key it's not, but Pericos has a solid reputation for serving good grilled meats, seafood, and fish in a boisterous, family-friendly atmosphere. Daily live music includes marimba that plays 7:30–10:30 P.M. and a roving mariachi band that begins playing at 10:30 P.M.

El Oasis (Alcatraces 57, no phone, 7 A.M.– 4 P.M. Mon.–Sat.) is a simple downtown eatery operated out of the front yard of the cook's home. Tasty *tortas* and hamburgers run US$1–2, main dishes with chicken or pork are US$3–4.

Your heart won't be pleased, but your belly sure will be at ◖ **Don Javier's Quesadillas** (Parque Las Palapas, 8 A.M.–midnight daily), a street-corner institution in Cancún's appealing central plaza. Day or night you can get Yucatecan snacks like *sopes, panuchos, salbutes,* tostadas, and—of course—quesadillas. All items come with your choice of a dozen stuffings, including *nopales* (cactus), *rajas* (sautéed chile), mushrooms, or potatoes. All items cost just under a buck. Two items will satisfy a small appetite, four might push you over the edge.

SEAFOOD

Almost every restaurant in Cancún serves seafood, regardless of the particular genre. The following are ones that specialize in seafood, especially lobster.

Zona Hotelera

At **Lorenzillo's** (Blvd. Kukulcán Km. 10.5, tel. 998/883-1254, www.lorenzillos.com.mx, 1 P.M.–midnight daily, US$18–45), live lobster is kept in an adapted rowboat at the entrance— select the one you want, weigh it on an old-time scale, and before long, dinner is served. Smaller tables line the narrow patio overlooking the lagoon and have small bowls with pellets to throw to the blue trumpet fish schooling below you. More upscale than its sister restaurant next door, Lorenzillo's doesn't have a kid's menu and isn't great for families. Prices are steep, especially on wine and specials.

The owners of **The Plantation House** (Blvd. Kukulcán Km. 10.5, tel. 998/883-1433, www.plantationhouse.com.mx, 1 P.M.–midnight daily, US$16–33) could have picked a more sensitive name, but they could hardly do better with the island-style seafood and ambience. The house specialty is the seafood *sabre* (sable): lobster or shrimp grilled on a small sword, kabob-like. As if that weren't enough, the grill is in a kiosk in the lagoon—live fish or lobster are rowed over in a little boat, and rowed back to your table when cooked. Lorenzillo's, a slightly more upscale sister restaurant, is next door.

Downtown

One of downtown's finest restaurants, ◖ **La Habichuela** (Calle Margaritas 25 at Parque Las

Palapas, tel. 998/884-3158, www.lahabichuela. com, noon–midnight daily) has been serving excellent Caribbean and Mexican dishes since 1977. The seafood here is especially good—try the giant shrimp in tamarind sauce or *cocobichuela,* the house specialty, with lobster and shrimp in a sweet Caribbean curry. For dessert, the Maya coffee flambé is a treat. Dishes range US$13–27.

Facing the Mercado 28 parking lot, **Ⅽ Pescado Con Limón** (Mercado 28, tel. 887-2436, 11:30 A.M.–7:30 P.M. daily, US$5–9) is a popular stop. Not a fancy place—patrons sit at plastic tables and chairs—the seafood is as fresh and good as it comes. Try a shrimp dish or one of the fried fish platters for a taste treat that has locals and expatriates returning regularly.

ITALIAN
Zona Hotelera

Ⅽ La Dolce Vita (Blvd. Kukulcán Km. 14.6 across from the Marriott Hotel, tel. 998/885-0161, www.cancunitalianrestaurant.com, noon–11:30 P.M., US$14–26) was the first stop in a January 2006 *New York Times* article called "36 Hours in Cancun." No surprise: this award-winning Italian restaurant and Cancún institution has excellent service and inventive dishes, including veal ravioli in rosemary sauce and *boquinete Dolce Vita:* white snapper stuffed with shrimp and mushrooms and baked in light golden pastry. The atmosphere is casual but elegant, and there's live jazz nightly except Sunday. It can get busy, so reservations are recommended. La Dolce Vita Centro, a downtown location (Av. Cobá 87 at Av. Nader, tel. 998/884-3393, noon–midnight), has similar prices and dishes.

Fantino's, at the Ritz Carlton Hotel (Retorno del Rey 36, tel. 988/881-0808, 7 A.M.–11 P.M. Mon.–Sat., US$30–60) is an extremely refined Italian-Mediterranean restaurant, and one of few places in laid-back Cancún with a dress code: slacks, collared shirt, and dress shoes for men. The intimate room—it has only 16 tables—is the epitome of elegance with plush chairs, gilt mirrors, heavy curtains, and a spectacular ocean view (get here before the sunset to see it!). Choose a main dish (such as Chilean sea bass in caramelized onions or lamb with basil risotto) or order a four-, six-, or nine-course tasting menu. It's not cheap: the nine-course menu with wines runs a cool US$208.

The chic decor and terrific food at **La Madonna** (Plaza La Isla, Blvd. Kukulcán Km. 12.5, tel. 998/883-2222, noon–midnight, US$15–25, US$28–42) will have you wondering "Are we really in a mall?" A huge modern replica of the Mona Lisa peers over a classy dining room with fine fixtures and settings. The Swiss and Italian menu includes veal, shrimp fettuccini, and risotto, plus specials such as live lobster and New Zealand lamb. Doubling as a martini bar (with 150 different martinis to choose from), this is also a nice place to stop for a mid-mall drink.

Downtown

Rolandi's (Av. Cobá 12, tel. 988/884-4047, 1 P.M.–midnight, US$6.50–13) is a Cancún institution, with sister pizzerias in the Zona Hotelera and Isla Mujeres. The food here—and at all of them—is consistently good; choose among thin-crust pizzas, calzones, and great homemade pastas. Pocket bread, warm and inflated right from the oven, and a dish of olive oil comes with every order—a nice touch. The atmosphere is casual; an easy-to-miss veranda in the rear has trellises draped in ivy, blocking out street noise.

Just half a block from Parque Palapas, **Trattoria La Veneziana** (Tulipanes near Av Tulum, tel. 998/860-5863, 4 P.M.–1 A.M. Mon.–Sat., 2 P.M.–1 A.M. Sun., US$5–11) offers authentic Italian cuisine—over 15 pasta dishes and 20 pizza combinations—with authentic Italian spirit. Service is boisterous and friendly and the setup is sidewalk casual. A tasty, affordable alternative on a balmy night.

STEAK HOUSES
Zona Hotelera

Puerto Madero (Blvd. Kukulcán Km. 14.1, tel. 998/885-2829, www.puertomaderocancun.com, 1 P.M.–1 A.M. daily, US$15–45) is a cool, classy place serving extremely fresh and carefully prepared meats in huge Argentinean-style portions. The dining rooms have dark bricks and exposed iron beams, reminiscent of a shipyard warehouse (in a good way), and there's an elegant half-moon patio. The menu includes salads, pastas, and grilled fish, in addition to the many cuts of beef, some of which serve two.

The name of the place says it all—**Cambalanche Argentinean Big Steak House** (Forum by the Sea, 2nd Fl., Blvd. Kulkulcán Km. 9, tel. 998/883-0902, 1 P.M.–1 A.M. daily, US$20–30). Excellent, huge cuts of beef serve two or more; the rib eye and top sirloin likely will leave you panting. The subdued ambience, frosted glass, and tuxedoed waiters help you forget the fact that, yes, you're in a mall. Pricey but worth it.

Ruth's Chris Steak House (Plaza Kukulcán, Blvd. Kukulcán Km. 12.5, tel. 988/885-0500, 1–11:30 P.M. daily, US$28–50) will already be familiar to steak aficionados, serving its signature USDA corn-fed Midwestern beef. Plaza Kukulcán underwent a major renovation in 2005, and Ruth's got dolled up too: guests now sip drinks in a demure lounge while waiting for a table in the sunken dining area.

Downtown

La Parrilla (Av. Yaxchilán 51, tel. 998/287-8118, 12:30 P.M.–2 A.M. Mon.–Thurs., 12:30 P.M.–4 A.M. Fri.–Sat., 12:30 P.M.–1 A.M. Sun., US$8.50–25) is one of the most popular of the restaurant-bars on this busy street, grilling a variety of delicious beef fillets, plus shrimp and lobster brochettes, chicken, fajitas, and tacos—the fiery spit in front is for *taquitos al pastor*, a Mexican classic. The breezy streetside eating area is comfortable and casual—good for families.

LIGHT FARE
Zona Hotelera

Deli-mart (Punta Cancún, Blvd. Kukulcán Km. 8.8, tel. 998/883-3818, 7 A.M.–11 P.M. daily, US$5–11) serves basic, affordable meals, from sandwiches and fries to fajitas and pasta dishes. A small outdoor eating area usually has a soccer game on the TV, and there's a full bar with a happy hour that runs from 6 P.M. to 8 P.M. The market has pre-made sandwiches, plus basics like chips, soda, water, and sunscreen. Nothing too memorable, but it's one of few genuinely cheap places to eat in the Zona Hotelera.

With locations in the Zona Hotelera and downtown, **100% Natural** (Blvd. Kukulcán Km. 9.5, tel. 998/883-1580, 8 A.M.–midnight daily, entrées US$5–11) is a well-known stop for travelers and locals alike. Popular for its fruit salads, veggie sandwiches, and freshly squeezed juices, it makes a great option for those seeking vegetarian meals. The downtown branch is located on Avenida Sunyaxchén at Avenida Yaxchilán (tel. 998/884-3617, 7 A.M.–10:30 P.M. daily).

Downtown

Part of the Hotel Xbalamqué downtown, **El Pabilo** (Av. Yaxchilán 31, tel. 998/892-4553, 8 A.M.–midnight, US$3.50–8), describes itself as a *cafebrería,* a classy but unassuming combination café, bookstore, and art gallery. Indeed, you can get excellent coffee and light meals here, and enjoy rotating exhibits and books in various languages, many for sale. Better still, every night but Sunday starting at 9 P.M., you're treated to great live music, a different genre each night from *bohemia cubana* to fusion jazz.

In nearby Parque Las Palapas, **El D'Pa** (Margaritas at Gladiolas, tel. 998/884-7615, 1 P.M.–1 A.M. Tue.–Sun., US$4–10) is an eclectic French-inspired restaurant offering creative crepes, baguettes, quiches, and salads. While the outdoor seating is great for people watching, the charming interior is worth a look—turn-of-the-20th-century prints, antiques, lamps with feathers, and even a pink sofa might just lure you in.

Also downtown, get a great baguette sandwich at **Ty-Coz Baguettería** (Av. Tulum at Av. Uxmal, tel. 998/884-6060, 8 A.M.–9 P.M. Mon.–Sat.), a small agreeable shop tucked behind the Comercial Mexicana supermarket opposite the bus terminal. Popular with local professionals and students, the menu includes

French- and German-inspired baguette sandwiches and *cuernos* (literally horns, they're large stuffed croissants). Most are US$3–5, but you can always order the *económica* with ham, salami and cheese for just US$1.25.

OTHER SPECIALTIES
Zona Hotelera

Classy but unassuming, **⟮ Laguna Grill** (Blvd. Kukulcán Km. 15.6, tel. 998/885-0267, www.lagunagrill.com.mx, 2 P.M.–midnight, bar area 6 P.M.–1:30 A.M., US$15–30) has an excellent lagoon-side patio with tables set well apart, diminishing the bustle found at other Zona Hotelera restaurants. The tables themselves are made of varnished tree trunks, with iron chairs and attractive glass candleholders. Contemporary gourmet offerings include sesame blackened ahi tuna with asparagus, and grilled lamb chops with pasta, grapes, and goat cheese. The bar has old-time armchairs and sofas set on a breezy deck.

Blue Bayou (Hyatt Cancún, Blvd. Kukulcán Km. 10.5, tel. 998/884-7800, 6:30–10:30 P.M. daily, US$12–30) is an award-winning Cajun restaurant, with dishes such as blackened grouper and "sailfish Mississippi"—grilled sailfish with mushroom-sauce risotto and vegetables. Chicken and meat dishes are also available. The space has dozens of hanging plants, and tables are set along a circular slow-sloping ramp, allowing maximum intimacy in the relatively small space. Enjoy great live jazz starting at 8 P.M. nightly; reservations recommended.

Hard Rock Café (Forum by the Sea mall, Blvd. Kukulcán Km. 9, tel. 998/881-2020, 11 A.M.–2 A.M. daily, US$10–20) has a dress code, which is that you must wear a shirt *and* shoes after 10 P.M. Otherwise, the place is pretty casual. Burgers, big sandwiches, and chicken-fried-chicken are popular, served with fries in a two-level circular eating area. Most tables have a view of the stage, where live rock bands play nightly. During the day, eat out on the outdoor deck, which overlooks the beach.

Rainforest Cafe (Forum by the Sea mall, Blvd. Kukulcán Km. 9, tel. 998/881-8130, 10 A.M.–1:30 A.M. daily, US$10–22) doesn't offer the best American fare in town but it is a fantastic place to take your kids. Trumpeting elephants, giant flapping butterflies, and life-sized gorillas set in a rainforest-themed room will have your children giggling within minutes. Be sure to keep an eye out for the resident clown, who entertains the young clientele while they're waiting for their burgers and shakes.

Downtown

⟮ Roots Jazz Club (Tulipanes 26, tel. 998/884-2437, 6 P.M.–1 A.M. Tues.–Sat., US$6–15) has good service and a varied menu with anything from hearty green salads to squid stuffed with cheese in a tomato and mango sauce. But the best reason to come is the great live jazz played from a small stage.

Great for a change of pace, **Sahara** (Calle Gladiolas, tel. 998/149-1492, noon–midnight Tue.–Sun, US$5–12) offers authentic Lebanese food in a casual setting. Traditional favorites like hummus, falafel, and tabbouleh are featured front and center but consider ordering a hookah hookup (so to speak, US$7) or having your coffee grounds read (US$10, including the coffee).

On the edge of Mercado 28, **Restaurante Taj Majal** (2nd Fl., tel. 998/887-6758, noon–10 P.M. daily, entrées US$7–11) has a good sampling of dishes from around India. While connoisseurs of Indian fare won't be blown away, the selection is tasty and especially ample for vegetarians.

SWEETS
Downtown

Pastelería Italiana (Av. Yaxchilán 67, tel. 998/884-0796, 8:30 A.M.–10 P.M. Mon.–Sat., 1–8 P.M. Sun.) offers good coffee and a large selection of fresh cakes—US$2 a slice, US$13–17 whole cakes—served at comfortable outdoor tables. Yaxchilán is a busy avenue, but a long awning and tall plants help block out the noise.

Boulangerie Patisserie Bordeaux (Av. Tulum at Av. Uxmal, tel. 998/887 6219, 9 A.M.–5 P.M. Mon.–Sat., 8 A.M.–4 P.M. Sun.) offers fresh-baked Danish pastries, cakes, and homemade chocolates, most for around US$0.50 apiece. There are no tables, so you have to take it to go. It's a bit hidden, on a narrow street behind Comercial Mexicana, a few doors past Ty-Coz sandwich shop.

GROCERIES
Zona Hotelera
If you just want to stock up for a picnic on the beach, numerous small markets along Boulevard Kukulcán in the Zona Hotelera have chips, water, and sunscreen and other basics. For a more complete grocery, head to **Super Express** (Plaza Quetzal, just west of Hotel Presidente-Intercontinental, Blvd. Kukulcán Km. 8, tel. 998/883-3654, 8 A.M.–11 P.M. daily), which has canned food, meats, fruit and veggies, bread, chips, drinks, and more.

Downtown
For mega-supermarkets with everything from in-house bakeries to snorkel gear, head to the downtown locales of **Chedraui** (Blvd. Kukulcán at Av. Tulum, 7 A.M.–11 P.M. daily) and **Comercial Mexicana** (Av. Tulum at Uxmal, 7 A.M.–midnight daily). Both supermarkets have ATMs just inside their doors.

Just a couple of blocks from the bus station, **Mercado 23** (Calles Ciricote and Cedro, three blocks north of Av. Uxmal via Calle Palmeras, 6 A.M.–6 P.M.) has stands of fresh fruits and vegetables, and almost none of the touristy trinkets that Mercado 28 has. The selection is somewhat limited, but the produce is the freshest around.

DINNER CRUISES
Operated by Dolphin Discovery, the **Lobster Dinner Cruise** (tel. 998/849-4748, www.the lobsterdinner.com, US$79 dinner and open bar, no children under 12 years, departures 5 P.M. and 8 P.M. nightly) serves three-course lobster and steak dinners aboard an 18.3-meter (60-foot) galleon. The ship cruises the lagoon at sunset or under a starry night sky, while diners enjoy the sounds of a soft jazz saxophone. Reservations required.

If the Lobster Dinner cruise sounds too staid, the **Galleon of Captain Hook** (El Embarcadero, Blvd. Kukulcán Km. 4.5, tel. 998/849-4451, www.capitanhook.com, US$67 steak, US$77 lobster or surf-and-turf, children ages 5–12 half price, under five free, 7–10:30 P.M. nightly) offers a larger, more boisterous alternative, including costumed crew members and a pitched pirate "battle" against an enemy galleon while cruising the bay.

Operated by AquaWorld, the **Cancún Queen** (Blvd. Kukulcán Km. 15.5, tel. 998/ 848-8300, www.aquaworld.com.mx, US$43 fish or chicken, US$65 surf & turf, including open bar) is the only dinner cruise aboard a paddle steamer. Meals are served in an air-conditioned dining room, and there's live music and dancing on the deck, all while the old-time river boat makes a three-hour tour of Laguna Nichupté. Departures are Wednesdays and Fridays at 5 P.M., or 6 P.M. in the summer. Reservations recommended.

Information and Services

TOURIST INFORMATION
Downtown, the **Tourist Office** (Palacio Municipal, Av. Tulum 5, tel. 998/881-2800 ext. 2175, www.cancun.gob.mx, 9 A.M.–4 P.M. Mon.–Fri.) is a bustling office with staffers who happily provide information on city and regional sights. A kiosk just outside of the office has brochures and maps. English spoken.

In the Zona Hotelera, try your luck with the **Secretaría Estatal de Turismo** (State Tourism Department, Convention Center, 1st Fl., tel. 988/ 881-9000, 9 A.M.–5 P.M. Mon.–Fri., 9 A.M.–1 P.M. Sat.)—it's tough to get useful information but occasionally it has maps and tourist magazines.

There are also several excellent publications that are worth picking up to supplement the information in this book: *Cancún Tips* is a free tourist information booklet available in many hotels and shops; *Restaurante Menu Mapa* is one of several ubiquitous brochures put out by

GETTING MARRIED IN CANCÚN

If you are thinking of getting married in Cancún – congratulations! In México, most weddings have two parts: a religious ceremony, which traditionally takes place in church – but can really take place anywhere – and a civil ceremony, which must be conducted by a judge. You can have the civil ceremony at the judge's office, or pay extra for him to come to the wedding site. The two ceremonies don't have to be on the same day, though the civil, not the religious, marks your "official" marriage date. The paperwork can be a bit time-consuming – definitely plan ahead – but many foreign couples come away having unexpectedly enjoyed the process. As weddings get more creative – on the beach, officiated by your best friend, with vows you wrote yourself and set to music – a civil wedding can provide a reassuring stamp of officialdom to the undertaking. If nothing else, your folks will appreciate it, and it's another chance to say "I do." Here's what's involved:

Go to a Registro Civil office (Calle Margaritas at Parque Las Palapas, tel. 998/884-9522, 9 A.M.-1 P.M. and 1-4 P.M. Mon.-Fri.) and request a list of the documents you will both need to submit. In Cancún, as in most cities, these include:

- Copies of your passport and valid visa (tourist visa is okay).

- Copies of the passports and valid visas (if not Mexican citizens) of two witnesses who will attend the service.

- A recently issued copy (six months or less) of your birth certificate plus an *apostille*, an internationally recognized certification. You typically obtain new birth certificates from the city you were born in, and then send it to a state office for the *apos-*

tille. Both must be translated into Spanish by an official translator; the Registro Civil will give you a list of its approved translators. Bring the originals and one copy of each. (There are a few special rules if either of you is divorced, widowed, or a Mexican citizen; ask the Registro Civil for details.)

- Certified blood test, which checks for reproductive compatibility and several infectious diseases, including HIV/AIDS. The Registro Civil has a list of clinics that perform prenuptial exams, which must be done no more than 15 days before the ceremony.

The Registro Civil needs at least three days to process your documents once they are all in order. Then make an appointment for the civil service. You can get married at the office (US$285), or have the judge come to your hotel or ceremony site (US$305); if one of you is a Mexican citizen, the costs are US$93 and US$103, respectively. Hold off on the champagne – neither you nor the witnesses are allowed to have consumed alcohol before the ceremony (and you cannot change witnesses once the forms are submitted). The ceremony takes around 30 minutes and consists mostly of the judge making declarations, and you, your witnesses, and your parents (if present) signing numerous forms, even taking fingerprints.

Once you're married, there's just one last hoop to jump through. After your ceremony, stop at the Registro Civil and order a few copies of your marriage certificate. Be sure to ask about getting *apostilles* – you'll need them back home to prove your marriage was genuine. *¡Felicidades!*

Cancún Travel (www.cancuntravel.com); this one has maps, restaurant menus, and reviews and discount coupons. *Map@migo* also has maps and coupons. The state cultural institute publishes the *Agenda Cultural* with listings of upcoming events, exhibitions, and workshops. It can be hard to find—ask at the Casa de la Cultura.

Booths with tourist information signs abound along Avenida Tulum and Boulevard Kukulcán, but they are virtually all operated by hotel and condo companies offering free tours and meals in exchange for attending a time-share presentation. Unless you are willing to spend a morning or afternoon in a hard-line sales pitch, stay clear of these kiosks.

NEWSPAPERS

In Spanish, *Novedades de Quintana Roo* is the state's oldest newspaper, centrist in coverage, with a good classified section. *¡Por Esto!* is a left-of-center Quintana Roo paper, while *Diario de Yucatán* is more conservative and covers the entire region. The Cancún version of the *Miami Herald Tribune* (US$1) is a good English-language alternative.

HOSPITALS

Although there is no hospital in the Zona Hotelera, there are several recommended private hospitals within a few blocks of each other in downtown Cancún. All have emergency rooms and English-speaking doctors: **Hospital de las Américas** (Av. Bonampak, behind Las Américas mall, tel. 998/881-3434), **Hospitén Cancún** (Av. Bonampak Lote 7, tel. 998/881-3700), and **Hospital Americano** (Retorno Viento 15, tel. 998/884-6133).

For diving-related injuries, try the **Hiperbárica Cancún** (Alcatraces 44, tel. 998/892-7680, www.hiperbarica-cancun.com)—it has a hyperbaric chamber. English spoken.

PHARMACIES

In the Zona Hotelera, try any of the malls or head directly to **Farmacia del Ahorro** (Blvd. Kukulcán Km. 9.5, tel. 998/892-7291, 24 hours). Downtown, **Farmacias Similares** (Av. Tulum at Calle Crisantemos, tel. 998/898-

0190, 24 hours) is a reliable national chain offering discounted generic medications.

POLICE

For **24-hour emergency assistance**—police department, fire station, and ambulance—dial toll-free **060** or **066** from any phone.

In the Zona Hotelera, the tourist police, ambulance, and fire station (Blvd. Kukulcán Km. 12.5, 998/885-2277, 24 hours daily) are in the same building, next to Plaza Kukulcán.

Downtown, the police station (Av. Xcaret at Av. Kabah, 998/884-1913, 24 hours daily) faces the Carrefour supermarket.

MONEY

In a town as popular as Cancún, you'll have no problem accessing or exchanging your money—banks, ATMs, and *casas de cambio* (exchange houses) are everywhere tourists are. In the Zona Hotelera, shopping centers are the easiest place to find them. Downtown, money services line Avenida Tulum and, to a lesser extent, Avenida Uxmal. Often, hotels will exchange your money, too (at pitiful rates, however).

For the best *casa de cambio* rates, head to the full-service **American Express** (Av. Tulum 208 at Calle Agua, tel. 998/881-4000, 9 A.M.–6 P.M. Mon.–Fri., 9 A.M.–1 P.M. Sat.). American Express also has a kiosk in the Plaza La Isla open 9 A.M.–3 P.M., 4–6 P.M., and 7–10 P.M. daily.

For a bank in the Zona Hotelera, head to Plaza Caracol (Blvd. Kukulcán Km. 8.5) where you'll find **Bancomer** (tel. 998/883-0834), **HSBC** (998/883-4652), and **Banamex** (998/883-3100), or Plaza Kukulcán (Blvd. Kukulcán Km. 12.5) where there's a **Banco Serfín** (998/881-4809). All have ATMs that accept foreign cards, and are open roughly 9 A.M.–4 P.M. Mon.–Fri.

Downtown, the best-located banks are on Avenida Tulum between Boulevard Kukulcán and Avenida Uxmal: **Bancomer** (Av. Tulum 20, tel. 998/881-6210, 8:30 A.M.–4 P.M. Mon.–Fri., 10 A.M.–2 P.M. Sat.) and **Banamex** (Av. Tulum 19, tel. 998/881-6403, 9 A.M.–4 P.M. Mon.–Fri., 10 A.M.–2 P.M. Sat.).

INTERNET AND TELEPHONE

Downtown Internet cafés charge around US$1–1.50 an hour, while those in the Zona Hotelera charge 5–10 times as much. Downtown, look for Internet cafés on Avenida Uxmal near the bus terminal; most offer reasonable national and international phone service as well. In the Zona Hotelera, all the malls have at least one place to check your email. Most of the cafés listed here can also download digital photos and burn them onto CDs (bring your own cables).

Cancún @ (Av. Uxmal 22-D, tel. 998/892-3484, 8 A.M.–2 A.M. daily) is a quiet, friendly downtown shop with fast Internet for under US$1 an hour; CD-burning US$4. Across the street, **Cyber-Office** (Av. Uxmal at Calle Pino, tel. 998/892-3854, 8 A.M.–midnight daily) has reliable Internet and cheap international phone service—under US$0.15 a minute to the United States and Canada.

In the Zona Hotelera, **Internet cafés** are located at Plaza Kukulcán (10 A.M.–10 P.M. daily, US$7.50/hr.) and Forum by the Sea (10 A.M.–10 P.M. Mon.–Sat., US$6/hr.).

POST OFFICE

The downtown post office is in front of Mercado 28 (Av. Sunyaxchen at Av. Xel-Ha, tel. 998/834-1418, 9 A.M.–6 P.M. Mon.–Fri., 8 A.M.–1 P.M. Sat.—stamps only). There is no post office in the Zona Hotelera, but your hotel may be able to send mail for you.

IMMIGRATION

Cancún's immigration office (Av. Nader at Av. Uxmal, tel. 998/884-1749, 8 A.M.–1 P.M. Mon.–Fri.) is an efficient, welcoming office—worlds better than the one in Playa del Carmen. For information on visa extensions and other immigration matters, see *Visas and Officialdom* in the *Essentials* chapter.

TRAVEL AGENCIES

There are literally scores of travel agencies in Cancún. Most prices are pretty uniform, both for area trips and international and domestic flights. In the Zona Hotelera, most large hotels have reliable in-house travel agencies. Downtown, there are numerous agencies on Avenida Tulum and Avenida Uxmal, including **American Express** (Av. Tulum 208 at Calle Agua, tel. 998/881-4000, 9 A.M.–6 P.M. Mon.–Fri., 9 A.M.–1 P.M. Sat.) and **PromoViajes** (Av. Uxmal 26, tel. 998/884-3128, www.promoviajesmexico.com, 9 A.M.–7 P.M., Mon.–Sat.). **Nómadas Travel Agency** (Hostal Soberanis, Av. Cobá near Av. Tulum, tel. 998/892-2320, www.nomadastravel.com, 10 A.M.–7 P.M. Mon.–Fri.) specializes in youth travel services, including international hostel cards and student air tickets, but it is still a full-service travel agency with professional service and good fares for all travelers.

LAUNDERETTE

Downtown, there are several launderettes on Av. Uxmal west of the bus terminal. On the other side of Parque Las Palapas, **Lava y Seca** (Retorno Crisantemos 22, tel. 998/892-4789, 10 A.M.–6:30 P.M. Mon.–Fri., 10 A.M.–6 P.M. Sat.) charges US$4.25 per three kilograms (6.6 pounds). Same-day service available if you drop off your laundry early.

In the Zona Hotelera, **Lavandería Lumi** (Plaza Quetzal, Blvd. Kukulcán Km. 7.4, tel. 998/883-3874, 8 A.M.–7 P.M. Mon.–Sat., 9 A.M.–3 P.M.) will wash, dry and fold your dirty clothes for US$10 for four kilograms (8.8 pounds) in 2–3 hours, or you can do it yourself for US$7, including soap. A cheaper but less central option is **Lavandería Happy Wash** (Blvd. Kukulcán Km. 3.5, tel. 998/155-4377), which charges US$3 for three kilograms (6.6 pounds).

STORAGE

On the 2nd floor of the bus station, **Guarda Volumen** (tel. 998/884-4352, ext. 2851, 7 A.M.–9:30 P.M. daily) is the only place to store your belongings, charging US$0.35–1 an hour, depending on the size.

Getting There and Around

GETTING THERE
Air
The Cancún International Airport (CUN) is 20 kilometers (12 miles) south of Cancún. Most flights arrive and depart from the airport's Terminal 2 (tel. 998/848-7200, ext. 107), which also has the airline, taxi, bus, and car rental desks, and ATMs. Charter flights, plus Spirit Airlines, use Terminal 1 (tel. 998/886-0341); a free shuttle van ferries travelers between the two.

FLYING TO CANCÚN

The following airlines service Cancún International Airport (CUN):

- **Aerocosta** (Av. Tulum at Av. Uxmal, tel. 998/884-0383)

- **Aerocozumel** (airport tel. 998/886-0083)

- **Aeroméxico** (Av. Cobá at Av. Bonampák, tel. 998/287-1860, airport tel. 998/287-1820, toll-free Mex. tel. 800/021-4010, www.aero mexico.com)

- **Air Canada** (airport tel. 998/886-0883, www.aircanada.com)

- **Alaska Airlines** (airport tel. 998/886-0803, toll-free Mex. tel. 800/426-0333, www.alaskaair.com)

- **American Airlines** (airport tel. 998/886-0086, toll-free Mex. tel. 800/904-6000, www.aa.com)

- **Asur** (airport tel. 998/886-0183)

- **Aviacsa** (Av. Cobá 37, tel. 998/887-4211, airport tel. 998/886-0093, toll-free Mex. tel. 800/006-2200, www.aviacsa.com)

- **Click Mexicana** (Av. Cobá 5, tel. 998/884-2000, airport tel. 998/886-0083, toll-free Mex. tel. 800/112-5425, www.clickmx.com)

- **Continental** (airport tel. 998/886-0006, toll-free Mex. tel. 800/900-5000, www .continental.com)

- **Copa Airlines** (airport tel. 998/886-0652, www.copaair.com)

- **Cubana de Aviación** (Av. Tulum 232, tel. 998/887-7210, airport tel. 998/886-0355, www.cubana.cu)

- **Delta** (airport tel. 998/886-0668, toll-free Mex. tel. 800/123-4710, www.delta.com)

- **Grupo TACA** (airport tel. 998/886-0008, www.taca.com)

- **LanChile** (airport tel. 998/887-9012, www .lanchile.com)

- **Líneas Aéreas Azteca** (Av. Cobá 5, tel. 998/892-3126, airport tel. 998/886-0831, www.aazteca.com.mx)

- **Lufthansa** (airport tel. 998/886-0122, www.lufthansa.com)

- **Magnicharters** (Av. Nader 93, tel. 998/886-0600, airport tel. 998/886-0833, www .magnicharters.com.mx)

- **Mexicana** (Av. Tulum 269, tel. 998/881-9093, airport tel. 998/886-0042, toll-free Mex. tel. 800/502-2000, www.mexicana .com)

- **Northwest Airlines** (airport tel. 998/886-0044, www.nwa.com)

- **Spirit Airlines** (Retorno Jazmines at Av. Yaxchilán, tel. 998/886-0708, airport tel. 998/887-1862, www.spiritair.com)

- **United Airlines** (toll-free Mex. tel. 800/003-0777, www.united.com)

- **US Airways** (airport tel. 998/886-0373, toll-free Mex. tel. 800/428-4322, www .usairways.com)

CANCÚN BUS SCHEDULES

Cancún's **main bus station** is located downtown at Avs. Tulum and Uxmal; call toll free 01-800-702-8000 for up-to-date schedules and prices.

DESTINATION	PRICE	DURATION	SCHEDULE
Campeche City	US$29-33*	7 hrs	7:45 A.M., 11:30 A.M., 3 P.M.*, and 10:30 P.M.
Cancún Int'l Airport	US$3.25	20 min.	every 30 min. 6:30 A.M.-8:30 P.M.; every 60 min. 4:30 A.M.-6:30 A.M. and 8:30 P.M.-11:30 P.M.
Chetumal	US$19-23*	5.5 hrs	every 1-2 hrs 5 A.M.-8 P.M., plus 11 P.M. and 12:30 A.M.
Chichén Itzá	US$12.50	3 hrs	9 A.M. or take any Pisté bus
Chiquilá	US$6.50	3 hrs	7:50 A.M. and 12:40 P.M.
Mahahual	US$15.50	5 hrs	7 A.M. and 11:30 P.M.
Mérida	US$20-32*	4 hrs	hourly 5 A.M.-7:30 P.M.; 10 P.M.; and midnight-2 A.M.
Mexico City	US$95-110*	24 hrs	eight departures 6:15 A.M.-8 P.M.
Palenque	US$44-51*	12 hrs	4:15 A.M., 3:45 P.M., and 5:45 P.M.*
Pisté	US$8.50	4 hrs	hourly 5 A.M.-12:30 A.M.

Bus

Buses leave Cancún's clean and modern bus terminal (Av. Tulum at Av. Uxmal) for destinations in the Yucatán Peninsula and throughout the interior of Mexico.

Shuttle vans also are a way to get from Cancún to Playa del Carmen. They queue up directly across Av. Tulum from the bus terminal, near the Comercial Mexicana, and depart every 10–15 minutes, 24 hours a day. The fare is US$2 to Puerto Morelos and US$3 to Playa del Carmen.

GETTING AROUND
To and From the Airport

Cancún's airport is served by taxi, shuttle, and bus. A taxi from the airport costs US$40, whether you're headed downtown or to the Zona Hotelera. It's the same to return to the airport from the Zona Hotelera, but much less from downtown, around US$15. A taxi to Playa del Carmen from the airport is US$62, and US$40 the other way around.

Shuttles can be booked at the service windows as you exit the airport; it's US$9 to Can-

DESTINATION	PRICE	DURATION	SCHEDULE
Playa del Carmen	US$3.25	1 hr	every 15 min. 4:30 A.M.- midnight
Puerto Morelos	US$2	30 min.	every 15 min. 4:30 A.M.- midnight
Río Lagartos	–	–	No direct service; connect through Tizimín
Tizimín	US$7.50-9	3-4 hrs	7:30 A.M., 1 P.M., and 1:30 P.M.
San Cristóbal (Chiapas)	US$54-63	18 hrs	2:15 P.M., 3:45 P.M., and 5:45 P.M.*
Tulum	US$5-6.50	2 hrs	nine departures 6 A.M.- 2 P.M., plus 8 P.M.
Valladolid	US$7-11	2-3 hrs	six direct departures 5 A.M.-5:30 P.M., second- class hourly 1:15 A.M.- midnight
Villahermosa	US$48-60	12 hrs	seven departures 7 P.M.- 11:30 P.M., plus 10 A.M. and 1 P.M.
Xpujil	US$26.50	7 hrs	seven departures 6:15 A.M.-11:30 P.M.

*Denotes deluxe service; not available for all departures

cún and US$18 to Playa del Carmen. You may have to wait a short time for the shuttle to fill up. There is no return shuttle service.

ADO's Riviera line has comfortable bus service every 20–30 minutes to and from the downtown bus station and the airport; service to Playa del Carmen is less frequent, but still convenient and affordable.

Bus

Frequent buses (US$0.60) run between downtown Cancún and the Zona Hotelera—you'll rarely have to wait more than five minutes for one to pass. These buses are red and have "R-1," "Hoteles," or "Zona Hotelera" printed on the front, and stop at or near most major hotels, beaches, the bus station, and ferry ports.

Taxi

You'll have no trouble finding a taxi around town or in the Zona Hotelera—they are everywhere tourists are. Before getting into one, however, make sure to agree upon a price—meters are often not used and drivers sometimes

TAXI SCAM

Beware of taxi drivers that try to convince you that the hotel you're going to is closed, roach-infested, flooded, burned down, has no running water, was destroyed by a hurricane, (add your disaster of choice). As sincere as the drivers might seem, they are more often than not retaliating against hotels that refuse to pay a finders fee. Taxi drivers in Cancún and throughout the Riviera Maya earn significant commissions – as much as US$10 per person *per night* – for bringing guests to certain establishments. Some hotels refuse to pay the fee and taxi drivers, in turn, try to take their clients to "cooperative" hotels instead. Don't fall for it. You may have to be firm, but insist that the driver take you to the hotel of your choice. Your best option is to call ahead for a room reservation, which also serves to confirm that the hotel actually is open and operational.

DRIVING DISTANCES FROM CANCÚN

LOCATION	DISTANCE
Airport	20 km (12.5 mi)
Akumal	105 km (65 mi)
Bacalar	320 km (199 mi)
Campeche	487 km (302.5 mi)
Chetumal	382 km (237.5 mi)
Chichén Itzá	178 km (110.5 mi)
Cobá	173 km (107.5 mi)
Izamal	266 km (166 mi)
Mahahual	351 km (218 mi)
Mérida	320 km (199 mi)
Paamul	82 km (51 mi)
Playa del Carmen	68 km (42.5 mi)
Puerto Aventuras	87 km (54 mi)
Puerto Juárez	5 km (3 mi)
Puerto Morelos	36 km (22.5 mi)
Punta Allen	182 km (114km)
Tulum	130 km (81 mi)
Valladolid	158 km (98 mi)
Xcalak	411 km (255.5 mi)
Xcaret	74 km (46 mi)
Xel-Há	122 km (76 mi)
Xpu-Há	101 km (63 mi)
Xpujil	501 km (311 mi)

overcharge. When we were here, the rate around downtown was US$1.60, from downtown to Isla Mujeres ferries was US$1.60, and from downtown to the Zona Hotelera was US$6–14, depending on the destination. Rates within the Zona Hotelera jump dramatically, and depend on how far you're going. Ask your hotel concierge for specific rates, but expect to pay US$4–12.

Car Rental

Although you won't need a car to visit Cancún proper, renting one is a great way to visit the nearest archaeological sites (i.e., Tulum, Cobá, Ek' Balam, and Chichén Itzá) without being part of a huge tour group. A rental also makes exploring the Riviera Maya a little easier, though buses cover that route fairly well. Driving in the Cancún area is relatively pain-free—unexpected speed bumps and impatient bus drivers are the biggest concern.

Car rentals are available at the airport, on Avenida Tulum and Avenida Uxmal, and at hotels and malls in the Zona Hotelera. Various sizes and types are available, from SUVs to Volkswagen bugs (optimistically dubbed VW "sedans"); prices with insurance and taxes start at around US$50 a day. The best rates are usually with online reservations, though some of the small agencies offer great deals during the low season. You also can get discounted rates if you can stomach spending half a day in a time-share presentation.

Most of the international chains have offices at the airport and in town; **Avicar** (Azucenas 1, tel. 998/884-9635, www.avicar.com.mx, 8 A.M.–1 P.M. and 4 P.M.–7 P.M. daily) and **Zipp Rent-A-Car** (Blvd. Kukulcán Km. 4 across from El Embarcadero, tel. 998/849-4193, or Avalon Grand Hotel, Blvd. Kukulcán Km. 11.5, tel. 998/848-9350, www.zipp.com.mx) are good local options.

Isla Mujeres

Just eight kilometers (five miles) long and no more than a quarter-mile wide, Isla Mujeres is a sliver of land fringed by white sand beaches amid the wide turquoise sea. It was actually one of the first places in the Mexican Caribbean to have hotels and other tourist developments, but attention quickly shifted to Isla Cozumel and then Cancún proper. It may have been a blessing in disguise: as those areas exploded, rushing to build high-rise hotels and cruise ship ports, Isla Mujeres developed more slowly, attracting backpackers, bohemians, and the occasional B&B, while remaining pretty much what it always was—a quiet, picturesque fishing community.

But even slow change adds up, and today Isla Mujeres is a well-established tourist destination. Thousands of day-trippers come from Cancún to shop, eat, and relax on the island's calm beaches. While still popular with backpackers, Isla Mujeres also attracts mid-range and upscale travelers with an ever-expanding selection of boutique hotels and B&Bs.

Despite higher hotel prices, and many more T-shirt shops, golf carts, and pushy tour operators, Isla Mujeres remains at its core a mellow tropical island, with a friendly and laid-back population. Passersby greet one another, people stroll in the middle of streets, and many businesses close for long lunches. Add that to beautiful beaches, and numerous options for snorkeling, biking, and other outdoor excursions, and it's no wonder so many visitors find themselves extending (and re-extending) their time here.

HISTORY

The history behind the name *Isla Mujeres* (Island of Women) depends on whom you ask or what book you read. One version is that pirates who trolled these waters kept their female captives here while they ransacked boats on the high seas. The other story is that when the Spaniards—ransackers of a different ilk—arrived they found a large number of female-shaped clay idols and named the island after them. The latter is the more likely story, and the one to which most archaeologists subscribe. It is thought that the idols were left behind by the Mayas using the island as a stopover on their pilgrimages to Cozumel to worship Ix Chel, the female goddess of fertility.

ORIENTATION

The town of Isla Mujeres (known as the *centro* or center) is at the far northwestern tip of the island, and at just eight blocks long and five blocks deep, is very walkable. This is where most of the hotels, restaurants, shops, and services are. There is no real "main" street, though Avenida Matamoros is notable for its bohemian shops and atmosphere, while Avenida Hidalgo has a busy pedestrian-only section and intersects with the town *zócalo* (central plaza) and city hall. Avenida Rueda Medina is a busy street that runs along the south side of the *centro* past the ferry piers and continues all the way to the island's other end, becoming Carretera Punta Sur at Parque Garrafón (for that reason it is also known as Carretera Garrafón). The road

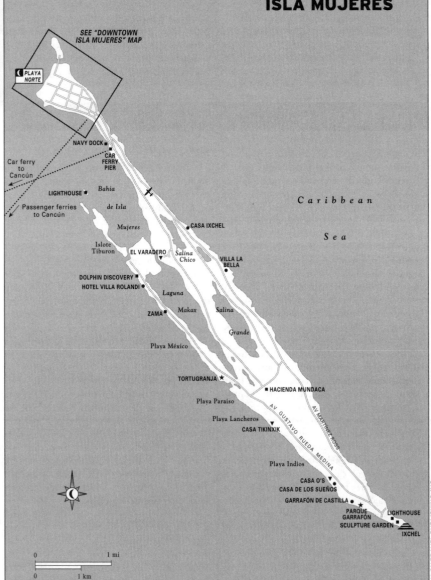

ISLA MUJERES

SEE "DOWNTOWN ISLA MUJERES" MAP

PLAYA NORTE

NAVY DOCK

Car ferry to Cancún

CAR FERRY PIER

LIGHTHOUSE   Bahia

de Isla

Passenger ferries to Cancún

Mujeres

CASA IXCHEL

Islote Tiburon

EL VARADERO   Salina Chico

VILLA LA BELLA

DOLPHIN DISCOVERY
HOTEL VILLA ROLANDI

Laguna

ZAMA   Makax   Salina

Grande

Playa México

Caribbean

Sea

TORTUGRANJA

HACIENDA MUNDACA

Playa Paraiso

Playa Lancheros
CASA TIKINXIK

AV GUSTAVO RUEDA MEDINA

AV MARTINEZ ROSS

Playa Indios

CASA O'S
CASA DE LOS SUEÑOS
GARRAFÓN DE CASTILLA

PARQUE GARRAFÓN   LIGHTHOUSE

SCULPTURE GARDEN

IXCHEL

0   1 mi

0   1 km

© AVALON TRAVEL PUBLISHING, INC.

that runs the length of the upper edge of the island is Avenida Martínez Ross.

SIGHTS
◖ Playa Norte

The closest downtown beach—and arguably the most beautiful on the island—is Playa Norte. It runs the width of the island on the northernmost edge of town. Here you'll find people sunning themselves on colorful beach towels, sipping margaritas at beachside restaurants, and relaxing under huge umbrellas. You'll also find plenty of people playing in the calm turquoise sea that is so shallow you can wade 35 meters (115 feet) and still be only waist deep.

At the north end of the beach **Buho's** (end of Av Carlos Lazos) rents beach chairs and umbrellas for US$5 apiece. Near the middle of the beach, **Water Sports Playa Norte** (end of Av. Guerrero at Playa Norte, 9 A.M.–5 P.M. daily) also rents chairs and umbrellas (US$15/day for a pair) plus snorkel gear (US$15/day), kayaks (US$10–20/hr.) and Hobie Cats (US$35/hr.). They also offer daily snorkel tours (US$25 pp, 2 hrs.) at 10 A.M., noon, and 2 P.M.

Other Beaches

Zama (Carretera Sac Bajo, near Hotel Villas Rolandi, tel. 998/877-0739, 10 A.M.–6 P.M. daily) is a small, very pleasant beach club and spa on the island's calm southwest shore. You can relax in a comfy beach-bed on the large clean beach or in a hammock in the shady garden. The water here has a fair amount of sea grass, but you can always swim from the pier or in one of the two appealing midsize pools. And it's all free, amazingly enough, if you eat at the small outdoor restaurant. Prices and selection are perfectly reasonable, including a kid's menu and everything from burritos to chicken fajitas to shrimp any way you like (US$5–20).

At the south end of the island, **Playa Lancheros** is less-manicured than Playa Norte, but has incredible views over the Caribbean to Cancún. The main feature of the beach is **Casa Tikinxik** (11 A.M.–6 P.M. daily, US$5–8), an Isla Mujeres institution whose specially grilled fish gives the restaurant its name. Playa Lancheros can get rowdy, especially on weekends when Cancúnenses and foreign tourists pack

Kick back under a palm tree at any of the mellow beaches on Isla Mujeres.

© LIZA PRADO

the beach clubs on either side of the restaurant, but it's a good place for a leisurely lunch.

Hacienda Mundaca

The ruins of a hacienda with a few paths and a sad little zoo is what you'll find if you stop at the **Hacienda Mundaca** (Av. Rueda Medina at Carretera Garrafón Km. 3.5, 9 A.M.–5 P.M. daily, US$2). It was built in the mid-1800s by Fermín Antonio Mundaca de Marechaga, a former African slave trader and pirate, to woo an islander with whom he'd fallen in love. Called La Trigueña because of her dark blond hair, the woman did not return his affections and instead, married another man before the hacienda was completed. It's said that Mundaca was left despondent and a bit crazed with the news, leaving his property to decay, the crops to rot, and the animals to die. He eventually left the island and died in Mérida. (Though Mundaca isn't buried on the Isla Mujeres, his tombstone, which he carved himself, is in the island's downtown cemetery—look for the skull and crossbones and the inscription *Como tú eres yo fui, y yo como soy, tu séras* (As you are, I was, and as I am, you will be). Hardly worth the admission fee, the most impressive aspect about the hacienda is that it somehow manages to attract enough visitors to stay open. It's the legend behind it, perhaps, that keeps people coming.

Sea Turtle Sanctuary

Commonly referred to as the **Tortugranja** (Turtle Farm; Carretera Sac Bajo, 5, tel. 998/888-0507, 9 A.M.–5 P.M. daily, US$2) this modest sea turtle sanctuary on the island's southwestern shore makes for a fascinating stop on your golf-cart tour of the island. The one-room cement structure contains several enclosures with sea turtles of different ages and species. The tank of just-hatched *tortuguitas* is always a hit; please respect the rules (and huge signs) and refrain from touching or picking them up. During the nesting season, one section of sand is fenced off, and eggs collected from nests are transplanted here for protection. Small aquariums along the walls contain sea anemones, sea horses, and the deadly rockfish, among others.

CANCÚN

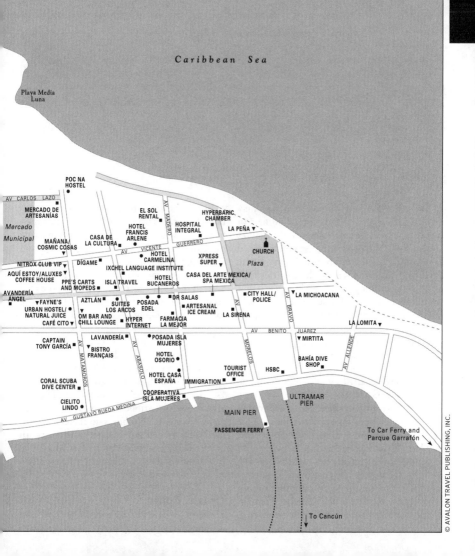

DOWNTOWN ISLA MUJERES

Caribbean Sea

Playa Media Luna

POC NA HOSTEL

AV. CARLOS LAZO

MERCADO DE ARTESANÍAS

EL SOL RENTAL

HYPERBARIC CHAMBER

HOTEL FRANCIS ARLENE

HOSPITAL INTEGRAL

LA PEÑA

Mercado Municipal

MAÑANA/ COSMIC COSAS

CASA DE LA CULTURA

AV. MADERO

AV. VICENTE GUERRERO

HOTEL CARMELINA

XPRESS SUPER

CHURCH

Plaza

NITROX CLUB VIP

DÍGAME

IXCHEL LANGUAGE INSTITUTE

AQUÍ ESTOY/ALUXES COFFEE HOUSE

PPE'S CARTS AND MOPEDS

ISLA TRAVEL

HOTEL BUCANEROS

CASA DEL ARTE MEXICA/ SPA MEXICA

AVANDERÍA ANGEL

FAYNE'S

AZTLÁN

SUITES LOS ARCOS

POSADA EDEL

DR SALAS

CITY HALL/ POLICE

LA MICHOACANA

URBAN HOSTEL/ NATURAL JUICE

ARTESANAL ICE CREAM

AV. BRAVO

OM BAR AND CHILL LOUNGE

HYPER INTERNET

FARMACIA LA MEJOR

LA SIRENA

LA LOMITA

CAFÉ CITO

AV. BENITO JUÁREZ

MIRTITA

CAPTAIN TONY GARCÍA

LAVANDERÍA

BISTRO FRANÇAIS

POSADA ISLA MUJERES

AV. MATAMOROS

AV. ABASOLO

HOTEL OSORIO

AV. MORELOS

TOURIST OFFICE

HSBC

BAHÍA DIVE SHOP

AV. ALLENDE

CORAL SCUBA DIVE CENTER

HOTEL CASA ESPAÑA

IMMIGRATION

CIELITO LINDO

COOPERATIVA ISLA MUJERES

AV. GUSTAVO RUEDA MEDINA

ULTRAMAR PIER

MAIN PIER

PASSENGER FERRY

To Car Ferry and Parque Garrafón

To Cancún

© AVALON TRAVEL PUBLISHING, INC.

© LIZA PRADO

Various organizations along the Riviera Maya protect sea turtles.

Between May and August, travelers may be able to accompany the center's workers in looking for fresh sea turtle nests on the island's eastern shore and re-locating eggs to protected areas, and, until October, helping release hatchlings into the sea. Both activities take place in the evening several nights a week, but are not formal tours. Those interested should inquire at the center, and having basic Spanish (and possibly your own vehicle) will make participating much easier. There's no charge, but a tip is customary.

Ixchel Ruins and Sculpture Garden

At the southern tip of the island, a crumbling Maya temple stands on a cliff overlooking the sea. Thought to be dedicated to Ixchel—the goddess of the moon, fertility, weaving, and childbirth—the ruins are believed to have been a pilgrimage site that also may have doubled as an observation post or as an astronomical observatory. In any case, when Francisco Hernández de Córdoba first reported their existence in 1517, they had been long abandoned.

By themselves, the ruins aren't too exciting—hurricanes have all but destroyed them—but a visit here also includes stopping in a tiny museum, climbing a renovated lighthouse, and enjoying the sculpture garden—a dozen or so multicolored modern sculptures lining the path to the ruins. Just past the ruins, the trail continues to the very tip of the island—the easternmost point of Mexico actually—before looping back along the craggy waterfront to the entrance. A decent side trip, especially if you have a golf cart at your disposal.

Admission to the site is included in the ticket price to Parque Garrafón; all others must pay US$3 (open 10 A.M.–5 P.M. daily). There is also a kitschy Caribbean "village" with shops and a restaurant. No buses go there, unfortunately. By moped or golf cart, continue south on the main road past Parque Garrafón. The road bends and you'll see the lighthouse down a small dead-end road.

◖ Isla Contoy

Decreed a national park in 1998, bird and nature lovers will enjoy a trip to Isla Con-

© LIZA PRADO

The path along the southernmost point of Isla Mujeres affords beautiful views of the Caribbean.

toy, a small island located just 24 kilometers (14 miles) north of Isla Mujeres. Surrounded by crystal-clear water, Contoy's saltwater lagoons, mangrove trees, and coconut palms make a perfect home to over 150 species of birds including herons, brown pelicans, frigates, and cormorants. In the summertime, you might also catch a glimpse of one of the three species of sea turtles that comes to lay its eggs on its shores. The island's only structures are a three-story viewing tower and a visitor's center, which houses a small museum. The rest of the island is tropical jungle that is accessible by hiking trails and the beach. To protect the local ecology, visitors can enter the park between 9 A.M. and 5 P.M. and are limited to 200 per day. The entrance fee is US$5 per visitor.

Isla Mujeres has lots of tour operators that offer the same basic trip to Isla Contoy for approximately US$50 (plus US$5 park entrance fee): bread and juice at the office between 8:30 and 9 A.M.; a departure shortly thereafter with nonalcoholic drinks served on the boat trip; snorkeling on the Ixlache reef a few minutes before arriving at Contoy; a walking tour of the island, including a trip to the museum and observation tower while lunch is prepared; lunch on the beach, which typically consists of barbecued chicken and grilled fish, rice, salad, guacamole, beer, and nonalcoholic drinks; afterward sunbathing, swimming, snorkeling, and general exploring are encouraged before the boat sets off at 3 P.M., arriving at Isla Mujeres around 4 P.M. What typically distinguishes one trip from another are the size of the boat, the number of tourists taken on each tour, the knowledge of the guide who takes you, the quality of the food, and whether there is an open bar. Tour operators or agencies that offer the trip include: **Captain Tony García** (Av. Matamoros near Av Benito Juárez, 998/877-0227), a friendly, English-speaking guide with over 20 years' experience, whose house doubles as his office—swing by to see if he's got a tour going; the local fishermen's coop, **Cooperativa Isla Mujeres** (Av. Madero pier, no tel., 8 A.M.–8 P.M. daily); and **Isla Travel** (Hidalgo 15, tel. 998/877-0845, 9 A.M.–2 P.M. and 4–7 P.M. Mon.–Fri., 9 A.M.–4 P.M. Sat).

ENTERTAINMENT AND EVENTS

Given Isla Mujeres' popularity with backpackers and people with generally laid-back attitudes, it's not surprising to find that the nightlife here tends strongly toward the bohemian, live-music and bar scene, rather than the pulsating nightclubs popular in Cancún.

Live Music

The Texan-owned **Jax Bar and Grill** (Av. Lopez Mateos at Av. Rueda Medina, tel. 998/877-1218, 8 A.M.–2 A.M. daily, drinks US$1–3) is known as a yacht crew hangout. In the high season, live country blues and classic rock fill the air 9–11 P.M. almost every night, and the partying continues until late into the night. Utilitarian breakfasts and burgers (US$4–7) are served until 10 P.M. Not everyone's scene, but those who like it come back again and again.

Fayne's (Hidalgo 12, tel. 998/877-0528, 5 P.M.–midnight daily, no cover, drinks US$1.50–3.50, food US$7–13) is a popular spot to listen to live and DJ music 9 P.M.– midnight daily. Music ranges from rock to salsa to reggae. The menu is likewise varied, from pasta to seafood.

Next door, **La Adelita** mixes tequila with revolution, with photos of Pancho Villa on the walls and an array of Mexican moonshine on shelves around the small bar and sitting area.

Bars

On the central plaza, **La Peña** (Av. Guerrero at Av. Bravo, tel. 998/845-7384, 7:30 P.M.– 3 A.M. daily) is a hip beach bar without the attitude, featuring low lighting and mammoth *roble* chairs imported from Thailand. A rambling place, with nooks here and there, the back deck has swings that overlook the ocean while the front room has shutters that transform into tables. Perfect for kicking back with a few friends or for meeting some new ones. There also are a few billiards tables if you feel like shooting some pool. The place gets going after midnight.

Om Bar and Chill Lounge (Matamoros 30, tel. 998/820-4876, 7 P.M.–1:30 A.M. Mon.–Sat.) is a bohemian bar with cool tunes, dim lighting, and low seating. Three tables have beer taps: Customers order the type of brew they want hooked up, drink their fill, and when they're ready for the tab, the keg's meter is measured for consumption. If you prefer harder stuff, kick off your night with the house specialty—*la viuda express* (the widow express)—which includes a shot of espresso, tequila, Baileys, Kahlua, and a little sugar.

Overlooking Playa Norte, **Buho's** (Av. Carlos Lazo at Playa Norte, 9 A.M.–1 A.M. daily) is a popular beach bar, with swings surrounding the bar, shells and buoys serving as decor, and hammocks well within reach. Happy hour runs 2–5 P.M. daily and features two-for-one beers and cocktails.

Discotheques

Nitrox Club V.I.P. (Av. Matamoros near Av. Guerrero, tel. 998/887-050568, 9 P.M.–3 A.M. Wed.–Sun., no cover) is the only dance club downtown and features mostly techno and reggae, although Fridays is Latin night. Unfortunately, it has a tiny dance floor but with two-for-one beer, you may end up spending most of your time at a table.

SHOPPING

As soon as you step off of the ferry, you will be surrounded by kitschy souvenirs and cheap T-shirts. Don't be discouraged! Isla Mujeres has a burgeoning market of specialty stores, most of which showcase the talents of Mexican artists. Poke around a bit, and you'll run into the following trailblazers and probably a few new ones.

A jewel hidden in a street of T-shirt shops, **Aztlán** (Hidalgo near Abasolo, tel. 998/887-0419, 9 A.M.–9 P.M. Mon.–Sat.; credit cards accepted) specializes in Mexican masks brought from every corner of the country. The owners, transplants from Mexico City, also make popular religious art that fills one corner of the shop.

La Sirena (Av. Morelos near Av. Hidalgo,

tel. 998/877-0223, 10 A.M.–6 P.M. Mon.–Sat.) is a tiny shop that's jam-packed with high-quality handicrafts from all over Mexico: beautiful textiles from Chiapas, masks from Guerrero, skeleton art from Mexico City, *alebrijes* from Oaxaca…you'll find a fine sampling of Mexican art here. The prices are a bit inflated but no worries, bargaining is welcome.

A bit kitschy around the edges, **Casa del Arte Mexica** (Hidalgo 6, tel. 998/877-1679, 10 A.M.–9 P.M. Mon.–Sat.) sells good Maya replicas as well as beautiful batik work made by islanders.

If you're in the market for decent diving or fishing gear, **Bahía Dive Shop** (Av. Rueda Medina 166, tel. 998/877-0340, bahiaisla mujeres@hotmail.com, 9:30 A.M.–7 P.M. Mon.–Sat., 8 A.M.–2 P.M. Sun.) has a wide—and pricey—range of equipment. A good source if you forgot your equipment at home.

Located in Mañana café, **Cosmic Cosas** (Av. Matamoros at Av. Guerrero, 9 A.M.–5 P.M. Mon.–Sat.) has long been one of the area's best foreign-language bookstores. You can buy, sell, and trade everything from beach trash to guidebooks to Maya history, with titles in English, German, Hebrew, and Spanish and ranging in price US$2–12. If you're hungry and out of pesos, trade-ins can also be used as credit at the café.

SPORTS AND RECREATION
Scuba Diving

Beginner divers will appreciate the still water and vibrant sealife on Isla Mujeres's western side, while the east side presents advanced divers more challenging options, with deeper water (up to 40 m./131 ft.), more varied terrain, and even a couple of shipwrecks. Favorite sites include **La Bandera** (a reef dive), **Media Luna** (a drift dive), **Ultrafreeze** (a shipwreck, in notoriously chilly water), and the famous **Sleeping Shark Cave**—a deep cave known to attract sharks where they fall into a strangely lethargic and nonaggressive state. The reason behind this phenomenon varies by the teller: salinity of the water, low carbon dioxide, or the flow of the water. Unfortunately, overfishing and overdiving has disrupted the slumber

© LIZA PRADO

Dive and snorkel boats use the same dock as many anglers.

party and there's only a 30–50 percent chance of seeing sharks there. Some guides say the chances of seeing the sharks increase in September, but you'll always find someone to disagree with that.

Isla Mujeres has a handful of dive operations. Rates are fairly uniform: around US$45 for one tank, US$50 for two, and US$5–10 for equipment if you need it. The sleeping shark cave and deep dives run a little higher. Open water certification courses are US$320–340, including equipment and materials.

Sea Hawk Divers (Av. Carlos Lazo at Av. Lopez Mateos, tel. 998/877-1233, www.islamujeres.net/seahawkdivers, 9 A.M.–10 P.M. daily) is a highly recommended dive shop owned and run by Ariel Barandica, a PADI-certified instructor. Service is friendly, professional, and dive groups are never larger than six. Sea Hawk also has a number of excellent rooms above and behind the shop; they're usually booked well in advance, but are definitely worth asking about.

At the end of Avenida Hidalgo on Playa Norte, **Sea Friends** (Playa Norte, tel. 998/860-1589, seafriendsisla@yahoo.com.mx, 8 A.M.–5 P.M. daily) is a professional and welcoming shop that has been in operation since 1974. It offers small groups—six or fewer—and most dives are led by instructors rather than dive masters.

Coral Scuba Dive Center (Matamoros 13-A, tel. 998/877-0763, www.coralscubadivecenter.com, 9 A.M.–10 P.M. daily) the island's largest dive shop, though that isn't always a good thing: On busy days boats carry 12–14 divers at a time and diving here can have a party-like feel. Then again, the shop has plenty of repeat customers, so they must be doing something right. Equipment is in top condition and prices are somewhat lower.

Snorkeling

Isla Mujeres's western side has calm shallow water (7–10 m./23–33 ft.) that's ideal for snorkeling. Tours can be booked at many hotels, on Playa Norte and at kiosks near the ferry pier, and typically cost US$25 per person for

1.5–2 hours. Most groups go to **Lighthouse** (by the ferry piers) and **Manchones** (off the southern end of the island), where the coral and sealife there are in relatively good shape despite the heavy traffic. Dive shops also offer snorkel trips, and are more apt to take you to a less-visited area. Another option is to take a trip to **Isla Contoy**, which usually includes an hour or more of snorkeling in addition to exploring the island.

You can snorkel on your own at **Garrafón de Castilla** (Carr. Punta Sur Km. 6, tel. 998/877-0107, 9 A.M.–5 P.M. daily, US$3.75), a modest beach club at the southern tip of the island. The club itself is a bit desultory, but you can explore over 300 meters (894.3 feet) of coral reef, including the part used by its much-hyped neighbor, Parque Garrafón. Snorkel gear rents for US$5.50, and lockers and towels are US$2 apiece. Hour-long tours to nearby Manchones reef can also be arranged (US$20 pp, including equipment).

Dolphin Discovery

Dolphin Discovery (Carretera Sac Bajo, just past Hotel Villas Rolandi, Isla Mujeres tel. 998/877-0875, reservations 998/849-4748, www.dolphindiscovery.com) offers various dolphin interaction programs at its large facility on the island's calm western shore. Programs vary in price according to the amount and type of direct interaction; the Royal Swim (US$139 pp; 30-minute orientation, 30 minutes in water) is the most interactive, with two dolphins per group of eight people doing a "dorsal tow," "footpush," and "kiss," plus some free swim time. Programs typically begin at 10:30 A.M., noon, 2 P.M., and 3:30 P.M. Most people come from Cancún, either on Dolphin Discovery's private ferry or on an all-day cruise/dolphin package. Oddly, there is no Dolphin Discovery kiosk in Isla Mujeres *centro*, but most hotels can arrange your visit or you can just go yourself. Taxi fare is US$5 from the center and US$7 from Playa Norte. Reservations required.

Eco-Parks

Built on a sloping bluff at the southern end

of Isla Mujeres, **Parque Garrafón** (Carretera Garrafón Km. 6, tel. 998/849-4748, 10 A.M.– 5 P.M. Sun.–Fri., US$65 adults, US$49 child; or US$89 adult, US$65 child, all-inclusive) is a combination eco- and water park that sells itself as one of the best in the Riviera. It falls short. While visitors do have a variety of activities to choose from—snorkeling, kayaking, snubaing (like scuba diving, but with a long tube instead of an air tank), or sea treking (a short underwater walking tour using a Martian-like helmet and breathing device)—it's hard to mask the damaged reef. The long curving infinity pool and zip lines are nice but for the price, you might as well swim at your hotel.

Sport Fishing

The fishermen's cooperative, **Cooperativa Isla Mujeres** (Av. Madero pier, no tel., 8 A.M.– 8 P.M. daily) offer *pesca deportiva* (sport fishing). Boats typically carry up to six people for the same price, and include nonalcoholic drinks, sandwiches, and bait. Two trips are usually available, depending on the season: Pesca Mediana (US$50 per hour, 3–4 hours minimum) focuses on midsize fish, including snapper, grouper, and barracuda; and Pesca Mayor (US$250, four hours or US$600, eight hours) goes after large catch such as marlin and sailfish. Reserve directly at the pier. Alternatively, many dive shops, including Sea Hawk Divers and Sea Friends, also offer fishing trips for comparable prices.

Body Work

In downtown Isla, **Spa Mexica** (Hidalgo 6, tel. 998/877-1679, 9 A.M.–10 P.M. Mon.–Sat.) offers a range of massages in a recently renovated spa. Massages begin at US$45 an hour and are given by certified masseuses. A great way to ease yourself into the island's rhythm.

The boutique resort, **Casa de los Sueños** (Carretera Garrafón Km. 9, tel. 998/877-0651, www.casadelossuenosresort.com, 9 A.M.– 6 P.M. daily) has a beautiful feng shui spa where clients can choose from a number of massages (US$89–149) and body treatments (US$70–115). For a treat, book the Day Escape

(US$140), which includes a welcome drink, a flower petal footbath, a 50-minute massage, a two-course meal at the hotel restaurant, and the use of many of the hotel's facilities for the day. Private yoga instruction also is offered for US$40 per person (two people minimum).

Yoga classes are offered at **Hotel Na Balam** (Calle Zazil-Ha #118, tel. 998/877-0279) at 9 A.M. Mon.–Fri. Classes are free for guests of the hotel, or US$14 per session for everyone else. Ask about monthly rates if you plan to stay awhile.

Spanish Classes

Opened in 2001, **Ixchel Language Institute** (Av. Abasolo near Av. Hidalgo, cell tel. 044-998/82-12-21-86, www.stormpages.com/ ixchel) offers Spanish lessons to travelers of all levels. Classes are taught by Laura Hernández, an experienced language teacher from Mexico City, and are scheduled around your day so that you can enjoy the island as much as possible. Standard offerings include "Survival Spanish" to learn basic phrases and vocabulary for traveling, beginner Spanish, and private tutoring where the course is tailored to the student's needs. Set courses are geared for one or two students and the rates are reasonable— US$11 per hour for one person, US$10 for two (minimum five hours). Tailored courses run US$18.50 per hour.

Art and Performance Classes

The **Casa de la Cultura** (Av. Guerrero at Av. Abasolo, tel. 998/877-0639, 9 A.M.–9 P.M. Mon.–Fri.) is a publicly funded organization that offers free or subsidized artistic workshops. Geared toward children and adolescents, classes include dance, painting, ceramics, and singing. Travelers are welcome.

ACCOMMODATIONS

Isla Mujeres has wide variety of lodging options, from youth hostels to upscale boutique hotels. Most budget and mid-range places are in the center, while higher-end resorts occupy secluded areas farther down the island. The latter means renting a golf cart or taking taxis

CANCÚN

(or else never leaving the hotel grounds, which may be just what you're looking for!).

Under US$50

For all the high-end hotels and day-trippers from Cancún, Isla Mujeres is still a backpacker's haven, the heart of which is the 【 **Poc Na Hostel** (Av. Matamoros 15, tel. 998/877-0090, www.pocna.com, US$6 pp camping, US$8.50–11.50 dorm, US$22–30 s/d, all with continental breakfast). In this large, labyrinthine hostel, dorms (including one for women only) have 6–10 comfy bunks and a small bathroom, while private rooms are simple and clean, with cement floors and whitewashed walls. Dorm and room prices vary by amenity: fan or a/c, private or shared bathroom, TV or no TV. The airy common area has food service and Internet; another room has Foosball and a pool table. The hostel hosts live music on Sundays and organizes daily activities, from volleyball tournaments to trips to Isla Contoy. The island's best beach is a three-minute walk away. The drawbacks are no kitchen access and the risk you'll never see Maya ruins because you couldn't bring yourself to leave. Visa and MasterCard accepted.

The new owners of **Urban Hostel** (Av. Matamoros at Calle Hidalgo, 2nd Fl., tel. 998/196-3824, US$10 dorm, US$17 s/d) have big plans for their little hostel: new kitchen, new patio bar and grill, new lockers, and new paint, plus a flat-screen TV, satellite Internet, even a massage area. The four dorm areas will continue to have 6–10 bunks apiece and ample space to move around. Private rooms with a shared bathroom have strong fans and are getting new beds. Although well located, Urban Hostel has never managed to reach its full potential as an alternative to Poc Na; completing even half these renovations would be a great start.

If you want a private bathroom but can't swing a mid-range room, consider the low-key **Posada Isla Mujeres** (Av. Juárez near Av. Abasolo, tel. 044-998/191-1531, US$18.50 s/d, US$28 s/d with a/c and TV). Less of a scene than the hostels, rooms are no frills and cramped, but they're clean enough. No charm here but then again, they're not charging for it.

Don't let the reluctant service at the **Hotel Osorio** (Av. Madero near Calle Juárez, tel. 998/877-0294, US$14 s, US$20 d, US$32.50 s/d with a/c and TV) dissuade you from staying here. Mint green floors, peach-colored walls, and flower bedspreads, the rooms not only have old-school character but are super clean and close to the ferry terminal too. Ask for one on the top floor—they open onto an outdoor corridor with decent light and get the best breezes.

If you've outgrown hostels but your wallet hasn't, the bright purple **Hotel Carmelina** (Av. Guerrero 4, tel. 998/877-0006, US$25.50–35 s/d with fan, US$45 s/d with a/c) is a decent choice. The exterior has a slight weekly-motel feel (the managers live in a few ground-floor rooms and another room houses a manicure shop), but the rooms are large, clean, have hot water, and get a good breeze from the open-air corridors. There's only one room with air-conditioning so be sure to call ahead if you want dibs.

Not only a fantastic deal but also perfectly located on Isla's pedestrian walkway, 【 **Posada Edel** (Av. Hidalgo 12-A, tel. 998/877-0474, hp_edelmar@hotmail.com, US$35 s with a/c, US$45 d with a/c) offers simple, clean rooms with tile floors, cable TV, mini-fridge, and coffeemakers. Doubles also have small kitchenettes—a major plus if you want to save a little money on food. There's no reception desk but the owner typically is around until 2 P.M. If you stop in and find no one, ask for assistance at the gift shop next door.

US$50-100

【 **Suites Los Arcos** (Av. Hidalgo 58, tel. 998/877-1343, www.suiteslosarcos.com, US$65–80 s/d) offers large, colorful rooms with gleaming bathrooms and wood furnishings. All have a small fridge and microwave for snacks and leftovers. Four of the 12 rooms have balconies—those overlooking Avenida Hidalgo are great for people watching, while those on the opposite side of the building are huge—perfect for relaxing in the sun.

Down the street, **Hotel Bucaneros** (Calle

Hidalgo 11, tel. 998/877-1222, www.bucaneros .com, US$40–55 s/d, US$65–72 s/d with kitchenette) has 16 nicely appointed rooms, all with modern bathrooms and air-conditioning. Basic rooms can be a bit stuffy, but those with a "kitchenette" (i.e., hot plate, mini-fridge, and toaster) are larger, often with a balcony and a separate dining area. Both are decent deals, considering the market.

(Hotel Casa España (Calle Madero near Av. Medina, tel. 998/877-1675, www.hotelcasa espanaislamujeres.com.mx, US$55–65 s/d with a/c, US$75 with a/c and kitchenette, US$100–110 suite with a/c) is a colorful hotel with a lush central garden and well-maintained pool. The rooms are airy and bright with rustic Mexican wood furnishings and small balconies. Some also come equipped with kitchenettes. As expected, suites are a step up—if you're want to treat yourself, ask for the one with the tub overlooking the Caribbean. The view is spectacular.

Posada del Mar (Av. Rueda Medina 15-A, tel. 998/877-0770, www.posadadelmar.com, US$80–100 s/d) is a friendly, longtime favorite. Spacious, modern rooms have spotless bathrooms, a balcony, air-conditioning, and cable TV. The pool is decent, fed by an attractive stone aqueduct; try a Maya Sacrifice cocktail at the adjoining bar. The advantage here is the location, near restaurants and the ferry terminal, and just across from a pleasant, active beach, where hotel guests have free use of the beach chairs, umbrellas, and kayaks.

Somewhat overpriced for the amenities and locale, the **Hotel Francis Arlene** (Av. Guerrero 7, tel. 998/877-0310, www.francisarlene.com, US$55–60 s/d with fan, US$60–65 s/d with a/c) can still hold its own with its 26 simple and spotless rooms. The decor is dated and only some have cable TV but all open onto a peaceful plant-filled courtyard. Larger, top-floor rooms have ocean views, which is a plus.

(Hotel Villa Kiin (Calle Zazil-Ha 129, tel. 998/877-0045, US$50–135 s/d, US$99–179 suite, including continental breakfast) has an eclectic combination of rooms, from thatch-roof bungalows, to hotel-like rooms with a/c,

to spacious suites with king-size bed and ocean views. The location can't be beat: walking distance to town, a semi-private beach (with no waves—perfect for kids), and Playa Norte just steps away. The hotel has two community kitchens, a TV room, and a leafy garden with hammocks. Rooms are a bit overpriced for what you get, although cooking a few meals will save you a bundle, and the seclusion, location, and family-friendly environment will prove priceless to some.

For a very homey place, **Cielito Lindo** (Av. Rueda Medina at Av. Matamoros, tel. 998/877-0585, joyw@prodigy.net.mx, US$80–90 s, US$100–112) is a great option. There are just two studio apartments, both charmingly decorated with Mexican bedspreads and artwork, tile floors, shelves of used books, and kitchenettes (fridge, coffeemaker, microwave, sink, and dishes in both; gas stove in one only). Both have air-conditioning—but can be rented with fan only, for US$10 a night less—and share a balcony overlooking a busy street. The owner, New York transplant Joy Williams Jones, has lived on the island since 1987. Three-day minimum and adults-only preferred. Reservations recommended.

US$100-300

The best hotel in the *centro* is **(Hotel Secreto** (Sección Rocas 11, tel. 998/877-1039, www.hotelsecreto.com, US$250–280 s/d), an angular glass and stucco hotel exuding discreet, understated class. Modern rooms have stone floors, CD players, thick mattresses, and huge private balconies with lounge chairs and excellent ocean views, especially from the 2nd and 3rd floors. A long curving infinity pool is framed by wide wooden patio, with comfortable deck chairs and a small bar. The rooms and pool overlook the attractive (though often very rough) Playa Media Luna. The hotel does not have a restaurant, but town is a short walk away, and a number of top restaurants deliver here. Continental breakfast included.

Next door to Hotel Secreto, **Hotel la Media Luna** (Sección Rocas 9–10, tel. 998/877 0759, www.playamedialuna.com, US$110–180 s/d) offers clean, classic rooms, many with the same excellent ocean view as the Hotel Secreto. Although not as cool as its neighbor—decor is a bit dated and air-conditioners are the boxy, old-school kind—the Media Luna is still one of the *centro*'s top hotels. Suites have a large balcony and whirlpool tub, and go for US$150 in the low season.

Right on Playa Norte, **Na Balam** (Calle Zazil-Ha 118, tel. 998/877-0279, www.nabalam.com, US$180–340) used to be one of Isla Mujeres's top hotels and is still one of the most popular. The restaurant and beach area are excellent—worth visiting even if you don't stay here—and there are daily meditation, yoga, and relaxation sessions for guests. (The hotel receives many yoga tour groups.) But the rooms and grounds leave something to be desired, especially the poolside rooms, which are dreary and not worth the price. Beachside and beachfront rooms have attractive whitewashed walls, stone floors, recessed lights, and (some) private whirlpool tubs. But it's the little insults—scum in the whirlpool tub, broken in-room safes, sometimes surly service, especially at reception—that guests consistently complain about. Not the end of the world, but certainly not what you expect for US$200-plus a night.

A block from Playa Norte, **Cabañas María del Mar** (Av. Carlos Lazo on Playa Norte, tel. 987/877-0179, www.cabanasdelmar.com, US$99–132) has three types of rooms: The cheapest ones are dated and have small bathrooms—there are better options in this range elsewhere. Middle-priced rooms, near the hotel's garden swimming pool, are larger and more comfortable with tile bathrooms and some patio space. The priciest rooms are smallish, but sleek and modern with king-size beds and good ocean views.

Casa Ixchel (Av. Martínez Ross s/n, tel. 998/888-0107, www.casaixchelisla.com, US$89–229) is one of the newer additions to a growing list of boutique hotels in Isla Mujeres. It has just nine rooms, all with names like Grace, Karma, and Serenity. Standard rooms are tiny, suites have a bit more breathing room, and you can actually unpack your bags in the apartments. But even in the small quarters, each room has a toy kitchenette, deep bathtub, luxurious beds, and classy decor. There are great ocean views from the pool and patio area, though for swimming—and eating—you'll have to head into town. The hotel has a few bikes (and snorkel gear) for guests to borrow, but you may want to rent a golf cart during your stay.

Villa La Bella (formerly Villa Las Brisas, tel.998/888-0342, www.villalabella.com; US$132–165) is run by an amiable American couple, who take pride in personalized service. Having just five rooms and one honeymoon suite certainly helps, and the owners have plenty of honest recommendations of things to do and places to eat, if you ask. Ground-floor rooms have bright paint and whimsical decor (and a/c), and are more cheerful than the *palapa*-roofed units upstairs. The pool is meticulously maintained, and a large, creative breakfast is included; the bar serves outstanding margaritas and other drinks. Taxis pass frequently, though many guests rent golf carts for their stay.

Over US$300

◖ Hotel Villa Rolandi (Carretera Sac-Bajo No. 15–16, tel. 998/877-0500, www.villarolandi.com, US$390–550 s/d) is one of two gorgeous boutique hotels on Isla Mujeres's calm, southwestern shore. Here, every suite has a private terrace with whirlpool tub, deep comfortable beds, two-person shower and steam bath, plus robes, slippers, and breakfast and one meal at the hotel's excellent oceanfront restaurant. An attractive infinity pool overlooks a small beach with umbrellas and beach chairs. The hotel can arrange personalized snorkel, scuba, and other activities, and delivers guests to and from Cancún in a private yacht. No children under 14. A taxi from town costs around US$4.

The boutique hotel, **◖ Casa de los Sueños** (Carretera Garrafón Km. 9, tel. 998/877-0651, www.casadelossuenosresort.com, US$350–400 s/d, US$450–500 suite) has eight luxurious rooms, most with breathtaking views of the

Caribbean and Cancún beyond. Each is decorated differently but all have high-end Mexican art and furnishings, marble bathrooms, large terraces, and feng shui touches like small gurgling fountains. The hotel also has a swank full-service spa and a meditation room. There's no beach—a drawback for sure—but then again, guests can swim from the hotel's pier or in the small infinity pool. Rates include continental breakfast, roundtrip ferry transportation, minibar consumption, and use of kayaks, bicycles, and snorkel gear. Adults only.

Long-Term Rentals

For weekly rentals, try the apartments at **Color de Verano** (Av. López Mateos at Rueda Medina, tel. 998/877-1264, colordeverano@prodigy.net.mx, www.colordeverano.com, one bedroom US$720–820/week, studio penthouse US$900/week). Over a classy boutique café, the apartments are attractive and fully furnished, with full-size kitchens and large modern bathrooms. All three have air-conditioning and large patios; two have outdoor whirlpool tubs. The studio penthouse is smaller than the one-bedrooms (queen bed instead of king) but has a larger terrace and better ocean view. There's maid service six days a week, and guests have free use of a washer/dryer, and two bicycles per apartment. In-room satellite Internet charged per minute.

FOOD

Seafood is the specialty in Isla Mujeres, even more so than in Cancún. In fact, much of the lobster and fish served on the Riviera Maya is caught near Isla Mujeres, so it stands to reason that it's freshest here. The island's popularity among backpackers, especially Europeans, means you'll also find a number of artsy bistros—look on Avenida Matamoros especially.

Mexican and Seafood

On Playa Lancheros, ◖ **Casa Tikinxik** (11 A.M.–6 P.M. daily, US$5–8) is a classic Mexican beach restaurant, with metal tables, cold beer, and finger-licking portions that make the long wait worth it. Be sure to try the specialty,

pescado tikinxik (TEEK'n-cheek), a whole grilled fish prepared in the parking lot grill using a spicy red sauce that dates to Maya times.

◖ **La Lomita** (Av. Juárez Sur 25-B, tel. 998/826-6335, 9 A.M.–11 P.M. Mon.–Sat., US$4.25–6), a brightly painted restaurant frequented by locals, offers standard, solid Mexican fare. *Comida corrida*—a two-course special with drink—is offered daily and often includes *chiles rellenos,* tacos, and stews. Ceviche, grilled whole fish, and other seafood meals are also featured at reasonable prices.

The **Zazil Ha** restaurant, part of the Na Balam hotel, (Calle Zazil-Ha 118, tel. 998/877-0279, 7 A.M.–11 P.M. daily, US$8–14) has a spacious indoor dining area, with a high *palapa* roof and moody lighting, and smaller beach area that is especially good for watching the sunset. The menu, available in both areas, includes excellent lunch items like ceviche and fish tacos, and equally tasty dinner entrées, like black pasta with calamari and tofu-and-veggie skewers, all in generous portions. Get here from along the beach or from Avenida Zazil-Ha.

A convenient, reliable place to get a meal, **Pinguino** (Rueda Medina 15-A, tel. 998/877-0044, 7 A.M.–11 P.M. daily, US$4–11) is part of Posada Del Mar, but is separated from the reception area so you don't feel like you're at a hotel restaurant. It offers three meals a day: Breakfasts are huge and the chef prepares excellent seafood dishes for lunch and dinner. With a view of the ocean, this is an especially good place to watch the sunset.

Italian

◖ **Casa Rolandi** at Hotel Villa Rolandi (Carretera Sac-Bajo No. 15–16, tel. 998/877-0500, noon–11 P.M. daily, US$10–20) is arguably the best restaurant on the island. With candlelit tables overlooking the calm southwest-facing shore, the restaurant has impeccable service and a creative Italian-Swiss menu. Everything sounds good, from seafood risotto to pumpkin-stuffed ravioli, plus many more pasta, meat, and fish dishes. The wine and drink selection is large—try a *mojito,* a classic Caribbean drink made of rum, lime, sugar, and fresh mint. Rolandi's also has a popular pizzeria in town (Av. Hidalgo between Avs. Abasolo and Madero) and two in Cancún.

Aquí Estoy (Av. Matamoros at Av. Hidalgo, noon–10 P.M. Mon.–Sat.) serves slices (US$1.50–3) and whole pizzas (US$8.50–10) from its appealing hole-in-the-wall on busy Av. Matamoros. Pesto, veggie, and Hawaiian pizzas are favorites, or try a specialty, like spinach and goat cheese pizza, for a taste treat. Other than a few high stools, it's takeout and standing-room only.

Cafés and Bistros

Operated by three Israelis and a Chilean, **Mañana** (Av. Matamoros at Av. Guerrero, 9 A.M.–5 P.M. Tues.–Sat., US$2–3) is a hip café with an eclectic menu, from kabobs and homemade hummus on pita to cheeseburgers and schnitzel. Great breakfast options include bagels, omelets, fruit, and granola. Half the dining area houses the Cosmic Cosas bookstore, which, along with the good food, cheerful decor and youthful ambiance, make this a natural hub for travelers. Opening and closing hours are somewhat flexible.

The preppy boutique café **Color de Verano** (Av. Lopez Mateos at Rueda Medina, 8–noon and 4–11 P.M. Mon.–Sat.) specializes in light sophisticated fare like quiche, pâté, and banana-flambé crepes, with which you'll feel almost duty bound to order a homemade dessert, glass of wine, or espresso. Three fully furnished apartments also are on the premises for long- and short-term rental.

Café Cito (Matamoros 42, tel. 998/888-0351, 7 A.M.–2 P.M. Mon.–Sat., 8 A.M.–2 P.M. Sun., US$2–6) is reminiscent of a Cape Cod eatery with its breezy blue and white decor and tables with sea shells beneath the glass. It's perfect for breakfast, serving tasty crepes, waffles, coffee, and big creamy *licuados* (milk- or water-based fruit shakes).

Bistro Françáis (Matamoros 29, 8 A.M.–noon and 6–10 P.M. daily, US$5–14) offers fantastic food in a quirky dining area decorated with bright bubble writing, cartoonish drawings, and Mexican hand-painted tiles. French

toast is a must for breakfast, while the *coq au vin,* beef kabobs, and lime and caper fish all make terrific dinners, and at surprisingly affordable prices. If vegetables are your thing, the veggie kabob is top-notch and features unforgettable portabella mushrooms. Instead of a beer, wash it down with wine, served by the glass for just US$2–4.

Other Specialties

Another of Isla Mujeres's best and favorite restaurants, █ **Casa O's** (Carretera Garrafón 9, tel. 998/888-0170, www.casaos.com, 1–10 P.M. daily, US$9–20) has a romantic *palapa*-covered dining area, with gorgeous views over the turquoise waters all the way to Cancún. The menu is varied and features some of the finest catches and cuts on the island; the filet mignon and shrimp kabobs are especially tasty. Portions are large, but don't miss out on the excellent appetizers and starters, like ceviche, heart of palm salad, and lobster bisque. Located one street below Casa de los Sueños; coming from town, the turnoff is just before the hotel entrance.

In a clapboard house facing the lagoon, with fishing boats crowded up next to it, **El Varadero** (noon–10 P.M. Tue.–Sun., US$7–14) doesn't really evoke the famous white-sand beach east of Havana that it's named for, but good food—and even better mojitos—have a way of trumping geography. Dig into classic Cuban fare while sitting at aluminum tables on an outdoor patio decorated with shipping buoys. Located at the mouth of Laguna Makax, near Puerto Isla Mujeres.

On Playa Norte, **Sunset Grill** (Av. Rueda Medina, tel. 998/877-0785, 10 A.M.–9 P.M. Mon.–Fri., 8 A.M.–9 P.M. Sat.–Sun., US$8–20) offers a great view with cool music on one of the best beaches on the island. Beachside chairs and umbrellas are also available for the day if you order from the menu. Food is standard but good, including grilled fish, ceviche, hamburgers, plus specials like rib eye and BBQ ribs.

Sweets

Aluxes Coffee House (Matamoros at Hidalgo, 7 A.M.–10 P.M. Mon.–Sat., US$1–3) is a great place to hang out with jazz playing in the background, comfy chairs, and artsy decor. Have a cup of caffeine, nibble on homemade brownies, muffins, and cheesecake, and catch up on your postcards. Milk shakes, ice cream sundaes, and smoothies are also offered.

La Michoacana (Av. Bravo at Av. Hidalgo, 9 A.M.–10 P.M. daily, US$0.60–1.50) offers homemade *aguas, paletas,* and *helados* (juices, popsicles, and ice cream). Choose from seasonal fruits including passion fruit, watermelon, pineapple, and mamey. Of course, chocolate- and vanilla-flavored treats are available too.

If you don't mind spending a bit extra on your frozen treats, try **Artesanal Ice Cream** (Av. Madero near Av. Hidalgo, 2–10 P.M. Tues.–Sat., 4–10 P.M. Sun.), a hipsterish ice cream parlor selling a variety of handcrafted ice creams at Häagen-Dazs prices.

Groceries

If you want to take snacks to the beach or prefer to cook your own meals, you can find a good selection of foodstuffs at several markets. **Mirtita** (Av. Juárez 14, tel. 998/887-0157, 7 A.M.–8:30 P.M. Mon.–Sat., 7 A.M.–4:30 P.M. Sun.) is a mom-and-pop grocery store run by the Magaña Family since 1965. **Xpress Super** (central plaza, Av. Morelos, 7 A.M.–10 P.M. Mon.–Sat., 7 A.M.–9 P.M. Sun.) is a chain supermarket offering a variety of all the usual suspects. Just inside the front door, you'll also find a small pharmacy. The **Mercado Municipal** (Av. Guerrero at Av. Matamoros, 6 A.M.–4 P.M. daily) is the place to go for fresh fruits and vegetables on the island, though selection can be slim depending on the season. There are also a handful of restaurants outside the market that serve cheap eats.

INFORMATION
Tourist Information

Across from the ferry docks, the **Oficina de Turismo** (Av. Rueda Medina 130, tel. 998/877-0307, www.isla-mujeres.com.mx, 9 A.M.–4 P.M. Mon.–Fri.) offers general information on the island, including hotel, res-

taurant, and tour options. It also gives out free brochures, maps, and copies of *Islander,* a twice-yearly tourist magazine.

Can-Do Isla Mujeres (www.cancunmap.com, US$8) is a series of fantastic professional-quality color **maps** of Isla Mujeres. It is extremely detailed, including annotated listings of almost every restaurant, hotel, and point of interest on the island. It is available at many restaurants and hotels or can be ordered online.

Hospitals

The general practitioner physician **Dr. Antonio E. Salas** (Hidalgo 18-D, tel. 998/877-0021, 24 hours tel. 998/877-0477, dr salas@prodigy.net.mx, 9 A.M.–3 P.M. and 4–9 pm daily) is highly recommended by islanders. He works directly with the Centro de Salud in town and has connections at most of Cancún's hospitals. He speaks fluent English and basic German.

Hospital Integral Isla Mujeres (Guerrero 7, tel. 998/877-0117, 24 hours daily) is equipped to handle walk-in consultations, simple surgeries, and basic emergencies. In case of a serious injury or illness, patients are taken to a Cancún hospital by boat. Cash only.

Isla Mujeres's primary **hyperbaric chamber** (tel. 998/877-0819, 9 A.M.–4 P.M.), or *cámera hiberbárica* in Spanish, is on the pedestrian-only extension of Avenida Morelos, just north of the center square. Recreational divers use it only very rarely; the main patents here are bent lobstermen, whose association collects monthly dues to help pay for the unit's operation and upkeep.

Pharmacies

Farmacia La Mejor (Madero 17, tel. 998/877-0116, 9 A.M.–10:30 P.M. Mon.–Sat., 9 A.M.–3:30 P.M. Sun.) has a fully stocked pharmacy. It also carries film, toiletries, sunscreen, and other personal items.

Police

The police (central plaza, tel. 998/877-0082) are available 24 hours daily.

FERRIES TO ISLA MUJERES

© LIZA PRADO

The ferry between Isla Mujeres and Cancún is known for its spectacular views of both destinations.

Various passenger ferries (and also a car ferry) leave for Isla Mujeres from Cancún every day. Those leaving from the Zona Hotelera are more expensive and take longer, but may be more convenient.

ZONA HOTELERA
Barcos Mexicanos (El Embarcadero/Playa Linda, Blvd. Kukulcán Km. 4, tel. 998/849-7515, US$10 one way, US$15 round-trip, 30 minutes each way). Departure: 9 A.M.*, 9:30 A.M., 10:30 A.M.*, 11 A.M., 11:30 A.M.*, 12:30 P.M., 2 P.M., and 2:45 P.M.* Return: 10:15 A.M.*, 11:50 A.M., 2 P.M.*, 3:30 P.M. and 5:30 P.M., and 6:15 P.M.* (Departures with an asterisk are available in the high season only.)

Playa Caracol Ferry (Blvd. Kukulcán Km. 8.5, no phone, US$15 round-trip, 30 minutes). Departure: 9 A.M., 11 A.M., and 1 P.M. Return: 11:50 A.M., 3:20 P.M., 5 P.M., and 6:15 P.M.

UltraMar/Playa Tortugas (Blvd. Kukulcán Km. 6.5, tel. 998/843-2011, US$15 round-trip, 30

SERVICES
Money
Immediately in front of the passenger ferry pier, **HSBC Bank** (Av. Rueda Medina between Av. Madero and Av. Morelos, tel. 998/877-0005, 8 A.M.–7 P.M. Mon.–Sat.) provides currency-exchange services and has 24-hour ATMs.

Internet and Telephone
A smattering of Internet and telephone places have popped up around the *centro,* which has helped to reduce the once-exorbitant prices. A couple of reliable and air-conditioned shops include: **IslaMujeres.com** (Madero 17, 8 A.M.–10 P.M. daily, US$1.50/hr.) and **Ciberco Lichos** (Av. Abasolo, between Av.

Hidalgo and Av. Juárez, 10 A.M.–11 P.M. daily, US$1.50/hr.).

For telephone calls, **DígaMe** (Av. Guerrero between Avs. Matamoros and Abasolo, 8 A.M.–10 P.M. Tue.–Sun.) had the best rates on the island at the time of research: US$0.27 per minute to the United States and Canada, US$0.37–65 per minute to Europe and Israel.

Post Office
The post office (Av. Guerrero at Av. Lopez Mateos, tel. 998/877-0085) is open 9 A.M.–4 P.M. Monday–Friday.

Immigration
The immigration office (Av. Medina near Av.

minutes). Departure: 9 A.M., 10 A.M., 11 A.M., noon, 1 P.M., and 4 P.M. Return: 9:30 A.M., 10:30 A.M., 11:30 A.M., 12:30 P.M., 3:30 P.M., and 5:30 P.M.

GRAN PUERTO

Passenger ferries operating from this pier (and neighboring Puerto Juárez) are faster, more frequent, and cost half as much as ferries in the Zona Hotelera. To get here, take the red R-1 bus (US$0.70, 20 minutes) on Blvd. Kukulcán or Av. Tulum; continue past the downtown bus terminal and north out of the city; you'll know Gran Puerto by its tall observation tower. The modern outdoor waiting area has two ATMs, a convenience store, gift shop, and even a McDonalds. Be aware that you may be approached by people dressed in UltraMar uniforms who are in fact selling timeshares.

UltraMar (tel. 998/843-2011, www.granpuerto.com.mx, US$3.50 each way, 15 minutes) boats feature comfy seats in an air-conditioned cabin, an open-air deck, and televisions playing a short promotional program on Isla Mujeres. Departure: every 30 minutes 5 A.M.-10 P.M., plus 11 P.M. and midnight. Return: every 30 minutes 5:30 A.M.-10:30 P.M., plus 11:30 P.M. and 12:30 A.M.

PUERTO JUÁREZ

Two blocks past Gran Puerto, Puerto Juárez is the original Isla Mujeres ferry pier, but the boats and waiting area are older and less comfy than at Gran Puerto.

Transportes Maritimos Magaña (Puerto Juárez, tel. 998/884-5479, US$3.50 each way, 15 minutes). Departure: every 30 minutes 6:30 A.M.-11:30 P.M. daily. Return: every 30 minutes 6 A.M.-8:30 P.M. daily.

PUNTA SAM VEHICLE FERRY

This lumbering vehicle ferry takes 45-60 minutes to cross between Punta Sam, on the mainland, and Isla Mujeres. Rates are according to your vehicle: US$17 for cars, $21 for SUVs, US$6.50 motorcycles, and US$5.50 for bicycles. Rates include the driver only – passengers (including walk-ons) are US$1.50 each way. On Isla Mujeres, the car ferry pier is a few hundred meters south of the passenger piers, past the naval dock. To get to Punta Sam, drive north on Av. Tulum, turn right on López Portillo and follow it to the pier, about five kilometers (3.1 miles) past Gran Puerto. The red R-1 bus also goes there (US$0.50, 30 minutes from downtown). Arrive an hour before your departure to get in line; tickets go on sale 30 minutes prior. Departure: 8 A.M., 11 A.M., 2:45 P.M., 5:30 P.M., and 8:15 P.M. Return: 6:30 A.M., 9:30 A.M., 12:45 P.M., 4:15 P.M., and 7:15 P.M.

Morelos, tel. 998/877-0189, 9 A.M.–3 P.M. Mon.–Fri., 9 A.M.–noon Sat.–Sun.) issues tourist cards to those arriving by boat from another country; for all other matters, including extending your visa, visitors must go to the Cancún office.

Travel Agencies

Isla Travel (Hidalgo 15, tel. 998/877-0805, islatravel@hotmail.com, 9 A.M.–7 P.M. Mon.–Sat., 10 A.M.–2 P.M. Sat.) is a good booking agency for tours—snorkeling, diving, Isla Contoy—on and off Isla Mujeres. Trips to Chichén Itzá, Xcaret, and Cuba also can be arranged. Travel services such as changing flights reservations or purchasing ADO bus tickets are provided as well.

Launderette

Tucked into Plaza Isla Mujeres, **Lavandería Ángel** (Av. Hidalgo, Local A3, tel. 998/151-3774, 8 A.M.–midnight daily) provides cheap laundry service with a smile. Same-day service is US$1 per kilogram (2.2 pounds), with a four-kilogram (8.8-pound) minimum. Express service is US$20 per kilogram, with the same four-kilogram minimum. If you call, they'll pick up and drop off your clothes at your hotel for no extra charge (though a tip to the driver is customary).

Lavandería (Av. Juárez at Abasolo, no tel. 7 A.M.–9 P.M. Mon.–Sat., 8 A.M.–2 P.M. Sun.) is a full-service launderette offering same-day service with a two-hour wait. Loads cost US$4.75 per four kilograms (8.8 pounds).

GETTING THERE

Isla Mujeres has a small airstrip but almost everyone takes the ferry—an inexpensive, quick, and scenic ride through the turquoise *Bahía de Mujeres* (Bay of Women).

Passenger Ferries

Passenger-only ferries leave for Isla Mujeres from Cancún in the Zona Hotelera and Puerto Juárez, about three kilometers (1.9 miles) north of downtown Cancún. If you are just going for the day, reconfirm the return times and remember that late-night ferries go to Puerto Juárez, not the Zona Hotelera.

Car Ferries

A vehicle ferry operates from Punta Sam, about five kilometers (3.1 miles) north of Puerto Juárez in Cancún. (See the *Ferries to Isla Mujeres* sidebar in this chapter for more details.)

GETTING AROUND

Isla Mujeres is a small and mostly flat island. In town you can easily walk everywhere. You could conceivably cover the length of the island on foot, but it's a long, hot walk with no sidewalks. Consider taking the bus, a taxi, or—better yet—rent a bike, moped, or golf cart for a little bit more adventure.

Bus

The bus is the cheapest way to get around Isla Mujeres—US$0.40 a ride. Unfortunately, it runs only between downtown and Playa Lancheros, about halfway down the island. Theoretically it runs every 30 minutes, but be prepared to wait from 45 minutes to forever (gas on the island is limited and sometimes runs out—ask at your hotel about the current situation). Bus stops are every couple of blocks on Rueda Medina and Avenida Martínez Ross

and are well marked with big blue and white signs—they're hard to miss.

Taxi

Isla Mujeres has many more taxis than seem necessary—in town, the danger isn't that you won't be able to hail a cab, but that you might get hit by one. They are especially numerous near the piers. Out of town, you shouldn't have to wait too long for a taxi to pass, and Parque Garrafón, Dolphin Discovery, and Playa Lancheros all have fixed taxi stands. From downtown, rates are US$1.25 around town or to Playa Norte, US$2 to Parque Garrafón, and US$4 to Playa Lancheros or Tortugranja or Punta Sur. Taxis are per trip, not per person, and drivers may pick up other passengers headed the same direction. You can also get a private driving tour of the island for US$13 per hour.

Bicycle, Golf Cart, and Moped Rental

Most rental operations on the island have fixed rates: golf carts—US$14 per hour, US$40 per day (store hours), and US$46 per 24 hours; mopeds US$9 per hour, US$22 per day, US$30 for 24 hours; and bicycles—US$2 per hour, US$8 per day. A word of caution: There are many road accidents, some very serious, involving tourists driving mopeds. Two people on a moped make it significantly less stable, especially for novice drivers, while renting separate mopeds will cost you more than a single golf cart, which carries four or more and is much safer.

Agencies right at the ferry pier may charge slightly more than those a few blocks away. Try **Ppe's Carts and Mopeds** (Hidalgo 19, tel. 998/877-0019, 9 A.M.–5 P.M. daily) or **El Sol Rental** (Av. Madero between Av. Guerrero and the ocean, 998/877-0791, 9 A.M.–5 P.M. daily).

Isla Holbox

At the northeastern tip of Quintana Roo where the Caribbean Sea mingles with the Gulf of Mexico, and completely within the Yum Balam national reserve, Isla Holbox (ohl-BOASH or hole-BOASH) is one of the last obscure islands in the Yucatán Peninsula. The town of Holbox is a fishing village (pop. 2,000) with sand roads, golf carts instead of cars, no ATMs, no cell phone service, no hospital, and no post office. Instead, you'll find brightly painted homes, *palapa*-roofed hotels, and a handful of Italian and Spanish expats who have opened B&Bs. The beaches are loaded with shells of all sorts but don't have the thick sand and reliably crystalline waters that Cancún has (though they are still awfully nice). In the summer, mosquitoes, sand flies, and horseflies can be vicious (come prepared with repellant!). Above all, Holbox offers a sense of peace and tranquility that is increasingly hard to find on Mexico's Caribbean coast, and the feeling of a place as yet untouched by big business. Holbox also offers great opportunities for sport fishing and bird-watching, and from June–September you can snorkel with whale sharks. Whale shark tours are monitored by the government and environmental groups to protect these creatures from harm. Sea turtles nest on Holbox as well, but tours are restricted to avoid disturbing them.

HISTORY

Mayas inhabited Holbox but abandoned the island more than 300 years before the first Europeans—wayward pirates—arrived. The name of the island and town is a matter of some dispute. Some say that "Holbox" means "black water" in a reference to the Maya founders who settled beside a spring whose water appeared to run black. A more popular story is that the pirate Francisco de Molas buried a treasure on the island and cut off the head of his African bodyguard to watch over the spot for eternity. De Molas was promptly killed by a snakebite, but the disembodied head of his bodyguard

appears occasionally to islanders, trying to divulge the treasure's location but succeeding only in scaring everyone away. By this latter account, the island was originally called "Pool-box," meaning "black head," and was apparently bastardized by subsequent Dutch arrivals.

Whatever the reason behind the name, this much is certain—the original town, located farther west, was destroyed by a hurricane and was rebuilt in the current location about 150 years ago. Storms are serious business on this

SEA TURTLES

At one time, sea turtles were plentiful and an important supplement to the regional diet. They were easy prey: Sea turtles were captured and killed as they clambered onto shore to lay eggs. The meat was sun-dried so that it could be eaten over time and the fat saved for soups and stews. The eggs – gathered from the nest or cut from the turtle – were eaten or saved for medicinal purposes.

Today, overfishing has placed all species of sea turtles on the endangered species list. Four of these eight – hawksbill, Kemp's ridley, green, and loggerhead – nest on the shores of the Yucatán Peninsula. Various environmental protection organizations in the Yucatán have joined forces with the Mexican government to save these ancient creatures; they have developed breeding programs and maintain strict surveillance of known nesting beaches to stop poaching.

It is strictly prohibited to capture and trade sea turtles or their products in Mexico. Do not buy their eggs, meat, or products like leather, oils, or tortoiseshell combs. By not participating in the trade of turtle products, you will help to promote the protection of these noble sea creatures.

low, flat island, which is buffeted by tropical conflagrations with some regularity; the most recent hurricane to strike was Wilma in 2005. *Nortes* are fall and winter storms that sweep down the Gulf coast bringing rain and turbid seas. *Maja' che* is the Maya name for sudden winds that can knock over trees; they are most common in April and May. In major storms, the whole island is evacuated.

Storms, however, have not managed to destroy Holbox's oldest house—a red wooden building with a *palapa* roof on the north (beach) side of the park. It belongs to Doña Trini, whose father bought it from the original owner almost a century ago. Doña Trini is a well-known hammock weaver; you can knock on the door to see her work or buy one of the finished products (Igualdad in front of the park, tel. 984/875-2262). Most of the town lives by fishing, though, and Holbox has almost 400 fishing boats and several fishing cooperatives. The town holds a land-and-sea parade on April 14 in honor of Saint Thelmo, patron saint of fishermen.

Other festivals include Environmental Week (July 1–5), when a group of local residents leads activities and presentations at local schools. Tourists can join the kids in one of the week's biggest events: picking up trash from the beach.

SIGHTS
◖ Whale Shark Feeding Grounds

Whale sharks congregate in shallow waters about 10 miles east of the village June–September. Snorkeling with whale sharks is a unique and (to some) nerve-wracking experience. The sharks themselves are harmless—like baleen whales, they eat plankton, krill, and other tiny organisms. But they are big: at 6–7.6 meters (20–25 feet) and more than 10 tons, they're the biggest fish in the world. The captain pulls the boat alongside a shark (at Holbox they tend to feed on the surface) and two guests and a guide slip into the water with life jackets, masks, snorkels, and fins. The water tends to be murky—it's all the sealife in the water that attracts the sharks

Snorkel with whale sharks, gentle giants that feed in these waters.

© LIZA PRADO

CANCÚN

in the first place—and the sharks are surprisingly fast. Still, you get a good view of these enormous, gentle animals, with their tiny eyes, bizarre shovel-mouths, and dark spotted skin. It's best to be on a small tour—since you go in two by two, you'll get more time in the water. Tours cost around US$80–90 a person, last 4–6 hours, and typically include snorkel gear, a life preserver, a box lunch, and nonalcoholic beverages. If there is time at the end of the tour, ask to stop off Cabo Catoche for a little snorkeling.

Isla Pájaros

Located in Yalahau Lagoon, **Isla Pájaros** (literally, Bird Island), is a wildlife sanctuary that is home to more than 150 species of birds throughout the year. Frigate birds, white ibis, double-crested cormorants, roseate spoonbills, and boat-billed herons are among the most frequently seen. In addition, between May and September, 40,000 flamingoes typically nest (and rest) here before they migrate to South America. Visitors are not allowed to wander on the island but two observation towers and walkways make spotting birds easy.

Town Beach

The town's main beach has no name but you can't miss it, extending eastward from town and fronted by a few hotels and private homes. It's ideal for beachcombing and shell-collecting, and only somewhat less-so for sunbathing, thanks to wind and a fair amount of dune grass. If you do swim, be sure to dry off immediately: horseflies (*tábanos* in Spanish) love skin still moist with seawater and they pack a mean bite.

Holbox's steady winds and shallow, waveless shore also make it ideal for kiteboarding and other wind sports. The strongest winds are September–March, while July and August tend to have lighter, novice-friendly breezes. Watching the kiteboarders zip and soar over the emerald waters is a sight unto itself. Holbox has a one-person kiteboarding operation if you want to try it for yourself.

© LIZA PRADO

The town beach caters to anglers and travelers alike.

Yalahau Spring

Said to have been used by pirates to fill their water barrels, **Yalahau Spring** is an *ojo de agua* (natural spring) on the edge of the mainland. Today, it is a picturesque swimming hole complete with a large *palapa,* picnic area, and pier. A trip here typically is combined with a stop to Isla Pájaros.

Isla de la Pasión

Just 15 minutes from town by boat, **Isla de la Pasíon** is a tiny deserted island just 50 meters (164 feet) wide. It's known for its white sand beach and beautiful emerald waters—perfect for a relaxing day at the beach. There are trees and a large *palapa* for shade. Be sure to bring plenty of water and snacks—there are no services on the island.

SHOPPING

La Bambina II(Av. Pedro Joaquín Coldwell, besomirosy@hotmail.com, tel. 984/875-2420, 10 A.M.–2 P.M. and 4–8 P.M. Tue.–Sun.) is an artsy shop run by a friendly multilingual Swiss expat named Rosy. Most of the items sold are handmade by locals or artists passing through town. Silver jewelry, bohemian clothes, handbags, and coconut objets d'art decorate this tiny shop. Located behind Hotel Faro Viejo; ask here about whale shark trips as well.

If you're into shells, **Lalo.com** (Abasolo 139, tel. 984/875-2118) is the place to go—it's filled with beautifully polished samples from all over the world. The owner—Maestro Lalo—lives below the shop so if you'd like to see his goods, ring the doorbell, and he'll open up.

If you're interested in buying a hammock or just seeing how they're made, wander over to **Doña Trini's** house (Igualdad in front of the park, tel. 984/875-2262). There, Doña Trini makes hammocks in endless colors and varying sizes. She also welcomes onlookers—whether they buy or not—and enjoys talking about her trade and her island. It takes Doña Trini about a month to complete a hammock so she often is steadily working away at one of her creations; if you want to be sure to see her at work, however, give her a call the night before to let her know

when you'll be stopping by. Hammocks cost US$45–80, depending on the size and material, and can be custom-ordered.

SPORTS AND RECREATION

There is a lot to do on Holbox, and lying in a hammock is one of the most popular activities. If you want to stretch your legs, hotels can arrange various tours, and there are a number of independent tour operators looking for your business. Either way, be clear on what you're getting before you sign up. Ask how many people will be on the tour, how long you will spend at the various sites (as opposed to getting there and back), whether any meals are included, whether the boat has shade from the sun, and whether the guide speaks your language (remembering that the person selling you the trip may not be the guide). You can also see about combining activities, such as going snorkeling before or after bird-watching or visiting the whale sharks. Although there are a handful of tour operators (and more certainly on the way), the following are well recommended: Carmelo at **Posada Mawimbi** (Av. Igualdad on the beach, tel. 984/875-2003, www.mawimbi .net) and Alberto at **Banana Tours** (Av. Igualdad between Avs. Palomino and Bravo, tel. 984/875-2366, 8 A.M.–9 P.M. daily, may close 1–4 P.M. in low season).

Snorkeling and Scuba Diving

Cabo Catoche, a coral reef in about 2–4 meters (6.5–13 feet) of water at the far eastern end of Isla Holbox, is the go-to spot for snorkeling. The water isn't as clear as in Isla Mujeres or Cancún, but the reef here is more pristine, and the animal life more abundant, including stingrays, moray eels, nurse sharks, sea stars, conch, and myriad fish. Because it is so far from town, tour operators usually prefer to combine it with another outing, such as an island tour or visiting the whale sharks. Posada Mawimbi and Banana Tours both offer snorkeling trips to Cabo Catoche for US$50–60 per person, lasting 4–5 hours. Less expensive tours (to nearer areas) can sometimes be arranged.

Posada Mawimbi also offers diving, though

Holbox is not known as a diving destination. The island lies on a huge shallow shelf, surrounded by sand. The best dive sites are a whopping 40–80 kilometers (25–50 miles) away, typically straight into the Gulf of Mexico. The effort is rewarding—shipwrecks, coral reefs, walls, and drift dives—but the long trip there and back is tiring and costly. Visibility is lower than in the Caribbean, although animal life is often more abundant. Posada Mawimbi offers two-tank dives for US$150–200 per person. Trips are small—maximum four divers—but cannot be arranged more than a day in advance because of variable weather in the gulf. Trips include lunch and all equipment.

Wind Sports

Take Off International (www.takeoff.nl/html-nieuw/mexico/index-mexico.htm) offers a three-day (three hours a day) introductory kiteboarding course for around US$335, all equipment included. If you want to improve your jumps, back loops, or just want a refresher, you can take a private two-hour lesson for US$135.

Certified kiters can rent kite and board for US$90 a day or US$350 a week. Take Off is a one-man operation with no fixed office, so you should email in advance to arrange a class; otherwise, ask at Hotel Faro Viejo for more information. Ask about windsurfing or sailing classes, as well, if those are more your style.

Bird-Watching

Holbox has more than 30 species of birds, including herons, white and brown pelicans, double-crested cormorants, roseate spoonbills, and greater flamingos (the brightest pink of the five flamingo species). A bird-watching tour (US$20–40 pp, 3–4 hours) generally includes taking a boat through the mangroves, to Isla Pájaros, and finally, to the flamingo nesting grounds. Most hotels can arrange a standard trip; Xaloc Resort has an island tour for US$25 per person that includes visiting Bird Island and Yalahau Spring, for swimming. Posada Mawimbi has bird-watching tours by kayak—you visit only the mangroves but typically succeed in seeing more birds since there is no motor

© LIZA PRADO

Fly high over the emerald waters of Isla Holbox, one of the best places in the region to kiteboard.

to scare them off (US$40 pp, 3–4 hours). More specialized bird-watchers may want to contact Juan Rico Santana (tel. 984/875-2021)—he leads many of the hotel trips, but he can arrange separate, more focused trips that are tailored to your interests.

Sport Fishing

Holbox is a good spot for sport fishing and still not very well known. A deep-sea fishing tour costs US$250–400, depending on how long you go out. A tour with a local fisherman, going after smaller and more plentiful catch, lasts 4–5 hours and costs around US$100. If you know how to fly-fish, a four- to six-hour tour in search of tarpon runs US$250–350. Most hotels can arrange trips, including Xaloc Resort, Faro Viejo, and Posada Mawimbi.

Baseball

Holbox has an amateur baseball team, known simply as *Selección Holbox* (Team Holbox). The season lasts all summer, and games against visiting teams are held most Sundays at noon at the baseball "stadium" on Avenida Benito Juárez a few blocks from the pier. It's a popular outing for island families, who typically bring tostadas and huge bowls of fresh homemade ceviche to go with the cold beer and soda on sale in the stands. Admission is US$1–2; bring a hat as there is little shade.

ACCOMMODATIONS

For many travelers, a big part of Holbox's charm is staying in one of the bungalow-style hotels that dot the island's long beach. The lodgings vary somewhat in style, amenities, and price, but all aim to offer simple rest and relaxation in a peaceful seaside setting. In town, hotels offer comfortable rooms a short distance from the beach, but at more accessible rates.

Under US$50

It is usually possible to camp on the beach, but **Ida y Vuelta Camping** (Calle Plutarco Elias Calles between Róbalo & Chacchi, tel. 984/875-2358, idayvueltacamping@yahoo .com, www.camping-mexico.com, US$8 per adult, US$5 per child) is a much better option. About 200 meters (650 feet) from the beach, the "campground" has five large *palapas* with sand floors and mosquito screens where you can hang hammocks or pitch a tent—the Italian owners will loan you either one, plus a pad and sheet, if you don't have them. There's a clean colorfully tiled common bathroom and a full kitchen for guests too.

Posada Los Arcos (Av. Benito Juárez at the park, tel. 984/875-2043, US$18.50 s, US$28 s with a/c, US$32.50 d with a/c, US$37 d with a/c and kitchenette) has long been a cheap, reliable option for budget travelers. The place is definitely starting to show its age in peeling paint, saggy mattresses, and so on. Rooms upstairs are better, brighter, and have a patio overlooking an interior garden. Good location and a friendly owner.

A few blocks from the park, **Posada Anhelyng** (Av. Porfirio Díaz s/n, kitty-corner from the soccer field, tel. 998/875-2006, US$37 s/d) has just five units; all have air-conditioning, TV, two beds, and are clean and spacious enough to make up for the somewhat sterile decor. Some rooms have a separate kitchen/eating area with a fridge, though you may have to borrow an electric stove and dishes from the owners. Reception is at the family's blue house on Avenida Porfirio Díaz nearer the park—look for the sign.

Rooms at **Posada D'Ingrid** (Av. Morelos at Av. Pedro Joaquín Coldwell, tel. 984/875-2070, US$32.50–46) are clean and comfortable, though rather small. Each has either a fan or air-conditioning, and either a queen and twin bed, and or two queens. The prices are a bit high for what you get, but there are a full common kitchen and *palapa*-covered eating area in the courtyard. Friendly owner.

US$50-100

◖ **Hotel Posada Mawimbi** (Av. Igualdad at the beach, tel. 984/875-2003, www.mawimbi .net, US$50 s/d with fan, US$60 s/d with a/c, US$60–80 bungalow with kitchenette, US$90 suite with a/c) is an upscale *palapa*-roofed posada with modern, comfortable rooms and bungalows that have lots of boho flair. Details like Guatemalan bedspreads, inlaid stones, colorful tile work, and exposed wood beams combine to give the rooms a personalized touch. There's a shady garden with plenty of hammocks and chairs, and the well-tended beach is just steps away. Italian owners Onny and Carmelo maintain a low-key friendly atmosphere, and offer recommended excursions, including whale shark tours, snorkeling, and scuba diving.

Each of the five colorful cabañas at **Villas Los Mapaches** (Av. Pedro Joaquín Coldwell s/n, tel. 984/875-2090, www.losmapaches .com, US$50 bungalow, US$50–75 bungalow with kitchenette) is decorated differently though all have a beachy, homey feel. All have solid wood frames and most have a large bedroom and bathroom, a loft with a queen-size bed, and a fully equipped kitchen and patio. The cabañas are set in a large palm-shaded garden that fronts the beach. It's about five blocks into town and a bit farther to the best swimming and beach areas. Use of the hotel's bicycles is included in the rate.

Opened in 1999, **Hotel La Palapa** (Av. Morelos at the beach, tel. 984/875-2121, www .hotellapalapa.com, US$60 s/d with a/c, US$80 suite with kitchenette) is owned and operated by an Italian family that's been on the island since 1989. Rooms vary in size and quality— some are a bit dim, but the ones facing the Gulf of Mexico have beautiful views. The hotel has a nice garden and small beach area, which the owners keep clean and free of boats (though boats pull up onshore on either side).

Over US$100

Xaloc Resort (Calle Chacchí s/n, Playa Norte, tel. 984/875-2160, www.holbox-xalocresort .com, US$111–165 s/d) is a classy, understated eco-resort about a 15-minute walk from town. It has 18 *palapa*-roofed cabañas sprinkled around two pools; each is large with thick beds, mosquito nets, red-tile floors, and large bathrooms. Though the grounds are nice, they're crowded—too many bungalows on the lot. Also, the beach-front units—definitely

the nicest—get noise from the sand street in front. Nevertheless, service here is excellent, which goes a long way toward a good experience. A full breakfast is included in the rate and is served in the hotel's bright Yucatecan restaurant. If you're interested in booking a tour, Xaloc also offers quality trips, often led by a working biologist.

For quality, amenities, and location, 《 **Villas Delfines** (Playa Norte, tel. 984/875-2196, www.holbox.com, US$90–150) gets our vote. Deluxe beachfront cabañas are spacious and attractive, with wood floors, two comfortable queen-size beds, fridge, and a large patio perfect for morning coffee. The pool and beach areas are often better maintained here than elsewhere, and the restaurant serves good, standard meals. About a 25-minute walk from town, the beach is large and boat-free, and there is less golf cart and moped traffic. Delfines is also an eco-friendly hotel, with waterless composting toilets (nicer than they sound), solar power, and fans only. Garden units are smaller, have concrete floors, and are missing the details that make the beachfront cabañas special.

FOOD

There are only a handful of restaurants on Isla Holbox—some at the beachfront hotels but most on or near the central park. If you stay for more than a couple days, don't stress about where to eat; by the end of your visit, you'll likely end up eating at every place in town.

Restaurants

Antojitos Los Chivos (Av. Benito Juárez at Av. Igualdad, 8 p.m.–midnight daily) is a classic snack shack serving good cheap Mexican food at plastic tables set up on the street. Everything is US$0.50, including Quintana Rooan staples such as *salbutes* and *panuchos,* variations of tostadas.

La Isla del Colibrí (central plaza, Benito Juárez at Av. Porfirio Díaz, 8 a.m.–1 p.m. and 6–11 p.m. daily, US$3.50–8) is especially good for breakfast, with big fruit juices and *licuados.* The fish dishes in the evening aren't bad.

A sister restaurant just down the street is a bit fancier and quite good, but it is open only in the high season.

The popular **Pizzería Edelín** (central park, Av. Palomino at Porfirio Díaz, tel. 984/875-2024, 11 A.M.–midnight daily, US$3.50–10) has decent thin-crust pizza—try the lobster or olive-and-caper toppings. Other options include fish, pasta, and Mexican finger foods. If you can, sit on the porch, as the tables there are much cooler.

Enjoy the breeze on the veranda of **Viva Zapata!** (Igualdad at Av. Benito Juárez, tel. 984/875-2204, 5 P.M.–11 P.M. daily, US$4–10). Specializing in grilled meat and seafood, this is a popular place with travelers. Be sure to check out the homage to Latin American revolutionary leaders inside.

Overlooking the park, **Cueva del Pirata** (central plaza, Av. Benito Juárez at Porfirio Díaz, tel. 984/875-2183, 8 A.M.–11 P.M. Mon.–Sat., US$5–16) is one of the classiest places in town. Soft jazz fills the room and spills out to the candlelit tables on the front porch. Offering a handful of homemade pastas, a dozen sauces to choose from, and imported wine—this is the place to go all-out. Try the lobster marinara sauce—it's worth the premium price. Meat, poultry, and seafood dishes are also offered.

Baked Goods and Ice Cream

A great local bakery, **Panadería La Conchita** (Av. Palomino at López Mateos, 7 A.M.–10 A.M. and 5–9 P.M. daily) makes bread, cookies, cakes, and other baked goods for the entire island's population. Even if you don't buy directly from the store, you're sure to eat some of its products in the town's restaurants and hotels.

Cool off with a homemade treat from **Paletería Ancona** (Morelos between Díaz and Igualdad, 9 A.M.–9 P.M. daily), which makes juices, popsicles, and ice cream from such varied flavors as coconut, peanut, tamarind, rice, and corn.

Groceries

Supplies ebb and flow in Isla Holbox, so you might have to go to more than one store to find everything you're looking for.

Super Monkey's (half a block south of the park on Av. Benito Juárez, 7 A.M.–11 P.M. daily) has canned and packaged food, bug repellent, sunscreen, and toiletries.

Frutas y Verduras (in front of Super Monkey's on Av. Benito Juárez, 7 A.M.–3 P.M. and 4–8 P.M. daily) has the best selection of fruits and vegetables on the island. You'll also find beans, pastas, and spices. Another option is **Frutería Ruby** (Av. Palomino at López Mateos), open daily 7 A.M.–10 P.M.

INFORMATION AND SERVICES

Holbox has no bank, no ATM, and no post office. Few hotels, restaurants, or tour operators take credit cards, so definitely bring enough cash for your stay and in case you decide to stay an extra day or two. (In a pinch, try buying your tours through the top-end hotels, where credit cards are accepted.) Hours of operation on the island are decidedly flexible—"open all day" usually means "closed for a couple of hours in the middle of the day for lunch."

Hospitals

The only health center on the island, **Centro de Salud** (Av. Benito Juárez between Oceano Atlántico and Adolfo López Mateos, 8 A.M.–2 P.M. and 5–7 P.M. Mon.–Sat., 9 A.M.–1 P.M. Sun.) has no phone, occasionally runs out of medicine, and is equipped to handle only minor injuries and illness. For more advanced medical attention, head to Cancún or Mérida; in emergencies you may be able to charter a small plane.

Pharmacies

Farmacia Pepe's (next to Super Monkey's on Av. Benito Juárez, tel. 998/875-2084, 8 A.M.–2:30 P.M. and 5–11 P.M. daily) is the only pharmacy on Holbox. The owners live on-site, so you can always ring if it's urgent.

Internet and Telephone

Facing the park and open late, **Internet El**

Parque (Av. Benito Juárez, 9 A.M.–midnight daily) charges US$1.50 per hour for reasonably fast Internet, and US$0.40 per minute for calls to the United States and Canada and US$0.80 per minute for calls to Europe.

Launderette

A number of women offer laundry service out of their homes, most charging around US$5 for three kilograms (6.6 pounds). Look for signs around town or ask at your hotel.

GETTING THERE
Car, Bus, and Ferry

To get to Holbox, you first need to get to the small coastal village of Chiquilá. There are direct buses from Cancún and Mérida (see those sections for fares and schedules). If you're driving, take old Highway 180 (not the *autopista*) to El Ideal, about 100 kilometers (62 miles) west of Cancún. Turn north onto Highway 5 and follow that about 140 kilometers (87 miles) to Chiquilá, passing though the town of Kantunilkín. (There are shortcuts from both Mérida and Cancún, but they follow smaller, less-maintained roads). You'll have to leave your car in Chiquilá. Several families run small overnight parking operations, charging US$4–5 a day.

The **9 Hermanos** (US$3.75; 25 minutes) ferry to Isla Holbox leave Chiquilá at 6 A.M., 8 A.M., 10 A.M., 11 A.M., noon, 2 P.M., 4 P.M., 5 P.M., and 7 P.M. Returning boats leave Holbox at 5 A.M., 7 A.M., 9 A.M., 10 A.M., 11 A.M., 1 P.M., 3 P.M., 4 P.M. and 6 P.M. Going to Holbox, it's a good idea to get to the dock a half hour early as the boat occasionally leaves ahead of schedule. Private boatmen make the trip in either direction for approximately US$23.50–32.50 for up to six people; ask at the dock.

From Chiquilá, second-class buses to Cancún (US$6.50) leave the dock parking area at 5:30 A.M., 7:30 A.M., and 1:30 P.M.; all wait for the boat arriving from Holbox. To Mérida, there's just one bus at 5:30 A.M. (US$14).

If you get stuck in Chiquilá, the **Hotel Puerta del Sol** (US$22 s/d with fan, US$30 with a/c) is your only option, located a short distance back down the main road from the dock. Rooms here are very simple, all with TV and private bath. Fan rooms are fairly dumpy, but those with air-conditioning are newer and nicer. There are several basic restaurants facing the dock parking area.

Air

Aerosaab (tel. 984/873-0804, www.aerosaab .com) offers a popular full-day tour to Isla Holbox from its home base in Playa del Carmen. Using one of two 4- to 5-passenger Cessna airplanes, the trip includes a scenic flight up the coast to Holbox, plus a tour of Isla Pájaros and Yalahau spring, and a chance to explore the village and beach. (US$305 pp, plus US$6–25 airport fees, minimum four people). If time is short, and money long, it's certainly a memorable way to visit.

GETTING AROUND

Holbox is very easy to get around on foot. Even the farthest hotels are no more than a half hour's walk from town, and it's very safe day or night. Though you can rent golf carts the only time you really need one is getting between the pier and your hotel with your bags. Golf carts serve as the island's taxis (some are even painted in yellow and black checkers). A ride from the pier into town is US$1 per person or US$2.50 to the hotels farther down the beach. There are always taxis parked around the plaza, or your hotel can call one.

Golf Cart Rental

It's hard to imagine really needing a golf cart, but if you find a reason there are numerous *rentadoras* (rental shops), including **Rentadora Glendy** (Av. Porfirio Díaz at Av. Morelos, tel. 984/875-2093, 7 A.M.–11 P.M.) and **Rentadora El Brother** (Av. Benito Juárez at Av. Igualdad, tel. 998/875-2018, 8 A.M.–10 P.M. daily). All charge about the same: US$8 per hour, US$30 for six hours, US$45 for 12 hours, and US$55 for 24 hours.

ISLA COZUMEL

All around Isla Cozumel, the Caribbean Sea glitters a hundred shades of blue. Beneath the waves, Cozumel's pristine coral reefs make for spectacular diving and snorkeling, the island's number one draw. San Miguel de Cozumel—usually just called Cozumel, since it's the only city on the island—is where the ferries from Playa del Carmen land. It's also where cruise ships, as many as 10 per day in the high season, arrive; it's then that the waterfront promenade becomes a human river, flowing slowly down a channel of jewelry stores, souvenir shops, and open-air restaurants.

Just a few blocks from the promenade, another Cozumel emerges, a small friendly community where old folks sit at their windows and dogs sleep in the streets. In spring, masses of orange *framboyán* (poinciana) flowers bloom on shade trees in the plaza, and festivals and religious celebrations are widely attended.

Cozumel's interior—including an important Maya ruin—and its eastern shore are yet another world, lacking even power lines and telephone cables. Heavy surf makes much of the eastern shore too dangerous for swimming, but you easily can spend a day beachcombing or relaxing on the unmanicured beaches and lunching at small restaurants overlooking the sea.

As Mexico's largest island, it shouldn't be surprising to discover that the island is so multifaceted. But it's hard not to marvel at how stark the differences are. Come for the diving and snorkeling, but leave time to experience a side of Cozumel you may not have expected.

© LIZA PRADO

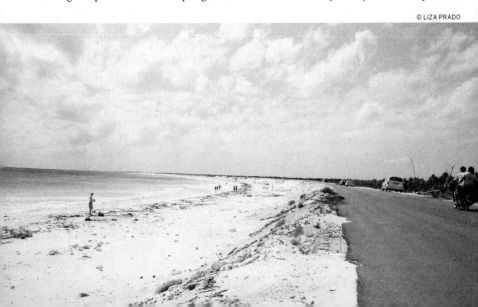

HIGHLIGHTS

◖ Museo de la Isla de Cozumel: Soak in the history and ecology of Mexico's largest island, a longtime Maya mecca and a bull's-eye for hurricanes (page 107).

◖ Santa Rosa Wall: Sit back and enjoy the ride at one of the island's favorite dive sites, where a strong current whisks you past a stony wall teeming with sealife (page 110).

◖ Palancar: Stretching a full three miles, this dive site has something for everyone, from snorkeler-friendly shallows to deep coral ravines (page 111).

◖ San Gervasio: Thought to be dedicated to Ixchel, the goddess of fertility, this is Cozumel's best Maya ruin (page 111).

◖ Parque Ecológico Punta Sur: Explore this popular national park, with a crocodile-infested lagoon, colorful coral reef, and even an ancient Maya lighthouse (page 120).

LOOK FOR ◖ TO FIND RECOMMENDED SIGHTS, ACTIVITIES, DINING, AND LODGING.

ISLA COZUMEL

PLANNING YOUR TIME

Don't let the cruise ship hubbub on Avenida Rafael Melgar turn you off from the town altogether. Besides the fact that most of the hotels, dive shops, banks, and other services are here, the town itself has much to offer, including a pleasant central plaza and a great museum. Budget a day or two to rent a car to explore the rest of the island, including the beach clubs, Maya ruins, family-friendly eco-parks, and the wild beaches and deserted coastline of Cozumel's eastern side.

HISTORY

Cozumel has been inhabited since 300 B.C. and was one of three major Maya pilgrimage sites in the region (the others were Chichén Itzá and Izamal in Yucatán state). The name is derived from the island's Maya name *Cuzamil* (Land of Swallows). The height of its occupation was A.D. 1250 to 1500, when Putún people (also known as the Chontol or Itzás, the same group who built Chichén Itzá's most famous structures) dominated the region as seafaring merchants. Capitan Don Juan de Grijalva "discovered" the island in 1518 and renamed it Isla de Santa Cruz, marking the beginning of the brutal dislocation of the native people by Spanish explorers and *conquistadores*. It eventually was overrun by British and Dutch pirates who used it as a base of operations. By the mid-1800s, however, the island was virtually uninhabited. The henequen, chicle, and coconut oil booms attracted a new wave of people to the Quintana Roo

ISLA COZUMEL

ISLA COZUMEL

Caribbean Sea

PUNTA MOLAS LIGHTHOUSE
Punta Molas
PUNTA MOLAS
AGUADA GRANDE
LAS GRECAS
CASTILLO REAL
Punta Norte
Isla de la Pasión
Playa San Juan
Playa Azul
CASA VIENTO
PLAYA AZUL
COZUMEL COUNTRY CLUB
SAN GERVASIO
LOS COCOS
COZUMEL INTERNATIONAL AIRPORT
To Playa del Carmen
CONDUMEL
MUSEO DE LA ISLA DE COZUMEL
SANTA RITA
SEE "SAN MIGUEL DE COZUMEL" MAP
San Miguel de Cozumel
CROSS-ISLAND HIGHWAY
SAN BENITO
Playa Punta
Punta Este
MEZCALITO'S BEACH BAR AND GRILL
SEÑOR IGUANAS
Paraíso Reef
SEE DETAIL
Playa Punta Morena
Playa Tortugas
HOTEL VENTANAS AL MAR
Bahía Chankanaab
COCONUTS BAR AND GRILL
Chankanaab Reef
Parque Nacional Chankanaab
RESTAURANT AND BAR CHEN RÍO
Tormentos
UVA'S
Yucab
EL CEDRAL
Playa Chen Río
Tunich
El Cedral
PARADISE BEACH
RANCHO PALMITAS
Playa San Martín
DETAIL
Playa San Francisco
NACHI COCOM
BUENA VISTA
Punta Chiqueros
Paraíso Reef
AIRPLANE WRECK
OCCIDENTAL ALLEGRO COZUMEL
Playa Bonita
INT'L PIER
EL CID HOTEL
Playa Palancar
PLAYA PALANCAR
PUERTO MAYA
San Francisco Reef
Playa Rasta
SANTA ROSA WALL
Paseo del Centro
PARQUE ECOLÓGICO PUNTA SUR
PARK ENTRANCE
Marina Caleta
Laguna de Colombia
PALANCAR
Laguna Chun Chacaab
EL CARACOL
PRESIDENTE INTERCONTINENTAL
Colombia Reef
Punta Sur
LIGHTHOUSE
DZUL-HA
FIESTA AMERICANA
Maracaibo Reef

0   2 mi
0   2 km

© AVALON TRAVEL PUBLISHING, INC.

territory (it didn't become a state until 1974) and Cozumel slowly rebounded, this time with a mostly Mexican mestizo population. With the establishment of Cancún in the 1970s, and the "discovery" of Cozumel's reefs by Jacques Cousteau, Cozumel's future as a tourist and diving destination was set.

ORIENTATION

The town of San Miguel de Cozumel is located on the west side of the island. The main pas-senger ferry lands here, across from the central plaza. Most streets are one-way in town; if you're driving, be aware that *avenidas* (avenues) run north–south and have the right-of-way over *calles* (streets), which run east–west. Once you leave town, there is a single road that circles the entire island.

Avenida Benito Juárez is one of the main streets in San Miguel de Cozumel, beginning at the central plaza, crossing town, and becoming the Cross-Island Highway.

ISLA COZUMEL

SAN MIGUEL DE COZUMEL

To Cozumel Country Club

SEE "DOWNTOWN SAN MIGUEL DE COZUMEL" MAP

MUSEO DE LA ISLA DE COZUMEL

Caribbean Sea

HACIENDA SAN MIGUEL

ALIANZA FRANCESA

BOULEVARD AEROPUERTO

To Airport

Benito Juárez Park

Mercado Público

CASA COLONIAL

AVENIDA BENITO JUAREZ

To Cross-Island Highway and SAN GERVASIO

AVENIDA ADOLFO ROSADO SALAS

JOSE MARIA MORELOS

CREPERIA LA DELICIA

MIGUEL HIDALGO

POLICE

CHEDRAUI/ CINÉPOLIS

To Parque Nacional Chankanaab and PARQUE ECOLÓGICO PUNTA SUR

SCALE NOT AVAILABLE

© AVALON TRAVEL PUBLISHING, INC.

HURRICANE WILMA

Hurricane Wilma was the worst hurricane of the worst storm season ever recorded in the Atlantic. There's a remarkable satellite image, which many shop owners in Isla Cozumel have tacked to their walls, of the huge spinning storm spread across the Caribbean, Isla Cozumel and Cancún visible in its eye. Both Cozumel and Cancún received direct hits, and the storm took its time leaving: for nearly three days, the region was pummeled with severe rain, wind, and surf.

Wilma struck Mexico in late October 2005, having already rampaged through the Caribbean and headed for Florida. It was the 13th hurricane that year, the fourth to reach Category 5 – the weather service's strongest classification – and only the third Category 5 hurricane ever known to have developed in the month of October. At its peak, Wilma was the single most intense hurricane ever recorded in the Atlantic basin (by barometric pressure) and had wind speeds of 185 mph (296 kph). The weather service even retired the name Wilma, assuring the massive storm's place in history.

Tens of thousands of travelers and residents rode out the storm, despite urgent evacuation orders in the days just before it hit. News reports showed vacationers huddled in hotel ballrooms, even as windows shattered and waves crashed against 3rd-story balconies. In Mexico alone, Wilma killed eight people and caused US$7.5 billion in damages; in all, however, Wilma hit a half-dozen countries, caused 63 deaths, and totaled US$25 billion in damages.

Wilma hit Mexico's tourism industry just as hard, coming just before the all-important holiday season. After intense media coverage of the storm itself and of the travails of tourists trying to get home afterward, scant attention was paid to the region's recovery and cleanup, which was amazingly quick and complete. Many businesses reopened within days. But shaken tourists stayed away and the high season was a total wash. Anticipating this, a number of hotels jump-started long-planned renovations, in some cases quite extensive. Ironically, one of Wilma's long-term effects has been the *improvement* of overall hotel quality and star rating, especially in Cancún. And while the storm stripped some beaches bare – and sand had to be pumped in to refill them – other beaches turned out even wider and more accessible than ever, and remain so today.

Hurricane Wilma also underscored the remarkable camaraderie of locals and expatriates throughout the entire region. Almost to a person, residents describe emerging from their storm-lashed homes and businesses, picking up shovels and wheelbarrows, and working side-by-side with their neighbors to put their communities back together. It's this same resilience and spirit that has long made the Riviera Maya and Yucatán Peninsula a special place to visit, and will continue to do so, even as those famous satellite pictures of Wilma, still tacked to store walls, fade to yellow and curl around the edges.

The highway passes the turnoff to the San Gervasio ruins before intersecting with the coastal road. The coastal road follows Cozumel's eastern shore, which is dotted with a few beach clubs and restaurants. Rounding the southern tip, the road heads north along the west shore before becoming Avenida Rafael Melgar, and returning to the central plaza. Continuing north, the road passes turnoffs to the airport and a country club before turning to dirt and eventually dead-ending.

Sights

THE CENTRAL PLAZA

In and around Cozumel's central plaza stand colonial and modern civic buildings, a boxy clock tower, and busts of the late Mexican president Benito Juárez and the general Andrés Quintana Roo. On Sunday evenings locals and tourists meet here. Families—sometimes three generations—gather around the white gazebo to hear Latin rhythms and tunes of the day played by local musicians. A few women still wear the lovely white *huipiles,* while men look crisp and cool in their traditional *guayaberas.* Children, dressed as miniatures of their parents, run, play, and chatter in front of the band. It's hard to say who does the best business—the balloon man or the cotton-candy vendor. In short, it's a pleasant place to spend an evening.

◖ MUSEO DE LA ISLA DE COZUMEL

The town's small but excellent museum (Av. Rafael Melgar at Calle 6, tel. 987/872-1434, 9 A.M.–5 P.M. Mon.–Sat., 9 A.M.–4 P.M. Sun., US$3) is on the waterfront in an old building that once housed a turn-of-the-20th-century hotel. Well-composed exhibits in English and Spanish describe the island's wildlife, coral reefs, and the fascinating, sometimes tortured history of human presence here, from the Maya pilgrims who came to worship the fertility goddess to present-day survivors of devastating hurricanes. Be sure to visit in the morning if you want to avoid the cruise ship crowds. The museum also has a small bookstore, a library, and a pleasant outdoor café overlooking the sea.

CORAL REEFS

Cozumel's coral reef—and the world-class diving and snorkeling it provides—is the main reason people come to the island. The reef was designated a national marine reserve more than two decades ago, and the waters have thrived under the park's rigorous protection and clean-up programs. Hurricane

ISLA COZUMEL

© LIZA PRADO

Cozumel's central plaza is a hub of social activity.

ISLA COZUMEL

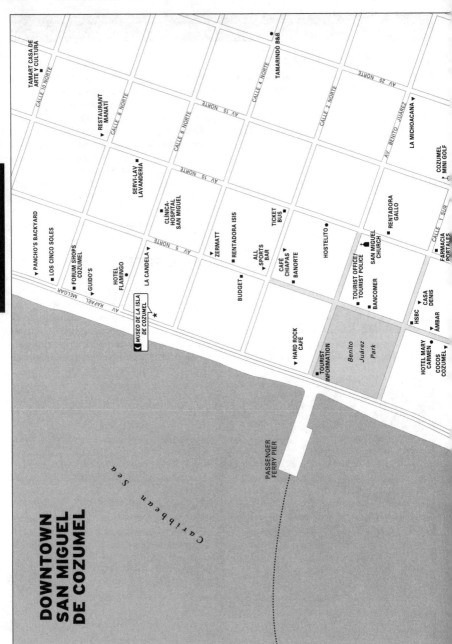

DOWNTOWN SAN MIGUEL DE COZUMEL

Caribbean Sea

PASSENGER FERRY PIER

TAMART CASA DE ARTE Y CULTURA
CALLE 10 NORTE
RESTAURANT MANATÍ
CALLE 8 NORTE
TAMARINDO B&B
CALLE 4 NORTE
CALLE 2 NORTE
AV. BENITO JUÁREZ
AV. 20 NORTE
LA MICHOACANA
COZUMEL MINI GOLF
CALLE 15 NORTE
CALLE 6 NORTE
AV. 10 NORTE
SERVI-LAV LAVANDERÍA
CLINICA-HOSPITAL SAN MIGUEL
AV. 5 NORTE
ZERMATT
RENTADORA ISIS
TICKET BUS
RENTADORA GALLO
CALLE 1 SUR
FARMACIA PORTALES
PANCHO'S BACKYARD
LOS CINCO SOLES
FORUM SHOPS COZUMEL
GUIDO'S
HOTEL FLAMINGO
LA CANDELA
ALL SPORTS BAR
CAFÉ CHIAPAS
BANORTE
HOSTELITO
TOURIST OFFICE/ TOURIST POLICE
SAN MIGUEL CHURCH
BANCOMER
HSBC
CASA DENIS
AMBAR
AV RAFAEL MELGAR
MUSEO DE LA ISLA DE COZUMEL
BUDGET
HARD ROCK CAFÉ
TOURIST INFORMATION
Benito Juárez Park
HOTEL MARY CARMEN
COCOS COZUMEL

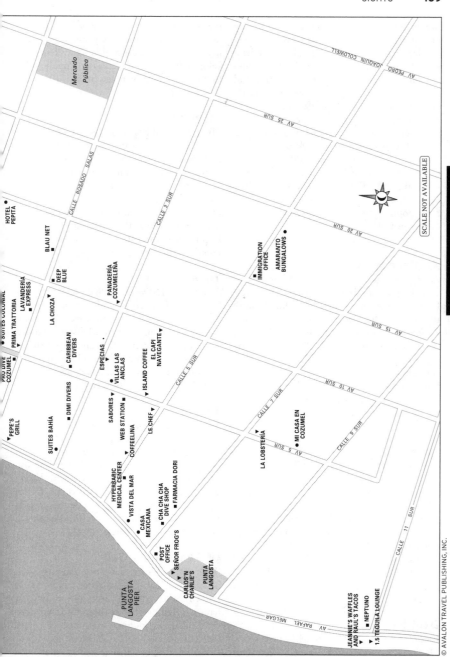

ISLA COZUMEL

SCALE NOT AVAILABLE

Mercado
Público

AV PEDRO JOAQUIN COLDWELL

AV 25 SUR

AV 20 SUR

AV 15 SUR

AV 10 SUR

AV 5 SUR

CALLE ROSADO SALAS

CALLE 3 SUR

CALLE 5 SUR

CALLE 7 SUR

CALLE 9 SUR

CALLE 11 SUR

AV RAFAEL MELGAR

HOTEL PEPITA

BLAU NET

DEEP BLUE

LAVANDERIA EXPRESS

PANADERIA COZUMELEÑA

LA CHOZA

PRIMA TRATTORIA

SUITES COLONIAL

PRO DIVE COZUMEL

CARIBBEAN DIVERS

ESPECIAS

VILLAS LAS ANCLAS

EL CAPI NAVEGANTE

ISLAND COFFEE

IMMIGRATION OFFICE

AMARANTO BUNGALOWS

PEPE'S GRILL

DIMI DIVERS

SUITES BAHÍA

SABORES

WEB STATION

COFFEELINA

LE CHEF

HYPERBARIC MEDICAL CENTER

VISTA DEL MAR

CASA MEXICANA

CHA CHA CHA DIVE SHOP

FARMACIA DORI

MI CASA EN COZUMEL

LA LOBSTERIA

POST OFFICE

SEÑOR FROG'S

CARLOS'N CHARLIE'S

PUNTA LANGOSTA

PUNTA LANGOSTA PIER

JEANNIE'S WAFFLES AND RAUL'S TACOS

NEPTUNO

1.5 TEQUILA LOUNGE

© AVALON TRAVEL PUBLISHING, INC.

Wilma took a major toll on the reef, snapping off coral and sponges with its powerful surge, and leaving other sections smothered under a thick layer of sand and debris. But hurricanes are nothing new to Cozumel or its coral, and reports of vast damage to the reef were greatly exaggerated. Cozumel's underwater treasure remains very much alive, supporting a plethora of creatures, its seascapes as stunning as ever. Dozens of dive and snorkeling sites encircle the island, and the 1,000-meter-deep (3,281-foot) channel between Cozumel and the mainland still provides spectacular drift and wall dives. Here is a list of some of the most popular dives, though by no means all of the worthwhile ones. (See *Sports and Recreation* for information on dive shops.)

Airplane Wreck

A 40-passenger Convair airliner lies on Cozumel's seabed, about 65 meters (195 feet) from the shore near the El Cid hotel. Sunk in 1977 for the Mexican movie production of *Survive II,* the plane has been broken into pieces and strewn about the site by years of storms. The site itself is relatively flat, though with parrot fish, damselfish, and a host of sea fans and small coral heads, there's plenty to see. With depth ranges from 3–15 meters (9–45 feet), this is a good site for snorkelers too.

Paraíso

Just south of the International Pier, and about 200 meters (656 feet) from shore, lies Paraíso, an impressive two-lane coral ridge. Medium-size coral—mostly brain and star—attract French and gray angelfish, squirrel fish, and sea cucumbers. This site is also popular for night dives because of its proximity to hotels, which means less time on the boat. Depth ranges from 11–15 meters (33–45 feet). Snorkeling is decent near the shore but be very careful of boat traffic.

Dzul-Ha

One of the best spots for snorkeling from shore, Dzul-Ha has small coral heads and sea fans that support a colorful array of fish like blue tangs, parrot fish, and queen angels. Steps lead into the ocean and concession stands rent snorkel gear (US$10) on the beach. Popular with tour groups. Depths range from 3–10 meters (10–30 feet).

Tormentos

About 60 coral heads can be seen at this site, each decorated with an assortment of sea fans, brain and whip corals, and sponges. Invertebrates like to hide out in the host of crevices—look for flamingo tongue shells, arrow crabs, and black crinoids. Lobster and nurse sharks like the scene too—keep your eyes peeled for them, especially at the north end of the site. Depth ranges from 10–20 meters (30–60 feet). Popular with photographers.

Yucab

A perfect drift dive, Yucab has archways, overhangs, and large coral heads—some as tall as 3 meters (10 feet)—that are alive with an incredible array of creatures: lobsters, banded coral shrimp, butterfly fish, and angelfish can almost always be found here. Video photographers typically have a field day. Depth ranges from 12–20 meters (36–60 feet).

Tunich

Tunich usually has a 1.5-knot current, which makes it an excellent high-velocity drift dive. The site itself has a white sand bottom with a gentle downward slope that ends in a drop-off. Along the way, the reef is dotted with basket sponges and intricately textured corals. Divers regularly encounter turtles, eagle rays, moray eels, bar jacks, and parrot fish. The depth ranges from 15–30 meters (45–90 feet).

⟨ Santa Rosa Wall

With a sensational drop-off that begins at 22 meters (72.2 feet), this spectacular site is known for its tunnels, caves, and stony overhangs. Teeming with sealife, divers encounter translucent sponges, mammoth sea fans, file clams, blennies, fairy basslets, gray angelfish, and groupers. Strong currents make this a good drift dive, especially for experienced divers. Depth ranges from 10–30 meters (30–90 feet).

Paso del Cedral

A strip reef lined with small corals like disk and cactus, this site attracts large schools of fish like blue striped grunts and snapper—perfect for dramatic photographs. Southern stingrays often are seen gliding over the sandy areas just inside the reef. Depths range from 10–20 meters (30–60 feet).

◖ Palancar

This spectacular five-kilometer-long (3.1-mile) dive spot is actually made up of five different sites—Shallows, Garden, Horseshoe, Caves, and Deep. It is known for its series of enormous coral buttresses. Some drop off dramatically into winding ravines, deep canyons, and passageways; others have become archways and tunnels with formations 15 meters (49.2 feet) tall. The most popular site here is Palancar Horseshoe, which is made up of a horseshoe-shaped series of coral heads at the top of a drop-off. All the sites, however, are teeming with reef life. Palancar ranges in depth from 10–40 meters (30–120 feet).

Colombia

An enormous coral buttress, Colombia boasts tall coral pillars separated by passageways, channels, and ravines. Divers enjoy drifting past huge sponges, anemones, and swaying sea fans. Larger creatures—sea turtles, groupers, and spotted eagle rays—are commonly seen here. This drift dive is recommended for experienced divers. Depths range from 10–40 meters (30–120 feet).

Maracaibo

At the island's southern tip, Maracaibo is a deep buttress reef interspersed with tunnels, caves, and vertical walls. It is known for its immense coral formations as well as its large animals—sharks (blacktips, hammerheads, tigers, and bulls) and schools of manta and eagle rays. A deep-drift dive, this site is recommended for

advanced divers only. Depths range from 30–40+ meters (90–120+ feet).

ARCHAEOLOGICAL ZONES

Isla Cozumel played a deeply significant role in the Maya world as an important port of trade and, more importantly, as one of three major destinations of religious pilgrimages (the others were Izamal and Chichén Itzá, both in Yucatán state). The island's primary site—known as San Gervasio today—was dedicated to Ixchel (Lady Rainbow), the Maya goddess of fertility (and of the Moon, childbirth, medicine, and weaving). Archaeologists believe that every Maya woman was expected, at least once in her life, to journey to Cozumel to make offerings to Ixchel for fertility—her own, and that of her family's fields. Cozumel's draw was powerful, as inscriptions there refer to places and events hundreds of miles away.

Twenty-four archaeological sites have been discovered, though only three are easily accessible, and only the largest—San Gervasio—can properly be called a tourist attraction. San Gervasio is certainly not as glorious as ruins found on the mainland, but well worth a visit all the same.

◖ San Gervasio

The area around San Gervasio (Cross-Island Hwy. Km. 7, www.cozumelparks.com, 7 A.M.–4 P.M. daily, US$5 Mon.–Sat., US$2 Sun.) was populated as early as A.D. 200, and remained so after the general Maya collapse (A.D. 800-900) and well into the Spanish conquest. In fact, archaeologists excavating the ruins found a crypt containing 50 skeletons along with numerous Spanish beads; the bodies are thought to be those of 16th-century Maya who died from diseases brought by the conquistadors.

Today's visitors will find a modest ruin, whose small square buildings, low to the ground with short doors, are typical of those found elsewhere on the island. This style, known as *oratorio,* almost certainly developed in response to climatic imperatives: Anything built here needed to withstand the hurricanes that have pummeled Cozumel for millennia.

ISLA COZUMEL

© LIZA PRADO

San Gervasio is known for its small structures, well-preserved *sacbés* (stone causeways), and this archway, which leads to the site's central plaza.

(Sure enough, Hurricane Wilma did no major damage to San Gervasio's structures.)

San Gervasio has three building groups, connected by trails that follow the same ancient causeways used by the city's original inhabitants. Entering the site, you'll come first to a structure known as *Las Manitas* (Little Hands), so named for the red handprints still visible on one of its walls. This structure is thought to have been the home of one of San Gervasio's kings, and the inner temple was likely a personal sanctuary.

Bearing left, the trail leads to the Plaza Central, a large courtyard surrounded by low structures in various states of decay. This served as the seat of power in San Gervasio's latest era, from A.D. 1200 onward.

A 0.5 kilometer (0.3 mile) from there is the site's largest and most important structure: *Ka'na Nah,* (Tall House). Also dating to San Gervasio's later era, this was the temple of the goddess Ixchel, and in its hey-day would have been covered in stucco and painted red, blue, green and black.

Other structures on the site include a somewhat precarious looking arch that served as an entrance to the central plaza and *Nohoch Nah,* (Big House), a boxy but serene temple at the edge of the city. With an interior alter, the temple might have been used by religious pilgrims to make an offering upon entering or leaving San Gervasio. It was originally covered in stucco and painted a multitude of colors.

Guides can be hired at the visitor's center for a fixed rate: US$17 for a one-hour tour in Spanish, English, French, or German. Prices are per group, which can include up to six people. Tips are customary and not included in the price.

El Cedral

South of town and just beyond Playa San Francisco, a paved turnoff leads to El Cedral (8 a.m.–5 p.m. daily, free), the oldest Maya structure on the island. Once the hub of Maya life on the island, it is the first Maya site that the Spaniards stumbled upon in 1518; allegedly, the first Catholic mass in Mexico was held here. Today, it is small and underwhelming though it still bears a few traces of the original paint and stucco. (Amazing, despite the passage of time—and its use as a jail in the 1800s—that these remnants are left). The ruin is located in the like-named village of El Cedral; tour operators often take visitors there to wander about and buy handicrafts.

El Caracol

Located inside Parque Ecológico Punta Sur, El Caracol is a small, conch-shaped structure that dates to A.D. 1200. It's believed to have been a lighthouse, where Mayas used smoke and flames to lead boats to safety. Small openings at the top of the structure also acted as whistles to alert Mayas to approaching tropical storms and hurricanes. The US$10 park admission includes access to the small site.

Castillo Real

Castillo Real is a partially excavated site with a temple, two chambers, and a lookout tower. It is believed to have been a Maya watchtower to protect against approaching enemies. It's located on the northeastern side of the island, on the sand road to Punta Molas. Unfortunately, at the time of research, it was prohibited to visit this part of the island because of a legal dispute (see *Northeastern Cozumel*).

BEACHES AND BEACH CLUBS

Cozumel isn't famous for its beaches, but it is not without a few beautiful stretches of sand. A series of beach clubs on the calmer west side are the best places to enjoy the sun and sand, but can get crowded. Beaches on the east side are windy and picturesque, and the surf can be fierce.

Western Cozumel

On the west side of the island with calm turquoise waters, a small beach, and lots of coconut trees, **Playa Palancar** (Km. 19.5, no phone, 9 A.M.–5 P.M. daily, minimum consumption US$10 pp) caters to visitors who just want to spend a quiet day lounging in a

hammock or snorkeling in the nearby Palancar reef. A *palapa*-roofed restaurant serves classic Mexican seafood and a wide range of drinks (US$5–12). Trips to the reef leave as soon as there is a critical mass of people (snorkel US$30, 1.5 hours, scuba US$80/two tanks). Snorkel gear also can be rented (US$10) but with no reef within striking distance, there's not much point in spending your cash on it. The club is 750 meters (0.5 mile) down a dirt road from the central road; a taxi between here and town is US$20.

With over three kilometers (1.9 miles) of thick white sand and calm turquoise waters, **Playa San Francisco** is certainly one of Cozumel's most attractive beaches. Its beauty is compromised somewhat—to say nothing of the tranquility—by two huge busy beach clubs right in the heart of it: **Nachi-Cocom** (Carr. Costera Sur Km. 16.5, tel. 987/872-1811, www.cozumel nachicocom.net, 9 A.M.–5 P.M. daily) is the rowdier of the two, catering to party-minded cruise shippers who pay US$69 for lunch, unlimited drinks, and a whirlpool tub that's usually teeming with minimally clad visitors. **Paradise Beach** (Carr. Costera Sur Km. 14.5, tel. 987/871-9010, www.paradise-beach-cozumel .net, 9 A.M.–sunset Mon.–Sat., 11 A.M.–6 P.M. Sun.) is also lively, but more geared toward families and people hoping to spend the day catching up on backlogged *New Yorker* magazines. Both clubs have huge open-air restaurants serving lots of finger foods and seafood (US$8–14), snorkel trips (US$35 pp, two hours), and other water sports. The sand and sea are gorgeous all the same, and the din evaporates just a hundred meters down the beach.

Uva's (Carr. Costera Sur Km. 8.5, tel. 987/800-9806, 8 A.M.–5 P.M. Mon.–Sat., cover US$7) exudes cool understatement, with minimalist furnishings and mellow beats, plus a small clean pool and a pretty patch of beach. The club offers guided snorkel tours every hour (US$15 pp, 45 minutes) and you can keep the snorkel gear for the rest of the day for exploring on your own. Or take a "dry snorkeling" tour in a clear acrylic kayak (US$40 pp, 45 minutes). A taxi here from town costs US$10.

Eastern Cozumel

On the east side of the island right where the Cross-Island Highway hits the Caribbean, you'll find a wild and windswept coastline dotted with beaches. Facing the open ocean, the surf here can be quite rough and only a few beaches are safe for swimming. The exception is when *nortes* (northern storm fronts) hit the island, and the west side turns choppy while the east side goes perfectly flat.

Right where the cross-island road hits the coast, two low-key restaurants sit alongside each other: **Mezcalito's Beach Bar and Grill** (tel. 987/872-1616, www.mezcalitos.com, 9 A.M.–6 P.M. daily) and **Señor Iguanas** (no phone, 8 A.M.–5 P.M. Mon. –Sat., 9 A.M.–5 P.M. Sun.). Both have similar menus (ceviche, fried fish, hamburgers, US$6–14), drinks (beer, margaritas, and tequila shots, US$2.50–5), and services (beachside chairs, hammocks, and *palapas,* free if you buy something from the restaurant). If you're feeling brave and have experience in rough waters, rent a boogie board from Señor Iguanas (US$3/two hours)—a lot of fun if you can handle the surf.

About six kilometers (3.7 miles) south is **Playa Tortugas,** a broad beautiful beach on the north side of the Ventanas al Mar hotel. Usually too rough for swimming, it's popular with surfers and is a good place to watch the wild and crashing waves.

A few steps away is **Coconuts Bar and Grill** (10:30 A.M.–sunset daily, US$5–13). Set on a magnificent bluff, tables and chairs are arranged so that patrons can enjoy the glorious views of the beach below and the Caribbean beyond. Meals are classic beach fare: nachos, ceviche, tacos—finger foods that go great with a cold beer. As long as you order something, you're free to hang out for as long as you'd like.

The best place to swim on the east side of the island is **Chen Río Beach** one kilometer (0.6 mile) south of Coconuts Bar and Grill fronting a wide protected bay and clear calm seas. It's popular with families, and lifeguards are usually on hand in case of any problems. Here you'll also find **Restaurant and Bar Chen Río**

(11 A.M.–6 P.M. daily, US$12–26), but the food is so expensive it's no wonder beachgoers bring a picnic.

Three kilometers farther south, **Playa Bonita** is another picturesque curve of sand with plenty of room to lay out a towel and soak in the sun. Heavy surf usually makes swimming here inadvisable, but provides for a dramatic scene. A small beach restaurant (10 A.M.–5 P.M. daily) serves hamburgers, fresh fish, and other standards.

Playa Rasta is the last beach you hit before turning west on the highway. It's mostly a rocky stretch of beach with a few sandy inlets and two restaurants blasting reggae at each other. It's not really the best place to spend the day, unless of course, you like rambling on rocks and have a craving for jerk chicken.

Northeastern Cozumel

Cozumel's northeastern coast has long been the "wild" part of the island. While paved roads run parallel to most of the island's shoreline, the northeast is reachable only by a rutted sand road extending 24.5 kilometers (15 miles) from the Cross-Island Highway up to Punta Molas, and passable only with a four-wheel drive vehicle. Now it's even harder to get there: Not only did Hurricane Wilma wash out large portions of the road, but the government environmental agency closed it entirely in January 2006, following an incident involving a foreign landowner. Evidently, the landowner was frustrated that the road hadn't been restored following the hurricane and decided to cut a new road—right through a protected mangrove swamp. A legal battle ensued, and no one seems in a hurry to re-open the area to visitors.

Presumably it *will* open eventually, and travelers will once again be able to explore this isolated and windswept part of the island. One way to visit is by joining an ATV tour, which are popular with cruise ship passengers (see *ATV Tours* in the *Sports and Recreation* section). More adventurous visitors can rent a jeep or even hike in, camping on the beach along the way. (If you drive in, be sure your four-wheel drive is engaged and that the insurance policy covers off-roading.) The first beaches you hit are nice beachcombing spots, and make for good places to pitch a tent. About 22 kilometers (14 miles) north, you'll pass the Maya site of **Castillo Real** and farther on is the **Punta Molas Lighthouse,** marking the northeastern-most tip of the island. Whether you come by Jeep or by foot, don't come alone or unprepared—there are absolutely no facilities, or even other people, out here. Take plenty of water and food, bug repellent, a flashlight, extra batteries, and a mosquito net if you plan to camp. Let someone know where you are going, and when you expect to return.

Entertainment and Events

DISCOTHEQUES AND BARS

The hottest spot in town when we were here, **1.5 Tequila Lounge** (Av. Rafael Melgar at Calle 11, tel. 987/872-4421, 9 P.M.–4 A.M. Mon.–Sat., US$4.75 cover) is an urban hipster lounge bar overlooking the Caribbean. It has comfy couches and chairs, outdoor decks, and cool fusion jazz playing in the background. Specialty shooters are the way to go, with an order of sashimi from the sushi bar as a chaser.

The urban chic **Ámbar** (Av. 5 between Calles 1 and Rosado Salas, tel. 987/869-1955, 11 A.M.–midnight Mon.–Thu., until 2 A.M. Fri.–Sat., and 5–11 P.M. Sun., no cover) is another go-to lounge on Friday and Saturday nights. Billowing white fabrics, dim lighting, modern white furniture, a martini bar, and a DJ spinning jazz, funk, and house make this a popular spot. An outdoor area with lounge chairs, umbrellas, and piped in (well, out) music is nice if you want to enjoy the ambience but still have a conversation. A small restaurant in front serves tapas and homemade pastas until 11 P.M. (US$8–14).

A classic Cozumeleño club, **Neptuno** (Av. Rafael Melgar at Calle 11, tel. 987/872-4374, 9 P.M.–4 A.M. Tues.–Sun.) is a good place to check out the local party scene. It has a large dance floor—check out the old-school lighting and disco ball—where revelers bump and grind to reggae, house, techno, and Latin beats. Things really get going after midnight.

If you're dying to catch the big game on a big screen (or at least a bunch of little ones), head to **All Sports Bar** (Calle 2 at Av. 5 Norte, tel. 987/869-2246, 10 A.M.–11 P.M. Mon.–Thurs.,

10–3 A.M. Fri.–Sun.). With a full line-up of sports channels and plenty of TVs, you're sure to feel right at home.

For a spring break atmosphere all day—and all year—long, head to the Punta Langosta shopping center where **Carlos'n Charlie's** (tel. 987/869-1648, 10 A.M.–1:30 A.M. Mon.–Fri., 11 A.M.–1:30 A.M. Sat., 5 P.M.–1:30 A.M. Sun.), **Señor Frog's** (tel. 987/869-2246, 8 A.M.–midnight Mon.–Thurs., 8 A.M.–2 A.M. Fri.–Sat.), and **Hard Rock Café Bar & Gift Shop** (8 A.M.–midnight Mon.–Sat., 10 A.M.–6 P.M. Sun.), make driving beats, drink specials, and dancing on tables the norm.

FESTIVALS
Carnaval

Cozumel is one of the few places in Mexico where Carnaval is celebrated with vigor, though the island's one-night celebration is still pretty mellow compared to the weeks or months of partying that mark the holiday elsewhere in the Caribbean and in South America. Held in February, Carnaval in Cozumel centers around a parade of floats and dance troupes, all decked out in colorful dress, masks, and glitter. Entire families come out together to participate and watch. Spectators dance and cheer in the streets as the floats go by, and many join the moving dance party that follows the floats with the largest speakers. Eventually the parade ends up in the center of town, where more music, dancing, and partying continue late into the night.

Festival de El Cedral

Residents of the village of El Cedral celebrate

ISLA COZUMEL

© GARY CHANDLER

Carnaval in Cozumel is celebrated with parades and dancing in the streets.

their namesake festival beginning around April 23 and culminating on May 3, the Day of the Holy Cross. Traditionally, the festival entails daily prayer sessions and ends with a dance called the *Baile de las cabezas de cochino* (Dance of the Pigs' Heads). The festival has morphed over the years into a somewhat more secular affair, with rodeos, dancing, music, and general revelry.

CALESA TOURS

Once a way for islanders to get around town, *calesas* (horse carriages) are now mainly used by tourists to see San Miguel. For US$25–30 you can hire a buggy to take you on a 30-minute tour of the town—from the waterfront to the interior. Look for the horses on Avenida Rafael Melgar by Calle 1.

CULTURAL AND MUSIC PERFORMANCES

Every Sunday evening, the city hosts an **open air concert** in the central plaza. Locals and expats come out to enjoy the show—put on

a clean T-shirt and your nicest flip-flops and you'll fit right in. Concerts typically begin at 7 P.M.

The **Alianza Francesa** (Blvd. Aeropuerto at Av. 20, 987/112-4826, 9 A.M.–1 P.M. and 4–9 P.M. Mon.–Fri., 9 A.M.–1 P.M. Sat.) is a worldwide educational and cultural center that offers a wide variety of French language classes and also sponsors cultural events for the community at large. The Alianza Francesa on Cozumel opened its doors in 2006. Although it was offering only language classes at the time we passed, the center was planning for events like film festivals, concerts, and other live performances. Worth a call to see what's on the schedule when you're in town.

CINEMA

Catch a relatively recent movie at **Cinépolis** (Av. Rafael Melgar between Calles 15 and 17, tel. 987/869-0799, US$4.25, US$2.75 before 3 P.M., US$2.50 all day Wed.) in the Chedraui supermarket complex.

Shopping

Shopping in Cozumel is aimed straight at cruise ship passengers—and its no wonder, they tend to spend a lot of money quickly. Avenida Rafael Melgar is where most of the action is, with a succession of marble-floored shops blasting air-conditioning to entice sweaty passersby in for a refreshing look around. Overpriced jewelry, T-shirt, and souvenir shops see the most buyer traffic, although, here and there are a few shops worth checking out.

For an impressive display of Mexican folk art, check out **Los Cinco Soles** (Av. Rafael Melgar at Calle 8, tel. 987/872-0132, www .loscincosoles.com, 8 A.M.–8 P.M. Mon.–Thurs., 8 A.M.–9 P.M. Fri.–Sat., 10 A.M.–4 P.M. Sun.). With room upon room of excellent examples of the country's artisanship—pre-Colombian replicas, *barro negro* pottery, colorful *rebosos* (shawls), and hand-carved furniture—it's definitely worth a stop, if even just to admire the art. There's a smaller satellite shop at the Punta Langosta mall.

Inspiración (5 Av. between Calles 3 and Rosado Salas, tel. 987/869-8293, www.inspiration cozumel.com, 10 A.M.–10 P.M. Mon.–Sat.) is a small gallery with a variety of quality Mexican artwork, from photos to jewelry to Maya replicas, all handpicked by the shop's friendly American owner.

Though a little pricey, **Pro Dive Cozumel** (Calle Rosado Salas at Av. 5, tel. 987/872-4123, prodivecozumel@prodigy.com.mx, www.pro divecozumel.com, 8 A.M.–10 P.M. Mon.–Sat., 9 A.M.–10 P.M. Sun.) has a great selection of snorkel and dive equipment—perfect if you've forgotten your mask or have lost a fin. For more options, try the **Cressi** retail shop kitty-corner to this one.

Punta Langosta (Av. Rafael Melgar between Calles 7 and 11, 9 A.M.–8 P.M. daily) is Cozumel's swankiest shopping center. An ultramodern open-air building, it's home to high-end clothing boutiques, air-conditioned jewelry stores, and even fancy ice cream shops.

A small shopping center on the north end of town, **Forum Shops Cozumel** (Av. Rafael Melgar at Calle 8, 8:30 A.M.–5:30 P.M. Mon.–Sat.) is nowhere near as nice as Punta Langosta, but it has a small collection of souvenir shops that are a bit more affordable.

ISLA COZUMEL

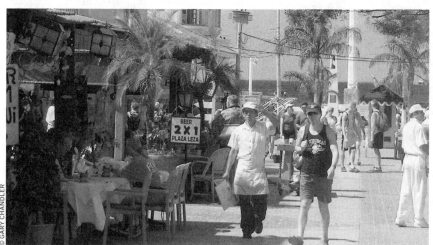

© GARY CHANDLER

Cozumel's main plaza has numerous shops and restaurants.

Sports and Recreation

SCUBA DIVING

Without a doubt, diving is the best reason to come to Cozumel. It should be no surprise then that Cozumel has a profusion of dive shops and operators—well more than 100 at last count. Rates are relatively uniform across the island: Expect to pay US$65–80 for a two-tank dive (plus US$10–20 for equipment rental, if you need it) and US$325–400 for a three- or four-day PADI open-water certification course. Most shops also conduct more advanced courses and offer discounts on multi-dive packages. Divers are also subject to a US$2 park entrance fee and a US$1 per day surcharge to support the *Servicios de Seguridad Sub-Acuática* (Underwater Safety Services) or SSS, which helps maintain Cozumel's hyperbaric chambers and marine ambulance.

Cozumel's diver safety record is good, and there are many more responsible, competent

© GARY CHANDLER

a beach break between dives on Cozumel's tranquil western shores

outfits in town than those listed here. Consider this list your base, to be augmented by the recommendations of fellow divers, travelers, locals, and expats—whose judgment you trust, of course. Most important, go with a shop you feel comfortable with, not just the cheapest, the cheeriest, or the most convenient.

Dimi Divers (Calle 3 between Av. Rafael Melgar and 5 Av., tel. 987/872-2915, www.dimi scubatours.com) is a small, locally owned shop that offers very reasonable rates, and whose many repeat clients are testament to the high quality of service.

Scuba Gamma (Calle 5 at Av. 5 Sur, tel. 987/878-4257, www.scubagamma.net, 9 A.M.–7 P.M. daily) is a mom-and-pop shop (literally) run by an amiable French family. The shop is one of few with specialized training in teaching and guiding divers with disabilities.

ScubaTony (www.scubatony.com, tel. 987/869-8628, in U.S. 626-593-7122) is one of a growing number of scuba operations run without an actual storefront—lower overhead typically means lower prices. American Tony Anschutz leads all his own dives and courses and offers excellent service before, during, and after your trip.

Deep Blue (Calle Rosado Salas at Av. 10 Sur, tel. 987/872-5653, www.deepbluecozumel .com) is a long-standing shop with a reputation and track record that keep it busy even through the low season.

Liquid Blue (5 Av. between Calle Rosado Salas and Calle 3, 987/869-7794, www.liquid bluedivers.com) has somewhat higher rates than most shops, but it offers small groups and attentive, personalized service.

Careyitos Advanced Divers (Caleta harbor, near Hotel Presidente InterContinental, tel. 987/872-1578, U.S. tel. 218/963-7578, www.advanceddivers.com) caters to experienced divers, allowing up to 75 minutes bottom time and offering top-notch service.

Caribbean Divers (5 Ave. at Calle 3, tel. 987/872-1145, www.caribbendiverscozumel

HOW TO CHOOSE A DIVE SHOP

There are over 100 dive shops on Isla Cozumel, and scores more at Isla Mujeres, Playa del Carmen, Cancún, Tulum, and elsewhere. Choosing just one – and then placing all your underwater faith into its hands – is not exactly easy.

Safety should be your number one concern in choosing a shop. Fortunately, the standards in Cozumel and the Riviera Maya are almost universally first-rate, and accidents are rare. But that's not a reason to be complacent. For example, don't dive with a shop that doesn't ask to see your certification card or logbook – if they didn't ask you, they probably didn't ask anyone, and an ill-trained diver is as dangerous to others as he is to himself.

Equipment is another crucial issue. You should ask to inspect the shop's equipment, and the dive shop should be quick to comply. Although few casual divers are trained to inspect gear, a good dive shop will appreciate your concern and be happy to put you at ease. If the staff is reluctant to show you the gear, either they aren't too proud of it or they don't see clients as equal partners in dive safety.

Of course, the most important equipment is not what's on the rack but what you actually use. Get to the shop early so you have time to **double-check your gear**. Old gear is not necessarily bad gear, but you should ask for a different BCD, wetsuit, or regulator if the one set out for you makes you uneasy. Learn how to check the O-ring (the small rubber ring that forms the seal between the tank and the regulator) and do so before every dive. Finally, open the tank and listen for any hissing between the regulator and the tank, and in the primary and backup mouthpieces. If you hear any, ask the dive master to check it and, if need be, change the regulator. Do all this before getting on the boat, so you can swap gear if necessary. Remember, *there are no stupid questions.*

Feeling comfortable and free to ask questions or raise concerns (of any sort at any time) is a crucial factor in safe diving. That's where a dive shop's **personality** comes in. Every dive shop has its own culture or style, and different divers will feel more comfortable in different shops. Spend some time talking to people at a couple of different dive shops before signing up. Try to meet the person who will be leading your particular dive – you may have to come in the afternoon when that day's trip returns. Chances are one of the shops or dive masters will "click" with you.

Finally, there are some specific questions you should ask about a shop's practices. Has their air been tested and certified? Do they carry radios and oxygen? Does the captain always stay with the boat? How many people will be going on your dive? How advanced are they? And how many dive masters or instructors will there be? How experienced are they?

And, of course, have fun!

.com) takes pride in its professional service and two 40-foot (12.2-meter) boats, which make surface intervals and getting to and from dive sites comfortable.

SNORKELING

If you don't have the time, money, or inclination to take up diving—and it's not for everyone—don't let that stop you from enjoying Cozumel's pristine coral reefs. In fact, many divers are also avid snorkelers, if for no other reason than plunking down US$100 a day for two 45-minute dives adds up really fast.

Many dive shops offer guided snorkeling tours, visiting 2–3 sites and spending a half-hour at each one (US$45–55 pp). Most often, snorkelers go out with a group of divers, and either snorkel in the same general location or go to a nearby site while the divers are underwater. While this can mean some extra downtime as divers get in and out of the water, you typically go to better, less crowded sites and have fewer people in your group. Be sure to agree beforehand on the number of sites you'll visit and for how long.

A number of shops sell snorkel tours from

DIVE INSURANCE

Although diving accidents are relatively rare on Cozumel, if you're planning on diving or snorkeling, consider purchasing secondary accident insurance through DAN (Divers Alert Network, toll-free U.S. tel. 800/446-2671, 24-hour emergency Mex. tel. 919/684-9111, accepts collect calls, www.diversalertnetwork.org), a nonprofit medical organization dedicated to the health and safety of snorkelers and recreational divers. Plans range from US$25 to US$70 per year and depending on the policy include medical and decompression coverage, lost equipment, airline and hotel costs, vacation cancellation insurance, accidental death and dismemberment benefits, as well as disability benefits. To be eligible for insurance, subscribers must become members of DAN, just US$29 per year.

booths on the central passenger pier. These trips tend to be less expensive (though with larger groups) and can be booked right as you debark from the ferry—handy if your time is short. **Cha Cha Cha Dive Shop** (Calle 7 between Avs. Rafael Melgar and 5 Sur, tel. 987/872-2331, www.chachachadiveshop.com, booth opens at 8 A.M.) offers 2–2.5-hour snorkeling trips on its glass-bottom boat for US$25 per person, including equipment. You'll snorkel for 30 minutes at each of three different sites. Its booth on the pier is easier to find than the actual shop, hidden down a narrow passage between souvenir stands and a tattoo parlor.

There are several terrific snorkeling spots right off the shore and not far from town where you don't need a guide at all; some of these are established snorkeling areas, others are recommended by locals. Cozumel's boat drivers are careful about steering clear of snorkelers, but even so do not swim too far from shore, look up and around frequently, and stay out of obvious boat lanes. If you plan to do a lot of snorkeling, especially outside of established snorkeling areas, consider bringing or buying

an inflatable personal buoy. Designed for snorkelers, they are brightly colored with a string you attach to your ankle or to a small anchor weight, alerting boat drivers of your presence. Also, be aware of the current, which typically runs south to north and can be quite strong.

KITEBOARDING

Kiteboarding has exploded in popularity around the world, eclipsing windsurfing among adrenaline seekers, in much the same way snowboarding has leapfrogged skiing. **Kite Cozumel** (tel. 987/103-6711, www.kitecozumel.com) is the kiting outfit of Cozumel-native Raul de Lille, a former Olympic-level windsurfer and now one of Mexico's top kiters and instructors. He doesn't come cheap: private lessons are US$125 an hour, and a three-day introductory course is US$900. For experienced kiters, de Lille offers clinics on kite control, tricks, and other specialties, plus adventuresome tours, like downwinding the entire island. Kite Cozumel operates out of the hotel Casa Viento, the island's only kiteboarding hotel and a short walk from the island's best kiting beach.

ECO- AND WATER PARKS
◖ Parque Ecológico Punta Sur

Parque Ecológico Punta Sur (Carr. Costera Sur Km. 27, tel. 987/872-0914, www.cozumelparks.com.mx, 9 A.M.–4 P.M. daily, US$10, children under 8 free) spans over 1,000 hectares (2,500 acres) of coastal dunes and mangroves at the island's southern tip. Declared a national reserve in 1996, it harbors dozens of animal species, including 30 types of seabirds and a vast array of sea creatures, reptiles, and amphibians (including some huge crocs). Just past the gate, a visitor center has displays about the history and ecology of the park, and a high platform overlooking Laguna Colombia, for spotting birds and crocodiles. A bit farther is a small Maya ruin known as *El Caracol*, believed to have been used for navigation and then the park's famous lighthouse and a small maritime museum. Private cars are not permitted beyond the lighthouse; a park truck ferries visitors to the beach area, where you can take a catamaran trip through the lagoon (US$3 pp, 40 minutes) or just spend time sunbathing, swimming, and snorkeling along the two kilometers (1.2 miles) of beautiful beaches. A small restaurant serves pricy food, and binoculars and snorkel gear can be rented at the visitor's center, if you don't have your own. Though this is a popular shore excursion for cruise shippers, it can still be rewarding for independent travelers.

Parque Nacional Chankanaab

Some 9 kilometers (5.6 mi.) south of town, Parque Chankanaab (Carr. Costera Sur Km. 14, tel. 987/872-9723, www.cozumelparks.com, 7 A.M.–5 P.M. daily, US$16 adult, US$8 children under 12) is a national park that doubles as a souped-up beach club. Visitors come to spend the day sunbathing, swimming in the ocean, and snorkeling. **Dolphin Discovery** (toll-free Mex. tel. 800/713-8862, www.dolphindiscovery.com, US$69–125 pp, 15–30 minutes) operates a popular dolphin and sea lion interaction program here. Reserve a spot as soon as you arrive, or better yet, book online. Park facilities include two thatch-roofed restaurants, a few gift shops, and a fully equipped dive shop. Popular with families, it is a good place to spend the day if you have little ones in tow.

SPORT FISHING

Cozumel boasts good deep-sea fishing year-round. It's one of few places anglers can go for the grand slam of billfishing: hooking into a blue marlin, a white marlin, a sailfish, and a swordfish all in a single day. It's also got plentiful tuna, barracuda, dorado, wahoo, grouper, snapper, and more. A **billfish tournament** is held every year in May, bringing fishing enthusiasts from all over—especially boaters from the United States who cross the Gulf of Mexico to take part in the popular event.

Albatross Fishing Charters (tel. 987/872-7904, in U.S. 888/333-4643, www.cozumelfishing.net) charges US$400 for four hours, US$500 for six hours, and US$550 for eight hours. It has a fleet of five boats, with experienced captains and crew. Boats carry a

maximum of six anglers. Trips include hotel pickup and drop-off, beer and soda, snacks, bait, and gear.

Other outfits include **Wahoo Tours** (www.wahootours.com, US$400/4hrs, US$545/8hrs, US$150 pp shared, up to six people) and **Go Fish** (book through www.cozumelinsider.com, US$270/4hrs, US$320/6hrs, up to four people).

GOLF

Jack Nicklaus designed the beautiful par-72 championship course at **Cozumel Country Club** (tel. 987/872-9570, www.cozumelcountryclub.com.mx, 6:30 A.M.–6 P.M. daily) located at the far end of the northern hotel zone. Green fees are US$149 until 1:30 P.M., when they drop to US$99. Carts are required, and included in the price; club rentals are US$29–50. In addition to the slightly rolling, moderately challenging course, the club has a driving range—the golf shop will loan you a club if you just want to hit some balls— putting and chipping areas, overnight bag storage, restaurant, retail shop, and available golf pro.

For something more laid-back, **Cozumel Mini Golf** (Calle 1 at Av. 15 Sur, tel. 987/872-6570, www.czmgolf.com, 10 A.M.–11 P.M. daily, US$7 adults, US$5 children under 11) features a fun and challenging 18-hole course set on a plot of 300 banana trees and a waterfall or two, just three blocks from the ferry. You'll get a walkie-talkie with your putter; use it to order dollar sodas and two-dollar beers and sangria, delivered to you right on the green. You can also pick out a CD (from a collection of 500) to be played over the course speakers. Watch for iguanas.

HORSEBACK RIDING

Located on the inland side of the highway across from Nachi Cocom beach club, **Rancho Palmitas** (Carr. Costera Sur Km. 16, tel. 987/878-7121) offers two horseback tours. A 2.5–3-hour tour (US$35 pp) includes stops at a cavern with a cenote, the archaeological site of El Cedral, and a few unexcavated Maya ruins. A shorter, 1.5-hour tour (US$25 pp) leads to the cavern only. Departures for either tour are at 8 A.M., 10 A.M., noon, 2 P.M., and 4 P.M. daily. A few additional ranches along this stretch of highway offer similar tours and prices.

ATV TOURS

For years, **Wild Tours** (tel. 987/872-5876 or toll-free Mex. tel. 800/202-4990, www.wildtours.com) has offered ATV excursions along the island's undeveloped northeast shore, including visiting isolated Maya ruins and snorkeling at deserted beaches (US$80–90 pp, 4.5 hours). However, the tours were suspended in January 2006, when the government's environmental agency shut down the road after a private landowner damaged a large portion of protected mangrove forest there. The tours will presumably resume, though no one seems to know when—ask at your hotel. Wild Tours caters to cruise ship passengers, but trips are open to all. They leave from a staging area next

to Mezcalito's restaurant on the east side of the island, where the Cross-Island Highway meets the coastal highway.

BODY WORK

Gym Club (Av. Benito Juárez between Calle 20 and Av. Pedro Joaquín Coldwell, tel. 987/872-7432, 6 A.M.–11 P.M. Mon.–Fri., 7 A.M.–6 P.M. Sat.) has free weights and weight machines in a smallish two-level exercise area. Use of the gym is US$5 a day or US$15 a week.

Though mainly geared toward children's dance instruction, **Tamart Casa de Arte y Cultura** (Calle 10 between Avs. 15 and 20 Norte, 987/869-8042, 8:30 A.M.–9 P.M. Mon.–Fri.) offers yoga and kickboxing classes for adults. Classes are typically offered two to three times per week and cost US$33–37 per month. Perfect if you're aching for a good workout and will be on Cozumel for more than a couple weeks.

Accommodations

Room prices can rise considerably during high season (mid-December–mid-April). Those listed here are high season (but not Christmas and New Year rates, which are even higher)—if you visit at another time rates may be 10–40 percent lower.

UNDER US$50

One block from the central plaza, **◖ Hostelito** (Av. 10 between Av. Benito Juárez and Calle 2 Norte, 987/869-8157, hostelitocozumelmx@gmail.com, US$11 dorm, US$10 dorm with a/c 4 guests minimum, US$35 s/d with a/c, US$50 studio with a/c) is an ultramodern hostel with a spacious coed dorm sporting 26 good beds and fans galore. Guests are provided with clean sheets, a huge locker, and continental breakfast; wireless Internet and cable TV are in the lobby. If you're traveling in a group, ask about the air-conditioned dorm with private bathroom, which is a steal at US$10 per head for four people. A spacious studio with a fully

equipped kitchen is a great deal for couples or families planning an extended stay on the island. The only drawbacks here: not much natural light and no communal kitchen (though one was in the works).

◖ Hotel Pepita (Av. 15 Sur between Calles 1 and Rosado Salas, tel. 987/872-0098, US$35 s/d, extra person US$5) is a modest but well-located and surprisingly comfortable hotel—a good value for traveler 'tweens: post-hostel but pre-B&B. The friendly owners keep the rooms very clean and well maintained. All have air-conditioning, ceiling fan, cable TV, minifridge, and two double beds (albeit a bit saggy), and there's fresh coffee every morning in the long inner courtyard. Same rates year-round.

Half a block from the central plaza, **Hotel Mary Carmen** (5 Av. Sur between Calles 1 and Rosado Salas, tel. 987/872-0581, www.cozumelisla.com.mx, US$39 s/d with a/c) is a simple but unexpectedly pleasant hotel. Smallish rooms have mosaic-tile headboards, good air-conditioners, and cable TV; bathrooms could stand to be remodeled but they're clean. Though not luxury, it's a good value for those on a limited budget. Ask for a room toward the back of the hotel, since some rooms get street noise.

US$50-100

€ **Mi Casa en Cozumel** (5 Ave. between Calles 7 and 9, tel. 987/872-6200, www.mi casaencozumel.com, US$55–90 s/d, US$170 suite) is perhaps Cozumel's first true boutique hotel, and surely its finest. Opened in 2006, the lofty structure is a study of curves and angles, the spiral staircase and curved interior walls counterbalancing the triangular patios and angled nooks occupied by whirlpool tubs. All units have king-size beds, sleek decor, and terraces with hammocks. The split-level suite has a full kitchen and a private hot tub. Free continental breakfast is served in a cozy cafeteria on the ground floor (where you can also get a wireless Internet signal).

Tamarindo Bed and Breakfast (Calle 4 between Avs. 20 and 25 Norte, tel. 987/872-6190, www.cozumel.net/bb/tamarind, US$44–47 s/d with fan, US$53 s/d with a/c, US$55 suite with a/c and kitchenette) is a pleasant bed-and-breakfast just a few blocks from the center of town, but comfortably removed from the hubbub. Owned by a friendly French expatriate who lives on-site, the hotel has seven units bordering a large, leafy garden. Each room is different from the other, from two boxy but comfortable hotel rooms to a whimsical *palapa* bungalow with boho flair. All have cable TV and wireless Internet. A good full breakfast is included in the rate (high season only; US$5 in low season) that is served on a sunny second-floor terrace. For those rooms without kitchenettes, there is a small communal kitchen. Rinse tanks and storage facilities also are provided for guests with dive gear.

Amaranto Bungalows (Calle 5 between Avs. 15 and 20 Sur, tel. 987/872-3219 or 987/103-1644, amarantocozumel@prodigy .net.mx, www.tamarindoamaranto.com, US$49 s/d, US$61 suite) offers seclusion and privacy, while still within easy walking distance from downtown. The three freestanding bungalows are fairly large and very clean, with modern bathrooms and attractive beachy decor. The two suites, however, are the Amaranto's shining stars. Occupying a three-story circular tower, both are spacious, with king-size beds, a separate sitting area, and nearly 360-degree windows. The lower suite has a high ceiling and more modern feel, while the upper unit looks up into the *palapa* roof, where a small lookout affords great town and ocean views. A large kitchen and dining room on the 1st floor has a TV and VCR and is open to all guests. Amaranto doesn't have a full-time attendant, so it's best to call ahead to let them know that you're coming.

Located on the main drag, **Vista del Mar** (Av. Rafael Melgar between Calles 5 and 7 Sur, tel. 987/872-0545, toll-free U.S. tel. 888/309-9988, www.hotelvistadelmar.com, US$83–94 with a/c) is a surprisingly charming hotel in the middle of a string of tacky souvenir shops. Rooms are classy and comfortable, with muted earth tones, beachy high-end decor, inlaid stone walls, and balconies (some with spectacular views of the Caribbean). All have cable TV, mini-fridges, safety deposit boxes, robes—even turndown service. There's also an outdoor mezzanine level with lounge chairs and a big Jacuzzi with a mosaic tile floor—a great space to hang out if it weren't for the rattling air-conditioners and the view of the souvenir shops.

Newly remodeled, the **Hotel Flamingo** (Calle 6 between Avs. Rafael Melgar and 5 Norte, tel. 987/872-1264 or toll-free U.S. tel. 800/806-1601, www.hotelflamingo.com, US$85 s/d with a/c, US$95 s/d superior with a/c, US$179 penthouse with a/c) offers three types of rooms: the standard are just that, basic hotel rooms with no views, air-conditioning, and cable TV; for US$10 more, superior units offer better beds and linens, mosaic tile bathrooms, and nice views—a good value; and for a big step up, the penthouse is a two-bedroom apartment with a fully equipped kitchen, a living room with ocean views, and one and a half bathrooms. All have wireless Internet; there's also a good restaurant/bar (7 A.M.–11 P.M. daily) on the ground floor. For a US$10–20 discount on accommodations, reserve online.

Suites Bahía (Calle 3 between Avs. Rafael Melgar and 5 Sur, tel. 987/872-9090 or toll-free Mex. tel. 800/227-2639, www.suites bahia.com, US$77–107 s/d with a/c) and **Suites Colonial** (Av. 5 Sur between Calles 1 and Rosado Salas, same tel., www.suitescolonial.com, US$77 s/d with a/c, US$79 suite with a/c) are sister hotels that rent unremarkable but functional rooms and studios, most with kitchenettes. The Colonial is on the pedestrian walkway downtown and feels newer, but the rooms at the Bahía (especially the ocean-view ones) are roomier and get more natural light. Neither hotel will win any awards for charm—both look as if they've been untouched since the early 1980s—but the rooms are clean and reasonably comfortable and a kitchen can definitely be nice for longer stays. Both include air-conditioning, cable TV, continental breakfast, and Internet service in the lobby.

OVER US$100

◖ **Villas Las Anclas** (Av. 5 Sur between Calles 3 and 5, tel. 987/872-5476, www.lasanclas.com, US$80–120 s/d with a/c) is a great option for those who want a little home away from home. Seven pleasantly decorated apartments each have air-conditioning, a fully equipped kitchen, a living room, and a loft master bedroom up a set of spiral stairs. Using the sofas as beds, the apartments can accommodate up to six people, making a good price even better. Apartments open onto a leafy, private garden. The friendly owner/operator is well informed of local dive shops, restaurants, and activities, and can help guests organize their stays.

In town, one of Cozumel's most modern hotels is **Casa Mexicana** (Av. Rafael Melgar between Calles 5 and 7, tel. 987/872-9090, U.S. tel. 877/228-6747, www.casamexicanacozumel.com, US$140–168 s/d with a/c) with its small infinity pool in its spacious lobby area and a view over the road to the big blue ocean beyond. The view is even better from the private

patio of the 20 oceanside rooms—notwithstanding the docked cruise ships and a large McDonald's sign. The other 70 rooms have views of the city or the soaring interior courtyard. The rooms are less inspired than the building itself, but are comfortable enough, with good beds, new air-conditioners, modern bathrooms, and large TVs. Rates include a full buffet breakfast in an impressive open-air dining room.

A long walk from town but worth every step, ◖ **Casa Colonial** (Av. 35 between Calles 8 and 10, tel. 987/872-6102, toll-free U.S., Canada, Europe 866/437-1320, www.cozumelrental villas.com, seven nights for US$1,036, villa with a/c) has four Mexican-style villas, each with two bedrooms. All are two stories with two-and-a-half bathrooms, a living room, a dining room, a fully equipped kitchen—even a washer and dryer and wireless Internet. It's like being home with the added bonus of daily maid service. All villas face a well-tended garden courtyard with a large pool and Jacuzzi. Dive rinse tanks also are available.

A leafy courtyard and gurgling fountain greet you at the **Hacienda San Miguel** (Calle 10 between Avs. Rafael Melgar and 5 Norte, tel. 987/872-1986, U.S. tel. 866/712-6387, www.haciendasanmiguel.com, US$100 studios with a/c, US$113–165 suites with a/c), a colonial-style hotel on the edge of town. Rooms need some sprucing up—a paint job and a little extra scrubbing in the showers would do wonders—but they're comfortable enough with air-conditioning, cable TV, and fully equipped kitchenettes. The two-story junior suites are the best units in the place with a comfortable living room and a balcony with nice views of the courtyard. Continental breakfast included in the rate.

OUTSIDE OF TOWN

Aptly named the House of Wind, **Casa Viento** (Country Club Estates, tel. 987/878-4537, www.casaviento.com, US$95–106) bills itself as a "guest house and kite camp" and caters almost exclusively to kiteboarders. Just minutes from some of the island's best kiteboarding spots, it is also home of Kite Cozumel, a kiting school and tour operator run by top Mexican kiteboarder Raul de Lille. Opposite the country club, Casa Viento has four charming detached rooms, and two in the main house where the kitchen and living room are located. A suite, complete with cupola, has terrific ocean views. A clean midsize pool completes the package. The place is almost too delightful—don't these kiters have a rep to keep?

Under US$150

The only hotel on the east side of the island, **Hotel Ventanas al Mar** (south end of Playa Tortugas, tel. 987/876-7687, www.ventanas almar.biz, US$89 s/d, US$169–189 d suite, includes full breakfast) has 12 large rooms and two suites, all with high ceilings and private patios or decks with marvelous ocean views. The interiors lack the detailing and upkeep you'd expect at this price, but are not uncomfortable, and suit the hotel's isolated feel. All have kitchenettes with microwave ovens and dishes; some have mini-fridges. Split-level suites can comfortably sleep four. There's no a/c, as the hotel runs almost entirely on wind and solar power. (Power lines have yet to reach the island's east side; the hotel was just installing a generator, but only for limited use.) Fortunately, the constant sea breeze keeps rooms cool. There's a good restaurant next door, but you'll probably want a car, as the east side has no ATM, grocery stores, or other services; the hotel does offer limited shuttle service, but only in the high season. Or you can embrace the isolation: Many guests spend a week or more without going to town at all. Playa Tortugas is a scenic windswept beach that's good for surfing—and has nesting turtles May to November—but it is often too rough for swimming or snorkeling.

US$150-200

An easy 15-minute walk north of town is **Condumel** (tel. 987/872-0892, www.aqua safari.com, US$159 apartment with a/c), an old school but well-kempt condominium complex on the main road. The 10 one-bedroom apart-

ments are spacious and have air-conditioning, a king-size bed, a sofa bed, marble bathroom, and a fully equipped kitchen—the refrigerator even comes stocked with regularly priced food items so that you don't have to go shopping right away. Oversized sliding-glass doors offer awesome views of the ocean, sunsets, and incoming airplanes. The coast here is iron shore, so it's rocky, but a small, semi-protected cove with steps and a ladder is perfect for swimming and snorkeling; there's even a diving board that screams cannonball. A small sandy area with lounge chairs also has been set up for guests who need a daily beach fix. Dive packages available.

Like many all-inclusives, the **Occidental Allegro Cozumel** (Carretera Sur Km. 16.5, tel. 987/872-9770, toll-free U.S. tel. 800/858-2258, www.allegroresorts.com, US$237 s with a/c, US$171 pp d with a/c) has a fantastic beach and pool area but rather unremarkable rooms and restaurants. The wide beach has powdery white sand dotted with beach chairs and umbrellas. On one side is a water-sports kiosk, where you can check out anything from snorkel gear (free) to small sailboats (extra charge). Two pools set end to end form a long corridor from the ocean toward the main building. Along the sides are two-story, *palapa*-roofed bungalows with four units apiece. Rooms are on the small side, and are showing their age—new furnishings would go a long way. The sister hotel **Occidental Grand Cozumel** (US$292 s with a/c, US$212 pp d with a/c), a five-star all-inclusive, is next door. The accommodations and installations are fancier there, but the beach is actually better at the Allegro. Daytime and nighttime activities include aerobics, cocktail parties, and theme nights.

Over US$200

After a year-long overhaul, the ■ **Presidente InterContinental Cozumel Resort Spa** (Carretera Sur Km. 6.5, tel. 987/872-9500, toll-free U.S. tel. 888/424-6835, www.intercontinental .com, US$370–570) may well be the best hotel-resort in Cozumel. It features spacious, classy rooms with details like flat screen TVs, stereos,

ISLA COZUMEL

turndown service, and bathrobes. While the views can either be garden or ocean, all roads lead to one of the best hotel beaches on the island—thick white sand and calm, turquoise waters with excellent access for snorkelers and shore divers. A well-regarded dive shop, two lighted tennis courts, three restaurants, and a full-service spa round out an already relaxing stay.

As the name suggests, the **Fiesta Americana Cozumel Dive Resort** (Carretera Sur Km. 7.5, tel. 987/872-9600, U.S. tel. 800/343-7821, www.fiestamericana.com, $150–300 s/d with a/c) caters to divers, most of whom come on package tours arranged from the United States or Canada. Recently refurbished, rooms are comfortable and attractive with terraces and excellent ocean views. The beach is constructed on iron shore with barriers to hold in the imported sand—not exactly what you expect when you think "Caribbean beach" but

nice enough if you just want to take in the sun. There's also a well-regarded, if pricey, dive shop on-site. Continental breakfast included.

North of town and near the country club, **Playa Azul** (Zona Hotelera Norte Km. 4, tel. 987/869-5160, www.playa-azul.com, US$240–320) caters mostly to golfers, but it has packages for divers and honeymooners as well. Even if you don't golf much, you may as well get in a round or two if you stay here—guests pay no green fees. Medium-size rooms have modern furnishings and large bathrooms; most have a terrace with chairs and excellent ocean views. Top-floor rooms have a little cupola on the bedroom, a nice touch. The pool is clean and attractive, but the beach (already small) can get crowded with day guests visiting the hotel's beach club. That said, the overall atmosphere here is calm and quiet, removed from the noise and activity downtown.

Food

Cozumel isn't known as a culinary hotspot, but you do have plenty of options. Like any island it has terrific seafood (though many people are surprised to learn that much of the catch actually comes from around Isla Mujeres because the waters around Cozumel are protected areas). And the island's popularity with Americans, especially hungry Texan divers, means you'll never want for a steak, plate of pasta, fajitas, or a big breakfast. And the island's tight-knit community of European expats, especially French, keep numerous cafés, bistros, and international eateries in business.

MEXICAN

Popular among locals, **(Sabores** (Av. 5 between Calles 3 and 5, noon–4 P.M. Mon.–Fri., US$4–11) is a family-run restaurant operated out of a bright yellow house. A wide variety of traditional Mexican dishes are served as *comidas corridas* with soup, main dish, and fruit drink running US$4–8. Clients can choose between eating in the converted living room or under

the shade trees in the backyard. Check out the dry erase board for the daily offerings.

The breezy *palapa*-roofed **(La Candela** (Av. 5 at Calle 6 Norte, 987/878-4471, 8 A.M.–6 P.M. Mon.–Sat., US$2.50–5) is a favorite among locals and expats. Every day, a line-up of Mexican and traditional Yucatecan dishes are offered in a cafeteria-style setting. Check out what's steaming behind the glass window cases, find a seat, then place your order with your waiter. Lunch specials typically include soup or pasta, a main dish, and a drink.

Serving customers since 1945, **Casa Denis** (Calle 1 between Avs. 5 and 10 Sur, tel. 987/872-0067, 7 A.M.–11 P.M. Mon.–Sat., 6–11 P.M. Sun., US$4–15) is a yellow clapboard house just steps from the central plaza. With wood tables set up on the porch and along the pedestrian walkway, it makes a great spot for people-watching that's made even better with a cold beer and fresh fish empanadas.

Located deep in one of Cozumel's residential neighborhoods, **El Moro** (Av. 75 Bis. Norte between Calles 2 and 4, tel. 872-3029, 1–11 P.M. Fri.–Wed., US$7–18) isn't a fancy place but it has won the loyal following of many expatriates. You'll find just about any Mexican specialty here—from *enchiladas suizas* to chicken *mole*—and big portions to boot. Unfortunately, prices are a bit inflated, especially considering the surroundings.

Mexican-food lovers pack **La Choza** (Av. 10 at Calle Rosado Salas, tel. 987/872-0958, 7 A.M.–10:30 P.M., US$6–19), a simple restaurant with high *palapa* roof that fills with the rich smells and sounds of traditional Mexican and Tex-Mex cuisine: almost everything on the menu involves some sort of sizzling meat. Always crowded with loyal aficionados, locals and visitors alike. Service is fast and friendly.

The setting at **Pancho's Backyard** (Av. Rafael Melgar 27 between Avs. 8 and 10 Norte, tel. 987/872-2141, 10 A.M.–11 P.M. Mon.–Sat., 5–11 P.M. Sun., US$10–20) is Mexico epitomized—gurgling fountains, colonial-style decor, and marimba music. Add creative haute cuisine such as *chiles rellenos* (peppers stuffed with bananas and walnut) and *camarones a la naranja* (orange shrimp flambéed in tequila) and you'll leave wanting to return. Popular with cruise ship travelers, the restaurant is big enough that it never feels crowded.

SEAFOOD

The nautical-themed 【 **El Capi Navegante** (Av. 10 Sur between Calles 3 and 5, tel. 987/872-1730, noon–10 P.M. daily, US$10–30) is a favorite on the island because it serves some of the freshest seafood around. For a treat, try the *Parrillada Capi Navigante*—a delectable dish of grilled fish, shrimp, octopus, conch, and squid—you won't be disappointed.

The Caribbean chic **La Lobstería** (Av. 5 Sur at Calle 7, tel. 987/100-2510, noon–11 P.M. Mon.–Sat US$5–15) is a good place to get a creative seafood dish such as fish sautéed in orange, garlic, and cumin (US$8), smoked marlin salad (US$4.50), and coconut shrimp (US$11.50). As the name suggests, lobster is a big seller as well but the smallish sizes don't quite merit the largish price tag. The outdoor patio, right on the corner, is nice on a warm evening.

ITALIAN

Specializing in northern Italian dishes, **Prima Trattoria** (Calle Rosado Salas at Av. 5, tel. 987/872-4242, 4:30–11 P.M. daily, US$7–23) serves handmade pastas and great salads in a charming rooftop garden.

With a shady courtyard and a seemingly endless list of sauces, 【 **Guido's** (Av. Rafael Melgar between Calles 6 and 8, tel. 987/872-0946, 11 A.M.–11 P.M. Mon.–Sat., US$8–17) is perfect if you're in the mood for a special pasta dish or brick-oven pizza. Add a glass of sangria and a warm breeze and you've got the makings for a classic Cozumeleño night out. Popular with expatriates and locals alike.

OTHER SPECIALTIES

Set in one of the oldest clapboard houses on the island, the artsy 【 **Restaurant Manatí** (Av. 10 Norte at Calle 8, tel. 987/869-8568, noon–11 P.M. Mon.–Sat., US$5–11) is a breezy place to get a creative meal. While not exclusively vegetarian, the menu veers in that direction (think spinach and cheese pasta, mixed vegetables in mango sauce, curry shrimp). The filling *comida corrida* also is one of the best deals in town: choice of soup and main dish as well as all-you-can-drink fruit juices for US$4.75. Be sure to save room for the homemade desserts—the lemon pie is a taste bud's delight. There's live music on Thursday and Saturday nights, starting at 9:30 P.M.

For a tasty change of pace, head to **Especias** (Calle 3 Sur near Av. 5 Sur, tel. 987/876-1558, 6:30–11:30 P.M. daily, US$5–10), a small restaurant serving world food—Argentinean, Jamaican, Thai, Indian, and more. The zucchini stuffed with cheese and tomatoes and the *chistorro* (rolled thin sausage) are especially good ways to start your meal.

If you're craving a big American breakfast, head straight to **Cocos Cozumel** (Av. 5 Sur between Calles Rosado Salas and 1, 987/872-0241, 6 A.M.–noon Tues.–Sun., US$3–6). After you've tried the Grand Slam, a serious meal with eggs, ham, hash browns, and coffee, it'll be tough to get your breakfast fix anywhere else. Just a block from the central plaza, this diner is popular among travelers and locals alike. Closed September and October.

Pepe's Grill (Av. Rafael Melgar between Calles Rosado Salas and 3, tel. 987/872-0213, 10 A.M.–11 P.M. Mon.–Sat., 5–11 P.M. Sun., US$12–24) has long been popular for its good food and sunset views over the Caribbean. It's definitely old school, harkening back to the mid-1980s in its nautical style and synthesizer jam sessions, but if you're in the mood for prime rib or a big salad, this is the place to come.

An old-time favorite, **Jeannie's Waffles and Raul's Tacos** (Av. Rafael Melgar near Calle 11, 6 A.M.–11 P.M. daily, US$6–10) serves made-to-order waffles in every shape, way, and form—they even replace tortillas as the base for traditional *huevos rancheros*. Other breakfast options include eggs, hash browns, and homemade bread. Portions are hearty so come hungry or be prepared to leave some for Mr. Manners. As the name suggests, the restaurant also serves decent tacos for lunch and dinner.

The world's smallest **Hard Rock Café** (Av. Rafael Melgar between Calles 1 and 3, tel. 987/872-5271, 10 A.M.–1 A.M. Sun.–Wed., until 2 A.M. Thu–Sat., US$6–18) has views of the Caribbean during the day and live music starting at 10 P.M. Thursday to Saturday night. Food is typical Hard Rock fare—burgers, potato skins, etc.—and a boutique near the entrance sells T-shirts and rock 'n' roll memorabilia.

CAFÉS AND BISTROS

With a tree growing in the middle of the main dining area, regular art exhibits on the walls, and Arabic tunes playing in the background, 【 **Coffeelia** (Calle 5 between Avs. 5 Sur and Rafael Melgar, tel. 987/872-7402, 7:30 A.M.–11 P.M. Mon.–Sat., 8A.M.–1 P.M. Sun., US$4–6.50) is a pleasing, bohemian place. The food, too, is a pleasure—light and varied with a dozen egg dishes, 18 crepe combos, and a small army of sandwiches and salads. A great place to kick back with a café au lait and catch up on postcards.

Owned and operated by a friendly French couple, **Crepería La Delicia** (Av. Felipe Ángeles near Calle 5 Sur, 5 –11 P.M. Sun.–Fri.,

US$3.50–6) is a breezy little place, serving more than 20 different crepes—delicious and filling for a meal, a dessert, or both. Three-item baguettes and omelets also are offered. Located deep in a residential neighborhood, it's worth the drive or long walk.

Restaurante del Museo (Av. Rafael Melgar and Calle 6, tel. 987/872-0838, 7 A.M.–2 P.M. daily, US$4–7) is a little outdoor café on the roof of the Museo Cozumel. Great for lunch after a morning at the museum or simply for a drink to watch the boats cruise past. Get there early on Sundays, when locals line up for the restaurant's famous *sopa de pancita* (cow's stomach soup)—an acquired, kind of furry taste.

A tiny bistro on a quiet corner, **Le Chef** (Av. 5 at Calle 5 Sur, 987/878-4391, 11 A.M.–4 P.M. and 6–10:30 P.M. Tues.– Sat., 6–10:30 P.M. Mon., US$5–20) serves up gourmet kosher meals and sandwiches, fancy cheese plates, fine steaks, and big salads. Service is molasses slow, but the ambiance makes up for it—a glass of wine often makes the time pass a little faster.

Across the street, the sterile-looking **Island Coffee** (Av. 5 near Calle 5 Sur, 987/872-1000, 7 A.M.–11 P.M. Mon.–Sat., 9 A.M.–2 P.M. Sun., US$2–5) doesn't have the charm its neighbor does but offers a fantastic array of coffee drinks, sandwich combos, and freshly made desserts. Great for an early morning caffeine kick or a mid-afternoon meal, the fact that it's open late and on Sundays makes it doubly special.

If you notice the aroma of roasting beans, follow your nose to **Café Chiapas** (Calle 2 between Avs. 5 and 10 Norte, tel. 987/869-2042, 8 A.M.–9 P.M. Mon.–Sat.). With just one stool and a countertop, this place sells some of the best coffee around—just take it to go.

SWEETS

Hands down, the best place to go for traditional Mexican baked goods is 【 **Zermatt** (Av. 5 Norte at Calle 4, tel. 987/872-1384, 7 A.M.–8:30 P.M. Mon.–Sat., 7 A.M.– 6 P.M. Sun.). Be sure to get a little something for the street dogs who like to sniff around outside—otherwise they'll follow you (and your bag of treats) back to your hotel.

If the bread is still baking at Zermatt, head to **Panadería Cozumeleña** (Av. 10 Sur at Calle 3, 7 A.M.–10 P.M. Mon.–Sat., 7 A.M.–9 P.M. Sun.) for a good sampling of Mexican breads and pastries.

For a cool treat, head to **La Michoacana** (Av. Juárez at Av. 20 Sur, 8:30 A.M.–11 P.M. daily), where there's always a changing variety of homemade *aguas* (fruit drinks), *nieves* (ice cream), and *paletas* (popsicles).

GROCERIES

If you are cooking for yourself, **Chedraui** (Av. Rafael Melgar between Calles 15 and 17, 7 A.M.–10 P.M. daily) is the largest supermarket on the island. For a traditional market experience—fresh produce and sides of beef hanging from hooks—head to the *mercado público* (Av. 25 between Calles 1 and Rosado Salas, 7 A.M.–3 P.M. daily).

Information and Services

TOURIST INFORMATION

The city tourist office has three **information booths** (8 A.M.–7 P.M. Mon.–Sat., 9 A.M.–2 P.M. Sun.) on the island—in the central plaza, at the International Pier, and at Puerta Maya pier. These booths are distinguishable from tour operators' kiosks by the staffers' uniforms—khaki pants and Hawaiian shirts with the tourism office logo—and the fact that they don't push area trips. English is spoken at all locations.

If the booths are packed or you simply prefer going to an office, the actual **tourist office** (Plaza del Sol, 2nd Fl., Av. 5 between Av. Juárez and Calle 1, tel. 987/869-0212, www.cozumel.gob.mx, 9 A.M.–7 P.M. Mon.–Fri.) is located in the central plaza.

Get a copy of the *Free Blue Guide to Cozumel* (tel. 987/872-1451, freeblueguide@hotmail.com) for a good map and listings for a range of services, from restaurants to dive shops. Look for the booklet as you get off the ferry.

HOSPITALS

The **Hyperbaric Medical Center** (Calle 5 between Avs. Rafael Melgar and 5 Sur, tel. 987/872-1430, cozumel@sssnetwork.com, 8 A.M.–11 P.M. daily, on-call 24 hours) specializes in diver-related medical treatment though non-diving ailments also are treated. English spoken.

Clínica-Hospital San Miguel (Calle 6 between Avs. 5 and 10 Norte, tel. 987/872-0103, 24 hours daily) offers both general and diver-related medical services.

Centro Médico de Cozumel (CMC, Calle 1 between Avs. 45 and 55 Sur, tel. 987/872-9400, www.centromedicodecozumel.com.mx, 24 hours daily) accepts many foreign insurance plans though prices are higher here than elsewhere.

PHARMACIES

Farmacia Portales (Calle 1 at Av. 10 Sur, tel. 987/872-1448, 7:30 A.M.–10:30 P.M. Mon.–Sat., 8:30 A.M.–9:30 P.M. Sun.) has a complete range of medication, plus sunscreen, film, and snacks.

Farmacia Dori (Calle 7 Sur near Av. Rafael Melgar; tel. 987/872-5519, 7 A.M.–11 P.M. Mon.–Sat., 8 A.M.–10 P.M. Sun.) has this and two other locations in town; delivery available.

POLICE

The **tourist police** (Plaza del Sol, 2nd Fl., Av. 5 between Av. Juárez and Calle 1, no phone, 24 hours daily) is located in the central plaza, next to the city tourist office.

The police (Palacio Municipal, Calle 13 between Avs. 5 and Rafael Melgar, tel. 987/872-0092, 24 hours daily) also can be reached toll-free at 066.

MONEY

Accessing your money is not difficult in Cozumel, especially near the central plaza. **HSBC** (Av. 5 Sur at Calle 1, 8 A.M.–7 P.M. Mon.–Sat.), **Bancomer** (Av. 5 Sur between Av. Juárez and Calle 1, 8:30 A.M.–4 P.M. Mon.–Fri.), and **Banorte** (Av. 5 Norte between Av. Juárez and Calle 2, 9 A.M.–6 P.M. Mon.–Fri., 10 A.M.–2 P.M. Sat.) exchange travelers checks and have ATMs.

INTERNET AND TELEPHONE

For emailing, **Blau Net** (Calle Rosado Salas between Avs. 10 and 15, tel. 987/872-6275, 9 A.M.–10 P.M. Mon.–Sat., US$1/hr., US$5 to burn photos onto CD) is a quiet and reliable place. Calls to the United States and Canada cost US$0.37 per minute.

Web Station (Av. 5 Sur between Calles 3 and 5, tel. 987/872-3911, 10 A.M.–11 P.M. Mon.–Sat, 10 A.M.–10 P.M. Sun.) offers fast Internet service on flat-screen computers (US$1/hr.), international telephone service (US$0.37/minute to most countries), and best of all, wicked air-conditioning.

POST OFFICE

The post office (Av. Rafael Melgar at Calle 7, 9 A.M.–5 P.M. Mon.–Fri., 9 A.M.–1 P.M. Sat.) is next to Punta Langosta shopping center.

IMMIGRATION

The immigration office (Av. 15 Sur at Calle 5, tel. 987/872-3110) is open 9 A.M.–1 P.M. Monday–Friday only. There's an office at the airport as well (tel. 987/872-5604, 7 A.M.–9 P.M. daily).

LAUNDERETTE

Servi-Lav Lavandería (Av. 10 Norte between Calles 6 and 8, tel. 987/872-3951, 8 A.M.–8 P.M. Mon.–Sat., US$1/kg (2.2 lbs)) typically provides next-day service; if you drop off your clothes first thing in the morning though, you'll have a shot at same-day service at no additional cost.

Lavandería Express (Calle Rosado Salas between Avs. 5 and 10, tel. 987/872-2932, 8 A.M.–9 P.M. Mon.–Sat., 8:30 A.M.–4:30 P.M. Sun.) offers full service (two hours, US$7 for up to eight kg/17.6 lbs) but will also let you wash your own clothes for US$2 a load to wash, US$1.25 every 10 minutes to dry.

Getting There and Around

GETTING THERE
Air

Cozumel International Airport (CZM, 987/872-0485) is approximately three kilometers (2 miles) from downtown. The airport has an ATM in the departures area, and AmEx currency exchange at arrivals, and a few magazine stands and duty-free shops. Taxis to or from the airport are US$10; shared vans are US$4.25 per person.

Bus

Although there are no long-distance buses on Cozumel (it is a pretty small island, after all), tickets for buses departing Playa del Carmen are sold at **Ticket Bus** (Calle 2 at Av. 10 Sur, tel. 987/869-2553, 6 A.M.–2 P.M. and 2:30–9 P.M. daily) at no extra cost.

Ferry

Ferries to Playa del Carmen (US$10 each way, 30 minutes) leave from the passenger ferry pier across from the central plaza. Two companies—**UltraMar** (Av. Rosado Salas at Av. 45, tel. 987/869-3223) and **Mexico Water Jets** (Calle 6 Norte between Av. 20 and 25, tel. 987/872-1578)—operate the boats; the service and fares are identical, though UltraMar's boats are somewhat newer. Between the two companies, at least one ferry leaves Cozumel every hour on the hour from 5 A.M. to 11 P.M. daily.

UltraMar has built a second ferry pier in Playa del Carmen at the end of Avenida Constituyentes, 10 blocks north of Playa's existing pier on the south end of town. When service begins there—it hadn't yet as we went to

ISLA COZUMEL

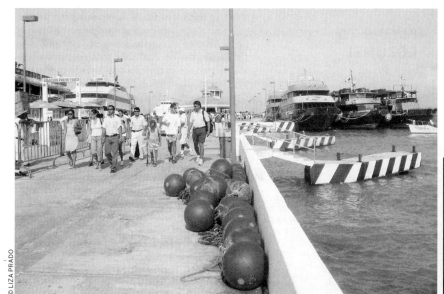

© LIZA PRADO

The passenger ferries from Playa del Carmen arrive in front of Cozumel's central plaza.

press—be sure to ask in Cozumel where your ferry is headed. If you're catching a bus straight from the ferry, the new pier will be more convenient to Terminal Alterna (long-distance service), while the main pier is just steps from Terminal Turística (for local service, including to Cancún and Tulum).

GETTING AROUND

In town, you can easily walk anywhere you like. However, the powerful taxi union has succeeded in quashing any and all efforts to start public bus service out of town and around the island. It is a shame, really, since it would be so easy and convenient to have a fleet of buses making loops around the island, or even just up and down the western shore. Until that changes (don't hold your breath), you'll need a car, moped, or bike to explore the rest of the island.

Bicycle

A bike can be handy for getting to beach clubs and snorkel sites outside of town. Traffic on Avenida Rafael Melgar can be heavy south of town, but once clear of that, the roadway is relatively unhurried. Both **Rentadora Isis** and **Rentadora Gallo** (see *Car and Moped Rental*) rent bicycles for around US$10 a day, as well as snorkel gear (US$10/day).

Taxi

Taxis (tel. 987/872-0236 or tel. 987/872-0041) are everywhere—you can easily flag one down on Avenida Rafael Melgar, near the main passenger pier, and around the plaza. Cabs have set prices—US$1.50–2 around town, and US$3.50 to the airport from the central plaza for instance. To and from hotels and beach clubs out of town, however, the rates jump significantly, to US$7–20. As always, before getting into a taxi, be sure to agree upon the price.

Car and Moped Rental

Renting a car is a nice way to get out of downtown and see the rest of the island. It is virtually impossible to get lost, and you can visit all the main spots in a day or two.

FLYING TO COZUMEL

The following airlines service Cozumel International Airport (CZM):

- **AeroCozumel** (airport tel. 987/872-0468)

- **Aeroméxico** (airport tel. 987/872-3454, toll-free Mex. tel. 800/021-4010, www.aeromexico.com)

- **American Airlines** (toll-free Mex. tel. 800/904-6000, www.aa.com)

- **Click Mexicana** (airport tel. 987/872-3456, toll-free Mex. tel. 800/112-5425, www.clickmx.com)

- **Continental** (airport tel. 987/872-0847, toll-free Mex. tel. 800/900-5000, www.continental.com)

- **Delta** (toll-free Mex. tel. 800/123-4710, www.delta.com)

- **Mexicana** (airport tel. 987/872-2945, toll-free Mex. tel. 800/502-2000, www.mexicana.com)

- **United Airlines** (toll-free Mex. tel. 800/003-0777, www.united.com)

- **US Airways** (toll-free Mex. tel. 800/428-4322, www.usairways.com)

If you do decide to rent some wheels, go to the agency yourself—do not allow one of the friendly guys at the pier to lead you there. They are *comisionistas,* freelancers who earn hefty commissions for bringing tourists to particular shops, which then pass the cost on to you. Shop owners go along begrudgingly; if they decline the "service," the same freelancers will actively steer future tourists away from the shop, saying it's closed, burned down, fresh out of cars—you get the idea.

Excluding commissions, rental cars in Cozumel start at US$40–50 a day for a VW bug or other small car, including insurance and taxes. Mopeds rent for around US$20 a day. Be aware that scooters account for the majority of accidents here, as speed bumps, potholes, and windy conditions can upend even experienced drivers. Also remember that unpaved roads are not covered by most rental car insurance plans.

Rentadora Isis (Av. 5 Norte between Calles 2 and 4, tel. 987/872-3367, rentadoraisis@prodigy.net.mx, 8 A.M.–6:30 P.M. Mon.–Sat., 8 A.M.–6 P.M. Sun.) consistently has the island's best rates, and friendly service to boot. **Rentadora Gallo** (Av. 10 Sur between Calle 1 and Av. Benito Juárez, tel. 987/869-2444, 8 A.M.–7 P.M. daily) is also eager to please. **Budget** (Av. 5 Norte between Calles 2 and 4, tel. 987/872-0903, www.budgetcancun.com, 7 A.M.–7:30 P.M. daily) is one of a handful of international companies on the island. **Hertz** and **Avis** have booths at the airport.

Cozumel has three **PEMEX** gas stations (7 A.M.–midnight daily). Two are in town on Avenida Benito Juárez (at Avs. Pedro Joaquin Coldwell and 75) and the third is four kilometers (2.5 miles) south of town on the Carretera Costera Sur across from Puerta Maya, the main cruise ship pier.

THE RIVIERA MAYA

Cancún may be the name everyone recognizes, but for many visitors, the best of Mexico's Caribbean coast belongs to the Riviera Maya. Defined as the 131-kilometer (79-mile) stretch of coastline between Cancún and Tulum, the Riviera Maya has no shortage of marquee attractions: the world's longest underground river, the world's second-longest coral reef, beautiful beaches packed with sun-worshippers, ancient Maya ruins, gourmet restaurants, hipster lounge bars, and beachside discotheques. With so much to see and do, the main trouble here may be fitting it all in. Then again, when you're on vacation in a place as beautiful as the Riviera Maya, doing nothing may well be the highlight of your trip!

PLANNING YOUR TIME

You'll probably want to pick a home base (or two) for your time here, and make day trips from there. Playa del Carmen is the area's only real city, with all the expected urban amenities, including nightlife. (It's also the gateway to Isla Cozumel.) Puerto Morelos and Akumal are smaller, and have numerous hotels and restaurants, but less hubbub. For even more isolation, the Riviera Maya has some secret getaways, like Xpu-Há, Punta Bete, and Tankah Tres. Day trips along the coast are easiest done in a rental car, though frequent public shuttles make getting up and down the coast fast and cheap. If you've got a week or more, consider spending half your time in the northern section—around Playa, for example—and then move farther south, to enjoy Akumal, Tankah Tres, and even Tulum.

© LIZA PRADO

HIGHLIGHTS

◖ **Puerto Morelos's Coral Reef:** Skip the tourist-trap snorkeling trips in Cancún and Playa del Carmen and go snorkeling where the reef is still healthy, the water uncrowded, and the price unbeatable (page 136).

◖ **Playa del Carmen's Quinta Avenida:** Ever growing yet wonderfully walkable, Playa's 5th Avenue has block after block of tempting restaurants, hipster boutiques, and lively bars (page 143).

◖ **Playa del Carmen's Beaches and Beach Clubs:** Chairs for rent, waiter service, and cool tunes make Playa's beaches – already among the Riviera Maya's most beautiful – some of the most enjoyable as well (page 146).

◖ **Xcaret Eco-Park:** Though not for everyone, the Riviera Maya's elaborate eco-parks are a hit with parents looking for a safe, active, friendly place to take the kids (page 151).

◖ **Laguna Yal-Ku:** A long elbow of water, where fresh and sea water mingle, and colorful fish live amid a jumble of underwater rocks and channels, makes this Akumal-area lagoon a favorite among snorkelers (page 171).

LOOK FOR ◖ TO FIND RECOMMENDED SIGHTS, ACTIVITIES, DINING, AND LODGING.

Puerto Morelos

Somehow little Puerto Morelos has escaped the mega-development that has swept up and down the Maya Riviera, and literally transformed its closest neighbors, Cancún and Playa del Carmen. Though Puerto Morelos can fill up with foreign tourists in the high season—and more and more condos and resorts are being built—it is still at heart a tranquil fishing town where kids and dogs romp in the streets, and life revolves around the central plaza. The beach isn't great, but Puerto Morelos has long been considered one of the best snorkeling spots on the coast. Local residents fought tirelessly (and successfully) to have the reef designated a national

reserve, and a town cooperative and local dive shops run well-recommended snorkeling and diving trips there. Puerto Morelos also is gaining popularity as a destination for yoga and meditation groups—no surprise given its serene atmosphere—and a growing number of hotels and resorts cater to that market. Be aware that the low season here is *very* low and many businesses close in May, September, and/or October.

SIGHTS
Beach

The beach here is disappointing—rocky in many places and strewn with seaweed that has

QUEEN CONCH

Tasty, easy to catch, and beautifully packaged – the Queen Conch (pronounced CONK) is a commercial angler's dream. Every part is sold: meat is exported to the United States and shells are bought as souvenirs by tourists. An easy way to make money – yes – but it's disappearing. Smaller conchs are being sold and anglers are being forced to go farther afield to make a profit.

It takes three to five years for this sea snail to grow from larva to market size. It also takes about that long for planktonic conch larvae, carried into fished-out areas by the currents, to replenish themselves. What's worse, the conch is easy to catch – large (up to 39 cm/15.4 in) and heavy (about three kg/6.6 lbs), the mollusk moves slowly and lives in shallow, crystalline water where it's easy to spot.

Biologists are working with various governments to impose restrictions on the fishing of Queen Conch, including closed seasons, minimum size, limits on the total numbers taken, and banning export.

Along with these proposed legal restrictions, science is lending a hand. Several mariculture centers, including one in Puerto Morelos, are experimenting with the Queen Conch. Raised in a protected environment, these creatures are released when they're large enough to survive in the wild. Unfortunately, this isn't always successful. One in 10 survives, as conch have to contend not only with humans but also with its other predators: lobsters, crabs, sharks, turtles, and rays.

The Queen Conch is not on the endangered species list yet but, by curbing our consumption – refusing to order it or to eat at establishments that serve it – we can help to save this creature.

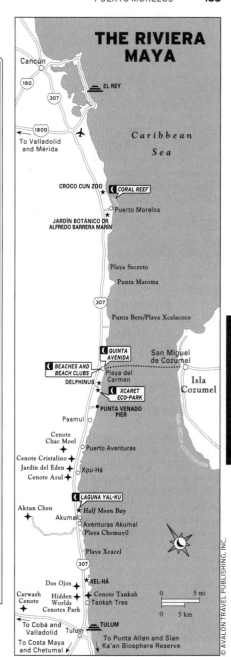

THE RIVIERA MAYA

© AVALON TRAVEL PUBLISHING, INC.

washed ashore. The best spot is at the Ojo de Agua hotel, where even a small purchase at the restaurant lets you use the beach chairs, umbrellas, and the pool. You can arrange snorkel and ATV tours here, as well.

☾ Coral Reef

Puerto Morelos's most spectacular attraction is snorkeling on the reef. Directly in front of the village, around 500 meters (0.3 mile) offshore, the reef here takes on gargantuan dimensions—up to 30 meters (99 feet) wide. Winding passages and large caverns alive with fish and sea flora make for great exploring. And since it's a marine reserve and fishing and motor traffic is limited, the reef is more pristine here than almost any place along the Riviera. (See *Snorkeling* for information on guided tours of the reef.)

The Plaza

The little plaza has restaurants and shops on three sides, and the ocean on the fourth. On Sundays, a small *tianguis* (flea market) is held here, and you can have fun browsing through someone else's old treasures. Otherwise, expect it to be quiet and unoccupied, save for a few people chatting on shaded benches.

Tropical Petting Zoo

A charming little tropical zoo, **Croco Cun Zoo** (tel. 998/850-3719, www.crococunzoo.com, 9 A.M.–6 P.M. daily, US$17 adults, US$11 children age 6–12, under 6 free) is located five kilometers (3.1 miles) north of the Puerto Morelos turnoff. Ninety-minute guided tours, offered in English or Spanish, bring visitors up close and personal to all sorts of local creatures—if you're up for it, you can feed spider monkeys on your shoulder, walk through a crocodile enclosure, and hold boas, iguanas, and baby crocs. Don't forget your camera. Well-managed and reasonably affordable—compare this to swimming with the dolphins!—Croco Cun is a sure hit for youngsters and adults alike.

Botanical Garden

A half kilometer (one-third mile) south of the

© AVALON TRAVEL PUBLISHING, INC.

Puerto Morelos turnoff is the **Jardín Botánico Dr. Alfredo Barrera Marín** (tel. 983/835-0440, 8 A.M.–4 P.M. daily, US$7), a peaceful botanical garden, study center, and tree nursery spread over 60 hectares (150 acres). Two kilometers (1.2 miles) of trails wind beneath a canopy of trees and past many of the peninsula's plants and flowers; each with its name labeled in English, Spanish, and Latin. Habitats vary from semi-evergreen tropical forest to mangrove swamp. Look for the epiphyte area, with a variety of orchids, tillandsias, and bromeliads. As you wander around you'll also find a re-creation of a Maya *chiclero* camp (showing how chicle was harvested to be used in chewing gum), a few ruins from the Postclassic period, and a contemporary Maya hut illustrating day-to-day life—from cooking facilities to hammocks. Wear long sleeves, pants, and closed shoes, and definitely bring bug repellent—the mosquitoes can be fierce, especially in the late afternoon and after it rains.

SHOPPING

The artisans' market of **Hunab Kú** (1.5 blocks south of the plaza, 9 A.M.–8 P.M. daily) may be your best bet for finding nice handicrafts. Here, you'll find a bunch of stands with colorful blankets, ceramics, hammocks, masks, jipi hats, shell art…pretty much anything you'll see sold up and down the coast.

The best English-language bookstore on the peninsula, **Alma Libre Bookstore** (central plaza, tel. 998/871-0713, www.almalibre books.com, 10 A.M.–3 P.M. and 6–9 P.M. Tues.–Sat., 4–9 P.M. Sun.) has a whopping 20,000 titles, ranging from "beach trash to Plato," in the words of the friendly Canadian couple who own and operate the store. Maya culture, Mexican cooking, learning Spanish, bird-watching, snorkeling guides, classics, philosophy, mysteries, fiction, nonfiction, and not just in English but Spanish, French, German, Dutch, Italian, Norwegian, and more—your taste in books would have to be extremely narrow to not find something you like here. Books are both new and used, and trade-ins (two for one) are possible; the store also has a

YUCATECAN HAMMOCKS

Yucatecan *hamacas* (hammocks) have the reputation of being the best in the world. Many locals prefer sleeping in them to mattresses. Cool and easy to store, they make great traveling beds and wonderful souvenirs. Here are a few tips for buying one:

Material: Nylon, cotton, or a blend of the two are the materials used to make hammocks. Nylon is more resilient but cotton is often more comfortable. Try a few out to see if you have a preference. If you're ambivalent, consider how much you plan to use it and which thread serves your needs best. Beware of vendors selling hammocks supposedly made of henequen; outside of miniature ones that hold fruit, they don't exist. (Even if they did, they would be incredibly itchy.)

Size: Hammocks typically come in *individual* (twin), *matrimonial* (queen), and *familiar* (king). While twins may be snug for a person taller than five feet, queen-size hammocks are roomy enough for most people. To judge whether a hammock will be long enough for you, hold one end of the body (the woven section) to the top of your head and let it drop; the other end of the body should touch the floor for you to be comfortable. A little extra material is optimal.

Loops: Check the end strings, which are called *brazos* (arms). At least 100-150 triple loops are in a good *matrimonial* hammock.

Shop Around: Finally, be sure to look at several hammocks before buying one. Feel the thread, check out the different sizes, count the *brazos,* and decide which patterns and color schemes you like best – vendors will always stretch out the hammock if asked. You'll soon hone in on one that best fits your needs, style, and budget.

wide selection of guidebooks and maps. Usually closed June to mid-October.

SPORTS AND RECREATION
Snorkeling

Puerto Morelos is justly famous for its snorkeling, with a protected stretch of coral reef running very near shore. A **local cooperative** (8 A.M.–3 P.M. Mon.–Sat.) offers excellent and affordable tours, visiting two spots on the reef for 45 minutes apiece, and using boats with sunshades. Prices are fixed: US$25 per person, including equipment, park fees, and a bottle of water. Boats leave every 30 minutes from the municipal pier; if there are fewer than three people, you have to wait up to 30 minutes (but no more) for additional passengers to come. Sign up at the cooperative's kiosk at the northeast corner of the plaza; late morning is the best time to go, as the sun is high but the afternoon winds haven't started.

The **dive shops** in town also offer snorkeling tours for US$25 pp for a two-hour trip visiting two different sites. Prices include snorkel gear, but you should ask whether the park fee is additional.

Caution: *Do not swim to the reef* from anywhere along the beach. Although it's close enough for strong swimmers to reach, boats use the channel between the reef and the shore, and tourists have been struck and killed in the past.

Scuba Diving

Divers have two shops to choose from in town, both offering one- and two-tank dives, night and specialty dives, cenote dives, and a range of certification courses. Reservations are strongly recommended in the high season.

Next to Posada el Moro, **Dive Puerto Morelos** (Av. Javier Rojo Gómez 14, tel. 998/206-9084, www.divepuertomorelos.com, 8 A.M.–6 P.M. Mon.–Sat., 8 A.M.–noon Sun.) offers reef diving (US$50 one tank, US$70 two tanks), cenote diving (US$85 one tank, US$125 two tanks), open water certification (US$325) and other courses, plus fishing, snorkeling and multi-dive packages. Rates include park fees and complete gear, except wetsuit.

Scuba Gecko (Hotel Ojo de Agua, tel. 998/871-0198, www.scubagecko.com, 9 A.M.–noon and 4–8 P.M. Tues.–Sat.) is part of Wet Set Adventures, a longtime dive and tour operator. Dives are US$45 for one tank, US$60 for two, and US$350 for open-water certification.

Sport Fishing

Both dive shops in Puerto Morelos also offer fishing trips beyond the reef. Scuba Gecko guarantees you will catch fish on its tour or the trip is free. Trolling trips (US$55/hr or US$175/day for two anglers) reel in wahoo, mackerel, bonito, and barracuda year-round, plus marlin and sailfish in the late spring and summer. Bottom-fishing tours (same prices) regularly bring home grouper, snapper, and other tasty fish—the crew will even prepare the fish for your hotel restaurant to cook. Dive Puerto Morelos offers tours on a local *panga* (US$250 for four hours, four people) or a modern fishing boat with cabin (US$450, four hours, 4–8 people).

ATV Tours

Puerto Morelos Adventure (Hotel Ojo de Agua, tel. 998/884-2314, www.puertomorelos adventure.com, 8 A.M.–7 P.M. daily) offers a four-hour ATV tour (US$58pp double, US$68 single) that weaves through sand dunes and coastal forest with stops at two cenotes to cool off. One cenote has a zip line for a bit of a rush. A bilingual guide and light lunch at Ojo de Agua hotel are included.

ACCOMMODATIONS
Under US$50

On a quiet street two blocks from the beach, **Hotel Eden** (Av. Andrés Quintana Roo No. 788, tel. 998/871-0450, US$31 s/d with fan) may not be the paradise its name suggests, but makes a good budget option all the same. Decor and flair are in short supply—not to mention TVs—but the spacious studios do have ceiling fans, clean hot-water bathrooms, and small kitchenettes. The kitchens aren't furnished (strangely) but the friendly proprietors usually have some extra pots and pans to loan you.

A half a block from the central plaza **Posada El Moro** (Av. Javier Rojo Gómez, tel. 998/871-0159, www.posadaelmoro.com, US$50 with fan, US$55 with a/c, US$75 suite with kitchenette) is one of Puerto Morelos's most charming hotels, and a great deal to boot. Operated by a friendly, English-speaking family, the hotel has 10 brightly painted units with polished cement floors, cable TV, wireless Internet (US$1.50/hr), and a pleasant little pool in a grassy courtyard in back. Continental breakfast is included.

In front of the Caribbean, **Amar Inn** (Av. Javier Rojo Gómez at Av. Lázaro Cárdenas, tel. 998/871-0026, amar_inn@hotmail.com, US$45–65 s/d with fan, US$75 suite) is a hurricane-battered inn run by the Aguilar family. The nine rooms vary from cramped garden cabañas with lofts, to spacious suites with amazing ocean views. All are reasonably clean and come with fans and refrigerators. Breakfast also is included.

The wine-red **Club Marviya** (Av. Rojo Gómez s/n, three blocks north of the central plaza, tel. 998/871-0049, in Canada 450/492-9094, www.marviya.com; US$95 Dec.–Apr., US$45 May–Nov.) is a laid-back Quebecois and Mexican-run hotel with six rooms and a communal kitchen, just a few steps from the beach. The rooms, all on the 2nd floor of a converted mansion, have firm beds, ceramic floors, and terrific views (and cool sea breezes) from small terraces. Breakfast is included, served in the covered downstairs corridor patio, where the owners and guests often hang out over beers at night. Bikes and beach gear can be rented or borrowed, and nine studio apartments were in the works when we passed by.

US$50-100

Formerly known as Rancho Libertad, **Rancho Sak Ol** (1 km/0.6 mi south of the central plaza, tel. 998/871-0181, www.ranchosakol.com, US$85 s/d with fan or a/c, US$120 jr. suite with fan and 2 night minimum) is a *palapa* hideaway on a broad beach south of town. Rooms have hanging beds and individual patios with hammocks. Downstairs rooms have air-conditioning, upstairs rooms have cross-breezes. A large buffet breakfast is included, and guests can use the community kitchen, located beachside. The beach here is decent, if not spectacular, marred somewhat by the cargo ferry on one side and a huge new condominium complex on the other. But there's enough breathing room so as not to spoil Rancho Sak Ol's relaxing, hideaway feel. Adults only, except during the low season when children over the age of 10 are welcome. Use of snorkel equipment and bicycles is also included in the rate.

One block south of the plaza, **Hacienda Morelos** (Av. Rafael Melgar, tel. 998/871-0448, www.haciendamorelos.com, US$70 s, US$100 d) took a beating in Hurricane Wilma, but has bounced back, completely renovated. Large airy rooms have simple but attractive decor, and the ocean views make up for the bathrooms, which someone hit with a 1970s stick. A concrete sunbathing patio with a small pool separates the hotel from the beach, and there's a good restaurant on-site.

Hotel Ojo de Aqua (Av. Javier Rojo Gómez, two blocks north of plaza, tel. 998/871-0027, www.ojo-de-agua.com, US$56–75 s/d) offers 36 basic rooms overlooking a pretty beach. Rooms come with cable TV and air-conditioning; standards feel a bit cramped, deluxes are bigger, and studios have a refrigerator, stove, and sink. All are clean and comfortable, though lacking in character—the flowered bedspreads and tile floors are classic hotel room. Families will appreciate the protected pool area, and on-site dive shop and tour operator, which rents snorkel gear and kayaks, and organizes ATV and snorkel tours.

Over US$100

A block from the beach, **Villas Shanti** (Av. Niños Héroes s/n, tel. 998/871-0040, www.villasshanti.com, US$123 d with a/c) offers eight one-bedroom units, each with a modern bathroom, fully equipped kitchenette, and private patio; all face a sunny courtyard that has a clover-shaped pool and a large *palapa* strung with hammocks. A spacious two-bedroom villa with full kitchen, living room, and dining room also is available for four to six guests, starting at around US$2,000 a week. Yoga workshops and retreats are regularly held here—classes are in a bright indoor studio or a large *palapa* in the garden. Check the website for more information. Although somewhat overpriced, **Ceiba Del Mar** (1.5 km/0.9 mi north of town, tel. 998/872-8060, www.ceibadelmar.com, US$437 s/d with a/c, US$493–840 suite with a/c, US$1008 suite with a/c and whirlpool, US$1,120 penthouse) offers a high-end resort experience in a laid-back town—something hard to come by. Located in eight three-story stucco buildings, the units are elegantly appointed and have the modern amenities you'd expect like flat-screen TVs with DVD, CD players, and minibars. Continental breakfast is included and is served in your room through a butler box—you won't even have to throw on your robe to open the door. The resort also boasts two glorious pools, a full-service spa, two restaurants, a dive shop, and tennis courts with night-lights.

FOOD

Who knows how it happened, but unassuming Puerto Morelos has an amazingly rich collection of restaurants and eateries, from cheerful holes-in-the-wall to international cuisine rivaling anything in Cancún or Playa del Carmen.

International

(**John Gray's Kitchen** (Av. Niños Héroes, half block north of plaza, tel. 998/871-0665, 6–10 P.M. Mon.–Sat., US$10–25) is a reincarnation of the now-closed but famously good Johnny Cairo Restaurant. It is without question the finest restaurant in Puerto Morelos (as was its predecessor), featuring an inventive menu that changes every other day. Specials include various fine cuts of beef and pasta prepared with almonds and chorizo. Occupying a boxy building two blocks from the plaza, the dining room is elegant and understated and the service is excellent. Cash only.

Giving Mr. Gray a run for his culinary money is **(** **Hola Asia** (central plaza, tel. 998/871-0679, 3–11 P.M. Mon.–Sat., 1–10 P.M. Sun., closed Tues., US$5–12) a small, popular restaurant serving a terrific pan-Asian menu of mostly Thai and Chinese inspiration. The simple one-room dining area can get crammed with diners, many who've come from Cancún or Playa del Carmen to eat here. For sweet and sour try General Tso's Chicken, for spicy go with Indian Yellow Curry. Closed in September.

The Argentinean and Uruguayan owners of **Los Gauchos** (Calle Tulum, tel. 998/871-0475, 4 P.M.–10 P.M. weekdays except Tues., 1 P.M.–10 P.M. weekends, US$1–5) serve homemade pizza and pasta, but don't leave without trying the *empanadas:* a classic Argentinean snack made of puffy, crispy fried dough filled with cheese or other goodies. At just US$1.25 apiece, a plate of five or six and a couple of sodas makes a great, cheap meal for two. Take them to go or eat at one of a few small tables on the sidewalk.

Everything you see at **Baraka** (Av. Rafael Melgar; 1 P.M.–10 P.M. Tue.–Sun., US$8–25)—the soaring *palapa,* the gorgeous wood floors, the sun-splashed patio—is in its second incarnation: the restaurant opened just days before Hurricane Wilma hit, destroying everything but the bathroom; check out the photo album while you're waiting for your meals. Lucky for everyone, it reopened and serves tasty Spanish-Mediterranean dishes, from *paella valenciana* to fresh sardines, accompanied by a full bar and friendly service.

A newcomer to the restaurant scene, **Tuna** (Av. Javier Rojo Gómez No. 801, tel. 998/206-9193, 8:30 A.M.–9:30 P.M. Tue.–Fri., 8:30 A.M.–11 P.M. Sat.–Sun., US$3–15) serves simple, tasty meals in a mellow, hip atmosphere. The menu sticks to Riviera Maya standards, like achiote chicken and garlic shrimp, but with a certain European flair: the French salad comes with chaya, pears, and blue cheese. Eat in the sleek dining area, then take a drink to one of the beach chairs and umbrellas. Saturday and Sunday evenings feature live music. By the way, *tuna* is the red fruit of the nopal cactus; *atún* is the fish you may have been expecting to see on the menu.

The Quebecois owners of **L'Oazis** (7:30 A.M.–10 P.M. Tue.–Sun.) serve mostly grilled dishes in their small, cheerful eatery. The menu includes tacos, burgers, NY steak, plus specialties like zucchini and eggplant with tzaziki sauce.

Mexican and Seafood

El Pirata (central plaza, tel. 998/871-0489, 8 A.M.–11 P.M. Mon.–Thurs., until 2 A.M. Fri.–Sun., US$5–15) has a good location on the central plaza just up from the pier where you take snorkeling tours. Choose from a large selection of hamburgers, fish burgers, *tortas,* tacos, and full entrées such as roast chicken or grilled beef, all served in a simple open-air dining area just off the street. Like many businesses here, El Pirata cuts back its hours in the low season, closing Mondays and the entire month of May.

◖ Doña Triny's (8 A.M.–1 A.M. daily; US$1–4) The bright orange and mural-bedecked exterior of this tiny restaurant on the northwest corner of the plaza make it impossible to miss. Come here for a friendly low-key ambiance and Mexican and Yucatecan standards, like quesadillas, huaraches, tacos, salbutes, and chile rellenos, all at great prices.

Los Pelícanos (central plaza, tel. 998/871-0014, 8 A.M.–10:30 P.M. daily, US$5–16) has a wraparound patio overlooking the plaza and the ocean—perfect for an afternoon beer or margarita. Food here can be a bit uneven, but with so many anglers it's hard to go wrong with shrimp, octopus, or fish, all served fresh in a half-dozen different ways.

Bakery and Sandwiches

A Puerto Morelos institution, **◖ Mama's Bakery** (Av. Rojo Gómez, one block north of plaza, tel. 044-998/845-6810, 7:30 A.M.–4 P.M. Tues.–Sat., 8:30 A.M.–1 P.M. Sun., US$3–5.50) is run by a friendly expat and baker extraordinaire—don't leave town without trying the sticky buns or carrot cake. Mama's is also a great place to come for fresh, healthy meals, like pancakes or breakfast burritos in the morning and smoothies and sandwiches on

homemade bread for lunch. Typically closed Labor Day to November 1.

Groceries

The supermarket (north side of the central plaza, 6 A.M.–10 P.M. daily) has a fairly large selection of canned foods, pastas, snacks, and drinks, and has a small produce section near the back.

INFORMATION AND SERVICES

Although this town sees a fair number of tourists, the services remain somewhat sparse.

Hospitals

Dr. Carlos Taboada Olvera (tel. 044-998/894-0832, 8 A.M.–9 P.M. Mon.–Sat.) heads a small clinic in a new commercial building a block west of the plaza, and comes well-recommended by expats living in town. For major medical issues, use the hospitals in Cancún or Playa del Carmen.

Money

There is no bank in Puerto Morelos. However, you can get cash from the HSBC ATM, which is just outside the supermarket on the plaza's north side.

Internet and Telephone

Next door to Dive Puerto Morelos, **PixanNET** (Av. Javier Rojo Gómez, tel. 998/206-9275, 9 A.M.–4 P.M. and 6 P.M.–10 P.M. Mon.–Sat.) has arguably the fastest connection in town, charging US$2 per hour. You can also download and burn your digital photos to a CD here for around US$2. Calls to the United States and Canada are US$0.30 a minute.

Papelería Computips (tel. 998/871-0361, 8 A.M.–10 P.M. Mon.–Sat., 2–10 P.M. Sun.) is located just off the southwest corner of the central plaza, and charges US$2 per hour for Internet.

Launderette

A block south of the plaza, the aptly named **La Lavandería** (Av. Javier Rojo Gómez s/n, no phone, 8 A.M.–8 P.M. Mon.–Fri. and 9 A.M.–5 P.M. Sat.) charges US$1.25 per kilogram (2.2 pounds) to wash, dry, and fold your dirty duds. Minimum three kilograms (6.5 pounds). The same distance north of the plaza, **Lavandería Las Vivas** (8 A.M.–9 P.M. Mon.–Sat., 10 A.M.–4 P.M. Sun.) charges US$1 per pound, or US$1.50 per pound for two-hour service.

GETTING THERE
Bus
Buses pass the Puerto Morelos turnoff on Highway 307, but do not enter town. The northbound stop is right at the turnoff, while the southbound stop is across the street and a block south (tel. 998/871-0759). For Cancún (US$1.50, 30 minutes) and Playa del Carmen (US$1–1.50, 20 minutes), second-class buses and *combis* (shared vans) pass every 10 minutes 6 A.M.–1 A.M. daily, and less frequently throughout the night. Some go as far as Tulum (US$3.50–5.25, 1.5 hours), but you should double-check before getting on. Buses to the **Cancún airport** (US$3, 25 minutes) pass every hour 8:30 A.M.–6:45 P.M. daily.

The only long-distance service from here is to Mérida (US$19.50, four hours), with daily departures at 9 A.M., 4 P.M., and 6 P.M. For all others (and many more to Mérida) go to Cancún or Playa del Carmen.

Ferry
The port here no longer offers car ferry service to islands. To get your car to Cozumel, head to Punta Venado, just south of Xcaret ecopark. For Isla Mujeres, head to Punta Sam, north of Cancún.

GETTING AROUND
Unless you're staying at Ceiba del Mar, Maya Echo, or Rancho Sak Ol, you'll have little need for a car. The town is compact—you can walk it from end to end in about 20 minutes—and the beach runs the length of it and beyond.

Taxis
Taxis line up day and night at the taxi stand on the northwest corner of the plaza. Prices are fixed and prominently displayed on a signboard at the taxi stand. A ride to the highway costs around US$2.

Punta Bete and Playa Xcalacoco

The turnoff to Punta Bete and Playa Xcalacoco is easy to miss from the highway—there's no sign and only a big "Cristal" water plant to mark the entrance. The access road is no more promising, unpaved and often waterlogged, winding through abandoned fields and past various construction projects. The reward for perseverance is a handful of hotels—from modest bungalows to one of the Yucatán's most exclusive resorts—and a mellow beach scene where locals and travelers alike lose themselves in the swaying palms and gentle blue waves. The beach is just okay (the sand is coarse and the shoreline rocky in places), but the snorkeling is reasonably good; you'll see more people beachcombing and reading books than playing beach volleyball or frolicking in the waves, and that seems to suit everyone just fine.

ACCOMMODATIONS
Hotel Kai-kaana (tel. 984/877-4000, www .kaikaana.com.mx, US$123) offers the comfort of a full-size hotel on this isolated stretch of beach, including a large pool, plenty of poolside lounge space, and a well-maintained beach area with *palapas* and hammocks. Rooms have one or two beds, cable TV, air-conditioning (though not mini-splits), and private balconies angled to provide everyone with a partial sea view. Breakfast is included in the rate, the restaurant serves up decent lunch and dinner. The staff is professional and affable.

Just steps from the beach **Bungalows Coco's** (tel. 998/874-7056, marsihel@hot mail.com, US$42 d queen, US$56 d king) has five *palapa*-roof bungalows squeezed onto a small, lush garden plot. The cabañas are charmingly decorated and have spotless bathrooms and private patios with hammocks to while away the day. There's a heart-shaped pool next to the open-air dining area and bar, and the beach is just 30 meters (100 feet) away. Reserve in advance so someone will be waiting for you when you arrive.

FOOD

Bungalows Coco's (see *Accommodations,* 7 A.M.–10 P.M., US$4–18) has a small outdoor bar and restaurant, serving dishes you don't often see in these parts, like fish, blackened rib eye, and banana flambé.

GETTING THERE AND AROUND

From the highway, follow the access road two kilometers (1.2 miles) until it forks at the Ikal del Mar resort. Bear left to reach the hotels and beach.

Taxis

There is no taxi stand in this tiny community. Ikal del Mar offers free daily van service to Playa del Carmen; otherwise your hotel can call you a taxi from Playa del Carmen or Puerto Morelos. A ride to the airport will cost you US$30, to Playa del Carmen around US$7.

Playa del Carmen

Not all that many years ago, your stroll through Playa del Carmen would have been escorted by children, dogs, little black pigs, and incredibly ugly turkeys; you might even have seen the milkman delivering milk from large cans strapped to his donkey's back. No more. With its population increasing nearly 20 percent annually, Playa del Carmen is the fastest-growing city in Quintana Roo. It is a full-blown tourist destination, no question about it.

Playa is not Cancún, however. For one thing, it is still much smaller and has almost none of the glitzy high-rises and all-night dance clubs. And unlike Cancún, Playa attracts mostly Europeans, and even has a nascent Italian quarter. Playacar, a planned community south of town, does have many high-end resorts but is also largely residential and does not have the "strip" atmosphere that Cancún's Zona Hotelera does. And while the southern section of Playa del Carmen—the area around the pier and local bus terminal—can be kitschy and intrusive, the northern section has a more low-key atmosphere with some excellent restaurants, cool bars, and offbeat shops. A hand-ful of huge condo and resort projects in the northern section may intrude on this pocket of funky charm, or push it farther north, but hopefully not destroy it.

Playa del Carmen has some pretty beaches (if you know where to go) and good snorkeling, diving, Maya ruins, cenotes, golf, and more are all nearby. It is a convenient base from which to explore and sample everything the Riviera Maya has to offer.

SIGHTS
◖ Quinta Avenida

Playa's main pedestrian and commercial drag is Quinta Avenida, or 5th Avenue, which stretches almost 20 blocks from the ferry dock northward. Pronounced KEEN-ta av-en-EE-da, you may see it written as 5 Avenida or 5a Avenida, which is akin to "5th" in English but refers to the same street. The first several blocks, especially around the ferry dock, are typical tourist traps, with souvenir shops and chain restaurants. Around Calle 10 or Calle 12, the atmosphere turns mellower, with bistros, jazz bars, and funky clothing stores. You'll

PLAYA DEL CARMEN

To Airport and Cancún

To Alltournative Expeditions

To Coco Beach Club

Caribbean Sea

EL JARDÍN DE SHANGRI-LA

LA CUEVA DEL CHANGO

SHANGRI-LA CARIBE

HOTEL LAS PALAPAS

MAMITA'S

Playa Tukán

CLUB TUKÁN

CHIQUITITA

NUDDY BEACH

BEACHES AND BEACH CLUBS

HOTEL RIVIERA CARIBE MAYA

MAKTUB CAFÉ

CALL HOME CASETA TELEFÓNICA

LA SIRENA

SEAC SUB GO CENOTES

CENTRO DE COMUNICACIONES 24

THE CREPES FACTORY

HOTEL LA RIVIERA

PLAYALINGUA

IKARUS

AVENTURA MEXICANA HOTEL

AH CACAO

VELOZ RENT A CAR

ARTESANÍAS MARKET

GRAN PORTO REAL

HSBC

CASA TEQUILA

SEE DETAIL

HAVANA CIGAR CO

ULA-GULA/BABE'S NOODLES AND BAR

BÁSICO

MR LAU

Plaza Pelicanos

BLUE PARROT

ALQUIMIA

100% NATURAL

THE BLUE PEARL SUITES

JAIME'S MARINA

Playa El Faro

TANK-HA DIVE CENTER

CAFÉ SASTA

Plaza 28 de Julio

PALACIO MUNICIPAL

TERMINAL ALTERNA

SAN FRANCISCO DE ASÍS

BASEBALL DIAMOND

UNIDAD DEPORTIVA VILLANUEVA MADRID

CALLE 30

CALLE 28

CALLE 26

CALLE 24

CALLE 22

CALLE 20

CALLE 16

CALLE 14

CALLE 14 BIS

CALLE 12 BIS

CALLE 12

AV CONSTITUYENTES

30 AV

20 AV

15 AV

5 AV

1 AV NORTE

1 AV NORTE

CALLE C CORAZÓN

CALLE 14

CALLE 12

CALLE 10

307

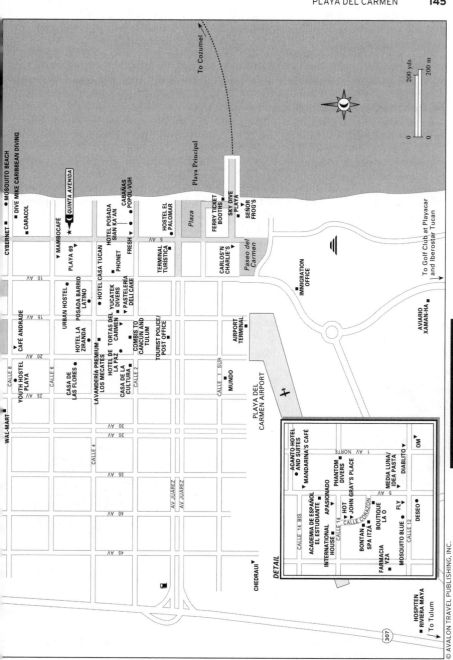

© AVALON TRAVEL PUBLISHING, INC.

probably walk the length of Quinta Avenida once or twice—the best beaches are in the northern part, the bus terminal and ferry dock in the southern—and everyone seems to find his or her favorite part.

◖ Beaches and Beach Clubs

With thick white sand and mild surf, **Playa Tukán** (entrance at 1 Av. Norte at Calle 26) is still the best beach in town. But it is being squeezed by condo developments, and its status as an accessible, truly public beach is definitely in peril. All beaches in Mexico are technically public, but resorts (like the ones being built) typically "claim" the stretch in front of them by setting up row after row of private chairs. The result is less and less space for non-guests, including locals, to lay out a towel for a day in the sun.

Several beach clubs on Playa Tukán rent chairs and umbrellas and have bar and restaurant service, along with small swimming pools, showers, and lockers for day guests. **Club**

Tukán and **Chiquitita** are mellow and good for families, while **Mamita's** (9 A.M.–6 P.M.) and **Nuddy Beach** (8 A.M.–6 P.M.) draw a younger, hipper set with techno music and beach beds. Prices are fairly uniform, around US$2–4 a day for chairs and umbrellas, US$8–15 for beach beds and large *palapas.*

There are also small tour operators on Playa Tukán that offer snorkeling tours, Hobie Cat trips, kayaks, and more.

Playa El Faro (between Calles 8 and 10) is an excellent beach just steps from the action on Quinta Avenida. Named for the large lighthouse *(faro)* at one end, there's still plenty of room to lay out your towel, unlike other stretches that have been snatched by encroaching hotels. Jaime's Marina (see *Snorkeling*), a well-recommended snorkel and sailing outfit, is located here.

Coco Beach Club is just a short distance north of Shangri La Caribe. It has good food, beach umbrellas, and sun beds, plus changing rooms and showers. The snorkeling here is the

© LIZA PRADO

Playa del Carmen's town beach is a popular spot, not only because it's beautiful but also because it's close to everything.

THE RIVIERA MAYA

best in the Playa area; you can rent gear here if you don't have your own.

Bird Sanctuary

A short distance inside the Playacar entrance off 10 Avenida, **Aviario Xaman-Ha** (Av. Xaman Ha, tel. 044-984/106-8766, 9 A.M.–5 P.M. daily, US$14 adults, free under 12) has more than 60 species of tropical birds, including toucans, flamingos, cormorants, and various types of parrots, all native to southeastern Mexico. The birds are divided by habitat and held in a variety of enclosures along a winding path—most people take a little less than an hour to see them all. Bring bug repellent, especially if you visit in the late afternoon or after it rains.

ENTERTAINMENT AND EVENTS

Playa del Carmen doesn't have the wild-and-crazy nightclubs that Cancún does, nor would many of the people who visit regularly want it to, but Playa does boast a great bar and lounge scene. You'll find plenty of lively spots along 5 Avenida any night of the week, but Playa's newest and hippest nightlife conflagration is happening at and around the corner of 1 Avenida and Calle 12, especially on weekends. The Blue Parrot, an oldy but goody, has been joined by a handful of newer bars, and you can dance from one to the next well into the wee hours.

Bars and Discotheques

One of Playa's classic hot spots, the **Blue Parrot** (Calle 12 at the beach, tel. 984/206-3350, www.blueparrot.com, 7:30 A.M.–4 A.M. daily, US$6–10 cover after 10 P.M.) is still going strong with a crowd most nights. Sand floors, swing bar seats, a candlelit *palapa* lounge, and a small dance floor all create the party feel that have kept customers streaming in for years. DJs play everything from retro to techno; be sure to check out the fire dancers—most nights shows start at 11 P.M. Service can be a bit brusque but seems to improve as your bikini (or Speedo) shrinks.

With retro tables and armchairs, and low beats and even lower lights, **Diablito** (1 Av. at Calle 12, tel. 984/803-3695, 1 P.M.–3 A.M.) is certainly the most stylish of the bars and clubs in this up-and-coming area. Order anything under the sun from the bar, and munch on unlikely Mexican-Japanese fusion snacks and meals. Quite pricey, but oozing cool.

Across the street, **Om** (Calle 12 near 1 Av., 984/879-4784, www.omplaya.com) is another popular spot, throwing rowdy parties and serving up cocktails made from fresh tropical fruit hanging at the bar.

Also nearby is the very cool and upscale **Fly** (5 Av. at Calle 12, tel. 984/803-1350, 1 P.M.–2 A.M. daily), which tries hard to be a New York hangout on the streets of Playa del Carmen. Lots of outdoor seating makes for prime people watching as you sip your martini. Service can be a bit uppity but then again, that's kind of the point.

Kitty-corner, DJs spin urban beats at **Deseo** (5 Av. at Calle 12, tel. 984/879-3620, www.hoteldeseo.com), a sleek minimalist lounge bar that attracts local and foreign hipsters most nights of the week. Part of a like-named hotel, the rooftop lounge is the centerpiece of the place; a candlelit stone stairway leads to a pool surrounded by queen-size cushions and billowing curtains.

One of Playa's only gay bars, **Playa 69** (5 Av. between Calles 4 and 6, tel. 984/876-9466, 9 P.M.–3 A.M.) is hopping on weekends, when tequila shots are almost mandatory. Popular with locals, the entrance is kind of hard to spot—look for it on the west side of 5 Avenida.

The beach club **Nuddy Beach** (Playa Tukán) turns into a lounge bar Thursday–Saturday nights (7 P.M.–3 A.M., no cover) with mellow, modern music and a cool attitude so thick you can cut it. On Thursdays women drink for free, and Saturday's "Sunset Party" features two-for-one champagne and wine.

The restaurant/bar **Apasionado** (5 Av. at Calle 14, tel.984/803-1101, 4 P.M.–midnight daily) features live Latin jazz on Friday and Saturday nights in its breezy, second-floor dining area that overlooks 5 Avenida. The music starts around 8 P.M.

The place to go for salsa dancing, **Mambocafé** (Calle 6 between Avs. 5 and 10, 984/803-2656, www.mambocafe.com.mx, 10 P.M.–4 A.M. Tue.–Sun., cover free–US$14) features live Latin bands every night. A packed party atmosphere rules with balloons, foam, and lots of sweating bodies moving to Latin rhythms. On Tuesdays there's no cover and on Wednesday women drink for free 10 P.M.–midnight.

And of course you can always find a party at **Señor Frog's** (Ferry pier, 10 A.M.–1 A.M. daily) and **Carlos'n Charlie's** (Plaza del Carmen, southern end of 5 Av., 984/803-3498, 10 A.M.–1 A.M. daily), both near the Cozumel ferry pier. These Mexican beach-town fixtures are famous for their yard-long drinks, dancing on the tables, and non-stop parties. Drink specials and special events are the norm. They also serve overpriced but familiar dishes, including barbecued ribs and hamburgers.

Cinema and Arcade

Cines Hollywood (Plaza Pelícanos, 2nd Fl., 15 Av. between Calles 8 and 10, tel. 984/803-1417, US$4.25 Thurs.–Tues., US$2.75 Wed) has three screens showing fairly recent Hollywood movies. The first show starts around 5 P.M.

Next to the movie theater, **Recórcholis** (Plaza Pelícanos, 2nd Fl., 15 Av. between Calles 8 and 10, tel. 984/803-1419, 2–11 P.M. Mon.–Fri., 11 A.M.–11 P.M. Sat.–Sun.) is a decent arcade—a perfect place to kill time before a movie.

SHOPPING

One of the most popular destinations on the Riviera Maya, Playa del Carmen offers some of the best shopping around and 5 Avenida is where it's at. You'll find everything from high-end clothing, Cuban cigars, specialty tequila, spectacular *artesanía,* jewelry, T-shirt, and postcard stands. You name it, Playa del Carmen probably has it.

Artesanía

La Sirena (5 Av. at Calle 26, tel. 984/803-3422, 8 A.M.–9 P.M. daily) is a boutique selling exceptional art from around Mexico. Italian shop owner Patrizia personally selects the beauties that she sells in her charming shop—whimsical skeleton art, colonial statuettes of La Virgen de Guadalupe, tin-framed mirrors, funky portraits, bright shawls—you're sure to find something you can't resist.

Caracol (5 Av. between Calles 6 and 8, tel. 984/803-1504, 9:30 A.M.–10:30 P.M. daily) is a pricey boutique selling beautiful and unique Mexican textiles. It makes a great stop, even if just to admire the spectacular fabrics—clothing, tablecloths, bedding, and decorative art—that the German owner handpicks herself on buying trips throughout southern Mexico.

A popular place, **La Calaca** (5 Av. between Calles 12 and 14, tel. 984/873-0174, 8 A.M.–12:30 A.M. daily) is jam-packed with Mexican masks, colorful *alebrijes* (fantastical wooden creatures), and quirky skeleton art. The quality is just all right but the variety is impressive. For collection pieces, check out its branch in Paseo del Carmen.

Bookstores

The best bookshop in the region is in nearby Puerto Morelos, and a stop there can be part of nice day trip from Playa. In town, **Alquimia** (1 Av. Between Calles 10 and 12, tel. 984/803-1575, 7 A.M.–midnight Mon.–Sat.) is a hip café plucked out of San Francisco, with baguettes and cappuccinos, and a small bank of used books for sale or trade (two-for-one).

For a larger selection, **Mundo** (Calle 1 Sur between 20 and 25 Av., tel. 984/879-3004, www.pequemundo.com.mx, 9 A.M.–8 P.M. Mon.–Fri., 10 A.M.–6 P.M. Sat.) has several cases of English-language titles, new and used. Mysteries, romances, and other beach-reads abound, but a close look turns up some good novels and nonfiction books. Prices run US$2–12, and the shop will buy the book back for 50 percent, cash or trade. You'll also find a small selection of regional maps.

Bontan (Calle Corazón near Calle 14, tel. 984/803-3733, 10 A.M.–10 P.M. daily) sells artsy Mexican specialty books—perfect if you're looking for a coffee table book to take home. A handful of guidebooks and regional maps also are for sale near the front of the shop.

Other Specialty Items

The local **Seac Sub** shop (1 Av. Norte between Calles 24 and 26, tel. 984/803-1192, 8 A.M.–9 P.M. Mon.–Sat.) has a large selection of masks, snorkels, fins, wetsuits, and other equipment, most decently priced. The shop has mostly Seac Sub products, of course, but carries other brands as well.

For a decent selection of specialty tequilas, check out **Casa Tequila** (5 Av. near Calle 14 Bus., 9 A.M.–midnight daily), where in addition to fine tequila, you'll find a nice variety of silver jewelry. A small sister store also is at 5 Avenida at Calle 16.

For the best in cigars, stop by **Havana Cigar Co.** (5 Av. between Calles 10 and 12, tel. 984/803-1047, 9 A.M.–11:30 P.M. daily). Cuban and Mexican *puros* are sold individually (US$5–10) or by the box (US$55–450).

For funky, bohemian-style beachwear, head to **Boutique La O** (Calle Corazón at 5 Av., tel. 984/803-3171, 9:30 A.M.–10:30 P.M. daily) where you'll find tie-dyed dresses, flowing linen pants, and cool cotton tops. Very comfortable and very Playa.

Shopping Centers

At the southern end of 5 Avenida, **Paseo del Carmen** (10 A.M.–10 P.M. daily) is a shady outdoor shopping center with high-end clothing boutiques, jewelry stores, art galleries, and restaurants. With a series of modern fountains, it makes for a pleasant place to window-shop—or enjoy an upscale lunch—after a day at the beach.

Plaza Pelícanos (10 Av. between Calles 8 and 10, 10 A.M.–10 P.M. daily) has a handful of low-end shoe and clothing stores plus a mediocre food court. The main—scratch that—the *only* reasons to come here are for the ATM, public bathrooms, arcade, and movie theater.

For trinkets to take home, check out the **outdoor market** at the corner of 5 Avenida and Constituyentes (8 A.M.–10 P.M. daily). You'll find everything from Maya pyramid key chains to silver jewelry.

SPORTS AND RECREATION
Scuba Diving

Playa del Carmen has decent offshore diving, and relatively easy access to Cozumel and inland cenotes. It's a logical base if you want a taste of all three, plus the convenience of being near the airport and in town. However, if diving is the main reason you came, consider basing yourself on Cozumel itself, or closer to the cenotes, such as at Akumal or Tulum. This will save you the time, money, and effort of going back and forth.

Prices in Playa del Carmen are reasonable, and fairly uniform from shop to shop. (See the *How to Choose a Dive Shop* sidebar in the *Isla Cozumel* chapter.) Two-tank reef dives are always a better deal than one; in fact, Cozumel and cenote trips are only offered as two-tankers. Reef dives cost around US$65–75 for two tanks, while Cozumel trips and cenote trips are around US$105–120. Only one shop (Tank-Ha) sends a dive boat directly to Cozumel from Playa; with the rest, you take the ferry (US$20 round- trip, not included in dive price) and board your dive boat there. Be sure to ask if lunch is included, as well as marine park fees (for Cozumel) and entrance fees (for cenotes). Same goes for gear—it's usually included, but can be pricey if not. Multi-dive packages are available at most shops, and earn you a 10–15 percent overall savings. Most shops also offer the full range of courses, from Discover Scuba and open-water certifications to nitrox and full cave diving courses.

Tank-Ha Dive Center (5 Av. between Calles 8 and 10, tel. 984/873-0302, www.tankha .com, 8 A.M.–10 P.M. daily) is one of the longest-operating shops in Playa, and the only one that takes divers to Cozumel by private boat instead of the ferry.

Dive Mike Caribbean Diving (Calle 8 between 5 Av. and the beach, tel. 984/803-1228, www.divemike.com, 8 A.M.–10 P.M. daily) is a very friendly, professional, reasonably priced shop. Check out its excellent and informative website for additional info and pictures.

Phantom Divers (1 Av. Norte at Calles 14,

THE RIVIERA MAYA

tel. 984/879-3988, www.phantomdivers.com, 8 A.M.–7 P.M. daily) is one of a handful of locally owned dive shops, offering friendly, casual service. No credit cards accepted.

Yucatek Divers (15 Av. between Calles 2 and 4, tel. 984/803-2836, www.yucatekdivers.com, 7:30 A.M.–6 P.M. daily) uses an area hotel's pool for beginner certification training and most fun dives are led by instructors.

Go Cenotes (1 Av. Norte between Calles 24 and 26, tel. 984/876-2629, www.gocenotes.com, 8 A.M.–8 P.M. daily) specializes in cave and cavern trips and courses for divers of all levels. Groups are always small (1–4 people) and the shop works hard to be sure you dive different cenotes every time.

Snorkeling

In Playa itself, you should take a tour since the snorkeling off the beach isn't too rewarding. The cenotes south of Playa also make for good, unique snorkeling.

Most of Playa's dive shops offer guided snorkeling tours to excellent sites. Ocean trips cost US$30–40, while cenote trips are US$50–60, all gear included. Be sure to ask how many people will be on the trip, how long the trip will last, and how many reefs you'll be visiting (for ocean trips). For cenote trips, we strongly recommend a wetsuit, even if it means renting one for a few extra bucks. The water is quite chilly, there's no sun, and you'll be better protected against cuts and scrapes.

Jaime's Marina (Playa El Faro, end of Calle 10, tel. 984/130-2034, www.jaimesmarina.bravehost.com, 9 A.M.–5 P.M. daily) is just a kiosk on the beach, but it offers friendly service and good snorkeling tours, among a number of water activities. Snorkel trips (US$30, two hours) include an hour of snorkeling and sailing to and from the reef in a Hobie Cat. If you come before 10:30 A.M., a 1.5-hour trip is just US$19 per person. Or you can rent a kayak and snorkel gear and create your own tour (US$15 single, US$20 double, three hours). Ask about a small anchor so your kayak doesn't float away, and about lockers and dry bags for your stuff.

Wind Sports

Kiteboarding, sailboarding, and sailing have grown in popularity along the Caribbean, a trickle-down effect from the world-famous wind belt on the Gulf Coast northwest of here. You can catch at least some breeze almost any time of the year, but the strongest, most consistent winds blow November–March.

Ikarus (5 Avenida and Calle 20, tel. 984/803-3490) is a retail shop that also arranges classes in kiteboarding. Beginning classes are often conducted at nearby Puerto Morelos, where the beaches are much less crowded. Private classes are US$75 an hour, while groups are US$45–55 an hour per person (maximum three to a group). The shop recommends 3–6 hours of instruction to learn the basics. Retail and rental gear is also available. A sister store is two blocks south at 5 Avenida and Calle 16.

Jaime's Marina offers friendly **sailing classes and rentals** from its kiosk on Playa El Faro. A four-hour beginner's class is just US$110 for up to four people. Rent a three-person Hobie Cat for US$25–35 an hour (depending on how long you stay out), or a five-seater for US$35–65 an hour, with or without a guide. Jaime's also has lockers and dry bags for your gear.

Fat Cat (tel. 984/876-3316, www.fatcatsail.com) is a spacious custom-designed catamaran used for day-long excursions (US$89/49 adult/child) that include sailing to secluded Xaac Cove, with a nice beach, good snorkeling, and a small Maya ruin nearby. You can also try "boom netting," in which you are pulled through the water behind the boat on a thick boom net.

Swimming with Dolphins

With tanks set up in the ocean, **Delphinus** (Hwy. 307 between Playa del Carmen and Paamul, toll-free Mex. tel. 800/335-3461, www.delphinus.com.mx, US$149) is a park all about swimming with dolphins in an environment that tries to replicate the "living conditions of pods in the wild." While being forced to work with humans in a closed-in pen isn't exactly wild, this park is as good as it gets for performing dolphins. For visitors, it's one of the most rewarding dolphin programs in the region. For US$149, participants are permitted to interact with a dolphin pod for 50 minutes; standard tricks are performed while visitors are in the water—a series of jumps, a foot push, and a dolphin kiss—along with extras like snuba-ing and just plain swimming with the pod. An additional 40 minutes is dedicated to touring the facility and listening to a lecture on dolphins. Admission includes a locker, towel, wetsuit, goggles, and round-trip transportation from many of the hotels on the Riviera Maya. There's a 10 percent discount if you book online.

◖ Xcaret Eco-Park

Popular for good reason, Xcaret (Hwy. 307 between Playa del Carmen and Paamul, toll-free Mex. tel. 800/292-2738, www.xcaret.com .mx, 8:30 A.M.–9 P.M. daily, US$58/29 adult/child, US$82/41 adult/child including buffet, US$104–110 adult including buffet and transportation, US$53–55 child including buffet and transportation) is a mega eco-park offering water activities like snorkeling in underground rivers and swimming with dolphins; up-close animal viewing areas including jaguar and puma islands, a butterfly pavilion, and an aquarium; and spectacular shows, like a Maya ballgame, regional dance, and music performances. Beyond this, the park also is dedicated to protecting the region's flora and fauna; there are scarlet macaw- and turtle-breeding areas, a section dedicated to the endemic stingerless bee, and an orchid greenhouse—all with educational exhibits for visitors. If you're into organized activities or you're traveling with kids, this definitely is a worthwhile stop.

Ecotours

Alltournative Expeditions (5 Av. between Calles 38 and 40, tel. 984/803-9999, www .alltournative.com) offers fun daily tours that include activities such as kayaking, rappelling, zip lines, off-road bicycling, caving, and snorkeling, plus (depending on the tour you choose)

visits to a small Maya village and Cobá archaeological zone. The agency has three principal tours to choose from (half or full day; US$94–104 pp adults and US$84–94 pp children under 12) and guides who speak English, Italian, French, German, Dutch, and Spanish.

Sport Fishing

Playa de Carmen has excellent sport and bottom fishing, with plentiful wahoo, *dorado,* mackerel, snapper, barracuda, and—especially April–June—sailfish and marlin. On average, trips for 1–5 people last 4–5 hours and cost US$200, including tackle and drinks. Most dive shops listed in the *Diving* section offer tours, as does Jaime's Marina (see *Snorkeling*).

Golf

The **Golf Club at Playacar** (Paseo Xaman-Há opposite Hotel Viva Azteca, tel. 998/881-6088 www.palaceresorts.com, 6 A.M.–6 P.M. daily) is a challenging, 7,144-yard championship course designed by Robert Van Hagge and located in Playacar, the upscale hotel and residential development south of Playa del Carmen proper. Green fees are US$190/90 adult/under 17 or US$130 after 2 P.M., including cart, snacks, and drinks; free hotel pickup for full-price rounds. Extra riders pay US$35/55 in low/high season and club and shoe rentals are US$30–50. Reserve at least a day in advance November–January.

Skydiving and Scenic Flights

Its gleaming white beaches and brilliant blue and turquoise seas make the Riviera Maya a spectacular place for skydiving. If you're up for it, **Sky Dive Playa** (Plaza Marina, tel. 984/873-0192, www.skydive.com.mx, 9 A.M.–6 P.M.) has been throwing travelers out of planes at 10,000 feet since 1996. You cover 4,500 feet in about 45 seconds, followed by a 6–7-minute parachute to a soft landing on the beach. Tandem dives (you and an instructor; US$200) are offered every hour—reserve 1–2 days in advance in summer and high season.

If you enjoy the view but prefer to stay buckled in, **Alas Sky Tour** (tel. 984/803-3718,

9 A.M.–4 P.M.) offers scenic flights in a modern ultralight aircraft. Flights last about 20–25 minutes and cost US$99. Sunset flights are gorgeous but can be bouncy; for a smoother flight, go in the morning. Each plane fits only one passenger (plus the pilot), but a couple can go up together in separate planes with radio communication.

Aerosaab (Playa del Carmen airport, tel. 984/873-0804, www.aerosaab.com) offers scenic full-day tours to Isla Holbox, a charming, little-developed island at the northeastern tip of the Yucatán Peninsula (see *Isla Holbox* in the *Cancún* chapter). The trip includes flying up the coast in a small Cessna airplane, touring the island's mangrove-fringed lagoons by boat, and exploring the beach and the tiny village there (US$305 pp, plus US$6–25 airport fees, minimum four people).

Body Work

Playa's swankiest gym is **Area Body Zone** (Paseo del Carmen shopping center, south end of 10 Av., tel. 984/803-4049, www.areabody zone.com, 6 A.M.–11 P.M. Mon.–Thu., 6 A.M.–10 P.M. Fri., 7 A.M.–5 P.M. Sat.–Sun.) with the latest exercise machines, a spacious free-weight and weight-machine areas, and regular sessions of aerobics, spinning, Pilates, and yoga. Day visits cost US$15, a 10-visit package US$55, and a month's membership US$110.

Across the street from the Shangri La Caríbe resort, **El Jardín de Shangri-la** (Calle 38 at Calle Flamingo, tel. 984/113-6151, 7:30 A.M.–9 P.M. Mon.–Fri., 8 A.M.–9 P.M. Sat.) is an undeveloped jungle lot reserved for, among others, yoga instruction, tai chi classes, and spiritual growth seminars. Instruction is mostly held under a huge *palapa* in the middle of the grounds but students are free to wander (and practice) on the lush property. Regular yoga, tai chi, capoeira, and meditation classes are offered weekly; classes cost US$7.50 per session, US$33 for a 10 pack, and US$47 per month (unlimited classes). Walk-ins welcome.

The well-tended **Unidad Deportiva Villanueva Madrid** (Av. 10 near Calle 30, 6 A.M.–10:30 P.M. daily) is Playa del Carmen's public sporting facility with a gym, tennis and basketball courts, track, and soccer field. All have night lighting and are open to the public at no charge; BYO equipment.

Treat yourself to an afternoon of pampering at **Spa Itzá** (Calle Corazón at 5 Av., tel. 984/803-2588, www.spaitza.com, 10 A.M.–9 P.M. daily), a full-service spa in the heart of Playa. Massage therapies (US$35–85), Maya healing baths (US$45), body treatments (US$45–75), and facials (US$45–85) are among the rejuvenating services offered.

Spanish Classes

Playa del Carmen is becoming a popular place to study Spanish, with several schools, plenty of options for cultural and historical excursions, and of course good nightlife and a great beach.

Solexico (35 Av. between Calles 6 and 6-Bis, tel. 984/873-0755, www.solexico.com) is a highly recommended school with a reputation for professionalism. Classes are offered in group (no more than five people) or individual settings, and for 15, 25, or 40 hours per week (US$159–564/wk). Students can stay with local families or at the school's 10-room student residence (US$25–35/night, including one or two meals), or arrange for hotel and condo rentals. Ask about volunteer opportunities.

Playalingua del Caribe (Calle 20 between 5 Av. and 10 Av., tel. 984/873-3876, www.playa lingua.com, 8 A.M.–8 P.M. daily) has a spacious learning center, with a leafy garden and small private pool. On-site rooms (small, clean, and air-conditioned) mean you can roll out of bed and be conjugating verbs in a matter of minutes. Most classes meet 10 or 20 hours a week, and the hourly cost is roughly US$9–25 per person, depending if you choose group, two-person, or private instruction. In addition to the rooms at the center (US$145–245 pp/week), students can also stay with a local family (US$150/week including half-board) or in a private apartment (US$50–100/day). One-time materials and inscription fees are about US$110; weekend excursions and extras classes, from salsa dancing to Mexican cooking, are also available.

International House (Calle 14 Norte between 5 Av. and 10 Av., tel. 984/803-3388, www.ihrivieramaya.com, 7:30 A.M.–9 P.M. Mon.–Fri., 7:30 A.M.–noon Sat.) occupies a pretty and peaceful colonial home, with a large classroom, garden, bar, and restaurant on-site. All instructors are university graduates with training in teaching Spanish as a foreign language. Intensive group classes (US$200/week) include four hours of class per day and can be joined on any Monday; classes typically have 3–4 students, and a maximum of eight. Private and two-person classes (US$29–35/hour) and packages including diving or Mexican cooking classes are also available. Age 16-plus only for group classes; all materials and inscription fees included. Family stays are US$175–US$200 a week, while a variety of furnished apartments and student rooms, with or without meals, run US$140–500 a week.

Academia de Idiomas El Estudiante (Restaurant Xlapak, 5 Av. between Calles 14 and 14-bis, tel. 044-984/876-0616, info@playaspanishschool.com, 8:30 A.M.–10 P.M. daily) is more low-key and backpacker-oriented, with a single open-air patio where classes are conducted over small wooden tables. Group classes (US$8/hr., 2–4 people only) meet four hours every weekday morning; private classes (US$15/hr.) can be conducted any time, including weekends. A one-time US$35 inscription fee covers books, copies, and other materials. The school helps organize outings, including trips to Cobá and Mérida, cooking and salsa classes, volleyball games, snorkeling tours, and more. Students can stay with a family (US$130/week, including breakfast) or in a shared apartment with a small kitchen and sometimes a pool (US$130/week d).

Art and Performance Classes

If you are staying for more than just a couple of weeks, consider taking a class or two at the **Casa de la Cultura** (Calle 2 at 20 Av., tel. 984/873-2654, 9 A.M.–10 P.M. Mon.–Sat.). Regional dance, guitar, painting, and singing are regularly offered.

ACCOMMODATIONS

Playa del Carmen has a huge selection and variety of accommodations, from youth hostels to swanky resorts to condos and long-term rentals. Most all-inclusives are located in Playacar, just south of town.

Under US$25

◖ **Youth Hostel Playa** (Calle 8 s/n at 25 Av., tel. 984/803-3277, US$10.25 dorm, US$28 d with shared bath) is Playa del Carmen's best hostel, despite being somewhat removed from downtown and the beach. The dorm rooms are narrow but clean, and have thick comfortable mattresses, individual fans, and free lockers. The simple private rooms are kept very clean, although light sleepers may be bothered by street noise. A well-equipped kitchen has plenty of space to work your culinary magic and a good cubby system to prevent groceries from disappearing. Best of all is the hostel's enormous common area, perfect for eating, playing cards, reading, watching TV, or whatever. Coffee and water are provided, but not breakfast. For better or worse, Playa's new Walmart is across the street.

Urban Hostel (10 Av. between Calles 4 and 6, tel. 984/803-3378, US$10 dorm, US$17.50–22 s/d with shared bath) has a welcoming entrance but the charm dries up somewhere in the narrow tunnel-like hallway that leads to the dorms and common area. Even a recent renovation didn't manage to improve the grubby, claustrophobic feeling here. Easy access to the bus terminal, free bike rental, and the cheapest rates in town (by a hair) are reason enough for some to stay, but there are better budget options to be had. This hostel is no longer affiliated with Urban Hostel in Isla Mujeres, but it remains to be seen who gets to keep the name.

Hostel El Palomar (5 Av. between Av. Juárez and Calle 2, tel. 984/873-0144, US$11 dorm, US$35 s, US$42 d) has giant dorm rooms crammed with row upon row of double bunks, and three smallish private rooms with a clean, shared bathroom and a terrace with hammocks and view of the ocean. The problem is there's no common area, save the rooftop

High-end resorts are popping up along one-time fishing village Playa del Carmen's gorgeous beachfront.

terrace with an open-air kitchen. The hostel is right across from the bus terminal; Internet access, continental breakfast, and large lockers are included.

US$25-50

Hotel Casa Tucan (Calle 4 between 10 and 15 Avs., tel. 984/873-0283, www.casatucan.de, US$38 s/d, US$50 studio) offers a labyrinth of basic rooms in a social environment. There are rustic cabañas with reasonably clean bathrooms, no-frill hotel rooms with fans, and small studios with even smaller kitchenettes. All of the units have fantastic murals, which spruce up the place quite a bit. There's also what is likely the deepest pool around—4.8 meters (15.7 ft.). (It's so deep, in fact, that it's used by dive shops for open-water certification training.) It's surrounded by lounge chairs and hammocks, perfect for whiling away an afternoon.

Near the bus station and with private access to a nice stretch of beach, **Cabañas Popol-Vuh** (Calle 2 near 5 Av., tel. 984/803-2149, pdcpopol_vuh@hotmail.com, US$20 s/d cabañas

with shared bath, US$30 s/d cabaña with private bath, US$54 s/d with private bath and a/c) is a decent budget option. As you walk through the gate, you'll take in the site at a glance: nine cozy cabañas and four hotel rooms that face a small sand lot. The cabañas are simple wood-paneled structures but they're comfortable, have good screens, and strong fans. Those with private bathrooms also have small private porches. Those with shared bathrooms should wear flip-flops in the shower—they need a serious scrub down. The hotel rooms definitely are a major step up: tile floors, cable TV, mini-split air-conditioning, and a private bathroom. In this town, these units are a steal—and go fast! Call ahead to reserve.

One of the first hotels in Playa, **Hotel Posada Sian Ka'an** (Calle 2 near 5 Av., tel. 984/873-0202, www.labnah.com, US$38–48 s/d with fan) doesn't looks like it has been remodeled in over three decades. Rooms are functional and clean but a coat of paint, updated bathrooms, and a few new beds would be nice. That said, the location and the price almost can't be beat. Sitting just half a block from both 5 Avenida and the Caribbean doesn't get much better around here. Most rooms also have balconies or terraces—some with partial views of the ocean, the rest overlooking the garden. Continental breakfast included in the rates.

A simple two-story motel, **Hotel La Paz** (Av. 20 between Calles 2 and 4, tel. 984/873-0467, www.hotel-la-paz.com, US$48–58 s/d with a/c) has 20 rooms with tile floors, hot-water bathrooms, and air-conditioning. Rooms open onto a lush courtyard with swaying palm trees, a well-tended garden, and a gazebo—a remarkably appealing place that makes you almost forget how no-frills the rooms are.

US$50-100

On a peaceful section of 5 Avenida, the inviting 【 **Hotel La Riviera** (5 Av. between Calles 22 and 24, tel. 984/873-3240, www .hotel-lariviera.com, US$65–75 s/d with a/c) has simple, recently renovated rooms. All have sponge-painted walls, tile bathrooms, cable TV, and quiet air-conditioners. Rooms in front also have balconies that overlook 5 Avenida—a great people-watching spot. Wireless Internet is accessible to all guests. Continental breakfast also is included if you book online.

【 **Casa de las Flores** (20 Av. Between Calles 4 and 6; tel. 984/873-2898, www.hotel casadelasflores.com, US$65–75 s, US$90 d) offers a slice of charm at very reasonable prices. The cheerful hacienda-esque exterior gives way to a leafy courtyard and garden, with a small stone-paved pool and rooms arranged on two levels in back. Americans will appreciate the air-conditioning, Europeans the bidet, and no one can complain about the whitewashed walls, simple but classy decor, and friendly service. Higher-priced rooms have better light or small terraces.

Recently remodeled, **Hotel Riviera Caribe Maya** (10 Av. at Calle 30, tel. 984/873-1193, www.hotelrivieramaya.com, US$89–101 s/d with a/c, US$135–146 suite with a/c) offers bright rooms with hand-carved Mexican furnishings and modern amenities like cable TV,

in-room phone, and mini-fridge. Most look out onto the hotel's inviting pool, which is tucked into a pleasant courtyard. Internet access and continental breakfast are included in the rate.

If you can overlook the uppity service, the **Posada Barrio Latino** (Calle 4 between 10 and 15 Avs., tel. 984/873-2384, www.posadabarriolatino.com, US$60–62 s/d with fan, US$72 s/d with a/c) offers 16 charming rooms with details like mosaic tile bathrooms, stone-inlayed floors, and private balconies. Continental breakfast is included in the rate and is served in a leafy courtyard with a *palapa*-roofed lounge—a good place to write postcards or play cards too. Bicycles available free of charge.

Hotel La Ziranda (Calle 4 between 15 and 20 Avs., tel. 984/873-3933, www.hotel laziranda.com, US$60 s/d with fan, US$70 s/d with a/c) offers 16 sparse rooms—all with private balconies or terraces—that are spread out between two modern buildings. Rooms are spacious, spotless, and have nice tile bathrooms. While all are well-kept, ask for a room on the 2nd floor—they have high ceilings and the best cross breezes. Look for the *palapa*-roofed lobby as you come down the street—it's unmistakable. Lots of ambivalent cats lounge about too.

US$100-150

Two hotels in one, **Aventura Mexicana Hotel** (Calle 24 between 5 and 10 Avs., tel. 984/873-1876, toll-free U.S. tel. 800/455-3417, www .hoteltierramaya.com, US$129–169 s/d with a/c, US$179–209 suite with a/c) is split into a family side and an adult-only side. Good idea but not-so-good execution—the adult-only side is significantly nicer. Boutiquey units have muted colors, elegant furnishings, and high-end amenities that open onto a nicely manicured garden with a "quiet" pool. In contrast, the family rooms are overly basic—tile floors, simple ironwork, and wood furnishings with a nondescript pool in the center—a classic mid-range room. If you have kids, your money is best spent elsewhere. Continental breakfast included in all the rates.

Over US$150

Just half a block from the beach, **⟨ Acanto Hotel and Suites** (Calle 16 near 5 Av., tel. 984/873-1252, toll-free U.S. tel. 866/655-8819, www.acantohotels.com, US$185 one-bedroom condo with a/c) is a charming little hotel on a shady street. This quiet hotel offers seven South Asian–inspired condominiums—dark woods, luxurious fabrics, Asian art—each with one bedroom, a fully equipped kitchen, a living-dining room, and a patio. A small swimming pool with a large Buddha to one side sits in the middle of the complex. There's also a sundeck for guests who want to take in the sun without leaving the premises.

The ultramodern **Mosquito Blue** (5 Av. between Calles 12 and 14, tel. 984/873-1335, www.mosquitoblue.com, US$208–236 s/d with a/c, US$265–405 suite with a/c) boasts lush interior courtyards with two amoeba-shaped pools, an impressive *palapa*-roofed lounge with comfy couches and striking modern art throughout. Rooms, though somewhat cramped, are beautifully appointed and have the most modern in amenities: digital safes, wireless Internet, plush bathrobes, minibar, and cable TV. It has a similarly luxurious sister hotel, the aptly named **Mosquito Beach** (Calle 8 at the beach, tel. 984/873-0001, US$230–291 s/d with a/c, US$445 suite with a/c), located on a nice stretch of beach in the heart of town. During high season weekends, both hotels raise their rates by 25 percent. Guests over age 16 only.

For extended stays, **⟨ The Blue Pearl Suites** (Av. 1 between Calles 10 and 12, tel. 984/803-2379, www.thebluepearl.com.mx, US$143–172 one-bedroom condo with a/c, US$229 two-bedroom condo with a/c, minimum seven nights) offers super-stylish, comfortable, and eco-friendly apartments that sleep between two and eight people. All have fully equipped kitchens (with recycling and composting bins) and a private terrace or garden with hammocks and outdoor tub. Rooms have gorgeous original art but otherwise minimalist decor, plus wireless Internet and daily cleaning (even your dishes!). The hotel doesn't have beach

club passes, but Playa El Faro—one of two good public beaches in town—is around the corner and there's a small pool and lounge area on the roof. Noise from nearby bars and clubs may be a problem for light sleepers, however.

Sitting on one of the best beaches in Playa, **⟨ Hotel Las Palapas** (Calle 34 between 5 Av. and the beach, tel. 984/873-4260, www .laspalapas.com, US$160–214 s with a/c, US$186–250 d with a/c) offers 75 thatch-roofed bungalows that open onto either a lush garden brimming with native flora or onto a white sand beach with breathtaking views. The peaceful units have comfortable beds, ample patios with hammocks, and radio access to an exceptional staff. No televisions or phones here. A stone-lined path leads guests to an inviting freshwater pool, a clubhouse, a full-service spa, a dive shop, and—of course—beach chairs and umbrellas on the Caribbean. Be sure to climb the tall lookout platform for a spectacular bird's-eye view of Playa del Carmen. Rates include a full buffet breakfast.

A sleek, urban-chic hotel, **Deseo** (5 Av. at Calle 12, tel. 984/879-3620, www.hoteldeseo .com, US$188–211 s/d with a/c, US$267 suite with a/c) boasts rooms that look as if they belong in a modern art museum. Think bananas, flip-flops, and a bikini top hanging from the walls. Add minimalist furnishings, including a low-lying bed, streamlined fixtures, and photoshoot lamps. Now, pump in some tunes—techno or modern bossa nova—and you've got your room. Outside your door, is the hotel's bar/lounge/pool area with queen-size cushions serving as beach chairs, and flowing white curtains strung high above. Very cool. Unless, of course, you want to sleep—music from the lounge blasts until 2 A.M. every night. The hotel even provides earplugs. Use 'em or join the party. Continental breakfast included.

Just a block away, Deseo's hip younger sister, **Básico** (5 Av. at Calle 10, tel. 984/879-4448, www.hotelbasico.com, US$188–211 s/d with a/c, US$267 suite with a/c) has high-end rooms with an industrial-warehouse style. Staffers say the inspiration comes from the oil tankers that ply the Gulf of Mexico. Needless to say, despite the stark, cement look, the rooms are ultra luxurious—plush beds, fine linens, flat screen TVs, even a Polaroid camera to capture a particular, er, moment with your partner. A retro Mexican seafood restaurant/bar/lounge is on the top floor with a glorious view of the Caribbean. Like Deseo, it's ultra cool and ultra loud: techno will keep you up—or keep you dancing—late into the night.

About 10 minutes from the hubbub on Avenida 5 but at the peak of the action on the beach, **Shangri-La Caríbe** (Calle 38 near 5 Av., tel. 984/873-0611, toll-free U.S. and Canada tel. 888/896-0690, www.shangrilacaribe .net, US$175–325 s with a/c, US$200–325 d with a/c) is the epitome of a Caribbean resort. Over 100 *palapa*-roofed bungalows are connected by sand paths that lead to the resort's facilities: two swimming pools, three restaurants, two bars, an Internet center, and a dive shop. Bungalows are beginning to show their age but are comfortable nonetheless with private balcony or terrace. It's definitely a party place but no worries—if you're looking to catch up on your romance novels, a quiet spot is never far away. Full breakfast and dinner are included in the rate.

All-Inclusive Resorts

Most of Playa del Carmen's all-inclusives are in Playacar, an upscale hotel and residential development south of town. But a slew of condo and resort projects are slated for north Playa proper, especially on Avenida Constituyentes, until now the "quiet" part of town.

Gran Porto Real (Av. Constituyentes 1, at 1 Av. Norte, tel. 984/873-4000, www.real resorts.com.mx, US$175–275 pp) is a family-oriented resort, so honeymooners may want to look elsewhere. The rooms and pool are nice, but the beach is disappointing—very small and used by a constant stream of anglers to haul up their boats. You may spot some huge fish being unloaded, but all in all we'd rather have the extra beach space. Another problem is the hotel's habit of overbooking the junior suites, especially in high season, and switching guests to inferior rooms.

Iberostar Tucan (Av. Xaman-Ha, tel. 984/877-2000, www.iberostar.com, US$252–310 s, US$222–280 pp d) has a spacious lobby-entryway and wide attractive beach with palm trees, beach chairs, and mild surf. Between the two is a broad patch of healthy, well-maintained coastal forest, where you can spot monkeys, parrots, and other native creatures in the treetops. After so many sterile and manicured resorts, this is a welcome change of scenery. The pool is huge, and near the beach. Rooms occupy large buildings along the property's edges, and are clean and comfortable, though plain. Junior suites have sea views.

Rental Properties

Playacar has scores of houses for rent of all different sizes and styles. Prices vary considerably, but expect to pay a premium for ocean views and during peak seasons. A number of property-management companies rent houses, including **Playacar Vacation Rentals** (Calle 10 s/n, two blocks south of Av. Juárez near the Playacar entrance, tel. 984/873-0418, www.playacarvacation rentals.com) and **Vacation Rentals** (tel. 984/ 873-2952, www.playabeachrentals.com).

FOOD

Playa del Carmen has scores of restaurants and eateries offering a variety of culinary delights. Walk a block or two down Quinta Avenida and you're sure to spot something that you like.

Mexican

◀ **La Cueva del Chango** (Calle 38 at 5 Av.; 8 A.M.–11 P.M. Mon.–Sat., 8 A.M.–2 P.M. Sun., US$4–12) means "Cave of the Monkey" but the restaurant is neither dim nor primitive: The covered dining area has light-hearted decor (and a back patio is ensconced in leafy vegetation) while the menu features crepes, empanadas, and innovative items like eggs with poleta and chaya. Well north of town, it's often packed with Playa's upper crust, though the prices make it accessible to all.

La Palapa Hemingway (5 Av. between Calles 12 and 14, tel. 984/803-0003, 8 A.M.–midnight daily) has a good all-you-can-eat

Mexican lunch buffet for under US$10. The menu has a varied selection of Mexican and Maya favorites, including chicken mole, *chile en nogada,* and Yucatecan grilled fish, and there are a full bar and wine list. Sit inside for the air-conditioning or outside for the pleasant tile-covered tables right on the avenue.

An old-school Mexican coffee shop, **Café Andrade** (Calle 8 near 20 Av., tel. 998/846-8257, 7 A.M.–11 P.M. daily, US$2–5) serves up mean breakfast and dinner plates with tacos, *chilaquiles, mole,* enchiladas...you name it, they'll whip it up. It's so typical, in fact, that you're likely only to see locals—during the week, businessmen puffing away at cigarettes, on weekends, families out for a bite.

For regional *tortas* (sandwiches), check out **Tortas del Carmen** (15 Av. between Calles 2 and 4, 984/129-7157, 8:30 A.M.–9 P.M. daily, US$2–4), serving massive sesame rolls piled high with refried beans, cabbage, avocado, *quesillo* (a soft cheese), tomatoes, and your choice of meat. Try the *Del Carmen,* with pulled pork and chicken fried steak, to fill up after a day at the beach. Outdoor seating only.

Other Specialties

◖ **John Gray's Place** (Calle Corazón near Calle 14, 984/803-3689, 6– 10 P.M. Mon.–Sat., US$10–20) is a sister restaurant to the original John Gray's Kitchen in Puerto Morelos, widely considered one of the best restaurants on the Riviera Maya. The new kid lives up to expectations, expertly fusing gourmet American cuisine with flavors from around the world. The menu changes daily, but expect dishes like asparagus soup or soy marinated tuna for starters, and entrées of roasted duck with tequila, chipotle and honey, or pork loin with Roquefort crust. Credit cards not accepted, so you may want to stop at the ATM before dinner. Don't worry, it's worth it.

◖ **Maktub Caffé** (5 Av. between Calles 28 and 30, 7 A.M.–1 A.M. daily, US$6–15) The first inklings of Arabic culture came to Mexico with the Spanish colonizers, whose food and architecture were deeply influenced by the Moors. Then came a wave of Palestinian and Lebanese immigrants who settled here in the 18th and 19th centuries. (Mexican actress Salma Hayek is of Lebanese descent, in fact.) So it's no surprise to find restaurants like this one, serving excellent tabbouleh, hummus, falafel, and more, and hookahs and flavored tobacco to relax by. It's on a hip, bustling block, with restaurants and bars on both sides and across the street.

Friendly and unassuming, **Ula-Gula** (5 Av. at Calle 10, 2nd Fl., tel. 984/879-3727, 5:30 P.M.–11:30 daily, US$9–25) serves outstanding international gourmet dinners in an appealing second-floor dining area overlooking the street corner. Argentinean owned and operated, the pasta and meat dishes are excellent as expected, but seafood is the real standout here: Start off with Kubik tuna with wasabi and soy sauce, then dig into the fish of the day, prepared one of several fashions, from parsley gorgonzola sauce to smoked tomato broth. For dessert, the chocolate fondant—a small chocolate cake filled with rich chocolate syrup and accompanied by ice cream—is divine.

Although occasionally missing the mark, old-timer **Babe's Noodles and Bar** (Calle 10 between 5 Av. and 10 Av., tel. 984/804-1998, noon–11 P.M. Mon.–Sat., 5–11 P.M. Sun., US$6–14) still serves up delicious Thai and Asian-fusion meals in a hip, bistro setting. Dishes come in half and full orders. Don't miss a chance at ordering the *limonmenta,* an awesome lime-mint slushie. It's not a huge place so you may have to wait for a table during high season, or if you prefer, head to its sister restaurant down the street (5 Avenida between Calles 28 and 30, 2–11 P.M. Mon.–Sat.). Cash only.

Another Puerto Morelos import holding its own in Playa del Carmen, **Mr. Lau** (10 Av. between Calles 8 and 10, tel. 984/873-2020, 2 P.M.–11 P.M. daily, US$8–15) is an offshoot of the wildly popular Hola Asia restaurant just up Highway 307. The pan-Asian menu is the same, including Japanese-style tempura, Indian yellow curry, and the ever-popular General Tso's chicken—breaded chicken in sweet and spicy sauce, all terrific. A sushi bar is planned for the courtyard in back—stay tuned.

Mandarina's Café (5 Av. at Calle 14 bis,

tel. 984/803-1249, 11 A.M.–1 A.M. daily, US$12–25) oozes cool, with low pulsing music, candles, and gleaming white tablecloths set in a semi-covered patio dining area. The sign says "pizza and champagne," both of which come in a number of varieties. The menu also has a long list of crepes, from egg and mushroom to asparagus and cheese, plus gnocchi, lasagna, and other pastas. Right on the avenue, this is also a great spot for people watching. Frequent two-for-one drink specials.

100% Natural (5 Av. between Calles 10 and 12, tel. 984/873-2242, 7 A.M.–11 P.M. daily, US$5–11) serves mostly vegetarian dishes and a large selection of fresh fruit blends. Service can be a bit inattentive here, but the food is fresh and well prepared. Tables are scattered through a leafy garden area and covered patio.

Cafés and Bakeries

Chocolate lovers will melt over **Ah Cacao** (5 Av. at Constituyentes, tel. 984/803-5748, www.ah cacao.com, 7:30 A.M.–midnight daily, US$1.50–4), a chocolate café where every item on the menu—from coffees to cakes—is homemade from the sweetest of beans. Try a spicy Mayan Hot Chocolate for a true tasty treat (US$3).

You'll smell **(Hot** (Calle Corazón at Calle 14, 7 A.M.–10 P.M. daily, US$2–8) from a block away—a café that makes freshly baked breads and pastries all day. Most people end up staying for more than just a brownie though—a full menu of sandwiches prepared on whole-wheat or sunflower-seed bread are almost impossible to resist. The shady outdoor eating area is a great place to enjoy a leisurely breakfast too.

The charming, old-world **(Café Sasta** (5 Av. between Calles 8 and 10, 7 A.M.–11 P.M. daily, US$1.50–4.50) offers a tempting display of muffins, scones, cupcakes—even cheese-cake—to go along with the full coffee menu. Seating is available indoors and outdoors.

Pastelería Deli Cake (15 Av. between Calles 2 and 4, 8 A.M.–10 P.M. daily, US$0.25–2) is a classic Mexican bakery selling typical baked goods—*cuernos* (croissants), *donas* (doughnuts),

galletas (cookies), and a case full of cakes. Not fancy by any means, but cheap and good.

The Crepes Factory (Calle 24 at 5 Av., no phone, 8:30 A.M.–11:30 P.M. daily, US$3.50–6) is a simple café that serves great smoothies and tasty crepes—you can oversee the production of both if you sit griddle-side at one of the counter stools, or have them delivered to tables set up on the sidewalk.

Groceries

Wal-Mart (Calle 8 between Avs. 20 and 25, 7 A.M.–midnight daily) has arrived in Playa, opening a huge superstore behind city hall, with everything from clothes, shoes, and snorkel gear to groceries, prepared food, and a full pharmacy.

INFORMATION
Tourist Information

Playa del Carmen has no reliable tourist information office, but does have a few free tourist magazines that are worth picking up, especially if you are here for more than a couple of days. *Sac-Be* and *Playa Maya News* are monthly magazines printed on newsprint and oriented toward the expat community. For tourists, they both usually offer a handful of useful articles, listings, and events calendars (and a dose of not-so-useful drivel, as well). *Dive 'n' Sports* (aka D'N'S) has good maps of Playa, Puerto Morelos, Cozumel, Tulum, and Akumal, plus hotel and restaurant listings and short articles about kiteboarding, skydiving, and other activities. *Que Pasa? Playa Pocket Guide* is a small booklet with a somewhat confusing map but a good selection of ads and coupons, all organized into a convenient directory.

Hospitals

Hospiten Riviera Maya (main highway, tel. 984/803-1002, www.hospiten.com, 24 hours) is a private hospital offering modern, high-quality medical service at reasonable rates. Many of the doctors have U.S. training and speak English, and are accustomed to treating foreign visitors and expats.

PLAYA DEL CARMEN BUS SCHEDULES

TERMINAL TURÍSTICA (5 Av. and Av. Juárez, 984/873-0109 ext. 2501 or 01-800-702-8000) is located near the ferry dock and has frequent service north to Cancún and south to Tulum, and most locations in between. Long-distance buses use the Terminal Alterna.

Most Tulum-bound buses stop at the turnoffs for destinations along the way, including **Xcaret** (US$1, 10min.), **Paamul** (US$1, 15 min.), **Puerto Aventuras** (US$1, 20 min.), **Xpu-Há** (US$1.50, 25 min.), **Akumal** (US$2, 30 min.), **Xel-Ha** (US$3, 30 min.), and **Hidden Worlds** and **Dos Ojos** (both US$3, 40 min.).

Most Chetumal buses stop at **Carrillo Puerto** (US$8, 2 hrs), and **Bacalar** (US$11, 5 hrs).

Most Cancún buses stop at **Puerto Morelos** (US$1.50, 20 min.) but *not* the airport or Cancún hotel zone.

DESTINATION	PRICE	DURATION	SCHEDULE
Cancún	US$3.25	1 hr	every 10 min., 5:45 A.M.-midnight
Cancun Int'l Airport	US$7.50	1 hr	hourly 7 A.M.-6 P.M.
Chetumal (2nd Class)	US$12.25	6 hrs	every 1-2 hrs 5:15 A.M.-5:15 P.M., plus 11:15 P.M. (making all stops)
Tulum	US$2	1 hr	hourly 5:15 A.M.-11:15 P.M.
Xcaret (main entrance)	US$3	15 min.	9 A.M., 9:40 A.M., 10:20 A.M., 11:20 A.M.

*Denotes deluxe service; there are many more deluxe departures from Cancún.

For emergency ambulance service, call 065 from any public phone.

Pharmacies

Farmacia Yza (tel. 984/873-2727) has two 24-hour pharmacies—one on 10 Avenida between Calles 12 and 14, and the other on 30 Avenida between Calles 4 and 6. Order at least US$10 of medicine or snacks (it's also a mini-mart) and they'll deliver to your hotel.

Police

The tourist police (tel. 984/877-3340, or 060 from any pay phone) have an office on Avenida Juárez and 15 Avenida, and informational kiosks along 5 Avenida, theoretically operating 24 hours a day.

SERVICES
Money

Banks and free-standing ATMs are scattered around town. To access your money or exchange foreign cash try **Banamex** (Calle 12 at 10 Av., 9 A.M.-4 P.M. Mon.-Fri., 10 A.M.-2 P.M. Sat.) or **Banorte** (Plaza Pelícanos, 10 Av. between Calles 8 and 10, 9 A.M.-6 P.M. Mon.-Fri., 10 A.M.-2 P.M. Sat.).

Internet and Telephone

Call Home Caseta Telefónica (5 Av. at Calle 28; 8 A.M.-11 P.M.) makes checking email cool and comfortable, with air-conditioning and solid armchairs. Internet is US$1.50 an hour and phone calls are just US$0.20 a minute to

TERMINAL ALTERNA (Calle 20 between Calles 12 and 12-Bis, tel. 984/803-0944, toll-free 01-800/702-8000) departures include:

DESTINATION	PRICE	DURATION	SCHEDULE
Campeche	US$30	8 hrs	10:20 A.M.
Chetumal	US$16	5 hrs	every 1-2 hrs 6:15 A.M.-11:55 P.M.
Chichén Itzá	US$15	4 hrs	8 A.M.
Cobá	US$5.50	1.5 hrs	8 A.M.
Mérida	US$24-30	5.5 hrs	every 1-2hrs 6:30 A.M.-6:30 P.M., plus midnight and 12:30 A.M.
Mexico City	US$92	24 hrs	five departures 7:30 A.M.-9:15 P.M.
Palenque	US$41	12 hrs	Take San Cristóbal bus
San Cristóbal (Chiapas)	US$51	19 hrs	3:30 P.M., 5 P.M., 7 P.M.*, and 9:40 P.M.
Valladolid	US$12.50	2.5 hrs	8 A.M., 10:20 A.M., 11:30 A.M., 6:30 P.M., and 12:30 A.M.
Villahermosa	US$45	12 hrs	nine departures 12:15 P.M.-12:30 A.M., plus 7:30 A.M.
Xpujil	US$22	5.5 hrs	7:30 A.M., 12:15 P.M., 3:15 P.M., 6:15 P.M., and 12:40 A.M.

the United States and Canada or US$0.40 to Europe.

Centro de Comunicaciones 24 (Calle 24 between 5 Av. and 1 Av. Norte, tel. 984/803-5778, Internet US$2.25/hr.) is often filled with clouds of cigarette smoke, but is open 24 hours and offers cut-rate international calling on Saturday and between midnight and 7 A.M.

Closer to the center, **Cybernet** (Calle 8 between 5 Av. and the beach, tel. 984/873-3476, 8:30 A.M.–11:30 P.M. daily) has a fast Internet connection for US$1.50 per hour, and international calling from US$0.50 a minute.

Phonet Centro de Comunicaciones (10 Av. between Calles 2 and 4, 8 A.M.–11 P.M. daily) is a quiet place to check email (US$1.50/hr) and to make calls (US$0.42/min to U.S. and Canada, and US$0.75/min to Europe).

THE RIVIERA MAYA

Post Office

The post office (9 A.M.–4 P.M. Mon.–Fri., 9 A.M.–noon P.M. Sat.) is next to the tourist police office at the corner of Avenida Juárez and 15 Avenida. Postcards and small letters cost US$1 to send to the United States, US$1.35 to Europe.

Immigration

Avoid using Playa del Carmen's immigration office (Plaza Antigua mall, 2nd Fl., Calle 10, tel. 998/881-3560, 9 A.M.–1 P.M. Mon.–Fri.), as the one in Cancún is much faster and friendlier. A simple tourist visa extension, or *prórroga,* can take a week or more in Playa and involves considerable documentation. In Cancún, the same process is simpler and takes as little as two hours.

Travel Agencies

Mayaluum Travel Agency (10 Av. at Calle 2, tel. 984/873-2961, www.mayaluum.com, 9:30 A.M.–2 P.M. and 3:30–7:30 P.M. Mon.–Fri., 9:30 A.M.–2 P.M. Sat.) handles plane tickets, package tours, and other travel arrangements.

Launderette

A convenient place to get your threads washed is **Lavendería Premium Los Mecates** (Calle 4 near 20 Av., 8:30 A.M.–8 P.M. Mon.–Fri., 8:30 A.M.–1 P.M. Sat.–Sun., US$1/kilogram). Same day service if you drop your clothes off early.

GETTING THERE
Bus

Playa del Carmen has two bus stations. **Terminal Turística** (aka Terminal Riviera, 5 Av. and Av. Juárez) is in the center of town and has frequent second-class service to destinations along the coast, including Cancún, Tulum, and everything in between. The **Terminal Alterna** (Calle 20 between Calles 12 and 12-bis) has first-class and deluxe service to interior destinations such as Mérida, Campeche, and beyond. There is some overlap, and you can buy tickets for any destination at either station, so always double-check

where your bus departs from when you buy a ticket.

Combis

Combis (public vans) are an easy way to get up and down the Riviera Maya. In Playa, northbound *combis* line up on Calle 2 near 20 Avenida, leaving every 15 minutes, 24 hours a day. The final destination is Cancún's main bus terminal (US$2.75, 50 minutes), but you can be dropped off anywhere along the highway, including Puerto Morelos (US$2, 20 minutes). *Combis* do not enter Cancún's hotel zone, but you can catch a bus there from outside the terminal. South from Playa del Carmen, *combis* leave from the same corner every 15 minutes, 5 A.M.–10 P.M. They go as far as the Tulum's bus station (US$2.50, 50 minutes), passing the turnoffs for Xpu-Ha (US$1.50, 20 minutes), Akumal (US$2, 25 minutes), Hidden Worlds (US$2.50, 40 minutes) and Tulum Ruins (US$2.50, 45 minutes) among others. To return, you can flag down *combis* anywhere along the highway.

Air

Playa del Carmen's airport does not receive regular commercial flights, though charters are available to and from locations around the peninsula and even Belize and Guatemala.

Car

If you are driving to Playa del Carmen look for the two main access roads to the beach—Avenida Constituyentes on the north end of town and Avenida Benito Juárez on the south. Playacar has its own entrance from the highway, but can also be reached by turning south on Calle 10 off Avenida Juárez.

Ferries to Isla Cozumel

Passenger ferries to Cozumel (US$10 each way, 30 minutes) leave from the pier at the end of Calle 1 Sur. **UltraMar** and **Mexico Water Jets** alternate departures and charge the same amount, though UltraMar's boats are newer. Their ticket booths are side-by-side at the foot of the pier, with the time of the next departure displayed prominently. The ticket seller will probably try to sell you a round-trip ticket, but it makes more sense, and costs the same, to buy a *sencilla* (one-way ticket) and wait to see which ferry has the next departure when you're ready to return. Between the two companies, there are ferries every 60–90 minutes 6 A.M.–10 P.M. daily.

South of Playa is **Punta Venado dock** (tel. 987/872-0916, www.maritimachankanaab. es.mw). Once used by the Calica Company to ship limestone products to the United States, today it is home to the only car ferry to and from Isla Cozumel. Ferries depart Punta Venado at 5 A.M., 7 A.M., 11 A.M., 5 P.M., and 9 P.M. Mon.–Sat. From Cozumel, the ferry leaves at 4 A.M., 9 A.M., 1 P.M., and 6 P.M. daily except Sunday. The trip takes about 1.5 hours and costs US$40 for a car including driver, and US$2.60 for each additional passenger. Arrive at least an hour in advance to get a spot.

GETTING AROUND

Playa del Carmen is a walking town, although the steady northward expansion is challenging that description. The commercial part of 5 Avenida now stretches 20 blocks and keeps getting longer. Cabs and bicycle taxis are a good option, especially if you have luggage. Parking in Playa in the high season can be a challenge, especially south of Avenida Constituyentes. Many hotels have secure parking, otherwise there are parking lots around town, including on Calle 2 at 10 Avenida (8 A.M.–10 P.M. daily, US$1/hour or US$8.50/day).

Taxi

Taxis around town cost US$1.50–5, or a bit more if you use a taxi stand or have your hotel summon one. All taxi drivers carry a *tarifario*—an official fare schedule—which you can ask to see if you think you're getting taken for a ride, so to speak. Prices do change every year or two, so ask at your hotel what the current rate is, and always be sure to agree on the fare with the driver before setting off.

Triciclos (bike-taxis) line up on Avenida Juárez alongside the Terminal Turística. The ride costs about the same as one in a taxi but makes an interesting alternative.

Car Rental

Playa has myriad car rental agencies and prices can vary considerably. Prices are highest at the major agencies, like Hertz, National, Avis and Executive, but they often have great deals online. At local agencies, like **Veloz Rent a Car** (Av. Constituyentes 111 between 5 Av. and 1 Av. Norte, tel. 984/803-2323, 8 A.M.–1 P.M. and 5 A.M.–8 P.M. daily) and **Zipp Rent-A-Car** (10 Av. between Calles 2 and 4, 998/873-0696, www.zipp.com.mx, 8 A.M.–6 P.M. daily) you may be able to negotiate lower rates, especially during low season and for rentals of a week or more. Expect to pay US$45–60 a day for a car, with taxes and insurance included.

THE RIVIERA MAYA

Paamul

What started out as an unassuming trailer park on a beautiful stretch of beach has now become a seaside community all its own. Located about 20 kilometers (12.4 miles) south of Playa del Carmen, Paamul has everything from RVs with elaborate wood and *palapa* structures over them to hotel rooms, a restaurant, and even a dive shop.

BEACH

Paamul stretches over a wide curving beach. It's clean and classically pretty with white sand and turquoise water—perfect for swimming and exploring. Watch your step on the south end of the beach, as its waters harbor prickly sea urchin—consider wearing water shoes.

SNORKELING AND SCUBA DIVING

The full-service **Scuba-Mex** (tel. 984/875-1066, toll-free U.S. tel. 888/871-6255, www.scuba mex.com, 8 A.M.–5 P.M. daily) offers one- and two-tank dive trips to open water sites and cenotes (US$29–80). A variety of packages and dive courses also are available at competitive rates. And if you're just interested in snorkeling off the beach, the shop rents snorkel gear for US$6 per day.

ACCOMODATIONS

Offering a little bit of everything, **Cabañas Paa Mul** (Carretera Cancún-Chetumal Km. 85, tel. 984/875-1051, www.paamul.com, US$10 pp tent, US$25 trailer spot, US$111 s/d cabañas, US$145 s/d with a/c) appeals to travelers of all budgets. Best of all are the modern hotel rooms, which were built in 2006. All are boutiquey in style, with muted colors, luxurious linens, gleaming bathtubs, mini-split air-conditioners, and gorgeous ocean views from private terraces. Next best are, surprisingly, the tent and trailer spaces.

Paamul's beach is a good place to spend the day.

© LIZA PRADO

Although set up in the main parking lot, all boast electricity, running water, and clean shared hot-water bathrooms—these are just steps from the Caribbean. Dead last—and with good reason—are the cabañas. Constructed in 2000, they look as if they've been through decades of wear and tear: wood floors with holes, cement walls with paint thrown on, and granny-style decor. Priced at over US$100, you're better off in a tent space.

FOOD

Open-air, modern, and with a great view of the Caribbean, the **Reefs of Paamul Restaurant and Bar** (8 A.M.–9 P.M. daily, US$5–15) serves up classic Mexican dishes along with a vari-

ety of international meals. There's something for everyone, which makes it easy to eat most of your meals here. (Good thing, since it's the only restaurant in Paamul).

For groceries, the very mini **Mini Super Paa Mul** (7 A.M.–7 P.M. Mon.–Sat., 8 A.M.–2 P.M. Sun.) sells basic food stuff. Look for it on the highway turnoff to Paamul.

INFORMATION AND SERVICES

There are no health, banking, Internet, or postal services in Paamul. The closest town—and one of the best places in the region—for a full range of services is Playa del Carmen, 20 kilometers (12.4 miles) north.

Puerto Aventuras

Puerto Aventuras is an odd conglomeration of condos, summer homes, and hotels, organized around a large marina, including a swim-with-dolphins area. It's more than a resort, but not really a town. Whatever you call it, Puerto Aventuras's huge signs and gated entrance are impossible to miss, located a few minutes north of Akumal on Highway 307.

SIGHTS
Museo Sub-Acuatico CEDAM

Short for the Conservation, Ecology, Diving, and Archaeology Museum, CEDAM (Bldg. F, 9 A.M.–1 P.M., 2:30–5:30 P.M. Mon.–Sat., donation requested) is a very worthwhile museum, displaying a wide variety of items: Maya offerings that were dredged from the peninsula's cenotes; artifacts recovered from nearby colonial shipwrecks; early diving equipment; and photos of open-water and cenote explorations, some from the halcyon days of diving when *jeans* were the preferred get-up.

SPORTS AND RECREATION
Snorkeling and Scuba Diving

Some 25 dive sites lie within a 10-minute boat ride from the marina, each boasting the same

rich coral, abundant sealife, and interesting features, like pillars and swim-throughs, found up and down the coast. **Aquanauts** (tel. 984/873-5041, www.aquanauts-online.com, 8:30 A.M.–5:30 P.M. daily) is a safe, full-service shop that has many repeat guests. Divers can count on personal details (such as storing dry gear) and guest-first practices (such as staying under as long as your air permits, not just the standard 45 minutes). The shop offers the full range of dives and courses, including reef dives (US$40/one tank, US$75/two tanks), cenotes dives (US$90/one tank, US$150/two tanks) and open-water certification (US$415 private, US$385 pp group). Multi-dive packages are available; equipment rental is included in courses but not fun dives (US$15/one tank, US$20/two tanks). The shop also offers a 2.5-hour snorkel tour (US$40, including equipment, snacks, and drinks, four people minimum) visiting two different reefs and has a good selection of new equipment for sale. Reservations recommended in high season.

Swimming with Dolphins

Dolphin Discovery (Marina, tel. 984/873-5078, in U.S. 800/417-1736, www.dolphin discovery.com, 8 A.M.–5 P.M. daily) offers several

CEDAM AND THE RIVIERA MAYA

In 1948, a small group of Mexican divers – active frogmen during World War II – created a nonprofit organization called Club de Exploración y Deporte Acuáticos de México (Exploration and Aquatic Sports Club of Mexico, or CEDAM). Their mission was to promote ocean conservation and educate others about its treasures and resources.

In 1958, the group set about salvaging the *Mantanceros*, a Spanish galleon that foundered offshore in 1741. It got permission to set up camp on present-day Akumal, then just a deserted beach owned by a man named Don Argimiro Arguelles. Argimiro leased CEDAM a workboat for their project, and even offered his services as captain.

It was this relationship that sealed Akumal's – and arguably, the Riviera Maya's – destiny. During a relaxed evening around the campfire, Don Argimiro sold Pablo Bush, the head of CEDAM, the bay of Akumal and thousands of acres of coconut palms north and south of it. For the next 12 years, CEDAM continued its work in the rustic and beautiful place – replacing their tents with sturdy *palapa* huts, and still using the creaky *SS Cozumel* to carry divers to sites up and down the coast.

It wasn't long before the idea of promoting tourism on Mexico's forgotten Caribbean coast arose. In 1968, the group – which had changed the words behind its initials to Conservation, Ecology, Diving, Archaeology, and Museums – donated 5,000 acres of land to the government, as well as the Cove of Xel-há, to create a national park. The aim was to open the isolated area to tourists, and in so doing, create jobs for local residents. CEDAM also provided housing, food, electricity, running water, a school for the children, and a first-aid station with a trained nurse.

Still based in Akumal, CEDAM has grown into an important international scientific and conservation organization. The group plays an active part in the archaeological exploration of cenotes, among other things, and hosts regular symposiums and seminars. A small but worthwhile museum in Puerto Aventuras – Museo Sub-Acuático CEDAM (Building F, 9 A.M.-2 P.M. and 3:30-6 P.M. Monday-Saturday) – displays some of the incredible items that the group has recovered in the region's waters.

dolphin-encounter activities, ranging in price and the amount and type of interaction you have. For the most contact, the Royal Swim program (US$139; 30 minutes' orientation, 30 minutes in water) includes two dolphins per group of eight people, with a chance to do a "dorsal tow," "foot-push," and "kiss," plus some open swim time. The Swim Adventure (US$99) and Dolphin Encounter (US$79) have somewhat less direct contact. The center also has manatee and sea lion programs that can be taken in combo with dolphins. Programs start at 9 A.M., 11 A.M., 1 P.M., and 3 P.M. daily; free shuttle service is available to and from Playa del Carmen.

Golf and Tennis

Puerto Aventuras Club de Golf (across from Bldg. B, tel. 984/873-5109, 7:30 A.M.–5:30 P.M. daily, last tee time 3 P.M.) offers a nine-hole, par-36 golf course right in town. The course, designed in 1991 by Tom Leman, is flat but has two par fives over a total 2,961 yards (3,255 championship). Green fees are US$80, including cart; after 1 P.M., they're US$65 with a cart, US$57 with a pull cart. Rates include a golf cart and are US$75 per person before 3 P.M. and US$55 per person afterward. Two tennis courts are also available for US$20 an hour. Golf club rentals cost US$24, tennis racquets run US$5.

Sport Fishing

Capt. Rick's Sportfishing Center (past Omni Puerto Aventuras hotel, tel. 984/873-5195 or toll-free Mex. tel. 800/719-6439, www.fishyucatan.com, office 8 A.M.–7 P.M. daily) offers customized fishing trips for groups and individuals. Trolling is the most popular, going for

© LIZA PRADO

Swimming with dolphins is one of the most popular activities along the Riviera Maya.

dorado, tuna, barracuda, sailfish, and even marlin. Bottom/drift fishing is also fun and targets "dinner fish" such as grouper, snapper, and yellowtail. You can also arrange time for visiting a deserted beach or Maya ruin, snorkeling on the reef, or just cruising by upscale homes and hotels. Choose between a 23-foot boat (two passengers maximum, US$250/450 half/full day), a 31- or 35-footer (eight passengers maximum, US$375/650 half/full day), or a 38-footer (10 passengers maximum, US450/800 half/full day). Shared trips are US$90 per person for half day and US$180 for full day. Full-day trips leave at 9 A.M. and return at 5 P.M.; half-day trips are 9 A.M.–1 P.M. and 1:30–5:30 P.M. Prices include equipment, bait, soft drinks, and water; full-day trips also include lunch. There's good fishing year-round, but April–July are best for hooking into a billfish.

Parasailing

Riviera Maya Parasail Adventures (past Omni Puerto Aventuras hotel, tel. 984/873-5623, www.snubamexico.com, office 8 A.M.–6 P.M. daily) offers single and tandem parasail trips (US$65 single, US$55 pp tandem, 9 A.M., 10 A.M., and 11 A.M.) several times daily. The flights last 10–12 minutes (although the whole excursion takes about an hour) and you reach up to 250 feet in the air. Others can accompany you on the boat for US$20 per person. The agency caters to cruise ships, so advance reservations are a good idea.

ACCOMMODATIONS

The main road bumps right into the **Omni Puerto Aventuras** (tel. 984/875-1950, www.omnihotels.com, US$308–342, includes breakfast), a small upscale hotel with the marina on one side and a fine, palm-shaded beach on the other. All 30 rooms have tile floors, one or two beds, colorful regional decor, and first-class amenities such as wireless Internet access. All rooms have private patios with hot tubs; those with an ocean view cost more. Large discounts in the low season.

◖ Casa del Agua (Punta Matzoma 21, tel. 984/873-5184, www.casadelagua .com, US$350 d, US$1,400 house) is a beacon of class and charm amid the plastic commercialism of Puerto Aventuras. At the far southern end of town, the hotel's four spacious suites—the bathrooms alone are bigger than some hotel rooms—all have king-size beds, air-conditioning and fan, and come with a hearty breakfast, served on a common patio overlooking the bay. There is a small sunny pool and the beach is quiet and private, although rather steeply sloped. Guests are free to borrow kayaks and snorkeling gear, as well as the hotel's wireless Internet signal. Casa del Agua caters to honeymooners and small yoga and meditation groups, so children are allowed only if you rent the entire building; otherwise 12 and older only. Service is superb. Three-night minimum stay for individual rooms, seven-night minimum when renting the house.

For info on long-term rentals or even buying a place, try **Paradise Beach Sales and Rentals** (next to Café-C@fé coffee shop, tel. 984/873-5029, www.puertaaventurasrentals .com, 7 A.M.–7 P.M. Mon.–Sat.).

FOOD

It is easy to find a place to eat in Puerto Aventuras: Stroll around the marina for a few minutes and you'll run into every restaurant in town. The variety is slim, however—most menus have a similar selection of Americanized Mexican food, pastas, and grilled meats. **Café Olé International** (Bldg. A, tel. 984/873-5125, 8 A.M.–10 P.M. daily, US$5–25) has something for everyone, and every price range. It's best known for its filet mignon and homemade desserts.

If you're in the mood for a big salad or a pizza—thin, regular, or deep dish—try **Richard's Quarterdeck Steakhouse and Pizza** (Bldg. A, tel. 984/873-5086, 11 A.M.–10 P.M. daily, US$6–32). Opened in 1994 by a Chicago native, food here is especially good if you're missing flavors from home.

If you've gone fishing, bring your catch to **Gringo Dave's** (Bldg. C, 7 A.M.–11 P.M. daily, US$6–31). For just US$5 per person, the chef will prepare your fish any way you want it and will even throw in rice, veggies, and a side of guacamole. The restaurant also hosts karaoke

Thursday and Sunday evenings, and has a direct view of one of the large dolphin enclosures.

Super Akumal (across from Omni Puerto Aventuras hotel, 8 A.M.–8 P.M. daily) is the local market and has a little of everything, including water, chips, sunscreen, toiletries, and so on.

INFORMATION AND SERVICES
Pharmacies

There is one local pharmacy, **First Aid Pharmacy** (Bldg. A, tel. 984/873-5305 or 984/206-6087, 9 A.M.–9 P.M. daily, or call by telephone 24 hours).

Money

Puerto Aventuras doesn't have an actual bank yet, but there's a **Banamex ATM** next to Capt. Rick's fishing shop and a **Santander ATM** near the entrance of Museo CEDAM. Both are accessible 24 hours.

Internet and Telephone

Café-C@fé (tel. 984/873-5728, www.cafe cafe-pa.com, 8 A.M.–6 P.M. Mon.–Sat low season, until 8 P.M. daily high season) has super-fast cable and wireless Internet for US$0.10 per minute, or at much better rates in prepaid plans of five hours (US$12) or 10 hours (US$18). You can also make **international calls** here for US$0.40 to the United States and Canada, US$0.80 to the rest of the world.

Azul Tequila Internet Bar (tel. 984/873-5673, 9 A.M.–11 P.M. daily) serves drinks along with Internet access (US$0.10/min or US$5/ hr) and CD burning (US$3.50, plus US$1.50 for disc).

Post Office

The post office (10 A.M.–3 P.M. Mon., Wed., and Fri.) is in a large kiosk a short distance from the golf club entrance.

Launderette

Opposite the post office, the friendly owner of **Fresh Bubbles** (8:30 A.M.–8 P.M. Mon.–Sat.) will wash, dry, and fold clothes for US$1.50 a kilogram (2.2 pounds) the same day, or US$3 a kilogram (6.6 pounds) for two-hour express service, both with a minimum of two kilograms (4.5 pounds). Ironing is US$1–1.50 per piece; local pickup and drop-off can be arranged.

GETTING THERE AND AROUND

By public transportation take a *combi* from Cancún, Playa del Carmen, or Tulum (US$2). Let the driver know where you're going and he'll drop you off on the side of the highway. From there, it's 500 meters (0.3 mile) into town. Arriving by car, there's a large control gate but no one who looks like a tourist is stopped.

In Puerto Aventuras, you can walk just about everywhere, as virtually all shops and services are centered around the marina.

Xpu-Há

A sleepy beachside community, Xpu-Há is made up of a sprinkling of hotels, a couple of restaurants, and a bunch of travelers just kicking back. On a spectacularly wide beach, it's definitely a known stop on the Riviera but it's managed to maintain a hideaway feel. Great for a couple of days (or weeks!) to catch up on that novel you've been meaning to read.

SPORTS AND RECREATION
Snorkeling

Besides the ocean, several privately operated cenotes on the inland side of Highway 307 north of Xpu-Há make for good snorkeling and swimming. They can get crowded with local families on weekends.

Cristalino Azul (Hwy. 307, 2 km/1.2 mi north of Xpu-Há, 8 A.M.–7 P.M. daily) charges US$3 for an adult, US$1.50 for a child, no rental gear. Much of this half-moon shaped cenote is shallow and covered in algae, but one section extends under a deep overhanging rock ceiling.

Jardín del Eden (Hwy. 307, 1.75 km/1 mi north of Xpu-Há, 7 A.M.–5 P.M. Sun.–Fri.) charges US$3.25 for an adult, US$2 for a child, mask and snorkel are US$3, life vest is US$3. Formerly known as Ponderosa Cenote, this is a much larger cenote than most—like a small lake—and can get busy with snorkelers, swimmers, and divers. A 6-meter (20-foot) cliff is fun to jump off.

At **Cenote Azul** (9 A.M.–6 P.M. daily, US$5 adult, US$3 child, mask and snorkel US$3, life vest US$3) a few large pools and a section of overhanging rock are the highlights here, and walkways along the edges facilitate getting in and out. Still, it's not clear why this one is the most expensive of the Xpu-Há area cenotes.

Scuba Diving

Bahía Divers (tel. 044-984/127-3872, www .bahiadivers.com), operates out of a small hut a short distance down the beach from La Playa. It offers the full gamut of fun dives, courses,

With a view like this, it's no wonder travelers come back so often.

© LIZA PRADO

THE RIVIERA MAYA

and snorkeling and fishing trips, with the advantage of small groups and personal service. Reefs dives run US$35 for one tank, US$65 for two, US$120 for four; gear is US$15 per day. Two-tank cenote dives are US$100, plus US$20 for gear. Snorkeling trips cost US$35–75 per person, depending where you go—reef, cenote, lagoon, or a combination of the three.

Beach Activities

La Playa Xpu-Há (entrance at Carr. Cancún-Tulum Km. 93, tel. 984/106-0024) is a bustling club that offers a slew of classic beach activities, including parasailing, fishing, banana boats, snorkeling, and kayaking, all at standard prices.

For just lounging on the beach, you'll find a much quieter scene at the **Hotel-Villas del Caribe,** which has free beach chairs and umbrellas if you order from the restaurant.

Not exactly a beach activity, **Duck Putt** (8:30 A.M.–2 P.M. and 5 P.M.–7 P.M. weekdays., 8:30 A.M.–6 P.M. weekends, closed Tue.) is nevertheless Xpu-Há's very own 18-hole miniature golf course. It lacks the crazy creatures and moving obstacles that are half the fun back home, but it's a nice walk down the beach and only costs US$4 for adults, US$3 for kids. It's also the nearest place to check Internet, though service is spotty at best.

Body Work

Hotel-Villas del Caribe offers twice-weekly **yoga classes** (US$9/session) and **Sunday sunrise meditation** (free); all levels welcome.

ACCOMMODATIONS
Under US$50

South of the Copacabana resort, **Xpu-Há Bonanza** (entrance at Carr. Cancún-Tulum Km. 93, tel. 984/116-4733, US$4.50 pp camping, US$40 s/d with fan) offers eight spacious rooms with clean cold-water bathrooms and space for two beds and two hammocks. The units are rather dark, but the quiet beach and bargain prices are reasonable consolation. Travelers with tents can set up in the sand under a palm tree, and have access to cleanish shared bathrooms.

US$50-100

Down a tiny sand road next to the Copacabana resort, **◖ Hotel-Villas del Caribe** (Xpu-Há X-4, tel. 984/873-2194, www.xpuhahotel.com, US$55–90 s/d with fan) is an oceanfront hotel with clean and comfortable rooms, most with terraces and/or hammocks. Rooms are repainted frequently in cheerful colors, and have simple, tasteful decor; the ocean breezes more than make up for the lack of air-conditioning. Rates vary according to the size and view: large or larger and garden or ocean. All that, plus a laid-back atmosphere and a fantastic restaurant make this an especially comfortable place to wind down for a few days.

FOOD

Wiggle your toes in the sand as you wait for your meal at **Café del Mar** (Hotel-Villas del Caribe, tel. 984/873-2194, 8 A.M.–9 P.M. Tues.–Sun., US$6–15). Right on the beach, this is an excellent open-air restaurant that offers an international menu made with the freshest of ingredients, and a full bar.

INFORMATION AND SERVICES

The only thing that qualifies under this heading is the unpredictable Internet service at **Duck Putt.** If you're lucky enough to find the shop open and the signal working, access is US$2 per hour. For everything else—cash machine, pharmacy, laundry, etc.—head to Akumal or Playa del Carmen.

GETTING THERE AND AROUND

The road to Hotel-Villas del Caribe is called "X-4" and runs along the north side of the Copacabana resort. It's poorly marked, but the Copacabana is easy to spot and most *combi* drivers know where to drop you. From the highway, it's about 500 meters (0.3 mile) to the beach and hotel. Xpu-Há Bonanza and La Playa Xpu-Há have a separate entrance, somewhat better marked and located a few hundred meters south of the Copacabana.

Akumal

Unreachable by land until the 1960s, Akumal (literally, Place of the Turtle) is a low-key, upscale community that has developed on two bays: Akumal and Half Moon. It's a quiet place with sand roads and dozens of condominiums and rental homes. The beach in town is decent—if you can handle the boats parked on the sand—and the one around Half Moon Bay is calm though rocky in places. What draws people here is a spectacular barrier reef, which protects Akumal's bays from the open sea and makes for ideal swimming and great snorkeling.

A short distance south of Akumal proper is Aventuras Akumal, another small bayside development. It doesn't have the townlike activity of Akumal (mostly private vacation homes, no restaurants) but two good condo-hotels and a truly gorgeous beach make this a tempting alternative. Aventuras Akumal has a separate access road from the highway, and walking there along the beach takes about 45 minutes.

SIGHTS
Beaches

Akumal Bay—the one right in front of town—has a long, slow-curving shoreline, with soft sand shaded by palm trees. The water is beautiful but a bit rocky underfoot, and you should be aware of boat traffic when swimming or snorkeling. Half Moon Bay can also be nice for swimming and snorkeling, but the shoreline is rocky in many parts; where there is beach, it is mostly narrow and covered with sea plants that have washed ashore.

◖ Laguna Yal-Ku

At the mouth of an elbow-shaped lagoon at the north end of Akumal, an endless upwelling of underground river water collides with the tireless flow of seawater—the result is a great place to snorkel, teeming with fish and plants adapted to this unique hybrid environment. Once a secret snorkeler's getaway, Laguna

© LIZA PRADO

At Half Moon Bay, top-notch diving and snorkeling are right outside your door.

THE RIVIERA MAYA

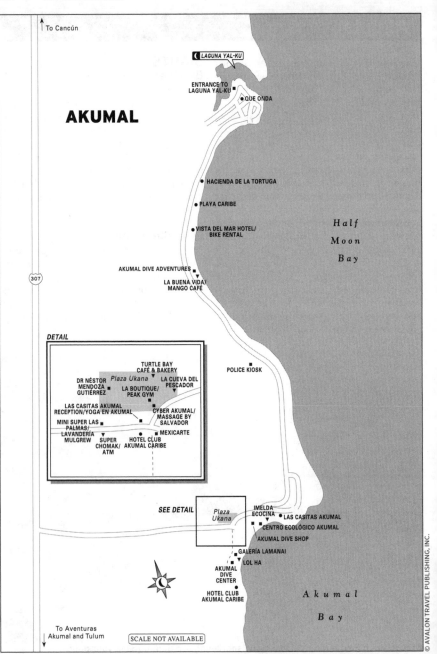

To Cancún

LAGUNA YAL-KU

ENTRANCE TO
LAGUNA YAL-KU
QUE ONDA

AKUMAL

HACIENDA DE LA TORTUGA

PLAYA CARIBE

VISTA DEL MAR HOTEL/
BIKE RENTAL

*Half
Moon
Bay*

AKUMAL DIVE ADVENTURES

LA BUENA VIDA/
MANGO CAFÉ

307

DETAIL

TURTLE BAY
CAFÉ & BAKERY

DR NÉSTOR
MENDOZA
GUTIÉRREZ

Plaza Ukana

LA CUEVA DEL
PESCADOR

LA BOUTIQUE/
PEAK GYM

LAS CASITAS AKUMAL
RECEPTION/YOGA EN AKUMAL

CYBER AKUMAL/
MASSAGE BY
SALVADOR

MINI SUPER LAS
PALMAS/
LAVANDERÍA
MULGREW

SUPER
CHOMAK/
ATM

MEXICARTE

HOTEL CLUB
AKUMAL CARIBE

POLICE KIOSK

SEE DETAIL

*Plaza
Ukana*

IMELDA
ECOCINA

LAS CASITAS AKUMAL

CENTRO ECOLÓGICO AKUMAL

AKUMAL DIVE SHOP

GALERÍA LAMANAI

LOL HA

AKUMAL
DIVE
CENTER

HOTEL CLUB
AKUMAL CARIBE

*Akumal

Bay*

To Aventuras
Akumal and Tulum

SCALE NOT AVAILABLE

© AVALON TRAVEL PUBLISHING, INC.

Yal-Ku (8 A.M.–5:30 P.M. daily, US$7 adult, US$4.25 child; US$14 snorkel gear; US$2 locker) now has a parking lot and a spot in every guidebook—come before 10 A.M., after 3 P.M., or anytime on Sunday for the least traffic. You can snorkel in the lagoons broad mouth, or up the narrow channel to its source. If possible, use a T-shirt or wetsuit instead of sunscreen—even the biodegradable kind can collect on plants and coral.

Akumal Ecological Center

Next to Akumal Dive Shop, the **Centro Ecológico Akumal** (CEA, tel. 984/875-9095, www.ceakumal.org, 9 A.M.–6 P.M. Mon.–Fri. 9 A.M.–1 P.M. Sat.) is a nonprofit founded in 1993 to monitor the health of Akumal's ecosystems, particularly related to coral and sea turtles. During turtle nesting season—May to July—you can join CEA volunteers on nighttime "turtle walks," covering about two kilometers (1.25 miles) of beach, looking for new nests and helping move eggs to protected hatcheries. From August to October, hatchlings are released back into the sea, which visitors can assist as well. Stop by the center for more details and to sign up; the activities are free but a US$5–10 donation is appreciated. The center also has free displays and frequent evening lectures on ocean ecology (in high season).

CEA also operates long-term volunteer projects on reef monitoring, sea turtles monitoring, and environmental education projects. Volunteers stay in the center's comfortable dorms, with kitchen and Internet access; minimum age is 21 and some fees are required. See website for details.

Aktun Chen

Maya for "Cave with an underground river," Aktun Chen (Carr. Cancún-Tulum Km. 107, tel. 998/892-0662, www.aktunchen. com, 9 A.M.–5 P.M. daily, last tour 4:30 P.M., US$24 adults, US$13 children under 11) is indeed that, and more. The cave itself has a breathtaking array of stalactites and stalagmites, and a 12-meter/40-foot-deep cenote filled with crystalline water at the end; lighting and a pathway make it accessible to all. Tours also include a brief nature walk (the park has almost 1,000 acres of protected forest) and a stop at the small zoo, where spider monkeys manage to charm everyone. Tours are offered in English and Spanish, and last about 75 minutes. Most hotels offer trips here that include transportation; otherwise, look for the turnoff just across from Aventuras Akumal, and continue three kilometers (1.9 miles) to the entrance. Mosquito repellent and a bottle of water are recommended.

SHOPPING

On the beach near Akumal Dive Center, **Galería Lamanai** (tel. 984/875-9055, 9 A.M.– 9 P.M. daily) was undergoing a major renovation at the time of research, but is sure to reopen with its consistently good selection of Mexican crafts and folk art.

La Boutique (Plaza Ukana, tel. 984/875-9208, 9 A.M.–5 P.M. Mon.–Sat., until 7 P.M. in high season) is the best of a cluster of three shops in the plaza area.

Mexicarte (9 A.M.–9 P.M. daily) is the small, bright pink shop just inside the arches on your right. The owner hand-selects the best folk art from around the region and country—prices are high, but so is the quality and artisanship.

SPORTS AND RECREATION
Scuba Diving

Some of the area's first scuba divers waded into the waves right here at Akumal Bay, and the area has been special to the sport ever since. While not as spectacular as other areas along the Riviera Maya, Akumal's diving is easy and fun, with a mellow current and few profiles that go below 20 meters (66 feet). The reef is predominantly boulder coral, which isn't as picturesque as other types, but still it teems with tropical fish and plant life. Visibility is decent by Caribbean standards—great by everyone else's—averaging 10–30 meters (33–99 feet).

Founded more than 30 years ago, **Akumal Dive Shop** (tel. 984/875-9032, www.akumal .com, 8 A.M.–6 P.M. daily) was the first dive shop in the Riviera Maya, long before any-one called it that. Still right on the beach, the shop offers fun dives and various certification courses in both open water and cave/cavern diving. Divers can take one- or two-tank reef dives (US$45/60), cavern or cenote dives (US$65/120), or buy packages of 4 or 10 dives for US$120/250. Fun dives do not include equipment rental (US$25/day, US$110/week). Open-water certification courses take 3–4 days and cost US$420, equipment and materials included.

Down the beach a short distance, **Akumal Dive Center** (tel. 984/875-9025, www.akumal divecenter.com, 8 A.M.–5 P.M. daily) has operated in Akumal almost as long and offers the same dives and courses at comparable prices.

On Half Moon Bay, **Akumal Dive Adventures** (next to La Buena Vida restaurant, tel. 984/875-9157, toll-free U.S. tel. 877/425-8625, www.akumaldiveadventures .com, 8 A.M.–5 P.M. daily) offers similarly priced diving and courses, as well as a package of three nights' lodging and four reef dives for US$270 per person double occupancy, US$360 per person single occupancy, with an option to extend your stay or swap reef dives for night or cenote dives at an extra cost. Rooms are at the affiliated Vista del Mar hotel.

On a calm bay with a healthy reef, Aventuras Akumal has good diving (and snorkeling) right at your doorstep. **Aquatech Villas DeRosa** (tel. 984/875-9020, U.S. tel. 866/619-9050, www.cenotes.com) is a full-service dive shop operated at the Villas DeRosa hotel, offering a complete range of dives and courses, but specializing in cenote and cave diving. Reef dives run US$40 for one tank, US$60 for two; cenote dives are US$65 one tank, US$120 for two; open-water certification is US$350; and a cavern diving specialty course US$650 private, US$440 per person in groups. Equipment is included in courses, but not fun dives (US$35 per day for a full set). Multi-dive packages, night dives, and even fishing are also available.

Snorkeling

Laguna Yal-Ku (see *Sights*) is a favorite among many snorkelers for its large area, calm water, and unique mix of fresh- and saltwater eco-systems. Look for several modern sculptures standing somewhat incongruously along the lagoon's edges.

The northern end of **Akumal Bay** also makes for fine snorkeling and you can wade in right from the beach. It's a great little nook of fairly shallow water, where tropical fish dart about a labyrinth of rocks, boulder coral, and plant life. Fishing boats do not pass through here (another reason it's good for snorkeling), but you should be careful not to drift out of the area and into boat channels. Many snorkelers make their way toward the large buoy at the edge of the bay, not realizing it marks a channel that boats use to get through the reef. Be smart and steer clear. Half Moon Bay has some good shore snorkeling as well.

You can **rent snorkel gear** at any of Akumal's dive shops for around US$10 a day or US$50 a week. Rentals at Yal-Ku cost US$14 and can only be used on-site. The dive shops also offer **guided snorkel tours,** which vary from 1–3 hours, depending on the number of sites you visit, and cost US$10–40 per person, including gear.

Sailing

Akumal Dive Shop offers a popular Robinson Crusoe cruise: a five-hour excursion on a catamaran sailboat, with stops for fishing and snorkeling (US$65 including lunch and equipment). Or try the two-hour Sunset Cruise, which doesn't include fishing and snorkeling, but offers beautiful evening views of the bay.

Sport Fishing

All three dive shops offer fishing tours for US$90–120 per boat (US$30–50/hr. extra, 1–4 passengers) including equipment and beverages. Fishing is excellent year-round, but the best months for trolling are April–June when sailfish and marlin are most numerous and active.

Body Work

In a breezy upstairs studio in the archway to town, **Yoga en Akumal** (tel. 984/875-9114, www.yoga-in-akumal.com) offers hatha, hatha flow, and anusana classes, for all experience levels. Sessions are 90 minutes and cost US$15 per class, US$75 for a two-week pass, or US$125 for a month.

Peak Gym (Plaza Ukana, 1st Fl., tel. 984/875-9208, 8 A.M.–7 P.M. Mon.–Sat.) has a small air-conditioned exercise space that's crammed with free weights and machines. Stationary bikes are the only cardio option—no Stairmaster or elliptical, unfortunately. Day passes cost US$10, 3-day passes US$27, weekly rates rise to US$46, and the monthly membership is US$60.

For a breezy outdoor massage, try **Massage by Salvador** (Plaza Ukana, 2nd Fl., no phone, Mon.–Sat., US$65/hour). Salvador speaks English and has two weeks' worth of sign-up sheets outside his door; just stop by and sign up for an appointment.

ACCOMMODATIONS

Akumal's hotel prices tend to run in the high range. There are numerous condos and villas for rent around the bend at Half Moon Bay, and south of town in Aventuras Akumal; at the right time and shared among several people, these can turn out to be reasonably affordable. Backpackers might snag a dorm room at CEA, but it's no sure thing.

In Town

Centro Ecológico Akumal (see *Sights*) has several large comfortable dorms—most even have air-conditioning—and a well-stocked communal kitchen. CEA's volunteers have priority for the rooms, and they are usually full, but if not they're available to walk-ins for US$15 a night. A long shot, but definitely worth asking.

Hotel Club Akumal Caribe (reception in the arches at the entrance to town, tel. 915/584-3552, U.S. 800/351-1622, Canada tel. 800/343-1440, www.hotelakumalcaribe.com, US$123 s/d bungalow with a/c, US$156 s/d room with a/c) was the first hotel in Akumal, when it was used by members of a local diving and conservation club. The bungalows sorely need a remodel, but are roomy and affordable—popular with families. The ocean-

front hotels are much more appealing, with whitewashed walls, air-conditioning, refrigerator, and private balcony; some have kitchenettes. The main complaint here is the beds, some of which are rock hard. In front, there is a well-kept swimming pool and beyond that, a palm-tree-laden beach. A good restaurant, pizzeria, private beach area, and a full-service dive shop also are on-site.

On the eastern end of the beach in town, **Las Casitas Akumal** (tel. 984/875-9071, toll-free U.S./Can. tel. 800/525-8625, www.lascasitasakumal.com) has 18 airy, furnished condominiums with two bedrooms, two baths, living room, fully equipped kitchen, and private patio. Some have two floors and space for six people; all have ocean views and direct access to a semiprivate section of the beach. High season rates range US$210–385 per night; holidays are more while rates drop significantly in May, September, and October. Reservations must be made for a minimum of seven nights and begin on a Saturday.

Half Moon Bay

Spacious one-, two-, and three- bedroom condominiums greet you at the ◖ **Vista del Mar** (tel. 984/875-9060, toll-free U.S. tel. 888/425-8625; www.akumalinfo.com, US$101–123 s/d with a/c, US$207–224 one bedroom condo with a/c, US$207–247 two bedroom condo with a/c, US$325 three bedroom condo with a/c). Located about halfway around the bay, the 15 units have glorious oceanfront views from their long balconies or porches. All have huge fully equipped kitchens, living rooms with flat-screen TVs, dining rooms, and master bedrooms with king-size beds. Mexican decor like *talavera* tiles, bright hand-woven bedspreads, and tapestries lend the place even more charm. Sixteen oceanfront hotel rooms also are on-site; small but comfortable, they're a good alternative for those on a tighter budget. All accommodations share a well-tended beach with lounge chairs and *palapa* shades.

Along Half Moon Bay's dirt road, **Hacienda de la Tortuga** (tel. 984/875-9068, www.haciendatortuga.com) offers spacious one-bedroom

(US$150) and two-bedroom (US$200) condos, all with huge windows overlooking the Caribbean. Although each is uniquely decorated, all units have a living room, fully equipped kitchen, (at least one) full bathroom, king-size beds, and air-conditioning in the bedrooms. A nice pool and the classy Mexican restaurant, **La Lunita,** only add to the relaxed feel of the place.

Nearby **Playa Caribe** (tel. 984/875-9137, www.amc-akumal.com, US$230 one-bedroom condo with a/c, US$275 two-bedroom condo with a/c) offers a similar deal: 12 one- and two-bedroom condos with fully-equipped kitchens and spectacular ocean views, each decorated differently from the other. There also is a well-tended pool that sits overlooking the beach. The main difference here is that the units have central air-conditioning in each room and satellite TV. That, and there's no on-site restaurant.

At the north end of Akumal and just a block from Yal-Ku Lagoon, **(Que Onda** (Caleta Yal-Ku, tel. 984/875-9101, www.queonda akumal.com, US$79 s/d, US$146–168 suite) has seven rooms, each lovingly decorated with tile floors, beautiful fabrics, and unique works of art, and two suites, including a split-level unit with wood floors and terrific views of the Caribbean and Yal-Ku. All face a verdant garden and a pool in the middle of the property. None have air-conditioning; the first-floor units can get a bit stuffy—the fans help—while upstairs rooms have terraces and sea breezes. Use of bicycles and snorkel gear are included in the rates—a big plus—and guests get 50 percent off admission to Laguna Yal-Ku. The Italian restaurant here can get busy.

Aventuras Akumal

Villas DeRosa (tel. 984/875-9020, U.S. tel. 866/619-9050, www.cenotes.com, US$79 s/d, US$150 one bedroom, US$207 two bedroom, US$263 three bedroom) offers hotel rooms with garden views, and one-, two-, and three-bedroom condominiums with ocean views and private balconies. The spacious accommodations have air-conditioning, cable TV, wireless Internet, stereos, and fully equipped kitchens

(in the condos). The bedrooms can feel a bit dark, but you're literally steps from a beautiful beach and the blue Caribbean water. The resort boasts a full-service dive shop, with a special emphasis on cenote diving; dive/accommodation packages available. Prices vary significantly depending on the season; call ahead.

Smaller and cozier than the DeRosa, **(Villa Las Brisas** (tel. 984/875-9263, www.lasbrisas akumal.icimx.com, US$90 s/d, US$101 studio, US$151 one-bedroom condo, US$213 two-bedroom condo) has just three units (two of which can be combined to make the two-bedroom condo), all spacious, spotless, and meticulously furnished, down to a stocked spice rack in the kitchen. Opened in 1998, the condos have large terraces with hammocks and stunning views; the smaller units have balconies that overlook a tidy garden. With comfortable beds, modern Mexican-style furnishings, and room to stretch out in, it's easy to feel at home here. Families are very welcome. Beach chairs and umbrellas are free, snorkel gear can be rented (US$5 per day), and there's a simple mini-mart at the entrance (8 A.M.–4 P.M. Mon–Sat.).

Rental Properties

The great majority of rooms for rent in Akumal are in privately owned homes along Half Moon Bay. For information and online listings, contact **Caribbean Fantasy** (U.S. tel. 800/523-6618, www.caribbfan.com), **Akumal Villas** (U.S. tel. 678/528-1775, www.akumalvillas.com), or **Loco Gringo** (www.locogringo.com). For retail and some rentals, stop by the office of **Akumal Real Estate** (entrance to town, tel. 984/875-9064, www.akumalrealestate.com, 9 A.M.–7 P.M. Mon.–Fri. and 9 A.M.–3 P.M. Sat.).

FOOD
In Town

Maya for "water lily," **(Lol Ha** (on the beach, tel. 984/875-9013, 7:30–11 A.M. and 6:30–10 P.M. daily, closed Oct.–mid-Nov., US$12–30) is Akumal's finest restaurant, easily living up to the class its name suggests. The beautiful wood and stucco dining room is topped with a high *palapa* roof and opens onto a pleasant veranda for outdoor dining. Expect excellent seafood and Mexican and American specialties, including prime USDA steaks, sushi-grade ahi tuna, and flambé specials prepared tableside. At breakfast, a basket of homemade sweet rolls comes immediately when you sit down, and the orange juice is freshly squeezed. The restaurant hosts Mexican folk dance performances on Mondays, flamenco on Wednesday, and jazz on Friday—a US$3 per person cover is added to the bill. For something especially romantic, ask about arranging a private dinner on the beach. Reservations strongly recommended, especially if you want to be on the veranda or by the window (though the views are nice throughout).

Next door to the mother restaurant, and nearly as big, **Snack Bar Lol Ha** (11:30 A.M.–8 P.M. daily, US$8–13) serves the best hamburgers on the beach, and tasty *tacos de cochinita,* a fusion of Maya flavor and Mexican packaging. Three 32-inch TVs always have a sporting event on, whether Monday Night Football, March Madness, or the Kentucky Derby. Hundreds of people turn out for the annual Academy Awards and Super Bowl parties (proceeds of which go to local community groups). Kids will love the adjacent game room, with air hockey and Foosball.

For a fresh, healthy meal, try **Imelda Ecococina** (no phone, 8 A.M.–3 P.M. daily., US$3–6) next to Centro Ecológico Akumal. Breakfast options include eggs, omelets, pancakes, French toast, and more. For lunch, the *comida corrida* comes with a choice of main plate and a side dish or two. On Mondays and Thursdays the restaurant hosts a popular Maya buffet (US$20; 7 P.M.) followed by *cumbia* tunes and dancing.

In Plaza Ukana, **Turtle Bay Café & Bakery** (tel. 984/875-9138, 7 A.M.–3 P.M. daily, 6–9 P.M. Wed.–Sat., US$5–18) offers scrumptious creations such as grilled portabella mushroom burgers, achiote chicken, and summer burritos. For breakfast, think French toast, eggs Benedict, fruit plate with yogurt and granola. Enjoy your meal surrounded by palm trees, either in the outdoor *palapa*-roofed dining room or on the porch of the main building.

For fresh seafood, check out **La Cueva del Pescador** (Plaza Ukana, tel. 984/875-9205, noon–10 P.M.daily, US$5–25). Sink your teeth into fish kabobs, shrimp prepared nine different ways (e.g., grilled, à la tequila, with curry salsa, and so on), and lobster—all caught the day that you order it. The bar is an especially popular stop on weekends.

For groceries, the best prices are across from the Akumal turnoff on Highway 307 in **Super Express Mar Caribe** (7 A.M.–11 P.M. daily); look for the store about 100 meters (328 feet) west of the highway. Otherwise, just outside the arch, **Super Chomak** and **Mini Super Las Palmas** (both 7 A.M.–9 P.M. daily) charge an arm and a leg for canned and dried food, soups and pastas, fresh and packaged meat, and other basics like sunscreen, booze, and film. The former has a larger selection, the latter is slightly cheaper. Both also sell fresh fruit and veggies, but you may find a better selection at the **farmers market** held Wednesdays and Saturdays in Plaza Ukana.

Half Moon Bay

A fantastic flying serpent skeleton greets you at the beachfront **La Buena Vida** (tel. 984/875-9061, 10 A.M.–11 P.M.daily, US$6–26) where clients enjoy the varied menu—from hamburgers to shrimp ceviche—under *palapa*-shaded tables. If you've already had lunch, consider just stopping in for a drink at the...er, swing bar, where swings line the sand-floored bar. Try the specialty—La Buena Vida—a smooth combo of Baileys, Kahlua, rum, coconut cream, and Grand Marnier; happy hour typically runs from 5–7 P.M. Next door, its sister restaurant, the brightly painted **Mango Café** (6 A.M.–noon daily) serves up a good variety of breakfasts on the beach. Look for both restaurants just before the Vista del Mar condominiums.

Right on the Caribbean, **La Lunita** (Hacienda de la Tortuga, tel. 984/875-9068, 5–10 P.M. Mon.–Sat., US$8–23) is a classy, intimate bistro serving gourmet Mexican and Maya specialties. Seafood is king here, though there are plenty of options for vegetarians and serious meat eaters. With only a handful of tables, La Lunita is a perfect place for a romantic dinner—just be sure to make reservations. Located on the ground floor of the Hacienda de la Tortuga.

If you're in the mood for Italian, try the open-air restaurant at the hotel **Que Onda** (4–10 P.M. daily except Tue., US$7–18). The homemade linguine comes with a wide choice of sauces, from gorgonzola to curry shrimp. The lasagna is famously tasty, though a bit pricey. For dessert, try the chocolate mousse.

INFORMATION AND SERVICES
Tourist Information
Akumal doesn't have an official tourist office, but it's a small town and you can probably find what you're looking for by asking the first person you see. If that fails, the folks at Centro Ecológico Akumal are friendly, well informed, and most speak English.

Hospitals
For an English-speaking physician, call or stop by the offices of general practitioner **Dr. Néstor Mendoza Gutiérrez** (Plaza Ukana, tel. 984/875-4051, 8 A.M.–4 P.M. Mon.–Sat., after-hours emergencies 044-984/806-4616). For major medical matters, head to Playa del Carmen.

Police
The police can be reached by calling 060 from any public phone.

Money
There is an ATM in Super Chomak grocery store, just outside the arch.

Internet and Telephone
Cyber Akumal (Plaza Ukana, tel. 984/875-9313, 7 A.M.–1 P.M. daily) is just past the arches as you enter town. Internet is fast, but runs a hefty US$0.10 a minute. From 9 P.M. to closing, it's US$6 for as much time as you like. Telephone calls to the United States and Can-

ada run US$0.55 a minute, or US$0.30 a minute after 9 P.M.

For much more reasonable Internet rates, head to the other side of Highway 307. Directly across from the turnoff to Akumal is a small community where a no-name **Internet café** (7 A.M.–9 P.M. daily) charges US$1.75 per hour. Look for it on the town's main road, about 150 meters (492 feet) from the highway.

Post Office
The post office (9:30 A.M.–3 P.M. Tues. and Thurs. only) is inside the Centro Ecológico Akumal, in the center of town.

Launderette
Next to the Mini Super Las Palmas, **Lavandería Mulgrew** (7 A.M.–1 P.M. and 5–7 P.M. Mon.–Sat.) charges US$1.60 a kilogram (2.2 pounds) and will provide same-day service if you drop off your load before 8 A.M.; two-kilogram (4.4-pound) minimum.

GETTING THERE AND AROUND
Having a car or bike will make getting to and around Akumal much easier. Vans and second-class buses stop at the Akumal turnoff, but it's a one kilometer (0.6 mile) walk into town. Likewise, you can manage the center area by foot, but walking to and from Half Moon Bay can be long, hot, and dusty. Many guests rent a car for their entire stay—which let's you take day trips as well—while the condo-hotel **Vista del Mar** (Half Moon Bay, tel. 984/875-9060) rents decent bikes for US$1 per hour, US$6 per day, and US$30 per week.

Taxis gather near the Super Chomak grocery store at the entrance of town, just outside of the arches. A ride from town to Laguna Yal-Ku costs US$2.50.

For Aventuras Akumal, the access road is south of the main Akumal entrance, and it's about 500 meters (0.3 mile) into the community. Look for the sign to Hotel Villas DeRosa, as the community itself isn't well signed.

Tankah Tres

Tucked innocuously between Tulum and Akumal, Tankah Tres sees only a fraction of the tourist traffic that its better-known neighbors do. But that's just the way visitors to this little stretch of coastline prefer it, enjoying excellent snorkeling, diving, and pretty (if not spectacular) beaches, with a sense of isolation that's hard to find in these parts. The area has three small bays, and the scattered hotels, villas, and private homes along their shores were once connected (together and to the highway) by a U-shaped access road. But new development cut the U right in half; the southern entrance is still marked Tankah Tres, while the northern entrance has a sign for Oscar y Lalo restaurant and *Bahías de Punta Soliman.* You have to return to the highway to get from one side to the other.

SIGHTS

The three bays that make up Tankah Tres have fine snorkeling, diving, and kayaking. Add to that a pleasant beach and relatively few tourists, and this becomes one of the better places on the Riviera Maya to spend a relaxing beach day.

Playa Tankah

Casa Cenote hotel fronts a pretty little beach, which non-guests are free to use if you order something at the restaurant.

Cenote Tankah

Across from Casa Cenote hotel, its namesake Cenote Tankah (no admission) forms a large lagoon perfect for snorkeling. The cenote's winding channels have crystal-clear water and a tangle of rocks, trees, and freshwater plants along their edges and bottoms. Look for schools of tiny fish near the surface, and some bigger ones farther down.

SCUBA DIVING AND SNORKELING

Run by a young American and based at the Tankah Inn, **Lucky Fish Diving** (tel. 044-984/129-6774, www.luckyfishdiving.com,

Small inlets and a healthy reef make snorkeling off of Playa Tankah a highlight of any trip.

© LIZA PRADO

THE RIVIERA MAYA

8:30 A.M.–6 P.M. and 9 A.M.–4 P.M. Sun.) is a small friendly shop offering personalized dive trips and instruction. Dive sites here get substantially less traffic than at nearby Akumal, but offer the same spectacular coral and sealife: "Mountains of the Moon" is a favorite, with huge coral mounds rising from 12 meters (40 feet) nearly to the surface. And no dive site is more than 10 minutes away by boat. Reef dives cost US$40 for one tank, US$75 for two, while cenote dives are US$60 for one tank and US$100 for two; all equipment and entrance fees are included. The shop also rents snorkel gear for US$7.50 a day, but it can be hard to find the best sections of reef; you'll have more fun on a guided trip (US$20 pp, 2.5 hours), hitting three different spots.

The restaurant **Oscar y Lalo** also rents snorkel gear (US$4.75/day) and kayaks (US$7.50/hour) and sometimes arranges snorkel and kayaking tours into the lagoon that extends behind the property.

ACCOMMODATIONS

The northern entrance to Tankah Tres extends almost to the beach before forking; to the left is **Oscar y Lalo** (tel. 984/804-4189) a restaurant and campsite on an isolated palm tree–lined beach. Here, you can set up a tent among the coconut trees for US$5 per person and feel, if only for a night or two, that you are on a idyllic deserted island (that happens to have a bathroom with running water, of course). When the restaurant closes at 8 P.M., the place is yours, starry night and all. Be sure to bring mosquito nets in the rainy season.

Five spacious rooms with murals of Maya temples make up the C **Tankah Inn** (southern entrance, 1.1 km/0.6 mi from the turnoff, U.S. tel. 918/582-3743, www.tankah.com, US$124 s/d with a/c). Right on the beach, each room has tile floors, a private terrace, and ocean views; all come equipped with five-gallon jugs of water and remote-controlled air-conditioning. A breezy common room has sweeping views of the Caribbean—comfy chairs and tables, a stereo, lots of board games, and an honor bar make this a popular area to hang out. Though the beach, with its lounge chairs and hammocks, is a tempting alternative. A full breakfast is included as is wireless Internet and the use of sea kayaks. There's also a dive shop on the premises. A perfect place to hole up for a few days or more.

Casa Cenote (southern entrance, 1.5 km/0.9 mi from the turnoff, tel. 998/874-5170, www.casacenote.com, US$150 s/d) was for many years the only life on this stretch of beach; more hotels have popped up, but this remains a favorite of old-timers and newcomers alike. All seven rooms have a/c, one or two large beds, wireless Internet and a stucco relief of Maya gods in each. A glass door opens onto a small patio with fine ocean views. The hotel built a new pool after Hurricane Wilma, and Cenote Tankah is just across the street. The hotel does its part for the earth by collecting rainwater and using natural wastewater processing. Breakfast is included.

Blue Sky Hotel (southern entrance, 1.7 km/1 mi from the turnoff, tel. 984/801-4004, www.blueskymexico.com, toll-free U.S. and Canada tel. 877/792-9237, US$168 s/d with a/c, US$213–258 suite with a/c) offers six breezy units with views of the Caribbean. All are modern and are decorated with Mexican flair—mostly high-end handicrafts with lots of recessed lighting. A nice pool opens onto the beach where there are plenty of toys—kayaks, boogie boards, and snorkel gear—for guests to use. Continental breakfast is included in the rate and served at the hotel's excellent *palapa* restaurant.

FOOD

Near the northern entrance to town, **Oscar y Lalo** (tel. 984/804-4189, 10 A.M.–8 P.M. daily, US$7–32) is an oceanside restaurant that serves excellent fresh seafood. All dishes come with fried banana, french fries, beans, and rice. Main dishes are definitely pricey—4–6 person specials run US$20–30 per person—but the view and the monster portions more than make up for it.

The restaurant at **Casa Cenote** (southern entrance, 2 km/1.25 mi from the turnoff, tel. 998/874-5170, www.casacenote.com, 8 A.M.–

9 P.M. daily, US$5–15) has a breezy patio dining area just steps from the sea's edge. You can order beach food such as quesadillas or a guacamole plate, or something heftier—the seafood is always tasty and fresh. Every Sunday at noon, the hotel hosts an awesome Texas-style barbecue, which is popular with locals and expats up and down the Riviera Maya. All settle in for an afternoon spent over heaping plates of great food and boisterous conversation. The regular menu includes fajitas, grilled fish, burgers, nachos, and more.

Worth treating yourself, the ◖ **Blue Sky** (Blue Sky Hotel, southern entrance, 1.7 km/ 1 mi from the turnoff, tel. 984/801-4004, 8–10 A.M., noon–4 P.M., and 4–10 P.M. daily, US$5–24) offers delicious Italian and Mexican specialties. Dishes are prepared to order and the presentation is beautiful—try the grilled calamari with vegetables, a simple meal that you'll remember long after you've gone home. With only a handful of tables, this is a perfect place for an intimate dinner. Just be sure to call for a reservation or arrive early.

INFORMATION AND SERVICES

There are no formal services here because it's not really a formal town. Head to Tulum for ATMs, medical services, Internet, groceries, and so on.

GETTING THERE AND AROUND

Arriving by car is definitely the best option—look for the Oscar y Lalo or Tankah Tres signs, depending on which part you want to go to. By bus, get off at either turnoff and start walking.

THE RIVIERA MAYA

TULUM AND SOUTHERN QUINTANA ROO

Set on a bluff overlooking the turquoise waters of the Caribbean Sea are the small but impressive ruins of Tulum. They represent a bridge between the bustling Riviera Maya and the state's decidedly less-traveled southern coast. Tulum is justly famous for its spectacular string of beaches and bohemian chic cabañas, but southern Quintana Roo holds even more: the pristine Sian Ka'an Biosphere Reserve; miles of deserted coastline; quiet fishing villages; rustic beaches; and eco-friendly B&Bs along the Costa Maya; the Caribbean-like colors of Laguna Bacalar; and Chetumal, the busy state capital and gateway to Belize. Take a few days (or weeks) to explore the region. You may find that Tulum and Southern Quintana Roo are just what you've been searching for: untouched seascape, tropical wildlife, and an easy Caribbean dream that seems to exist just for you.

PLANNING YOUR TIME

Tulum is the first stop, of course, and for many people their main destination in this area. If you can tear yourself from the beach, the Sian Ka'an Reserve makes a great day or overnight trip. Farther south, you'll probably want a rental car as bus service is significantly less frequent. The seaside towns of Mahahual and Xcalak are great places to spend three or more days snorkeling, kayaking, and catching up on summer reading. Laguna Bacalar is worth a day or two, time enough to take a boat trip on the Caribbean-like water, swim in Cenote Azul, and visit the surprisingly good piracy museum in

© LIZA PRADO

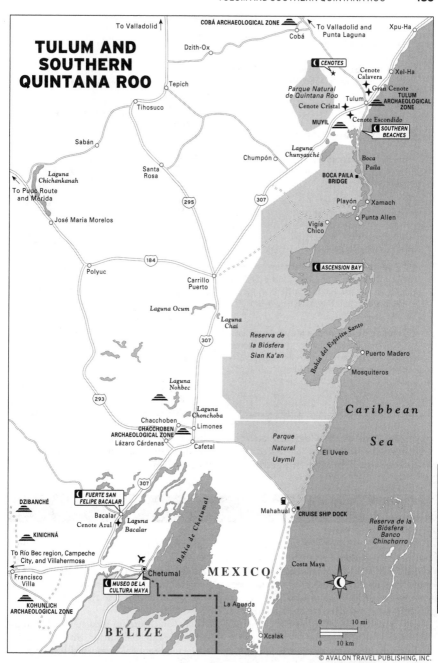

TULUM AND SOUTHERN QUINTANA ROO

To Valladolid

COBÁ ARCHAEOLOGICAL ZONE

Cobá

To Valladolid and Punta Laguna

Xpu-Ha

Dzith-Ox

Tepich

CENOTES

Cenote Calavera

Xel-Ha

Gran Cenote

Tihosuco

Parque Natural de Quintana Roo

Tulum

TULUM ARCHAEOLOGICAL ZONE

Cenote Cristal

Sabán

Santa Rosa

Chumpón

MUYIL

Cenote Escondido

SOUTHERN BEACHES

Laguna Chunyaxché

Laguna Chichankanah

To Puuc Route and Mérida

Boca Paila

BOCA PAILA BRIDGE

295

307

Playón

Xamach

José Maria Morelos

Punta Allen

Vigía Chico

184

Polyuc

Carrillo Puerto

ASCENSION BAY

Laguna Ocum

Laguna Chai

307

Reserva de la Biósfera Sian Ka'an

Bahía del Espíritu Santo

Puerto Madero

Mosquiteros

Laguna Nohbec

Caribbean

293

Laguna Chonchoba

Chacchoben

Limones

CHACCHOBEN ARCHAEOLOGICAL ZONE

Lázaro Cárdenas

Cafetal

Sea

Parque Natural Uaymil

El Uvero

307

DZIBANCHÉ

FUERTE SAN FELIPE BACALAR

Mahahual

CRUISE SHIP DOCK

Reserva de la Biósfera Banco Chinchorro

Bacalar

Cenote Azul

Laguna Bacalar

KINICHNÁ

To Río Bec region, Campeche City, and Villahermosa

Bahía de Chetumal

Francisco Villa

Chetumal

Costa Maya

MEXICO

MUSEO DE LA CULTURA MAYA

KOHUNLICH ARCHAEOLOGICAL ZONE

La Aguada

0   10 mi

0   10 km

BELIZE

Xcalak

© AVALON TRAVEL PUBLISHING, INC.

HIGHLIGHTS

◖ **Tulum's Southern Beaches:** Beaches like these – the white sand, the azure water, and the softly bending palms – are the reason you came to the Caribbean in the first place (page 189).

◖ **Cenotes near Tulum:** Explore an unforgettable realm of crystal-clear water and eerily beautiful stalagmites and stalactites in the world's longest underground river system (page 190).

◖ **Ascension Bay:** A huge untouched expanse of calm ocean flats and tangled mangrove forests make this a world-class destination for birders, anglers, and everyday travelers (page 203).

◖ **Fuerte San Felipe Bacalar:** The museum in this star-shaped fort has excellent exhibits on piracy and the Caste War, plus it overlooks a lagoon the Maya called "Lake of Seven Colors" (page 219).

◖ **Museo de la Cultura Maya:** Chetumal's phenomenal museum mirrors Maya cosmology with three levels of excellent exhibits on the religion, astronomy, writing, artwork, and daily life of ancient Mayas (page 224).

LOOK FOR ◖ TO FIND RECOMMENDED SIGHTS, ACTIVITIES, DINING, AND LODGING.

town. Chetumal can be a logical stopover for those headed west toward the Río Bec region or crossing into Belize. But as a destination, Chetumal is far down the totem pole, and wouldn't rank at all but for the superb Maya museum there.

TULUM AND QUINTANA ROO

Tulum

Tulum has long captured the imagination of independent, beach-loving travelers. Maya ruins overlooking turquoise seas and picturesque cabañas set on deserted beaches were (and still are) the ideal anti-Cancún. Tulum has definitely grown and changed, but travelers of all sorts can still enjoy its remarkable natural beauty and isolated charm.

Tulum has three distinct parts. The Tulum ruins are the popular Maya temples. Tulum Pueblo (literally, Tulum Town) is south and inland from the ruins. And the Zona Hotelera (Hotel Zone) hugs the coast from the ruins to the entrance to the Sian Ka'an Biosphere Reserve.

The Zona Hotelera used to be a haven for backpackers and bohemians, with simple cabañas facing beautiful untouched beaches. The beaches are still beautiful, but the prices have long since gone through the *palapa* roof, catering more to urban escapists and upscale yoga groups. It's still a lovely place to stay, no matter who you are, just not as cheap as it used to be.

Tulum Pueblo used to be quite dumpy, but now has many small cafés, cool restaurants, and more and better hotels, as travelers who are priced out of the Zona Hotelera choose to stay there and go to the beach by day. A beachside cabaña will always be the most appealing place to stay, of course, but staying in town is no longer the huge step down that it was.

TULUM ARCHAEOLOGICAL ZONE

Perched on a cliff 12 meters (40 feet) above the turquoise Caribbean waters, Tulum (8 A.M.– 5 P.M. daily, US$4.25) is justly the subject of thousands of postcards and is one of Mexico's best-known archaeological sites. While the structures themselves lack the grandeur of ruins in the interior, they are still interesting and well worth a visit.

The most important advice regarding Tulum is **get there early.** Thousands of package tourists arrive daily by bus from resorts in Cancún and Playa del Carmen; it used to be that the crush didn't begin until 11 A.M., but it creeps earlier and earlier every year. Still, if you're there right at 8 A.M., you'll have a good hour before the hoards descend; there is sometimes a lull 1:30 P.M.–2:30 P.M. as well. Consider wearing your swimsuit and bringing a towel—this may be the only Maya ruin with a great little beach right inside the archaeological zone.

History

Tulum was part of a series of Maya forts, watchtowers, and ports established along the coast as far south as Chetumal and north past Cancún. Its original Maya name was Zama (Sunrise) but was changed to Tulum (Wall), almost certainly in reference to the thick stone barrier that encloses the city's 60 main structures. Measuring

© LIZA PRADO

TULUM AND QUINTANA ROO

A spectacular setting, Tulum ruins have a nice little beach – perfect for cooling off after exploring the site.

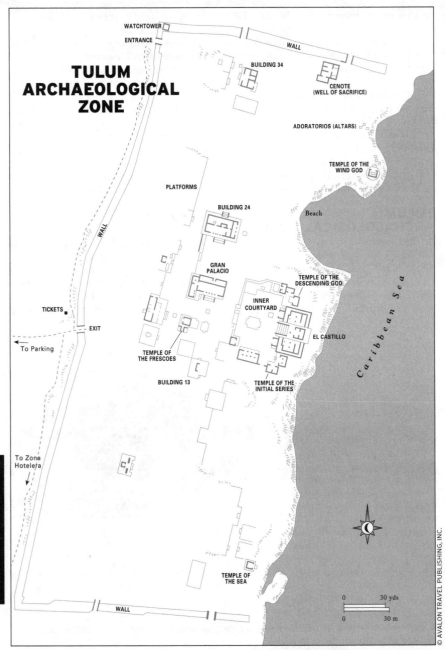

TULUM ARCHAEOLOGICAL ZONE

WATCHTOWER

ENTRANCE

WALL

BUILDING 34

CENOTE (WELL OF SACRIFICE)

ADORATORIOS (ALTARS)

TEMPLE OF THE WIND GOD

PLATFORMS

BUILDING 24

Beach

GRAN PALACIO

TEMPLE OF THE DESCENDING GOD

INNER COURTYARD

TICKETS

EXIT

← To Parking

TEMPLE OF THE FRESCOES

EL CASTILLO

Caribbean Sea

WALL

BUILDING 13

TEMPLE OF THE INITIAL SERIES

To Zona Hotelera

TEMPLE OF THE SEA

0   30 yds

0   30 m

WALL

© AVALON TRAVEL PUBLISHING, INC.

DECIPHERING THE GLYPHS

Mayanist and scholar Michael D. Coe's *Breaking the Maya Code* (Thames and Hudson, 1992) is a fascinating account of the decipherment of Maya writing.

For many years, scholars could not agree whether Maya writing contained anything more than numbers and dates. Many thought the text was not "real writing" as it did not appear to reproduce spoken language. Even those who believed the writing to be more meaningful despaired at ever reading it.

In 1952, Russian scholar Yuri Valentinovich Knorosov jump-started Maya scholarship by showing that Maya writing did in fact convey spoken words. Using a rough alphabet recorded by Fray Diego de Landa (the 16th-century bishop who, ironically, is best known for having destroyed numerous Maya texts), Knorosov showed that ancient texts contain common Yucatec words such as *cutz* (turkey) and *tzul* (dog). Interestingly, Knorosov conducted his research from reproductions only, having never held a Maya artifact or visited an ancient temple. When he did finally visit Tikal in 1990, Coe writes, Knorosov wasn't very impressed.

By the mid-1980s decipherment picked up speed. One of many standouts from that era is David Stuart, the son of Maya experts, who went to Cobá with his parents at age eight and passed the time copying glyphs and learning Yucatec words from local playmates. In high school he served as chief epigrapher on a groundbreaking exploration in Belize, and at age 18 he received a US$128,000 MacArthur Fellowship to, as he told Michael Coe, "play around with the glyphs" full-time.

Researchers now know that Maya writing is like most other hieroglyphic systems. What appears at first to be a single glyph can have up to four parts, and the same word can be expressed in pictorial, phonetic, or hybrid form. Depending on context, one symbol can have either a pictorial or phonetic role; likewise, a particular sound can be represented in more than one way. The word cacao is spelled phonetically as "ca-ca-u" but is written with a picture of a fish (*ca*) and a comblike symbol (also *ca*, according to Landa) and followed by -u. One of David Stuart's great insights was that for all its complexity, much of Maya glyphic writing is "just repetitive."

But how do we know what the symbols are meant to sound like in the first place? Some come from the Landa alphabet, others are suggested by the pictures that accompany many texts, still others from patterns derived by linguistic analyses of contemporary Maya languages. In some cases, it is simply a hunch that, after applying it to a number of texts, turns out to be right. If this seems like somewhat shaky scientific ground, it is – but not without a means of being proved. The cacao decipherment was confirmed when the same glyph was found on a jar with chocolate residue still inside.

Hundreds of glyphs have been deciphered and most of the known Maya texts can be reliably translated. The effort has lent invaluable insight into Maya civilization, especially dynastic successions and religious beliefs. Some archaeologists lament, not entirely without reason, that high-profile glyphic studies have diverted attention from research into the lives of ordinary ancient Maya people. Without question, there is much to be learned on that front. But it is hard not to marvel at how one of the world's great ancient civilizations is revealed in the whorls and creases of fading stone pictures.

380 by 165 meters (1,247 by 541 feet), it's the largest fortified Maya site on the Quintana Roo coast, although small compared to most archaeological zones.

Tulum's enviable patch of seashore was settled as early as 300 B.C., but it remained little more than a village for most of its existence, overshadowed by the Maya city of Tankah, a few kilometers to the north. However, Tulum experienced a boom around A.D. 1200, during which time most of its main structures were built. These exhibit strong influences from the reigning power of that time, Mayapán. Around A.D. 1440, the influence of central Mexican civilizations grew, as it did across the Yucatán Peninsula. Strangely, the structures built during that time were of rather shoddy construction, so Tulum's temples are much more decayed than structures at other sites, built hundreds of years prior.

The Spanish got their first view of the then brightly colored fortress when Juan de Grijalva's expedition sailed past the Quintana Roo coast in 1518. This was also the Spaniards' first encounter with the indigenous people of the new continent, and according to ships' logs, the image was awe-inspiring. One notable entry describes "a village so large, that Seville would not have appeared larger or better." The city remained an important port well into the conquest, but was abandoned when European diseases decimated its population.

Visiting the Ruins

The Tulum ruins are made up of mostly small, ornate structures with stuccoed gargoyle faces carved onto their corners. By far the site's most impressive structure is **El Castillo** (The Castle), a large pyramid standing on the edge of a 12-meter (39-foot) limestone cliff overlooking the sea. The building was constructed in three different phases. A wide staircase leads to a two-chamber temple at the top; visitors are no longer allowed to climb this stairway, but the view from the hill on which the Castillo stands encompasses the sea, the surrounding jungle (with an occasional stone ruin poking through the tight

brush), and scattered clearings where small farms are sprouting.

In the **Temple of the Frescoes,** looking through a metal grate you'll see a fresco that still bears a trace of color from the ancient artist. Archaeologically, this is the most interesting building on the site. The original parts of the building were constructed around 1450 during the late Postclassic period, and as is the case with so many Maya structures, it was added to over the years.

Across the compound, the small off-kilter **Temple of the Descending God** has a *palapa*-cover to protect a carving of an upside-down winged creature on the main lintel. The name is purely descriptive. Some archaeologists believe the carving depicts the God of the Setting Sun, while others say it represents the bee; in pre-Hispanic times, honey was revered and valued almost as much as maize.

Practicalities

Tulum's massive parking lot and strip mall–like visitors center ought to clue you in to the number of tourists that pass through here every day. (Did we mention to get here early?) You'll find a small museum and bookshop amid innumerable souvenir shops, fast food restaurants, and ATM machines that give U.S. dollars instead of pesos. Don't let the scene here turn you off to all Maya ruins—even Chichén Itzá is less commercialized, and most sites are not at all.

The site entrance and ticket booth are about one kilometer (0.6 mile) from the visitors center; if you don't feel like walking, a **trolley** ferries guests there and back for US$2 per person (kids under 10 ride free). Professional bilingual guides can be hired at the entrance for around US$33.

Getting There

Tulum ruins are seven kilometers (4.5 miles) south of Akumal on Highway 307. Arriving by bus or *combi*, be sure to ask the driver to let you off at *las ruínas* as opposed to the town, which is another 1.5 kilometers (one mile) south. To return, vans may be waiting near the site exit; otherwise flag a bus or van down on the highway. They pass frequently well after the ruins have closed. If you're driving, parking is US$2.50.

OTHER SIGHTS
Northern Beaches

The area north of the turnoff has two easy-to-reach beach areas that are ideal for people staying in town, at least for now: Most of this beautiful stretch of sand—right up to the ruins, in fact—was bought by the developers of The Tides, a huge condominium complex in Playa del Carmen. Plans to build condos had to be scrapped, thankfully, because of environmental laws against high-density development here. But it may be inevitable that this area sees the construction of high-end bungalows, which will be delightful for guests but will make getting to the beach as an ordinary traveler more and more tricky.

Nuddy Beach Club (tel. 984/130-0285, between La Vita Bella restaurant and Mar Caribe, 8 A.M.–6 P.M. daily, restaurant noon–6 P.M., beach bar 8 P.M.–2 A.M. Thu.–Sat.) occupi, wide beautiful stretch of sand known as Play, Paraíso. Once little more than a bar and some hammocks, the beach club has morphed into a bustling expanse of lounge chairs and umbrellas (for rent US$2–6/day), with waiters weaving between them, and a full-service water sport center offering snorkeling, diving, kiteboarding, and more. Busy but still wonderfully relaxing.

Travelers looking for less of a scene have migrated one beach north to the area known by the nearby bungalows, **Mar Caribe.** Broad and unspoiled, this is the place to come to lay out your towel or sheet on the white sand, which you share with a picturesque array of moored fishing boats. This is where backpacker shuttles operated by The Weary Traveler and Hostel Tulum come.

◖ Southern Beaches

Tulum's very best beaches—thick white sand, turquoise blue water, no one around—are toward the southern end of the hotel zone. Not

© LIZA PRADO

Tulum's southern beaches are classic Caribbean – powdery sand and turquoise waters that are seemingly endless.

most exclusive hotels are in the ... access to the beach can be dif- ...t staying at one of them. That ..., ... south of the Zona Hotelera's mini-village there is a rocky public beach, the end of which marks the beginning of the southern beaches; from here just walk down the shore until you find a spot that fits your fancy—hotels are allowed to restrict use of their chairs and umbrellas, but the beach itself is public.

◖ Cenotes

Hidden Worlds Cenotes Park (Hwy. 307 between Tulum and Akumal, tel. 984/877-8535, www.hiddenworlds.com, 9 A.M.–5 P.M. daily) is an excellent place for first-timers to experience underground snorkeling or diving. Although sometimes crowded, Hidden Worlds earns its popularity by offering excellent tours and professional service. Snorkeling tours (US$40 pp for 2.5 hours, US$25 pp for 1.5 hours, gear

included; 9 A.M., 11 A.M., 1 P.M., 2 P.M., and 3 P.M. daily, maximum 10 people/group) visit two different cenotes. You will explore huge caverns, see light beams penetrate distant pools, and (if you want) swim through channels with just a head's worth of airspace. One- and two-tank cavern dives (US$50 one tank, US$90 two tank, gear rental US$5–15, four divers maximum, 9 A.M., 11 A.M., 1 P.M. daily) also visit two cenotes and follow guidelines set by cave explorers. Exploration is ongoing—ask about Dreamgate, a stunning cavern opened to divers in September 2003. Hidden Worlds offers free hotel pickup if you're staying in or between Puerto Aventuras and Tulum. It's recommended to reserve at least a day in advance.

Just north, **Dos Ojos** (tel. 984/877-8535, 8 A.M.–5 P.M. daily) also offers guided snorkeling and dive trips. Like Hidden Worlds, it offers daily snorkeling tours (US$28 pp), with on-site guides leading visitors through

---

CENOTES: THEN AND NOW

One of the Yucatán Peninsula's most intriguing features is its cenotes, large freshwater sinkholes. Cenotes owe their formation to the massive meteorite that hit the Yucatán Peninsula 65 million years ago, near present-day Mérida. The impact shattered the peninsula's thick limestone cap like a stone hitting a car windshield. Over millions of years, rainwater seeped into the cracks, forming what is today the world's largest underground river system. Cenotes are former caverns whose roofs collapsed. (Caveins are extremely rare today, however.) Cenotes can be hundreds of meters deep and are usually filled with fresh water (occasional seawater intrusion in some cenotes forms haloclines – a bizarre and interesting sight).

Cenotes were sacred to the Mayas, who relied on them for water. They also were seen as apertures to the underworld, and sacrificial victims were sometimes thrown into their eerie depths, along with finely worked stone and clay items. Archaeologists have learned a great deal about early Maya rituals by dredging cenotes near archaeological sites.

Still revered by many Mayas, the peninsula's cenotes have attracted other worshippers: snorkelers and scuba divers. The unbelievably clear water – 100-meter (328-foot) visibility in places – attracts many underwater enthusiasts. But the real joy of snorkeling or diving here comes from the amazing stalactite and stalagmite formations. Formed in the ice age when water levels were extremely low, they were submerged in water as the climate warmed. Today, you can snorkel and dive past beautiful formations that you would walk around in a dry cave.

Divers with open-water certification can dive in the cenotes. Though "full-cave" diving requires advanced training, most cenote tours are actually "cavern" dives, meaning you are always within 40 meters (130 feet) of an air pocket. It's a good idea to take some open-water dives before your first cenote tour – buoyancy control is especially important in cenotes, and you'll be contending with different weights and finning technique.

TULUM AND QUINTANA ROO

this massive and spectacular cave system. *Dos Ojos* (Two Eyes) is a reference to the twin caverns that you can explore here. You can also snorkel independently for a small admission fee (US$7.50).

Other favorite cenotes include **Car Wash, Kolimba/Kin-Ha, Cenote Grande,** and **Calavera Cenote** (all west of Tulum on the road to Cobá); **Casa Cenote** (at Tankah Tres); **Cenote Azul** and **Cristalina** (Hwy. 307 across from Xpu-Há); and **Chaac Mol** (Hwy. 307, two km/1.2 mi north of Xpu-Há). All can be visited on a tour or by yourself, and most have snorkel gear for rent (US$6). Most are on private or *ejido* (collective) land and charge admission fees, usually US$5–8 for snorkelers and US$10 for divers. If you take a tour, ask if admission fees are included in the rate. Most cenotes are open 8 A.M.–5 P.M. daily.

Tours of Sian Ka'an Biosphere Reserve

CESiaK (Hwy. 307 just south of the Tulum ruins turnoff, tel. 984/871-2499, www.cesiak .org, 9 A.M.–2 P.M. and 4–8 P.M. daily) is a nonprofit environmental organization that offers several excellent trips into the rich Sian Ka'an Biosphere Reserve. The most popular is an all-day excursion (US$68 pp) that begins with a short introduction to the reserve and guided walk along the coastal dunes, followed by a motor boat tour of the lagoon complex and its many habitats and ecosystems (plus a remote Maya ruin), and then floating down a canal in the mangroves and snorkeling in one of the many cenotes. A sunset bird-watching tour (US$70 pp) starts in the afternoon and includes visiting (by motor boat) known nesting areas, including the aptly named Bird Island. A bird-watching tour by kayak is also available (US$45) or you can rent kayaks (US$20 single, US$30 double, three hours) and explore the lagoon yourself. Don't worry—a guide will give you tips on where to go, and how to get back! Fishing, mountain biking, and archaeological tours can also be arranged; most tours include hotel pickup, lunch, and a bilingual guide. CESiaK also

has well-recommended lodging just inside the reserve.

Sian Ka'an Ecoturismo (Av. Tulum between Calles Beta and Osiris, tel. 984/871-2363, 10 A.M.–7 P.M. Mon.–Sat.) also offers similar tours at similar prices—in fact, the two agencies used to be one. But whereas CESiaK typically enters from the Tulum-Boca Paila road, the canal tour here starts with a visit to Muyil archaeological site, south of Tulum on Highway 307, and enters the reserve from that side.

For more information on Sian Ka'an or if you want to spend more than just a few hours there, check out the *Punta Allen/Sian Ka'an Biosphere Reserve* section later in this chapter.

SHOPPING

Mixik Artesanía Mexicana (Av. Tulum between Calles Alfa and Jupiter, tel. 984/871-2136, 9 A.M.–9 P.M. Mon.–Sat.) has a large selection of quality folk art, from green copper suns to carved wooden angels and masks, plus T-shirts, jewelry, cards, and more. There's a sister shop in the Zona Hotelera by the same name. Also in the hotel zone and near Mixik's sister store, **Joyería Studio** (Hotel Posada del Sol, tel. 984/876-6206, 8 A.M.–10 P.M. daily) sells good handmade *artesanía,* especially jewelry, from a small shop at the hotel entrance.

SPORTS AND RECREATION
Scuba Diving

The reef here is superb, but Tulum's diving claim-to-fame are the slew of freshwater cenotes and caves, all within easy reach. Divers with open-water certification can make "cavern" dives, defined as no more than 30 feet deep or 130 feet from an air pocket. (Full-cave diving requires advanced training and certification.) If you haven't dived in a while, definitely take several open-water dives before your first cenote trip, as buoyancy control is especially important in cavern environments.

Prices for cenote dives are fairly uniform among the various shops, around US$70–80 for one tank, US$120–140 for two tanks, including equipment, transportation, and entrance fees. Tulum's shops also offer multi-dive packages and cavern, intro to cave, and full-cave certification courses; they also offer snorkeling and reef diving, of course. As always, choose a shop and guide you feel comfortable with, not necessarily the least expensive one. (See *How to Choose a Dive Shop* sidebar in the *Isla Cozumel* chapter.)

The easiest introduction to cenotes is at **Hidden Worlds Cenote Park,** which runs excellent daily cavern diving (and snorkeling) trips on a private cenote system right at its shop, located a short distance north of Tulum.

Cenote Dive Center (Av. Tulum at Calle Osiris, tel. 984/871-2232, www.cenotedive .com, 8:30 A.M.–8 P.M. daily, low season closed Sun.) is affiliated with the Abyss Dive Center located by the turnoff to the Tulum ruins.

Aptly named after the Maya underworld, **Xibalba Dive Center** (Av. Tulum between Av. Satelite and the road to Zona Hotelera/Boca Paila, tel. 984/807-4579, www.xibalbadive center.com, 9 A.M.–7 P.M. daily) has a good reputation for safety and professionalism.

In Tulum's hotel zone, **Mexi-Divers** (Zama Hotel, 998/185-9656, mexidiverstulum@ hotmail.com, 8:30 A.M.–5 P.M. daily) in the mini-village area or **Dive Ollin** (984/876-4385, 9 A.M.–6 P.M. daily) at Playa Paraíso are both reliable operators.

Other recommended cenote-diving shops include **Aquatech** (tel. 984/875-9020, www .cenotes.com) in Aventuras Akumal and **Lucky Fish Divers** (tel. 044-984/129-6774, www .luckyfishdiving.com) in Tankah Tres, both a short distance north of Tulum.

Snorkeling

Like divers, snorkelers have an embarrassment of riches in Tulum, with great reef snorkeling and easy access to the eerie beauty of the area's many cenotes. Dive shops listed here offer snorkel trips of both sorts; reef trips cost around US$20 for a 2.5-hour trip, while cenote trips run US$30–45. Hidden Worlds is again the easiest introduction to cenotes, offering guided snorkeling tours offered several times daily.

To **rent snorkel gear** ask at any of the dive shops in town or along the beach. In the Zona Hotelera, a kiosk in front of Cabañas Punta Piedra (mini-village area, 7:30 A.M.–6:30 P.M. daily) rents snorkel gear for US$5 a day, and also offers tours.

Kiteboarding

Extreme Control (Playa Paraíso, 984/745-4555, www.extremecontrol.net, 8 A.M.–sunset daily) is based at the water sport center at Playa Paraíso and Nuddy Beach Club. Tulum's only kiteboarding outfit—for now, anyway—is run by an American-Italian couple and offers courses and rentals for all experience levels. A private full introductory class of four hours costs US$220, plus US$70 an hour for additional lessons; group classes are somewhat less. Multiday packages, including lodging at the shop's studio apartments, are a great deal if you're serious about learning and practicing the sport. Diving and specialty courses also available.

Eco-Parks

Snorkel in the ocean, snuba in a lagoon, float down a river, or swim with dolphins at **Xel-Há** (Hwy. 307, 9 km/5.6 mi north of Tulum, tel. 998/883-3293, www.xel-ha.com, 8:30 A.M.–6 P.M. daily, US$39/27 adult/child, US$59/41 adult/child including snorkel gear, meals, and beverages, US$74–88 adult including transportation, US$52–82 including transportation child). Promoted as a water lovers and marine life paradise, children and beginner snorkelers will probably list this as a highlight of their trip; others may find the waters overrun with tourists and underpopulated by fish and other sea creatures. Dolphin interaction program costs extra.

Cycling

Along with renting well-maintained bicycles, **Iguana Bike Shop** (Av. Satélite near Calle Andromeda, tel. 984/119-0836, 9 A.M.–7 P.M. Mon.–Sat.) offers mountain bike tours to snorkeling sites in various cenotes and beaches as well as turtle nesting grounds on Xcacel beach. Prices vary depending on the tour, which typically last four hours and are limited to six cyclists.

Body Work

A holistic spa set over the beach at Copal hotel, **Maya Spa Wellness Center** (Carr. Tulum-Punta Allen Km. 5, tel. 984/871-2750, www.maya-spa.com, 8 A.M.–8 P.M. daily) offers a variety of massages (US$73–100 60 minutes, US$109–165 90 minutes), body wraps (US$79–165), and spiritual treatments like Reiki and Maya crystal therapy (US$36–73). Yoga instruction also is offered. For a full listing of offerings, check the website.

Located at the Ana y José hotel, **Om...Spa** (Carr. Tulum-Punta Allen Km. 7, tel. 998/887-5470, www.anayjose.com, 10 A.M.–6 P.M. daily) is a full-service spa set in a beachfront, ultra chic setting. Choose from a menu of massages (US$75–95) and body treatments (US$60–85); if you want a treat, ask about the Yumka Chocolate Spa (US$150, 120 minutes), which includes a chocolate body mask and a chocolate foaming bath. Just don't drink the water.

ACCOMMODATIONS

Chances are you've come to Tulum to stay in one of the famous beachside bungalow-type hotels. There are many to choose from, each slightly different, but most sharing a laid-back atmosphere and terrific beaches. However, the area has no power lines or fresh water wells, and some travelers are surprised by just how rustic some lodgings are. Even top-end hotels may have very limited nighttime lighting—or none at all, providing candles instead—and virtually all use salt water in the showers and sinks. (Air-conditioning is available in only a couple places.) At the same time, many hotels use generators to power their restaurants and reception area. Always ask for a room away from the generator but be ready to pay for it. Nothing is a bigger kill-joy than a giant diesel motor pounding outside your window, especially since the whole point of coming here is for the peace and quiet.

The Zona Hotelera has a short "northern section" (north of the turnoff to Tulum Pueblo) and a longer "southern section" (south of there). Addresses are designated by kilometer number, but there are no kilometer mark-

© LIZA PRADO

Grab a book and a hammock and you're set for a day in Tulum.

ers, so the point is moot unless you set your odometer. Both sections of the road are now paved, but you should drive slowly as there are several blind curves.

Hotels in town have improved steadily over the years, as prices on the beach make it harder for even mid-range travelers to stay there. With the beach a short cab or bike ride away, and prices for food, Internet, laundry so much lower than in the Zona Hotelera, it's not a bad option.

Under US$25

In Town: Weary Traveler Hostel (Av. Tulum between Calles Jupiter and Calle Acuario, tel. 984/871-2390, www.wearytravelerhostel.com, US$11 dorm, US$28 d) is Tulum's longtime backpacker gathering spot. It operates on a largely do-it-yourself basis: breakfast is whatever you feel like making from the eggs, bread, pancake batter, etc. Ditto for the nightly barbecue (US$5 pp), which brings guests together over a hot grill and sizzling meat. There's a common kitchen, free salsa lessons, and free

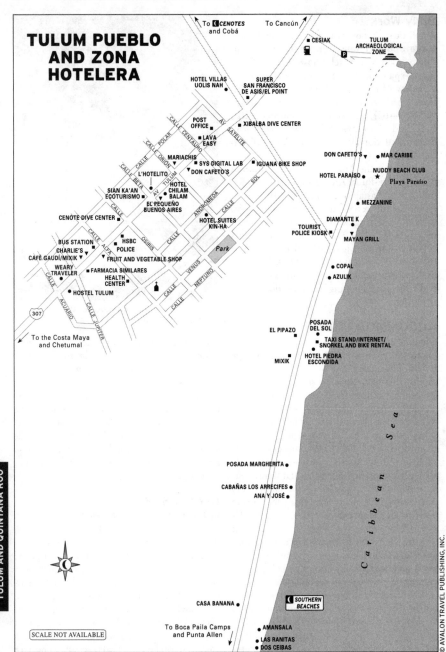

TULUM PUEBLO AND ZONA HOTELERA

To CENOTES and Cobá

To Cancún

CESIAK

TULUM ARCHAEOLOGICAL ZONE

HOTEL VILLAS UOLIS NAH

SUPER SAN FRANCISCO DE ASIS/EL POINT

POST OFFICE

LAVA EASY

XIBALBA DIVE CENTER

MARIACHIS

SYS DIGITAL LAB

DON CAFETO'S

IGUANA BIKE SHOP

DON CAFETO'S

MAR CARIBE

L'HOTELITO

HOTEL PARAÍSO

NUDDY BEACH CLUB

Playa Paraíso

SIAN KA'AN ECOTURISMO

HOTEL CHILAM BALAM

EL PEQUEÑO BUENOS AIRES

MEZZANINE

CENOTE DIVE CENTER

HOTEL SUITES KIN-HA

DIAMANTE K

TOURIST POLICE KIOSK

MAYAN GRILL

BUS STATION

HSBC POLICE

CHARLIE'S

CAFÉ GAUDÍ/MIXIK

FRUIT AND VEGETABLE SHOP

Park

WEARY TRAVELER

FARMACIA SIMILARES

HEALTH CENTER

COPAL

AZULIK

HOSTEL TULUM

307

To the Costa Maya and Chetumal

POSADA DEL SOL

EL PIPAZO

TAXI STAND/INTERNET/ SNORKEL AND BIKE RENTAL

MIXIK

HOTEL PIEDRA ESCONDIDA

Caribbean Sea

POSADA MARGHERITA

CABAÑAS LOS ARRECIFES

ANA Y JOSÉ

CASA BANANA

SOUTHERN BEACHES

To Boca Paila Camps and Punta Allen

AMANSALA

LAS RANITAS

DOS CEIBAS

CALLE CENTAURO

CALLE POLAR

CALLE ORION

CALLE BETA

CALLE

AV SATELITE

AV TULUM

CALLE SOL

CALLE ANDROMEDA

CALLE

CALLE ALFA

OSIRIS

CALLE VENUS

CALLE NEPTUNO

CALLE

CALLE

CALLE ACUARIO

CALLE JUPITER

SCALE NOT AVAILABLE

© AVALON TRAVEL PUBLISHING, INC.

twice-daily shuttle service to and from the beach. The hostel also provides large safety deposit boxes and luggage storage if you've got a late bus. The big drawback here are the rooms, which are dim, grubby, and in serious need of renovation. Each dorm—which can be converted to a private—has just four bunks, a fan, and small unappealing bathroom. Fortunately, the hostel's environs and the allure of the beach mean you probably won't be spending much time inside anyway.

Across the street, **Hostel Tulum** (Calle Jupiter 20, tel. 984/871-2089, tulumhostel@hotmail.com, US$10 dorm, US$18.50 d shared bath, US$28 t with private bath) is for backpackers happy to forgo the scene at Weary Traveler in exchange for newer, cleaner dorms, including one for women only. Thick mattresses and bright linens are a plus, though the bathrooms could use a scrubbing and the "private" rooms have thin walls that don't reach the ceiling. Lockers, continental breakfast, use of a small communal kitchen, and once-daily shuttle to the beach are all included.

In Zona Hotelera: The rustic **Mar Caribe** (between Nuddy Beach Club and Tulum ruins, no phone, US$2.75 pp camping, US$10 s/d cabaña BYO hammock, US$14 s/d cabaña with bed) occupies a broad, windswept beach with a handful of fishing boats tied ashore and views of the Tulum ruins. There are plenty of spots to set up a tent and a handful of extremely basic cabañas with sand floors, hammock hooks or saggy beds, and sand blowing through the gaps in the walls. All share three grubby bathrooms—definitely wear your flip-flops when you use them. Not very pleasant, Mar Caribe nonetheless is cheap and on a beautiful beach.

US$25-50

In Town: Although the rooms at **Hotel Chilam Balam** (Av. Tulum between Calles Beta and Orion, tel. 984/871-2042, US$33–37 s/d with a/c) are showing their age, they're spacious and very clean. All have air-conditioning, flat-screen TVs, sponge-painted walls, and bright bedspreads. Many rooms open onto an interior hallway—if you like natural sunlight, ask for one facing the street.

L'Hotelito (Av. Tulum between Calles Beta and Orion, no tel., hotelito@viaggiland.it, US$33 s/d with fan, US$37 s/d with a/c) has 10 worn rooms that open onto wide corridors. Rooms are made more cheerful by colorful walls and Mexican *artesanía,* but there's no hiding the fact that the bathrooms need scrubbing and many of the beds are saggy. At least it's cheap and well-located. And if you like *palapa* roofs, the fan units on the 2nd floor have them.

Villa Matisse (Av. Satelite 19, tel. 984/871-2636, shuvinito@yahoo.com, US$40) has six simple comfortable rooms, a pleasant garden and reading area (with book exchange), and a community kitchen. The rooms are spotless, and the grounds and common areas equally well maintained; the multilingual owner sets out coffee and small snacks in the morning, and often supplies rooms with fresh flowers. No air-conditioning, but rooms have fans and good cross-ventilation. Use of the hotel's bikes are included in the rate.

In Zona Hotelera: Diamante K (north of intersection, tel. 984/876-2115, www.diamantek.com, US$42 s/d with shared bathrooms, US$100–223 suite) is a classic Tulum cabaña hotel and a good midrange option. Although there are a handful of suites, most of the units are simple wood bungalows with *palapa* roofs, concrete floors, and hanging beds; all share decent bathrooms. The shore here is a jagged rocky shelf, and the hotel has various nooks and crannies with cushions, chairs, or hammocks where guests can watch the waves crash ashore. For swimming or sandcastles, there's a tiny private beach or, better yet, follow a path that leads a few hundred meters north to a broad unkempt beach. Other than the litter, which is avoidable, it's all part of the rustic, unpolished charm of the place. The hotel also has a bohemian chic restaurant and bar.

Behind an enormous sand dune, **Cabañas Los Arrecifes** (Carr. Tulum-Punta Allen Km. 7, tel. 984/879-7307, www.losarrecifes tulum.com, US$30 s/d with shared bathroom,

US$50 s/d bungalow with shared bathroom, US$100–150 s/d with private bathroom) offers a range of accommodations on an ample palm-tree-laden property. The beachfront bungalows are basic—sand floors and a bed—but the view can't be beat; and the modern hotel rooms are clean and comfortable though charmless. The remaining rooms are at the back of the property; be sure you're not stuck in there—these rooms are effectively cement boxes, dark and gnarly.

More than an eatery, **Mayan Grill** (north of intersection, tel. 984/116-3292, marelmerida@ yahoo.com.mx, US$24–42 s/d with shared bathroom) has six basic cabañas that are squeezed into a *tiny* beachfront lot. All have cement floors, decent beds, and mosquito netting on the windows. A generator is run until 10 P.M. nightly—if you can, try to get a cabaña as far from it as possible.

US$50-100

In Town: Arguably the best place in town, ◖ **Hotel Villas Uolis Nah** (Carr. Tulum-Cobá Km. 0.2, tel. 984/745-2898, www.uolis nah.com, US$65 studio with kitchen, US$75 studio with kitchen and a/c) also is about the only place that has fully equipped kitchens in each guest room. Set in a leafy garden, units are simple, clean, and comfortable with little touches like mosaic tile bathrooms and *palapa*-shaded terraces with hammocks. With Super San Francisco just steps away, it's also no problem to get groceries if you don't have a car. Affiliated with the kiteboarding school Extreme Control, guests receive discounts on courses too.

Set in a leafy tropical garden, **Hotel Suites Kin-Ha** (Calle Orión near Calle Andromeda, tel. 984/871-2321, www.hotelkinha.com, US$55 s/d with fan, US$70 s/d with a/c) offers 10 colorful rooms with thick mattresses, tile floors, and mosaic tile accents. Each has a small *palapa*-shaded patio—perfect for writing postcards. The hotel also has a sister hotel on the beach **Playa Kin-Ha** (Carr. Tulum-Punta Allen Km. 5.5, US$110 s/d, US$130 suite); guests of the Kin-Ha in town are welcome to enjoy the

beach amenities there. Transportation between the two is even included in the rate.

In Zona Hotelera: Posada del Sol (minivillage, tel. 984/876-6206, www.laposada delsol.com, US$75–150) has seven attractive rooms—three on the ocean side of the road, four on the other—all with private bath, fan, and most with terrace and hammock. The hotel has an artesanía shop in the reception area, so it's no surprise the rooms also have an artsy feel, from driftwood beams to Mexican rugs. Stay here if you prefer to spend a little less and have a little more atmosphere—in this cluster of hotels are also a few restaurants, Internet access, a market and some stores, plus money exchange, taxi post, and a place to rent bikes.

Hotel Paraíso (Playa Paraíso, north of intersection, tel. 984/130-0285, US$83 d, US$91 t) offers 10 small artful rooms, a beautiful beach, and Maya ruins within walking distance, which all make this a comfortable and reliable choice. The decor is simple but pleasing: blue walls, modern porcelain sinks, cement floors inlaid with stone. There's a water-sports center on the beach, and a bar and restaurant (though Don Cafeto's, nearby, is better and cheaper). On the downside, the hotel is definitely secondary to the beach club, so service can be slow; guests can use the beach chairs, you pay for the beach beds like everyone else. While not the classic Tulum locale—it's a hotel, not bungalows, and the beach can get busy with day-trippers—but a comfy room, 24-hour electricity, and easy access to food, beach, and activities may be just the amount of "experience" you're after.

Neither too rustic nor too chichi, **Dos Ceibas** (Carr. Tulum-Punta Allen Km. 10, tel. 984/877-6024, www.dosceibas.com, US$50–133) offers comfortable affordable bungalows on a beautiful stretch of beach. Units have polished cement floors, brightly painted walls, and firm beds with mosquito nets hanging from the *palapa* roof. Like many hotels here, the shower and sink use salt water. All but the two breezy oceanfront rooms have fans, though the power is turned off during daylight hours. The eight units range from a 2nd-floor honeymooner just steps from the beach, to a bargain bungalow with a detached bathroom (and near enough the road to hear passing cars). Children are welcome and service is consistently superb. The restaurant, though overpriced, serves tasty meals in a shady, sand-floor dining area. At night, a profusion of candles set in niches along the back wall light up the restaurant area, while more glow in paper bags, marking the path to the beach.

Posada Lamar (Carr. Tulum-Punta Allen Km. 4.5, tel. 984/876-6206, www.posada lamar.com, US$100–150) has eight comfortable and beautifully decorated bungalows. The painted cement floors with inlaid tile and stones, the salvaged-wood detailing, even the exposed water pipes, all lend an appealingly artistic flair. Managed by an amiable Mexican couple, service is friendly but definitely hands-off; come here for a real getaway, not to be pampered. Bungalows have fans, but the electricity is on only from 6–11 P.M.; oceanfront rooms have the best sea breeze, and may be worth the higher rate in the summer. The beach here is stunning, and the hotel has a well-maintained beach area with chairs, beds, and *palapas*. Posada Lamar is a sister hotel to Posada del Sol, a kilometer away in the mini-village area.

Over US$100

In Zona Hotelera: While Tulum has many beach bungalows with a touch of class, **Mezzanine** (1.5 km/1 mi north of intersection, tel. 998/112-2840, www.mezzanine.com .mx, US$250 d) is a high-class boutique hotel that happens to be on the beach. Seven rooms (four with ocean view) exude modern design, from unexpected color combinations to chic dark-wood furnishings. The pool here is more decorative than functional, and beach beds aren't on the beach at all, but on a platform overlooking it. (A path leads down to the sand, if you must.) The restaurant serves outstanding Thai-fusion dishes and a full bar stirs up mixed drinks to hip beats.

Beachy and hip, **◖ Posada Margherita** (Carr. Tulum-Punta Allen Km. 4.5, tel. 984/100-3780, www.posadamargherita.com,

US$120–180 s/d) boasts just eight rooms on its oceanfront property. Each is decorated differently but all have stone-inlaid showers, private porches, and art from around the world. All are located just feet from a nice stretch of beach and an open-air lounge. Posada Margherita also is run on solar energy, which means 24 hours of silent electricity—a luxury in this part of the Riviera. Don't miss eating dinner at the hotel restaurant, as it's one of the best in Tulum.

Known as the "Bikini Boot Camp," **Amansala** (north of Las Ranitas, tel. 984/100-0805, www.amansala.com, US$111–263 s/d, six nights all-inclusive US$2,777 s, US$1,959 pp d) is a chic resort that caters to people who are looking to buff up in the sun. Located on a stunning white sand beach, the 14 eclectic rooms are set in two-story *palapas* with wood floors that are beautifully appointed with stone-inlaid walls, paper lanterns, and fine linens. All-inclusive packages include yoga and Pilates instruction on the beach, outdoor cardio and strength workouts, low-calorie meals, and body treatments. Biking and kayaking excursions are included as is a tour of the Tulum archaeological site. Popular with women, though everyone is welcome. And unlike the army, no one is forced to do push-ups.

Perfect for a romantic getaway, **Azulik** (Carr. Tulum-Punta Allen Km. 5.1, toll-free U.S. and Canada tel. 877/532-6737, www.ecotulum .com, US$325–350) has 15 spacious villas set on high rocky bluffs overlooking the Caribbean. The *palapa* villas are luxurious, soothing, and private—with floor-to-ceiling windows, a large deck with lounge chairs, two tubs each (a dugout tree indoors, a mosaic tile one outdoors), and hanging king-size beds. There's no electricity—the moon and candles rule at night—and access paths lead to a nude beach below (like the beach, the hotel is nude friendly). The two end units lend a bit more privacy, while three others are on the beach itself. Waiters come by in the morning to take your breakfast order (not included in rate), and deliver it for you to eat on your patio, a perfect way to start the day. Adults only.

TULUM AND QUINTANA ROO

Ana y José (Carr. Tulum-Punta Allen Km. 7, just south of Cabañas Los Arrecifes, tel. 998/892-0910, www.anayjose.com, US$202–320) stands out as one of the few hotels on the beach to offer 24-hour air-conditioning and a swimming pool. It sports a gorgeous beach, full spa, restaurant, car rental agency, and concierge, and hosts numerous weddings. The standard rooms are pleasant but with a cookie-cutter style that's odd for a resort of this caliber. The suites are a cut above, with king-size beds, living rooms, ocean views, and chic decor…which they ought to be for the even higher price they fetch. In fact, rates (for rooms and meals alike) are the main complaint here, being inflated even by Tulum's standards. Still, for those who require air-conditioning and a pool and other comforts, there's no real competition.

An upscale eco-resort, **Las Ranitas** (Carr. Tulum-Punta Allen Km. 9, tel. 984/877-8554, www.lasranitas.com, US$120–250 s/d, US$300–420 suite) boasts one of the most spectacular beaches in Tulum—expansive white sand, huge palm trees, and a mellow turquoise sea. Rooms themselves are set in bungalows that are surrounded by lush vegetation; each is ample and airy with a private terrace or balcony. The decor is a little tacky—think ceramic frogs—but the rooms are comfortable and very private. Stone-inlaid walkways lead guests to an inviting pool, a paddle tennis court, and the welcoming main house, where there's a lounge, reading room, and good restaurant.

FOOD

Most of the hotels and beach clubs in the Zona Hotelera have restaurants, which are usually rather pricey, but handy for the days you don't feel like going anywhere. If you can drag yourself from the beach, a few eateries in town and in the hotel zone definitely stand out from the crowd.

Mexican

Charlie's (Av. Tulum between Calles Alfa and Jupiter, tel. 984/871-2573, 7:30 A.M.–11 P.M. Tues.–Sun., US$5–12) is one of Tulum's most popular restaurants, with a large airy dining area under a high *palapa* roof. The menu has classic Mexican dishes, such as *chiles rellenos,* enchiladas, tacos, and even a vegetarian plate or two. The restaurant hosts live music on Saturday nights during the year-end high season.

As popular as Charlie's is, locals and visitors looking for truly home-style cooking head to **Don Cafeto's** (Av. Tulum between Calles Centauro and Orion, tel. 984/871-2207, 7 A.M.–11 P.M. daily, US$5–9) for fresh seafood and grilled meat platters, Mexican staples like mole and enchiladas, and ceviche plates that are meals unto themselves. On a hot day, try a tall cold *superlimonada* or a *chayagra,* an uplifting blend of pineapple juice, lime juice, cucumber, and chaya (similar to spinach). On the beach, try the like-named **sister restaurant** (8 A.M.–10:30 P.M. daily) at Mar Caribe cabañas.

Open late every night, **Mariachis** (Av. Tulum at Calle Orion, tel. 984/871-2972, 9 A.M.–3 A.M. daily, US$4–20) is good for a midnight plate of tacos or just to throw back a couple of beers. Grilled seafood is the specialty—the *parrillada del mar* comes with thick grouper fillets, octopus, and shrimp—a meal big enough for two.

In the Zona Hotelera, the restaurant at **Cabañas Zahra** (mini-village, 7 A.M.–11 P.M. daily, US$6–16) offers reliable Mexican fare with a good number of vegetarian options—not surprising considering the number of health-conscious travelers in Tulum. A good place to have breakfast before you head out for a day on the beach.

Other Specialties

One of the best restaurants in Tulum, is at **Posada Margherita** (Carr. Tulum-Punta Allen Km. 4.5, tel. 984/100-3780, 7:30–10:30 A.M., noon–9 P.M. Mon. –Sat., US$6–18). Serving gourmet Italian meals, dishes are prepared with the freshest of ingredients, including organic products and homemade pastas and breads. A huge tree-trunk plate of appetizers also is brought to each table (think olives, roasted red peppers, and artichoke hearts)—almost a meal in and of itself. Beyond the extraordinary food, the beachside setting—a chic sand-floored restaurant with billowing white fabrics and candles—leave you wanting to come back.

€ **El Pequeño Buenos Aires** (Av. Tulum between Calles Orion and Beta, tel. 984/871-2708, 10 A.M.–11 P.M. Mon.–Sat., US$5–17) serves excellent cuts of beef, plus an array of crepes and even a few vegetarian dishes—not exactly a norm for Argentinean grills! The *parrillada Argentina* comes piled with different cuts and sausages—a perfect sampler if you can't decide exactly what you want. For lunch on a budget, try the *menu ejecutivo*—the special of the day plus a drink for US$4–5.50.

Fusion Thai is the specialty at **Mezzanine** (8 A.M.–10 P.M. daily, US$10–25), Tulum's newest, chicest hotel on the beach. Curries—red, green, or pineapple—and fried Thai tofu in peanut sauce are among the dishes served in a fashionable dining area or shaded outdoor patio, both with fine sea views. Full bar and cool music make this a nice place to linger.

Pizzería Il Basilico (Av. Tulum at Calle Beta, tel. 984/876-2632, 11 A.M.–11 P.M. daily except Tues.) is a reliable Italian restaurant specializing in pizza from its *forno a legna* (wood-burning oven).

Cafés

€ **Café Gaudí** (Av. Tulum between Calles Alfa and Jupiter, no phone, 7 A.M.–10 P.M. daily, US$3–6) is a small café-restaurant serving light fresh fare. Breakfast options are named after works by the Catalan architect and namesake, like Sagrada Familia and Park Guëll, and include fruit and yogurt, or eggs any way you like; the authentic Spanish tortilla and salami or roasted vegetable sandwiches make a good lunch.

On the inland side of the Zona Hotelera road, **Casa Banana** (Carr. Tulum-Punta Allen Km. 8.5, 7:30–11 A.M. and 6–9 P.M. Wed.–Mon., US$5–7) offers a good variety of breakfast dishes, sandwiches, and other light fare. Set under a high *palapa* and surrounded by the jungle, it makes a great place to linger over your iced coffee while you catch up on postcards.

Groceries

Tulum has a great local **fruit and vegetable shop** (6 A.M.–9 P.M. daily) on Avenida Tulum at Calle Alfa.

For basics and them some, head to the **Super San Francisco de Asis** (Av. Tulum at the turnoff to the Zona Hotelera, 7 A.M.–10 P.M. daily).

The Zona Hotelera's largest market, **El Pipazo** (mini-village, 9 A.M.–9 P.M. daily) is attached to Nohoch Tunich hotel; it has one room filled with essentials such as snack food, canned food, water, liquor, and sunscreen.

INFORMATION
Hospitals

Tulum's modest clinic is known as **SESA** (Calle Andrómeda between Calles Jupiter and Alfa, tel. 984/871-2050, 24 hours). For serious medical matters, go to Playa del Carmen or Cancún.

Pharmacies

Farmacia Similares (Av. Tulum at Calle Jupiter Sur, tel. 984/871-2736) is open 8 A.M.–10 P.M. Monday–Saturday, and until 9 P.M. Sunday. A doctor is available for simple consultations 5 P.M.–9 P.M. Monday–Saturday.

Police

The police station is in the city hall on Avenida Tulum and Calle Alfa, next to the HSBC bank. Dial 066 from any public phone for emergency assistance.

SERVICES
Money

HSBC (Av. Tulum at Calle Alfa next to city hall, 8 A.M.–7 P.M. Mon.–Sat.) has a reliable ATM machine and will change foreign cash and AmEx travelers checks 10 A.M.–5 P.M. Monday–Saturday.

An **exchange booth** (9 A.M.–9 P.M. daily) in the Zona Hotelera will change euros, U.S. dollars, and AmEx travelers checks.

Internet and Telephone

In town, **Sys Digital Lab** (Av. Tulum near Calle

TULUM BUS SCHEDULES

Departures from the **main bus terminal** (Av. Tulum between Calles Alfa and Jupiter, tel. 984/871-2122) include:

DESTINATION	PRICE	DURATION	SCHEDULE
Cancún (1st class)	US$6	2 hrs	12 times daily 7:15 A.M.-10 P.M.)
Cancún (2nd class)	US$5	2.5 hrs	16 times daily 6:25 A.M.-10:15 P.M.
Chetumal	US$13	3.5 hrs	six times daily 8:20 A.M.-4:25 P.M., plus 10 P.M.
Chichén Itzá	US$8.50	2.5 hrs	9 A.M. and 2:30 P.M.
Cobá	US$2.75	1 hr	7:30 A.M., 9 A.M., 10 A.M., 11 A.M., 5 P.M. and 6 P.M.
Carrillo Puerto	US$5	1 hr	8:20 A.M., 11:45 A.M., 12:50 P.M., 4:25 P.M. and 10 P.M.
Mérida	US$15.25	4 hrs	1:25 A.M., 12:25 P.M., and 2:30 P.M., and 7:40 P.M.
San Cristóbal, Chiapas	US$48.50	15 hrs	4:40 P.M. and 6:10 P.M.
Valladolid	US$4.50	2 hrs	1:25 A.M., 9 A.M., 12:25 P.M., and 2:30 P.M., and 7:40 P.M.
Xpujil	US$18.50	5 hrs	8:40 A.M., 1:25 P.M., 4:40 P.M. and 4:45 P.M.

Centauro, 8:30 A.M.–11:30 P.M. Mon.–Sat., 10 A.M.–4 P.M. Sun.) charges US$1.50 an hour for Internet, US$0.37 a minute for calls to the United States, and US$0.46 a minute to Europe.

Next to the grocery store at the turnoff to Cobá, **El Point** (tel. 984/871-2715, 8 A.M.–11 P.M. Mon.–Fri., 9 A.M.–9 P.M. Sat.–Sun.) has modern computers and a fast connection for US$2.25 a minute.

In the Zona Hotelera, **Cabañas Zahra** (7 A.M.–11 P.M. daily) has Internet access for US$3 per hour. Two coin-operated public phones are just outside the front door of **El Pipazo** market.

Post Office

The easy-to-miss post office is located on the north end of Avenida Tulum between Avenida Satelite and Calle Centauro (9 A.M.–4 P.M. Mon.–Fri.).

Launderette

Lava Easy (Av. Tulum between Av. Satelite

and Calle Centauro, 8 A.M.–8:30 P.M. Mon.–Sat.) charges US$1.50 per kilogram (2.2 pounds), with a three-kilogram (6.6-pound) minimum; two-hour rush service costs US$2.50 per kilogram, with a one-kilogram (2.2-pound) minimum.

Storage
The main bus terminal (open 24 hours) has luggage storage for US$0.50–0.75 an hour depending on the size of the bag.

GETTING THERE
Bus
Tulum's main bus terminal is at the south end of town, a block up from The Weary Traveler hostel. (If you're returning for the first time in a while, you're not losing your marbles: The terminal used to be on the other side of the street.)

White vans known as *combis* also go to Cobá (and all the spots in between), albeit less frequently. Catch them at the intersection of Highway 307 and the Cobá/Boca Paila road (US$2, one hour).

Combis
By now you probably know about *combis,* white collective vans that zip between Tulum and Playa del Carmen (US$2.50, 50 min) all day, every day. They leave more frequently than buses, and are handier for intermediate stops, like Hidden Worlds, Dos Ojos, Akumal, and Xpu-Ha. Flag them down anywhere on Avenida Tulum or Highway 307.

Car
Highway 307 passes right through the middle of Tulum Pueblo. Whether heading south from Cancún or Playa del Carmen, or north from Chetumal and Carrillo Puerto, you can't miss it.

GETTING AROUND
Bicycle
A high-end bike shop, **Iguana Bike Shop** (Av. Satélite near Calle Andromeda, tel. 984/119-0836, hugo_bike@hotmail.com, 9 A.M.–7 P.M. Mon.–Sat.) rents beach cruisers (US$4.75/24 hours) and mountain bicycles (US$10–14/24 hours) in excellent condition. Rates included a helmet, front and back lights, lock, basket, as well as life and accident insurance. English spoken.

Car
Tulum Pueblo is very walkable, but if you're staying in the Zona Hotelera—or plan to go there during your stay—a car will come in very handy. It's three kilometers (2 miles) just to the coast, and significantly farther to many of the hotels and best beaches.

Taxi
Taxis are plentiful and fares run about US$2 in town and US$3–8 to get to the Zona Hotelera (depending where exactly you're going). In the Zona Hotelera, there is a taxi stand at the mini-village area; rates are roughly the same, within the Zona Hotelera or back into Tulum Pueblo. From either area, a ride to Tulum ruins costs about US$3, and US$55 to the Cancún airport.

Sian Ka'an Biosphere Reserve

Sian Ka'an is Maya for "where the sky is born," and it's not hard to see how the original inhabitants arrived at such a poetic name. The unkempt beaches, blue-green sea, bird-filled wetlands and islets, and humble accommodations are manna for bird-watchers, artists, snorkelers, and kayakers. But most of the visitors come here for the fishing—Sian Ka'an is one of the best fly-fishing spots in the world, especially for the "big three" catches: bonefish, tarpon, and permit.

The reserve was created in 1986, designated a UNESCO World Heritage Site in 1987, and expanded in 1994. It now encompasses around 1.3 million acres of coastal and mangrove forests, wetlands, and some 113 kilometers (70

TULUM AND QUINTANA ROO

miles) of pristine coral reefs just offshore. A huge variety of flora and fauna thrive in the reserve, including four species of mangrove, many medicinal plants, and about 300 species of birds, including toucans, parrots, frigate birds, herons, and egrets. Monkeys, foxes, crocodiles, and boa constrictors also populate the reserve, and are spotted by locals and visitors with some regularity. Manatees and jaguars are the reserve's largest animals, but also the most reclusive: You need sharp eyes and a great deal of luck to spot either one. More than 20 Maya ruins have been found in the reserve, though most are unexcavated.

A long spit of land extends south from Tulum, separating the ocean from a tangle of lagoons, mangroves, and channels. At the far end is tiny **Punta Allen** (pop. 400, also known as Rojo Gómez), where around 100 families survive by lobster fishing and (increasingly) tourism—not surprisingly, many of the local young men have become uncannily sharp fly-fishing guides.

Spending a few days in Sian Ka'an is the best way to really appreciate its beauty and pace. Hotels and tour operators there can arrange fishing, bird-watching, and other tours, all with experienced local guides. But if time is short, a number of tour operators in Tulum offer day trips into the reserve as well.

SIGHTS
Muyil Archaeological Zone

The most accessible Maya site within the Sian Ka'an reserve is Muyil (Hwy. 307, 25 km/15.5 mi south of Tulum, 8 A.M.–5 P.M. daily, US$2.50), on the western edge of the park. Also known as Chunyaxche, it is one of the oldest archaeological sites in the Maya world, dating back to 300 B.C. and occupied continuously through the Conquest.

Resting on the edge of a limestone shelf near Laguna Muyil (aka Laguna Chunyaxche), the site is believed to have been an ancient Maya seaport. Only a small portion of the city has been excavated, however, so it makes for a relatively quick visit. There are six main structures ranging from two-meter-high (6.6-foot) plat-

© LIZA PRADO

A small site, Muyil has a handful of excavated structures.

forms to the impressive **Castillo** (Castle). At 17 meters (51 feet), it is one of the tallest structures on the peninsula's Caribbean coast. The Castillo is topped with a unique solid round masonry turret from which the waters of the Caribbean Sea can be seen. Unfortunately, climbing it is prohibited.

A *sacbé* (raised stone road) runs about a half kilometer (a third of a mile) from the center of the site to the edge of the lagoon. Part of this *sacbé* is on private property, however, so if you want to walk to the lagoon from the ruins there is an additional—and hefty—charge of US$3.75 per person. Along the way, there is a lookout tower, which adds some bang to your buck.

Boat tours on the lagoon also are offered for US$25 per group; a pleasant way to enjoy the water, you'll also get a view of several otherwise inaccessible ruins along the edge of the water. Visitors can either walk to the lagoon on the *sacbé* mentioned here or can drive there for free. Follow the signs on Highway 307, just south of the entrance to the archaeological site.

Ascension Bay

Ascension Bay covers about 20 square kilometers (12.4 square miles) and its shallow flats and tangled mangrove islands teem with bonefish, tarpon, and huge permit—some of the biggest ever caught, in fact. It is a fly fisher's dream come true, and it has been attracting anglers from around the world since the mid-1980s. And not just guys in waders—the spin fishing is fantastic, too, and the offshore reef yields plenty of grouper, barracuda, *dorado,* tuna, sailfish, and marlin.

SPORTS AND RECREATION
Sport Fishing

Ascension Bay has world-class fishing. All of the hotels listed in this section arrange tours, and most specialize in it, using their own boats and guides.

Bird-Watching and Ecotours

Sian Ka'an is also an excellent place for bird-watching. Trips to Bird Island and other spots afford a look at various species of water birds—in the winter, male frigates show off their big red balloonlike breasts. Tours often combine bird-watching with time snorkeling and walking around one or more bay islands. Hotels in Punta Allen and along the coastal road can arrange tours, as do outfits in Tulum.

ACCOMMODATIONS

Punta Allen is the only real town on the peninsula and has the most options for lodging, food, tours, and other services. A smattering of lodges and private homes are on the long unpaved road to Punta Allen; the nearest to Tulum, Boca Paila Camps, just four well-maintained kilometers (2.5 miles) from the entrance of the reserve, is also perhaps the best. Past Boca Paila—an inlet between the ocean and the lagoon, spanned by a bridge—you'll see a lot of deserted coastline and not much else until reaching Punta Allen.

Road to Punta Allen

Boca Paila Camps (four km/2.5 mi south of the entrance to the reserve, tel. 984/871-2499, www.cesiak.org, US$73–95, including continental breakfast) is perfect for eco-minded travelers looking for an outdoorsy experience with the comforts of a Caribbean vacation. Spacious "tent cabins"—heavy-duty canvas tents set on platforms—are surprisingly comfortable, with real beds, quality linens, and tasteful decor, including hand-painted headboards. Cabins are spread well apart, and have private terraces with views of the Caribbean or lagoon. Shared bathrooms are spotless and have rainwater showers, modern compost toilets, and 24-hour lighting. The cabins themselves don't have electricity, but guests are provided with candles and battery-powered lamps. The main building, completely solar- and wind-powered, houses a good restaurant too. Operated by CE-SiaK, an environmental foundation that offers excellent kayak and bird-watching tours, it also rents bikes and kayaks to guests so that they can explore the lagoon on their own.

Eight kilometers (five miles) before Punta Allen, **Rancho Sol Caribe** (fanny@cancun.net, www.locogringo.com/siankaan/sol-caribe.html, US$107 s/d, US$162/135 s/d per person all-inclusive) has four comfortable cabañas, each with two double beds, private hot-water bathroom, patio with hammocks and chairs, and 24-hour electricity. The hotel owners organize sport- and fly-fishing trips, departing from a private pier on the lagoon. Fishing trips can be combined with lodging and meal packages—email for rates and availability. Snorkeling, bird-watching, and other boat tours also can be arranged. Transfer to and from Cancún International Airport is included for all-inclusive guests staying seven-plus nights.

Also north of town is **Ascension Bay Beach Club** (toll-free U.S. tel. 866/787-9676, www.letitbeinn.com, three nights/two days fishing US$2,395 s, US$1,100 pp d; seven nights/six days fishing US$3,595 s, US$2,400 pp d). It has just three oceanfront *palapa* cabañas, each with two beds, private hot-water bathroom, tile floors, and a porch with chairs and hammocks. With a maximum of just six guests at any one time, the hosts give friendly and personalized service. Everything here is geared toward anglers, down

TULUM AND QUINTANA ROO

TULUM AND QUINTANA ROO

© LIZA PRADO

Sian Ka'an has miles of little-visited beaches.

to rod racks in the cabins and beers and fly-tying in the main cabin. Fishing trips begin at 7:30 A.M. and don't return until 4:30 P.M., with a prepacked lunch and a cooler full of drinks onboard. Visits typically run Friday-to-Friday, including airport pickup at the Cancún Airport; shorter stays begin and end on Saturdays.

Punta Allen

One of the original fishing lodges in town, **Cuzan Guesthouse** (tel. 983/834-0358, www .flyfishmx.com, US$30–90 s/d, four nights/three days fishing US$1,358 s, US$1,289 pp d; seven nights/six days fishing US$2,158 s, US$2,089 pp d) still has a loyal following despite the ever-growing pool of competitors. Basic *palapa*-roofed wood cabañas have private bathrooms, porches with hammocks, and ocean views. The hotel also boasts one of the best restaurants in town. Beyond fishing trips, Cuzan Guesthouse also can arrange bird-watching, snorkeling, and kayaking tours.

About 100 meters (328 feet) from the beach **Posada Sirena** (tel. 984/877-8521, www.casa sirena.com, US$30–50 s/d) offers large, simple "Robinson Crusoe-style" bungalows. Each sleeps up to eight people and have private bathrooms and fully equipped kitchens. All-day fly-fishing trips run US$140 per person or US$190 for solo anglers. Half- and full-day tours of the bay, including snorkeling and bird-watching also can be arranged.

On the coastal road just past Punta Allen, **Serenidad Shardon** (tel. 984/876-1827, www .shardon.com, US$10 dorm, US$80–90 s/d with kitchen, US$100 large room maximum eight guests, US$150 two-bedroom apartment) offers a variety of accommodations for all sorts of budgets; rooms vary from dorms with shared bathrooms to private cabañas with fully equipped kitchens. Right on the beach, Serenidad Shardon makes a good place to just kick back and relax. If you want a little more action, the owners are also happy to arrange area tours.

FOOD

Punta Allen isn't a foodie's village but it does have a handful of eateries in town, all specializing in fresh seafood. A few mini-marts and a bakery round things out a bit, especially if you're planning on staying more than a couple days. Most of the hotels also offer meal plans.

Restaurants

◖ Cuzan Guest House's (8 A.M.–9 P.M. daily, US$5–15) sand-floor restaurant may be the best in town. Beyond mouthwatering seafood dishes (the ceviche is a must), the menu has a good variety of Mexican and Yucatecan cuisine—all cooked with fresh herbs and spices.

With a beautiful view of the Caribbean, **Muelle Viejo** (near the main pier, 11 A.M.–10 P.M. Mon.–Sat.) is an excellent choice for seafood and enjoying a breezy evening with a beer.

Chary's, near the central plaza, is a locals' joint with good, cheap eats.

Worth the drive back toward Tulum, the restaurant at **Boca Paila Camps** (8 A.M.–9 P.M. daily, US$5–15) serves an unexpectedly creative menu, including cilantro fish fillet and nopal (cactus) salad. Tables are set up on the rooftop patio—come for lunch or an early dinner for stunning views of the lagoon to the west and the Caribbean to the east.

Groceries

Tienda Socorro (one block south of the central plaza) is one of a few mini-marts that sells basic food stuff and snacks.

INFORMATION AND SERVICES

Don't expect much in the way of services in Sian Ka'an—if there is something you can't do without, definitely bring it with you. There are **no banking services** and none of the hotels or tour operators accept credit cards. Punta Allen does have a modest **medical clinic** and **pharmacy.** A few local entrepreneurs buy **gas** in Tulum and sell it for a small premium, and most hotels offer laundry service.

GETTING THERE

Many of the hotels include airport pickup/drop-off, which is convenient and helps avoid paying for a week's car rental when you plan on fishing all day. That said, a car is useful if you'd like to do some exploring on your own.

Bus

The only public transportation to Punta Allen is from Carrillo Puerto, via the village of Playón. Shuttles to Playón (US$10, two hours, 9:30 A.M. and 3 P.M.) leave Carrillo Puerto twice daily from a stop kitty-corner to the market area; look for a "Playón" sign in front of a hair salon). From there you take a water taxi across the lagoon to Punta Allen (US$2 pp, 10 minutes, 6 A.M.–10 P.M. daily). On the return trip, shuttles leave Playón at 5 A.M. for Tulum, and 6:30 A.M. and 3:30 P.M. to Carrillo Puerto.

Car

There are two good ways to enter the reserve. The first entrance is about eight kilometers (five miles) south of the Tulum ruins on the Zona Hotelera/Boca Paila road. From the control kiosk—where you pay a US$2 park fee—it's almost 60 kilometers (37 miles) of unpaved and sometimes rutted road to Punta Allen. The drive is no piece of cake, with sections of deep mud and others of deep sand. A four-wheel drive is best, but an ordinary car can make it as long at it hasn't rained in the last 2–3 days. If you get stuck, you may have to wait several hours before another vehicle passes. Leave early, and fill up on gas before leaving Tulum.

The other entrance is from the west, off Highway 307 between Tulum and Carrillo Puerto. From Tulum, go south of Highway 307 for 24 kilometers (14.4 miles) to the Playón/Punta Allen turnoff—it's a tiny road and tiny sign, so keep your eyes peeled. (The turnoff is about two km/1.25 mi past a much more visible road and sign to the right for Chaccoben.) This is also a rough and sometimes muddy road but it's much shorter than the northern route. You weave through tangled wetlands to the port of Playón. From there, ferries take passengers across the bay to Punta Allen. You'll have to leave your car; someone in Playón usually watches vehicles, and theft isn't common, but don't tempt fate by leaving anything valuable in plain view.

Carrillo Puerto

Highway 307 from Tulum to Chetumal passes through Carrillo Puerto, a small city that holds little of interest to most travelers except to fill up on gas. Historically, however, it played a central role in the formation of Quintana Roo and the entire peninsula.

HISTORY

The town of Noj Kaj Santa Cruz (present-day Carrillo Puerto) was the center of a pivotal movement during the Caste War. As the Mayas lost ground in the war, two indigenous leaders enlisted a ventriloquist to introduce— or invent, to some—the *Cruz Parlante* (Talking Cross) in Noj Kaj Santa Cruz. The cross "spoke" to the battle-weary population, urging them to continue fighting, even issuing tactical orders and predicting victory in the long, bitter conflict. Thousands joined the sect of the cross, calling themselves Cruzob (People

of the Holy Cross, a conflation of Spanish *cruz* or "cross" and the Maya pluralization -*ob,* in this case, "people of"). Some accounts portray the talking cross as little more than political theater for a simpleminded audience, but it seems likely that many or most of the Cruzob understood the ruse behind the Talking Cross and saw it as a form of channeling or simply much-needed motivation. Whatever the case, it reinvigorated the Maya soldiers, and Noj Kaj Santa Cruz remained the last redoubt of organized indigenous resistance, finally submitting to federal troops in 1901. Today, the Talking Cross itself is housed in a small sanctuary in town.

The town's name was changed in 1934 in honor of a former governor of Quintana Roo, much revered by indigenous and working-class people for his progressive reforms, for which he was ultimately assassinated.

TULUM AND QUINTANA ROO

THE CASTE WAR

On July 18, 1847, a military commander in Valladolid learned of an armed plot to overthrow the government that was being planned by two indigenous men – Don Miguel Antonio Ay and Cecilio Chí. Ay was arrested and executed. Chí managed to escape punishment and on July 30, 1847, led a small band of armed men into the town of Tepich. Several officials and Euro-Mexican families were killed. The military responded with overwhelming force, burning villages, poisoning wells, and killing scores of people, including many women, children, and elderly. The massacre galvanized indigenous people across the peninsula, sparking what came to be called the Caste War.

Supplied with arms and ammunition from Britain, the indigenous troops tore through colonial cities, killing and even enslaving terrified non-Mayas. Valladolid was evacuated in 1848 and was left abandoned for nearly a year. By 1849, the peninsula's indigenous people, draw-

ing on centuries of misery and abuse, were close to expelling the colonial elite. However, as they were preparing their final assaults on Mérida and Campeche City, the rains came early, forcing the Maya soldiers to choose between victory and famine. The men returned to their fields to plant corn.

Mexican troops immediately took advantage of the lull, and the Mayas never regained the upper hand. For the next 13 years, captured indigenous soldiers (and increasingly *any* indigenous person) were sold to slave brokers and shipped to Cuba. Many Mayas eventually fled into the forests and jungles of southern Quintana Roo. The fighting was rekindled when a wooden cross in the town of Noj Kaj Santa Cruz (today, Carrillo Puerto) was said to be channeling the voice of God, urging the Mayas to keep fighting. The war ended, however, when troops took control of Noj Kaj Santa Cruz in 1901. An official surrender was signed in 1936.

SIGHTS

The **Santuario de la Cruz Parlante** (Calle 69 at Calle 60, irregular hours) is a sacred place where the Talking Cross and two smaller ones are housed in a small wooden church. Shoes and hats must be removed before entering. Ask permission before snapping any photographs.

Like many places of worship in the region, Carrillo Puerto's main church, the **Iglesia de Balam Nah** (central plaza) was built by slaves, but they weren't Maya or African. During the Caste War, indigenous troops captured Spaniards and white Mexicans, some of whom they enslaved and forced to work.

Despite outward appearances, Maya nationalism is still very much alive and aware of the sometimes invasive effects of mass tourism. Check out the beautifully painted **mural** in the central plaza that reads: *La zona Maya no es un museo etnográfico, es un pueblo en marcha* (The Maya region is not an ethnographic museum, it is a people marching forward).

ACCOMMODATIONS

Owned and operated by one of the founding families of the city, **Hotel Esquivel** (Calle 63 between Calles 66 and 68, tel. 983/834-0344, esquivelhotel@quintanaroo.com, US$23–28 s/d, US$30–35 s/d with A/C, US$46 s/d with a/c and kitchenette) offers 37 rooms in four buildings, each with private bathroom and cable TV. The main building has by far the best rooms—gleaming tile floors, simple furnishings, decent beds, and some with small balconies overlooking a pleasant park. The property across the street—once the family home called La Casona—is pretty sad. Dilapidated and dark, they're clean enough to be acceptable in a pinch.

FOOD

 La Casona (5:30 P.M.–midnight daily, US$5–10) opens right onto the central plaza and offers excellent Mexican fare at reasonable prices. Although it's not obvious, this is actually part of the Hotel Esquivel—you can reach the restaurant from the plaza or from the other side by going through the hotel.

El Faisán y el Venado (Av. Benito Juárez at Calle 67, tel. 983/834-0043, 6 A.M.–10 P.M. daily, US$5–7) is Carrillo Puerto's best-known restaurant, as much for its location and longevity than for any particular noteworthiness of its food. The menu is mostly reliable Yucatecan standards, including 8–10 variations each of fish, chicken, and beef, plus soup and other sides.

INFORMATION
Tourist Information

Although the tourist office (Av. Benito Juárez at Av. Santiago, 9 A.M.–4 P.M. Mon.–Fri.) is relatively helpful, the city's official website, **www.fcarrillopuerto.com.mx**, is an especially good source of information, if you can get it to load.

Hospitals

The Hospital General (Calle 51 between Av. Benito Juárez and Calle 68, tel. 983/834-0092) is open 24 hours daily.

Pharmacies

Farmacia Similares (Av. Benito Juárez at Av. Lázaro Cárdenas, tel. 983/834-1407) is open 8 A.M.–10:30 P.M. Monday–Saturday and 9 A.M.–10:30 P.M. on Sunday.

Police

The police department (central plaza, 983/834-0369, 24 hours daily) is located in the *Palacio Municipal* (city hall).

SERVICES
Money

Next to the Pemex station, **HSBC** (Av. Benito Juárez at Calle 69, 8 A.M.–7 P.M. Mon.–Sat.) has one 24-hour ATM.

Internet

Facing the central plaza, **Balam 'Nah Internet** (tel. 983/834-1026, 7 A.M.–1 A.M. Mon.–Fri., 8 A.M.–1 A.M. Sat.–Sun.) charges US$0.75 an hour for Internet access.

Post Office

The post office (Calle 69 between Calles 64 and 66) is open 9 A.M.–4 P.M. weekdays.

CARRILLO PUERTO BUS SCHEDULES

DESTINATION	PRICE	DURATION	SCHEDULE
Bacalar	US$5	1.5-2 hrs	take any Chetumal bus
Cancún	US$9-US$12*	3.5-4 hrs	30-60 min. 12:30 A.M.-9:30 P.M.
Chetumal	US$6-8*	2-2.5 hrs	every 30-90 min. 5:45 A.M.-11:15 P.M.
Mahahual	US$5.50	2 hrs	3 A.M. and 10:30 A.M.
Mérida	US$11-13*	5-6 hrs	13 departures 12:30 A.M.-7:15 P.M.
Ticul	US$9	4 hrs	take any Mérida bus
Tulum	US$4.50	1 hr	take any Cancún bus
Valladolid	US$6	2 hrs	9 A.M.-4:30 P.M.
Xpujil	US$15	5 hrs	6:15 P.M.

*Denotes first class service; not available for all departures.

GETTING THERE
Bus

Carrillo Puerto's main bus terminal (tel. 983/834-0815) is just off the central plaza, with new service to Mahahual, and long-standing routes to Cancún, Chetumal, Mérida, and elsewhere.

Car

Fill your gas tank in Carrillo Puerto, especially if you're headed to Mahahual, Xcalak, Xpujil, or Ticul. There are other roadside gas stations ahead (and in Chetumal), but they get less and less reliable—having either no gas or no electricity to pump it—just as the stretches of empty highway grow longer and longer.

La Costa Maya

The coastline south of Tulum loops and weaves like the tangled branches of the mangrove trees that blanket much of it. It is a mosaic of savannas, marshes, lagoons, scattered islands, and three huge bays: Bahía de la Ascensión, Bahía del Espiritu Santo, and Bahía de Chetumal. Where it's not covered by mangroves, the shore has sandy beaches and dunes, and just below the turquoise sea is one of the least impacted sections of the great Mesoamerican Coral Reef. Dozens of Maya sites have been located here, but few excavated, and much remains unknown about pre-Hispanic life here. During the conquest, the snarled coastal forest proved an effective sanctuary for indigenous rebels and refugees fleeing Spanish control, not to mention a haven for pirates, British logwood cutters, and Belizean anglers.

In the 1990s, Quintana Roo officials launched an effort to develop the state's southern coast, which was still extremely isolated despite the breakneck development taking place in and around Cancún. (It has always been a famous fly-fishing area, however.) The first order of business was to construct a huge cruise ship port, which they did in the tiny fishing village of Mahahual. They also needed a catchy name: Riviera Maya was already taken, so this area was dubbed the Costa Maya. The moniker applies to the coastal areas south of Tulum, especially the Sian Ka'an Biosphere Reserve; the towns of Mahahual and Xcalak; Laguna Bacalar; and Chetumal, the state capital and by far the largest city in the area. Few locals use it.

Okay, it's hard not to be cynical when cruise ships lumber into this remote stretch of the Caribbean, and their passengers belly about Mahahual, beer bottles in hand. Then again, it's doubtful the area would have paved roads, power lines, or telephone service if not for the cruise ships. Driving the rutted coastal road to Xcalak—an even smaller town south of Mahahual—took a half-day or more; today, a two-lane paved road has cut the trip to under an hour. The state government has vowed to control development by limiting hotel size and density; monitoring construction methods; and protecting the mangroves and coral reef. Small eco-friendly B&Bs have thrived, not surprisingly, and more and more independent travelers are drawn to the Costa Maya for its quiet isolation and pristine natural beauty.

MAHAHUAL

Mahahual is a place of two faces—cruise ship days, when the town's one road is packed with day-trippers looking to buy T-shirts and throw back a beer or two; and non-cruise ship days, when Mahahual is sleepy and laid-back and the narrow, seaweed-strewn beaches are free to walk for miles. Whether you stay here a night or a week, you're likely to see both. It's a good thing. You can be in a major party zone one day, and the next be the only snorkeler

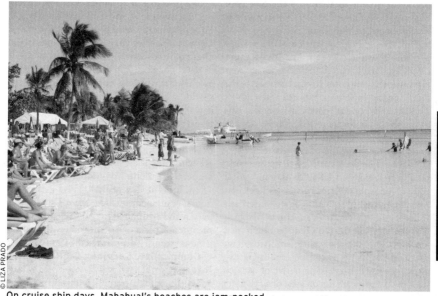

© LIZA PRADO

On cruise ship days, Mahahual's beaches are jam-packed.

in town—all without changing hotels. If what you seek are long quiet days every day, definitely stay outside of town. You'll see a few ATVers flying by now and again but that's as much partying as you'll see.

Orientation

Mahahual is pretty easy to manage. Most of its hotels and services are located on the sand road that runs through town and south along the coast. One inland street runs parallel to this coastal road, you'll find a supermarket and the police station on it. Just northwest of town, the tiny residential community of Nuevo Mahahual (aka Las Casitas) has a good supermarket, a few decent restaurants, and a launderette. To get there, head west on the paved road that leads out of town and turn north at the Nuevo Mahahual sign.

Sports and Recreation

Scuba Diving: Mahahual has terrific diving on the coral reef just off shore, with dozens of sites a short boat ride away. It's also one of two jumping-off points for trips to Chinchorro Bank, the largest coral atoll in the Northern Hemisphere. The other departure point is Xcalak, south of Mahahual.

Don't be deterred by the slew of cruise shippers who crowd into **Dreamtime Dive Resort** (Av. Mahahual Km. 2.5, 983/834-5823, www.dreamtimediving.com) almost every day—the shop is an indy operation at heart, and sends its students and "regular" guests on separate boats in groups of six divers or less. On non-cruise ship days, instructors may take small groups to unchartered portions of the reef for exploratory trips. Fun dives cost US$40 for one tank, US$75 for two, and US$25 a day for rental equipment. Snorkel trips run US$35 per person, including equipment. Open-water, advanced, and other courses are also available.

Bucanero del Caribe (Tequila Beach pier, tel. 983/120-5306, www.bucanerodiving.com, 9 A.M.–4 P.M. daily) is run by Arturo García, a friendly English-speaking native of Mexico City. He offers great rates on local dives (US$65 two tanks, including gear), plus trips to Chin-

chorro and other distant sites. Tequila Beach is a beach club just outside of Mahahual proper, catering to cruise shippers, though García's trips can be personalized for indy travelers.

Blue Ocean Safari (Av. Mahahual Km 1.6, 983/834-5742, www.blueoceansafari .com) operates in affiliation with the Luna de Plata hotel and offers fun dives and courses for similar prices. Ask for Phil or Julie, or at Luna de Plata.

Snorkeling: You can rent snorkel gear for around US$10 a day from a number of kiosks that pop up on cruise ship days and swim or kayak out to the reef. However, you'll see more on a guided tour—not every spot on the reef is worth snorkeling—and have extra safety and convenience.

Mahahual's dive shops all offer snorkel trips for around US$35 per person. Or contact Joaquín Corrales Solís, aka **Huacho** (Av. Mahahual Km. 9, brumars@hotmail.com), a friendly, English-speaking former diver who leads custom snorkeling tours, also for US$35 per person. Most trips last four-plus hours, and guests can set the agenda, whether it's maximum snorkeling time or a more laid-back outing including lunch and sunbathing on an isolated beach. Huacho typically stops by hotels to talk to new arrivals, or you (or your hotel) can contact him ahead of time to arrange a trip.

Kiteboarding: Kiteboarding has taken off as one of the hottest new wind sports in the world; with optimal winds between January–April, Mahahual is a good place to learn or practice. You can rent kiteboarding equipment or take lessons from Luca Sancinelli, an experienced kiteboarder and Italian expatriate who runs the gelateria and kiteboarding school, **Kite Zone** (Av. Mahahual, 983/130-7898, luca4685@virgilio.it). Five classes (10 hours, equipment included) run US$200 per person and are limited to two students. Equipment rental costs US$40 per hour, with an additional security deposit of US$100.

Community Service: Global Vision International (www.gvi.co.uk, 984/116-4208) operates a popular volunteer-for-pay program in Mahahual, in partnership with

© LIZA PRADO

Whether or not there is a ship in town, kayaking is a favorite activity.

Amigos de Sian Ka'an, a local nonprofit. GVI "expeditions," as they are called, typically last 5–10 weeks and require open-water diver certification. The Mahahual center (Av. Mahahual s/n) has a dorm for around 12 volunteers, plus cold-water bathrooms and a community kitchen. Fees are not cheap: US$2,500 for five weeks, US$4,450 for 10 weeks, including room board and equipment, but not airfare. Advance registration is required, as the center is not designed to handle walk-ins. GVI has programs in Tulum and Sian Ka'an Biosphere as well.

Shopping

Mahahual is no shopper's heaven—pretty much all you'll see are folding tables laden with knickknacky souvenirs that are set up on the main drag. The one exception—and a pricey one—is **El Ziricote** (Av. Mahahual, just south of Kite Zone, 9 A.M.–5:30 P.M. Mon.–Fri., 9 A.M.–noon Sat.), which has mostly high-end handicrafts from the states of Chiapas and Michoacán. It's definitely worth at least a peek to check out the beauties that are created in other parts of the country.

Accommodations

UNDER US$25

Recently renovated, **Las Cabañas del Doctor** (Av. Mahahual between Calles 2 and 4, tel. 983/832-2102, primomm@hotmail.com, US$4.75 pp camping, US$24 s/d with bathroom, US$33 s/d with shared bathroom) offers spotless *palapa*-roofed bungalows across from the town beach. All have cement walls, tile floors, and fans. Campers (BYO gear) set up on grassy areas on the lot and share cold-water bathrooms with the guests in bungalows. An excellent value.

US$25-50

Another excellent value, **Kohunbeach Cabañas** (Carr. Antigua Km. 7, no phone, www.kohunbeach.o-f.com, US$37 s/d) offers three spacious and modern cabañas that have comfortable queen beds with beautifully hand-carved headboards, picture windows with views

TULUM AND QUINTANA ROO

of the Caribbean, and mosaic tile bathrooms. Each is spotless and solar powered. Continental breakfast is included in the rate and is served under a huge *palapa*. Kayaks also are available for guest use. If you make online reservations, be sure to email well in advance—the owner doesn't check email daily.

Xiq'ita Kabah-Nah (Carr. Antigua Km. 8, tel. 983/700-5917, www.kabahna.com, US$35 s/d with shared bath, US$40 s/d with private bath) has five simple *palapa* cabañas, each with two beds, concrete floors, and good mosquito nets. Three have clean, brightly painted private bathrooms; the others share a bathroom that could use a scrubbing. Bring a good book as you'll surely while away an afternoon or two in the beachside hammocks. The beach here isn't fantastic—few in this area are—but the seaweed and driftwood manage to complement the hotel's rustic, laid-back atmosphere. There's also a simple boho-style restaurant that offers light meals.

US$50-100

One of Mahahual's finest hotels, **⬤ Balamkú** (Av. Mahahual Km. 5.7, tel. 983/839-5332, www.balamku.com, US$75 s/d including breakfast) combines comfort and style with ecological awareness, and at a great price to boot. Rooms occupy a series of circular two-story buildings and are spacious, clean and artfully decorated with Mexican and Guatemalan *artesanía*. The friendly Canadian owners have eschewed diesel generators and septic tanks for solar panels, wind turbines, and a nonpolluting wastewater system—ask for a short tour of the green technology used here. A full breakfast is included, and guests have free use of the hotel's wireless Internet, kayaks, and library, with plenty of books, board games, and music. Yoga classes, snorkeling tours, and other outings are described in a binder at reception, and can be arranged by the hotel.

A peaceful spot along the coast, **⬤ Maya Luna** (Av. Mahahual Km. 5.6, tel. 983/836-0905, www.hotelmayaluna.com, US$65/75 s/d) offers four modern bungalows, all with 24-hour solar/wind power, rainwater showers, and *palapa*-shaded porches. Each has a fantastic mural depicting a different regional scene—Banco Chinchorro and a set of ruins in the jungle, for instance. Best of all, each unit has a private rooftop terrace with glorious views of the Caribbean in front, and the jungle in back; lounge chairs and hammocks make it an easy place to while away a few hours with a good book and a drink. A hearty and healthy breakfast also is included in the rate. An excellent value.

One of the only hotels offering rooms with fully equipped kitchens, **Margarita del Sol** (Av. Mahahual Km. 7, www.margaritadelsol.com, US$95 studio) is a perfect option if you want to save a bit and cook on the road. The units themselves are spacious and very modern in style; each has an eating area, a private porch or terrace with an ocean view, and features like wireless Internet and DVD players (there's a decent library of DVDs). Use of kayaks and snorkel gear also is included.

Dreamtime Dive Resort (US$65 d) has eight free-standing wooden cabañas—six with two beds and two with king-size beds—surrounding a palm-shaded sandy lot; all have a ceiling fan, a painted stucco interior, and a private front patio. Breakfast is included, served in the lodgelike main building, which also has wireless Internet (BYO laptop). There's an okay beach in front, and a better one a short walk away. Most guests here are divers, or learning to dive, but not exclusively so. Guests of the resort receive a 10 percent discount on all trips, including snorkeling.

A friendly Italian couple runs **Luna de Plata** (Av. Mahahual Km. 2, tel. 983/834-5741, www.lunadeplata.info, US$40–80 d), a popular place with a restaurant in front and seven hotel rooms in back. All have plain but tasteful decor, like ruddy ceramic floors and painted *talavera* sinks, and simple boxy furniture, including firm wood-frame beds. Hot water, ceiling fan, and wireless Internet cover the basic creature comforts. Town is a pleasant walk away, while a patch of beach and a dive shop in front give you plenty of reason to stay nearby.

Right in the middle of town, **La Posada de Los 40 Cañones** (tel. 983/834-5803, www.los 40canones.com, US$70 standard, US$80 superior, US$160 suite) has fared better than its namesake, the best-known shipwreck off Chinchorro Bank. Smallish standard rooms have comfy beds, modern baths, and a clean, bright feel. Superior rooms and two huge suites have more artful decor—the hanging beds are very Tulumesque—and extras like king-size beds, jet baths, and (for one) a big private patio. All have mini-split air-conditioners, but only numbers 2 and 8 have full sea views—get 'em if you can. The rooms form a horseshoe around an attractive entrance and patio area. The hotel also has an Internet café, a recommended restaurant, and a beach area with chairs and full bar across the street.

At three stories high, **Arrecifes** (Av. Mahahual Km. 2.5, tel. 983/834-5956, arrecifescostamaya@prodigy.net.mx, US$80 d, US$100 d with ocean view) is a veritable skyscraper in low-lying Mahahual. Its gleaming white exterior gives way to 10 plain but very clean and comfortable rooms, all with two double beds, wireless Internet, and mini-split air-conditioners (6 P.M.–8 A.M. only), but no TV. The manager, a former dive instructor, can arrange snorkel and fishing trips; if he's not at reception, check one of the stools at the beach bar (also part of the hotel) across the street.

OVER US$100

About 21 kilometers (12.5 miles) north of Mahahual, **Mayan Beach Garden Inn** (no tel., www.mayanbeachgarden.com, US$103 s/d, US$146 suite) has five spacious cabañas with 24-hour solar power. Simple but pleasing, each has whitewashed walls, Mexican-style decor, and thick mattresses. All also have gorgeous ocean views from private porches. A hearty breakfast is included in the rate, as is use of the kayaks. All-inclusive meal packages are available and, if you don't want to venture far, a must (the nearest restaurant is in Mahahual). In the high season, there's a three-night minimum.

Food

Just outside of town, **Luna de Plata** (Av. Mahahual Km. 2, tel. 983/834-5741, 11:30 A.M.–3:30 P.M. and 6 P.M.–midnight daily, US$4–15) serves tasty and well-prepared Italian dishes, from a slice of good, crispy pizza to fresh-made pasta with shrimp or lobster. There are a few international variations as well, such as veggie curry pasta, and a full bar. The Italian owners also operate the **Blue Iguana** (8 A.M.–6 P.M. daily, US$3–5), right across the street and a great spot for breakfast.

Toward the southern end of town, but still very much in the thick of things, little **Casa del Mar** (7 A.M.–9 P.M. daily, US$3–6) serves sandwiches, waffles, beer-batter shrimp tacos (the specialty), and other cheap eats perfect for the beach. A cook shack on the inland side of the road has a handful of tables, or you can eat in the restaurant's small beach area. Beer and cocktails also served.

In Nuevo Mahahual, **Aroma** (Av. Paseo del Puerto, 7 A.M.–noon and 5 P.M.–midnight, Sun.–Fri., US$4–13) is a cool corner bistro, open to the street on two sides, with plastic tables and chairs before a open kitchen. An international menu offers respite from standard Mexican fare: gazpacho, mousaka, beef medallions in soy balsamic sauce. Worth the trip.

Around the corner from Aroma, **Restaurante Monserat** (Paseo Chac Choben at Av. Paseo del Puerto, 7 A.M.–9 P.M. daily, US$4–10) serves up Mahahual's best tacos and other authentic Mexican dishes, in a large no-frills, family-friendly dining area. Service can be abrupt, but it's all part of the experience.

The restaurant at ◖ **La Posada de Los 40 Cañones** (center of town, 7:30–10:30 A.M., 12:30–2:30 P.M., 7–9 P.M. Mon.–Sat., 7:30 A.M.–11 P.M. Sun., US$5–15) serves breakfasts of various international extractions: the Italian is bread and Nutella, the Mexican is eggs any way you like, the American is pancakes and bacon. For lunch or dinner, choose among items like fajitas, grilled fish, and homemade pasta, which comes with your choice of sauce, from olive oil and garlic to shrimp and lobster sauce. Eat on the shaded patio for entertaining people-watching.

◖ Travel In' (Carr. Antigua Km. 6, 8 A.M.–12:30 P.M. and 5:30 P.M.–11 P.M. Mon.–Sat., US$4–15) is a great little restaurant a few kilometers down the coastal road. Pita bread is baked fresh daily and makes for great sandwiches—hamburger, fish, BLT, etc.—as well as a curious but tasty "pita pizza." The curry is popular here, and daily seafood specials vary according to the day's catch and what's available in town. Well worth the walk (or ride) down the coast.

For groceries, the best mini-mart is **Los Hermanos Martín** (Paseo Chac Choben, 8 A.M.–11 P.M. daily) in Nuevo Mahahual. If you just need the basics, try **Chepemart** (6:30 A.M.–9 P.M. daily), which is located on the sand road that runs parallel to Avenida Mahahual.

Information and Services

Cruise ships have brought considerable modernization to this once-isolated fishing village, but tourist services are still somewhat limited, including no bank, ATM, or post office.

Hospitals: The **Centro de Salud** (8 A.M.–2:30 P.M. daily, after 5 P.M. emergencies only) is located two blocks from the beach, on the road to the elementary school.

Pharmacies: Farmacia del Caribe (9 A.M.–9 P.M. Mon.–Fri., until 5 P.M. Sat.) is on Avenida Paseo del Puerto in Nuevo Mahahual, three blocks from the turnoff on the left.

Police: The police department (toll-free tel. 066, 24 hours daily) is located on the sand road that runs parallel to the main drag in town.

Internet and Telephone: Check email and make international phone calls at **Mobius Playa Internet** (tel. 983/834-5973, 9 A.M.–9 P.M. Mon.–Sat.) inside La Posada de Los 40 Cañones. Internet is US$3 an hour, and calls to the United States and Europe are US$0.30–0.60 a minute. A number of restaurants and beach bars (in addition to hotels) offer free wireless Internet to customers; just look for laptops and the bottles of *Leones* beer.

Launderette: Lavandería Lavahual (8 A.M.–2 P.M. and 5 P.M.–8 P.M. Mon.–Sat., and 8 A.M.–2 P.M. Sat.) is kitty-corner from Aroma restaurant, at the entrance to Nuevo Mahahual. Wash, dry, and fold is US$1.50 per kilogram (2.2 pounds) with a three kilogram (6.6 pound) minimum.

Getting There and Around

Just south of the grubby roadside town of Limones, a good paved road with signs to Mahahual breaks off Highway 307 and cuts through 58 kilometers (36 miles) of coastal forest and wetlands tangled with mangroves. It's a scenic stretch, whether in car or on a bus, along which you should see egrets, herons, and other water birds.

Bus: Mahahual's ADO "terminal" is a modest affair—an open-air lot near the entrance of town—but daily first-class service makes coming and going a breeze. Buses to Cancún (US$15.50, 5.5 hours) leave at 8:30 A.M. Monday–Saturday, 12:30 P.M. Sunday, and 5:30 P.M. daily, stopping at the major towns in between. To Chetumal (US$6.50, 2.5 hours) buses depart at 7:30 A.M., 1 P.M., and 6:30 P.M. daily, plus 10:30 A.M. and 3 P.M. on Sunday. The ticket booth is open a short time before and after scheduled departures only.

Taxi: Cabs abound in this town, especially on cruise ship days. In general, rates run US$1 per kilometer (1.6 miles).

Car: There is a **PEMEX** gas station (24 hours daily) on the main road to Mahahual, just east of the turnoff to Xcalak. It runs out of gas occasionally, so definitely fill your tank in Carrillo Puerto or Chetumal on your way here.

Mahahual proper is very walkable—in fact, town leaders are trying to have the beach-front road converted to a pedestrian walkway, and divert cars down the back street. However, if you're staying outside of town, you'll definitely need some wheels, whether car, scooter, bike, or taxi to get around.

XCALAK

The tiny fishing village of Xcalak lies just a short distance from the channel that marks the Mexico-Belize border, and a blessed long ways from anything else. The town started

© LIZA PRADO

Still relatively untouched, Xcalak's beaches and small eco-hotels make a perfect getaway.

out as a military outpost, and didn't get its first real hotel until Costa de Coco opened in 1988 (and still going strong, by the way). Villagers had to wait until another decade to get a paved road; before that, the only way in or out of town was by boat or via 55 kilometers (34 miles) of rutted beach tracks. Electrical lines were installed in 2004 but only in the village proper, so many outlying areas (including most of the better hotels) still rely on solar, wind, and generators. The town has no bank, no public phones, and no gas station. That is to say: Perfect!

The area doesn't have much beach but makes up for it with world-class fly-fishing, great snorkeling and diving, and a healthy coral reef and lagoon. A growing contingent of expats, mostly American and Canadian, have built homes, some for personal use, others for rent, others as small hotels. Large-scale tourism may be inevitable but still seems a long way off, and Xcalak remains a small and wonderfully laid-back place, perfect for those looking for some honest-to-goodness isolation.

Sports and Recreation

Scuba Diving and Snorkeling: The Xcalak Reef National Park (Parque Nacional Arrecifes de Xcalak) was established at the end of 2003, affording protection to the coastal ecosystem as well as Xcalak's nascent tourist economy. The park spans nearly 18,000 hectares (44,479 acres), from the Belize border well north of town, and includes the reef—and everything else down to 100 meters (328 feet)—as well as the shoreline and numerous inland lagoons. A US$4 a day fee technically applies to all divers and snorkelers (and kayakers and anglers); dive shops typically add it to their rates, while most hotels have a stack of wristband-permits to sell to guests snorkeling right from shore. The somewhat steep fee, uneven enforcement, and bonehead features like using paper wristbands that disintegrate in water have stirred some grumbling and scattered noncompliance by locals and hoteliers alike. With luck (and time) the problems will be resolved and everyone will contribute a fair share. For the time being, ask at your hotel for the latest.

The main coral reef lies just 90–180 meters (100–200) yards from shore and the water is less than 1.5 meters (five feet) deep almost the whole way out. Many snorkelers prefer the coral heads even closer to shore, which have plenty to see and less swell than the main reef. The shallow waters keep boat traffic to a minimum and anglers are good about steering clear of snorkelers (you should still stay alert at all times, however).

Divers and snorkelers can also explore the reef at around 20 official sites and many more unofficial ones. Most are a short distance from town, and shops typically return to port between tanks. "La Poza" is one of the more unique dives, drifting through a trench where hundreds, sometimes thousands, of tarpon congregate, varying in size from one-meter (three-foot) "juveniles" to two-meter (seven-foot) behemoths.

And, of course, there is **Banco de Chinchorro** (Chinchorro Bank), which is by some measurements the largest coral atoll in the Northern Hemisphere and a paradise for divers and snorkelers alike. About 48 kilometers (30 miles) northeast from Xcalak, Chinchorro is a marine reserve and is known for its spectacular coral formations, massive sponges, and abundant sealife. Scores of ships have foundered on the shallow reefs through the years, but (contrary to innumerable misreports) the wrecks cannot be dived. Not only are they protected as historical sites, most are on the eastern side of the atoll where the surf and currents are too strong for recreational diving. The famous "40 Cannons" wreck, in about three meters (10 feet) of water on the atoll's northwest side, is a good for snorkeling but not diving, and there are nowhere near 40 cannons there, thanks to looters. There are small government and fishermen's huts on one of the three cays, but tourists are not permitted to stay the night.

To get to Chinchorro, it's a 1.5–2-hour boat ride, which can be pretty punishing depending on conditions. You typically set out around 7:30 or 8 A.M., dive three tanks, have lunch onboard, and return to port around 4:30 or 5 P.M. Dive shops usually require at least four divers (or eight snorkelers) and may not go for days at a time if the weather is bad.

XTC Dive Center (north end of town, across bridge, www.xtcdivecenter.com, 9 A.M.–5 P.M. daily) is a full-service dive shop that specializes in trips to Chinchorro Bank; its acronym officially stands for "Xcalak to Chinchorro," though the ecstasy-inducing dives here certainly figured into the name. Trips to Chinchorro are US$160 per person for three tanks or US$100 per person for snorkelers, including lunch and drinks. Closer to home, reef dives cost US$45 for one tank, US$65 for two, and US$85 for three; equipment is an extra US$15 a day if you need it. Snorkel tours run US$25–50 per person depending on how long and far you go; five-hour trips include jaunts into the lagoon and Bird Island, which can be fascinating, especially in January and February when the birds are most plentiful. A 10 percent tax applies to most rates.

Costa de Cocos also offers diving, as does **Casa Carolina** though for its own guests only. Prices at all three shops are comparable.

Sport Fishing: Xcalak also has world-class sport fishing, with huge saltwater and brackish flats where hooking into the grand slam of fly-fishing—tarpon, bonefish, and permit—is by no means impossible. Add a snook and you've got a super slam. Oceanside, tarpon and barracuda abound, in addition to grouper, snapper, and others. **Costa de Cocos** is the area's only true fishing resort, with highly experienced guides and numerous magazine write-ups, including *Fly Rod & Reel* and *Gray's Sporting Journal*. Options range from half-day outings (US$175, including gear and guide) to 2–7-night packages including lodging, meals, open bar, and of course nonstop fishing (US$1,020–3,820). All the dive shops also arrange guided fishing tours.

Accommodations

Xcalak's most appealing accommodations are on the beach road heading north out of town. Few places accept credit cards on-site, but many have payment systems on their websites.

UNDER US$50

Right at the entrance of town, **Cabañas Tío Bon** (983/836-6954, US$23) are very basic but reasonably clean and the cheapest digs in town. Three pink-painted wooden cabins right alongside the owners' home—you share a front gate—have tiny private bathrooms, fan, and 24-hour electricity. A queen bed and a hammock mean up to three people can squeeze into each cabin. Plywood interior and lack of hot water will prevent any confusion between Uncle Bon's and the Westin.

US$50-100

Four cheerful units with fully equipped kitchenettes make **Casa Carolina** (2.5 km/1.6 mi north of town, no tel., www.casacarolina.net, US$95 s/d) a fine choice. Add perfect ocean views from the private balconies, free use of kayaks and bicycles, and a wide beach with palm trees, and you've got the formula for a relaxing beach vacation. Owner Bob Villier is an experienced NAUI dive instructor trainer and offers personalized certification classes plus diving and snorkeling trips. Continental breakfast, including divine homemade muffins, is included.

Hotel Tierra Maya (2.1 km/1.3 mi north of town, toll-free U.S. tel. 800/216-1902, www.tierramaya.net, US$90–101 s/d) is a pleasant hotel on a well-tended stretch of beach. Its six rooms are ample and decorated with simple furnishings, Mexican tile accents, and bright blankets. All have private terraces and balconies with views of the Caribbean. Continental breakfast is included in the rate and is served in the hotel's excellent beachfront restaurant. All-inclusive fly-fishing packages also are available.

Xcalak's first hotel and only true fishing and diving lodge, **Costa de Cocos** (3 km/2 mi north of town, tel. 983/839-8537, www.costadecocos.com, US$73 s, 84 d) eschews fluff and formality for a laid-back sportsman's atmosphere that's perfectly suited to its clientele. Individual wood-paneled cabañas are clean and comfortable, with tile floors and hot water, and surround a well-kempt sandy lot. Travelers looking for "cute" or "charming" won't find it here—certainly not like at neighboring B&Bs—and that seems to be just how the staff and guests prefer it. The restaurant is open late, serving up pizza, steak, beer, and all manner of tall tales—though with fishing as good as it is, many just happen to be true.

OVER US$100

It's hard not to feel at home at **⬛ Sin Duda** (eight km/five mi north of town, www.sindudavillas.com, US$84 d, US$112 studio, US$125 apartment), one of Xcalak's best-loved hotels. The three standard rooms, one studio, and two two-bedroom apartments are all charmers: beautifully furnished, whimsically decorated, most with breathtaking views of the turquoise Caribbean Sea. Two roof decks offer an even better angle: uninterrupted 360-degree views of the jungle, lagoon, and sea. On arrival, owners Margo and Robert (and their four corgis) show you around the delightful villa, tell you where to find the self-serve snorkel gear, kayaks, and bicycles, and even point out the best coral heads to snorkel to. Evening time brings cocktail hour, when guests can join the hosts for a "margo-rita" in the cozy lounge that doubles as a common kitchen and library. A home away from home, without a doubt.

Run by friendly Minnesota retirees, **Sand-Wood Villas** (7.9 km/4.9 mi north of town, tel. 983/839-5428, www.sandwood.com, US$122 d, 145 t) has three apartments, each with two bedrooms, two small bathrooms, a full kitchen—from gas stoves to juicers—and gorgeous sea views. The decor veers from plain to old-fashioned and back again, but the units themselves are comfortable and roomy. Snorkel gear, kayaks, and canoes are available for exploring the reef or the lagoon, and bikes for getting in and out of town. The owners here also manage **Coral Garden Inn** (www.coralgardeninn.com, US$675–800/wk) which has two spacious two-bedroom apartments with kitchens about one kilometer (0.5 mile) farther north.

A hotel where "all you need is your smile," **Playa Sonrisa** (6.9 km/4.3 mi north of town, tel. 983/114-9895, www.playasonrisa.com,

US$112 s/d, US$146 s/d with a/c) is a clothing-optional resort on a palm-tree-laden beach. Rooms are divided between beachfront units and garden view cabins. The beachfront units are comfortable and clean—the stand alone bungalows are the nicest—but lack charm. The garden view cabins are worn and depressing and not worth the US$112 price tag. What you pay for here is the freedom to enjoy the Caribbean in the buff without being ogled or disrespecting local mores. Couples and nudist families only. Continental breakfast, kayaks, and snorkel gear included in the rate.

Food

◖ **Xcalak Caribe** (noon–8 P.M. Wed.–Fri., 11–5 P.M. Sat.–Sun., US$6–12) serves seaside standards like shrimp quesadillas and garlic grilled fish, plus an ever-changing selection of specials. Restaurant options are slim in Xcalak, but the large tasty dishes, friendly service, and casual watering hole would make this a popular watering hole anywhere. Look for the yellow *palapa*-roofed building just south of the lighthouse, facing the beach.

Xcalak's hoteliers heap praise onto the ◖ **Leaky Palapa Restaurant** (no phone, 11:30 A.M.–9 P.M. Sat.–Mon., US$4–16) like Cuban guys scooping sugar into their coffee. A small bohemian *palapa*-roofed restaurant run by two Canadian expats, the menu varies according to the day's catch and what the food truck brings but is invariably delicious. A must for any stay here. Open November–May only.

The restaurant at **Costa de Cocos** (7 A.M.–10 P.M. daily, US$5–18) serves solid familiar fare, like burgers, steak, grilled fish, and pizza. Not particularly outstanding, but the kitchen is open daily, no reservations required, and the full bar and casual atmosphere make this a reliable choice.

The Maya Grill (Tierra Maya Hotel, 2.1 km/1.3 mi north of town, toll-free U.S. tel. 800/216-1902, 6:30 A.M.–1:30 P.M. and 5–9 P.M. daily, US$5–17) is a beachside hotel restaurant offering fresh ingredients in its Mexican-inspired meals. Seafood is the focus but chicken and meat dishes edge their way onto the menu too. Dinners are pricey but hearty, including an appetizer, soup, and dessert.

If you are cooking for yourself, a **grocery truck** passes through town and down the coastal road on Tuesdays, Fridays, and Sundays every week. It comes stocked with eggs, yogurt, grains, basic produce, fresh meats, and canned food. You can also buy a broom or two. In town, try the no-name **mini-mart** (one and a half blocks south of the elementary school, 9 A.M.–9 P.M. daily), which sells basic canned and dried foods along with a good variety of chips.

Information and Services

Xcalak has no bank, ATM, or currency exchange office, and only a few places take credit cards. Plan accordingly!

Hospitals: There's a basic health clinic (8 A.M.–noon and 2–6 P.M. Mon.–Fri.) near the entrance of town.

Internet and Telephone: There was no reliable Internet café when we passed through, though many hotel owners will let you use their computers in a pinch. To place an international or domestic call, head to **Telecomm/ Telégrafos** (near The Leaky Palapa, 9 A.M.–3 P.M. Mon.–Fri.).

Getting There and Around

Bus service is somewhat erratic in Xcalak. Theoretically, buses leave every day at 5 A.M. and 2:30 P.M., though departures are sometimes delayed or cancelled without notice. From Xcalak, buses pass Mahahual (including a portion of the coastal road south of town), then continue to Limones and Chetumal. If you're arriving, your hotel may send a car to pick you up; otherwise a taxi from town is about US$1 per kilometer (0.6 mile).

Most travelers come in a rental car, which certainly simplifies life here. The closest gas station is on the main road to Mahahual, near the turnoff for Xcalak. However, it occasionally runs out of gas, so you should fill up on Highway 307 as well—Carrillo Puerto is a good spot. In a pinch, a few Xcalak families sell marked-up gas from barrels in their front yards; ask your hotel owner for help locating them.

CHACCHOBEN ARCHAEOLOGICAL ZONE

Chacchoben (8 A.M.–5 P.M. daily, US$3, free on Sundays) got its name from archaeologists, who, after uncovering no inscription indicating what the city's original residents called it, named it after the Maya village to whom the land pertained. The exact meaning of the name is lost, even to local villagers, though the accepted translation is "Place of Red Corn." The area may have been settled as early as 1000 B.C., and most of the building activity probably took place A.D. 200–700, the Classic period.

Visiting the Ruins

Entering the site, a short path leads first to Temple 24, a squat pyramid that is the primary structure of a small enclosed area called Plaza B. Across that plaza—and the larger Plaza Central beyond it—is a massive raised platform with the site's largest pyramid, Temple 1, atop it. Also on the platform, two smaller structures, dubbed Las Vasijas and Los Gemelos, were likely used for ceremonial functions. The site has some well-preserved stucco paint and for that reason none of the pyramids can be climbed. Though it can get crowded on cruise-ship days, Chacchoben has an appealingly remote feel, nestled in the forest with towering mahogany and banyan trees.

Practicalities

Turismo Chacchoben (www.chacchobenruins.com) is a small friendly tour operation run by David Villagómez and Ivan Cohuo, both born and raised in Chacchoben village, and extremely knowledgeable about the ruins and Maya history, culture, and belief systems. Tours are of the ruins alone (US$43 pp, 3–4 hours) or in combination with a visit to the guides' home village (US$70 pp, six hours); all tours are offered in Spanish, English, or Italian, and include air-conditioned transport from Mahahual, entrance fees, and drinks. The tours are geared for the cruise ship crowd (as they must) but are limited to 14 people and are warmly recommended by hotel owners to independent travelers as well.

Laguna Bacalar

Almost 50 kilometers (31 miles) long, Laguna Bacalar is the second-largest lake in Mexico and certainly among the most beautiful. Well, it's not technically a lake: A series of waterways do eventually lead to the ocean, making Bacalar a lagoon; but it is fed by natural springs and the water on the western shore, where the hotels and town are, is 100 percent *agua dulce* (fresh water).

The Maya name for the lagoon translates as "Lake of Seven Colors." It is an apt description, as you will see on any sunny day. The lagoon's sandy bottom and crystalline water turn shallow areas a brilliant turquoise, which fades to deep blue in the center. If you didn't know better, you'd think it was the Caribbean.

ORIENTATION

The hub of the Laguna Bacalar region is the town of Bacalar. Located on the west side of the lake, it won't win any prizes for charm but it does have a terrific museum, one of the best hotels around, a handful of good restaurants, and of course, gorgeous views of the lagoon. A handful of hotels are sprinkled a few kilometers on either side of town and the enormous Cenote Azul is just south of it.

SIGHTS
◀ Fuerte San Felipe Bacalar

The 17th-century Fuerte San Felipe Bacalar (central plaza, Av. 3 at Calle 20, 9 A.M.–7 P.M. Tues.–Thurs. and Sun., 9 A.M.–8 P.M. Fri.–Sat., US$4.75) was built by the Spanish for protection against the pirates and Mayas that regularly raided the area. In fact, attacks proved so frequent—and successful—that the fort was destroyed in 1858 during the Caste

© LIZA PRADO

A beautifully restored fort, Fuerte San Felipe Bacalar has one of the best museums in the region.

War. Today, the star-shaped stone edifice has been restored to its former glory: drawbridge, cannons, moat, and all. The fort also houses the excellent **Museo de la Piratería,** a state-of-the-art museum with exhibits on the history of the area with a focus on the pirates who regularly attacked these shores.

Cenote Azul

As good or better than the Laguna Bacalar for swimming, Cenote Azul (Carretera Chetumal-Bacalar Km. 15, tel. 983/834-2038, 8 A.M.–8 P.M. daily, free) is said to be the widest cenote in Mexico, measuring 185 meters (607 feet) across and 61 meters (200 feet) deep. Filled with crystalline blue water, short ladders make getting into the water easy. A rope stretches clear across, so even less-conditioned swimmers can make it to the far side. A large, breezy restaurant (US$6–16) has smallish portions of unremarkable seafood, but the pretty waterside tables are perfect for fries and a beer. Located two kilometers (1.25 miles) south of town.

ENTERTAINMENT AND EVENTS
Fiesta de San Joaquín

Every July, the town of Bacalar celebrates San Joaquín, its patron saint. For nine consecutive days, different neighborhoods host festive celebrations, each trying to outdo the other for the year's best party. Visitors are welcome and should definitely join the fun—expect plenty of food, music, dancing, and performances of all sorts. Cockfights also are popular, and a three-day hydroplane race usually follows the festivities in early August.

SPORTS AND RECREATION
Ecotours

A friendly German couple founded **Active Nature** (Villas Ecotucan, tel. 983/834-2516, www.activenaturebacalar.com) in 2006 after fate and car trouble cut short their planned tour of the Americas and left them in lovely Laguna Bacalar. Tour options include kayaking through mangrove channels to hidden

TULUM AND QUINTANA ROO

lagoons and freshwater beaches, sunset and moonlight canoe rides, biking to a Great Curassow breeding reserve and research center, and morning bird-watching walks. Prices range from US$10–40 per person, including gear and often lunch and water; children under 10 are free, under 14 half-off. Tours begin at Villas Ecotucán and guests there get a 10 percent discount. A portion of proceeds is donated to the Great Curassow center.

Swimming and Boating

In town, on the waterfront, the **Club de Vela Bacalar** (Av. Costera at Calle 20, tel. 983/834-2478, 9 A.M.–6 P.M. daily) rents sea kayaks for US$7 an hour single or US$9.50 an hour double. The pier here is one of the best places to swim in town; a wooden footbridge leads water babies from land to a swimming dock, where the water is crystal clear and deep.

Other good swimming spots include those at Rancho Encantado and Hotel Laguna; plan on ordering something from the hotel restaurant to be able to use the waterfront.

ACCOMMODATIONS
In Town

Located in the heart of town, **C Casita Carolina** (Av. Costera between Calles 16 and 18, tel. 983/834-2334, www.casitacarolina .com, US$23–42 s/d with shared kitchen, US$37–US$42 s/d, US$51 s/d cabaña with kitchen) is one of the area's most charming and convenient accommodations. Three of the six units occupy a converted family home and share a common living room and kitchen. The other units—a cabaña apartment, a cozy casita, and a *palapa* bungalow—face a large grassy garden that runs to the lakeshore. The rooms vary in size and decor, but all have private bath, fan, and a homey feel. American host and owner Carolyn Niemeyer Weiss lives on-site and loves to visit with guests; she also hosts a weeklong artist's retreat in February.

Hotelito Paraíso (Av. Costera at Calle 14, tel. 983/834-2787, US$37 s/d with fan, US$47 s/d with a/c) has six aging units surrounding a large grassy area that runs right to the lakeshore. There's a generally downtrodden feel about the place, however, with cavernous rooms, nonfunctioning kitchens, and rather saggy beds. Newer units are better, in a pinch.

Outside of Town

Located on approximately 40 hectares (98.8 acres) of mostly undeveloped land, **Villas Ecotucán** (Carr. Chetumal-Cancún Km. 26.5, tel. 983/834-2516, www.villasecotucan .info, US$5/tent camping, US$50 s/d cabañas including breakfast) is a perfect place to enjoy the outdoors. There are plenty of activities for everyone—jungle walks, swimming, kayaking, badminton as well as excellent bird-watching and lake tours. Accommodations consist of just five *palapa*-roofed cabañas. Each is spacious and simple with a separate sitting area and checkerboard floors. Camping is permitted near the lake on a broad expanse of grass. A family-orientated place, rates include two adults and two kids.

If you can get used to the persistent hum of traffic from nearby Highway 307, **Rancho Encantado** (two km/1.25 mi north of town, tel. 983/101-3358, U.S. tel. 505/894-7074, www.encantado.com, US$160–190 s/d, US$245 suite) is a good option. A New-Agey hotel on a lush lakeside property, it has 12 spacious casitas featuring Mexican tile floors, good beds, and small porches that overlook either the garden or the lagoon. The prettiest spot here, however, is a pier that leads to a shady dock strung with hammocks—it's perfect for swimming and relaxing. There's also a small kiosk built over the lake where guests receive massages and body treatments; a Jacuzzi is nearby. Rates include buffet breakfast and dinner.

Built on a bluff overlooking the lagoon, **Hotel Laguna Bacalar** (Blvd. Costero 479, tel. 983/834-2206, www.hotellagunabacalar .com, US$51 s/d with fan, US$64 s/d with a/c) has spacious rooms, most with a balcony and an impressive view of the lake. The decor is seriously tacky and worn—seashells and animal prints figure prominently—but the rooms are clean. Stairs zigzag down to the water, where a pier, ladder, and a diving board make swimming fun and easy. Otherwise, there's a small pool (filled only during high season) near the rooms. The hotel **restaurant** (7:30 A.M.–9 P.M. daily, US$4–15) serves basic, predictable meals. From the highway, look for the large sign and white and aqua structure on the south side of town.

FOOD
Restaurants
El Carboncito (central plaza, Av. 5 near Calle 20, 5–11:30 P.M. Wed.–Mon., US$2.50–5.50) is a popular *puesto* (outdoor food stand with tables) that serves up grilled favorites like hot dogs, hamburgers, and tacos.

For a laid-back, indoor eatery, **Señor Café** (central plaza, Av 5. at Calle 22, tel. 983/834-2852, 7 A.M.–11 P.M. daily, US$3.50–5.50) offers Mexican favorites like tacos and enchiladas along with sandwiches and egg dishes. Service is excruciatingly slow but the wait is worth it.

For a more formal option, try **La Cosa Nostra** (central plaza, Calle 22 between Avs. 3 and 5, 1–11 P.M. Wed.–Mon., US$5–7), a pleasant little restaurant serving up a variety of salads, baguettes, and pasta dishes.

The lagoon-front **Club de Vela Bacalar** (Av. Costera at Calle 20, tel. 983/834-2478, 9 A.M.–6 P.M. daily, US$8–15) serves seafood and regional food in its open-air restaurant. The prices are somewhat inflated for what you get but the view and the variety are welcome.

Groceries
On the central plaza, **Dunosusa** (Calle 22 between Avs. 3 and 5, 7:30 A.M.–9 P.M. Mon.–Sat., 8:30 A.M.–8 P.M. Sun.) is a surprisingly well-stocked supermarket.

INFORMATION AND SERVICES
Tourist Information
Bacalar does not have a tourist information office yet but www.bacalarmosaico.com is a bilingual website offering useful information on the area's sights, activities, and businesses.

Hospitals
The **Centro de Salud** (Av. 3 between Calles 22 and 24, tel. 983/834-2756, 24 hours daily) is located a block from the central plaza, across from the post office.

Pharmacies
Farmacia San Joaquín (Av. 7 between Calles 20 and 22, 8 A.M.–3 P.M., 6–9 P.M. daily) is just a couple blocks north of the central plaza.

Police
The police station (Calle 20 near Av. 3, 24 hours daily) is just east of the central plaza, across the street from the Fuerte San Felipe Bacalar.

Money
There is no bank in town but there is a **Banorte** ATM on the west side of the central plaza. If you need any other money services or the ATM has run out of cash, the closest bank is in Chetumal.

Internet and Telephone
The most convenient place to email is the **Nave de Papel** (central plaza, Av. 5 between Calles 20 and 22, 2–10 P.M. daily, US$0.75 per hour).

For telephone calls, your best bet is to use the public phones on the central plaza; Ladatel telephone cards can be purchased at the supermarket and at most corner stores.

Post Office
The post office (Av. 3 near Calle 24, 9 A.M.–3 P.M. Mon.–Fri.) is just east of the Fuerte San Felipe Bacalar.

Launderette
Lavandería Lolita (Av. 7 between Calles 24 and 26, tel. 983/834-2069, 9 A.M.–10 P.M. daily) offers same-day service for US$1 per kilogram (2.2 pounds). Pickup and delivery available.

BACALAR BUS SCHEDULES

DESTINATION	PRICE	DURATION	SCHEDULE
Cancún	US$14-17*	6 hrs	every 1-2 hrs, 5:30 A.M.-7:15 P.M., plus 10:45 P.M., and 12:45 A.M.
Chetumal	US$1.75	45 min.	every 30-60 min. 5:30 A.M.-11:15 P.M.
Carrillo Puerto	US$5	2.5 hrs	take Cancún bus
Mahahual	US$5	2 hrs	3-4 times daily
Playa del Carmen	US$11-14*	5 hrs	take Cancún bus
Tulum	US$8.50-9*	4 hrs	take Cancún bus

*Denotes first-class; not available for every departure.

GETTING THERE
Bus
Just one block south of the central plaza, Bacalar's modest bus terminal (Av. 5 near Calle 18, tel. 983/834-2517) has mostly *de paso* (mid-route) service, which means you have to wait for the bus to arrive before buying your ticket, space permitting. Arriving from the north, be sure get off in front of the church; because of the one-way streets, the bus doesn't stop at the station itself. Leaving, first-class ADO buses to Cancún (US$18, 5.5 hours) pass at 9:15 A.M. and 3:15 P.M. daily, while second-class Mayab buses (US$15, 6 hours) pass every 1-2 hours 5:30 A.M.–12:45 A.M.

Buses to Chetumal pass at roughly the same frequency, but most people catch a *taxi colectivo* or **combi** (US$1.25–1.75, every 30 minutes) in front of Iglesia San Joaquín on Avenida 7, one block up from the lake. You can also flag down Chetumal-bound buses along the highway, if your hotel is closer to there than the terminal.

GETTING AROUND
You can easily walk to all the sites of interest in Bacalar, with the exception of Cenote Azul. A taxi there from town costs US$1–2; you can usually find one around the central plaza or on Avenida 7.

TULUM AND QUINTANA ROO

Chetumal

Chetumal is the capital of Quintana Roo and the gateway to Central America. Not the prettiest of towns, most guidebook-toting travelers just pass through, on their way to or from Belize or southern Campeche. However, Chetumal's modern Maya museum is one of the best you'll find, and well worth a visit. In fact, many tour groups stop here just to visit the museum. And if you're dying to see the Guatemalan ruins of Tikal, a shuttle from Chetumal can get you there in eight hours (cutting through Belize), and back again just as fast. The beautiful Laguna Bacalar, north of town, and intriguing Kohunlich and Dzibanché ruins, west of town, make for easy day trips (sans border crossings) too.

SIGHTS
◖ Museo de la Cultura Maya

One of the best museums in the Yucatán, Museo de la Cultura Maya (Av. de los Héroes at Calle Cristóbal Colón, tel. 983/832-6838, 9 A.M.–7 P.M. Tues.–Thurs. and Sun., 9 A.M.–8 P.M. Fri.–Sat., US$4.75) extends over three levels—the upper represents the world of gods, the middle the world of humans, and the lower *Xibalba*, the underworld. Each floor has impressive, well-designed exhibits describing Maya spiritual beliefs, agricultural practices, astronomy and counting, and more, all in English and Spanish. The exposition area

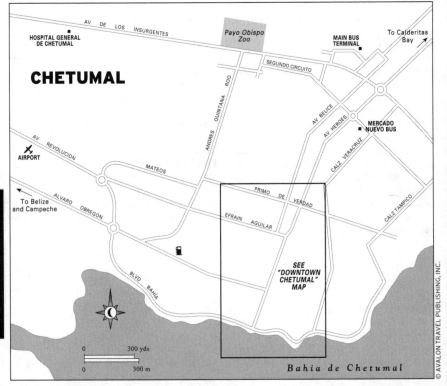

CHETUMAL

To Calderitas Bay

HOSPITAL GENERAL DE CHETUMAL

Payo Obispo Zoo

MAIN BUS TERMINAL

AV DE LOS INSURGENTES

SEGUNDO CIRCUITO

ANDRES QUINTANA ROO

AV BELICE

AV HEROES

MERCADO NUEVO BUS

CALZ VERACRUZ

AIRPORT

AV REVOLUCION

MATEOS

PRIMO DE VERDAD

CALZ TAMPICO

To Belize and Campeche

ALVARO OBREGON

EFRAIN AGUILAR

SEE "DOWNTOWN CHETUMAL" MAP

BLVD BAHIA

0   300 yds
0   300 m

Bahía de Chetumal

© AVALON TRAVEL PUBLISHING, INC.

TULUM AND QUINTANA ROO

DOWNTOWN CHETUMAL

To Main Bus Terminal and Mercado Nuevo Bus Terminal

AV PRIMO DE VERDAD

AV BELICE

AV 18 DE SEPTIEMBRE

MINIBUS TERMINAL

CRISTÓBAL COLON

BODEGÓN III

FARMACIA SIMILARES

ADO TICKET OFFICE

MUSEO DE LA CULTURA MAYA

AV JOSE MARIA MORELOS

AV FRANCISCO I MADERO

AV MAHATMA GANDHI

MONUMENTO AL MESTIZO

HOTEL UCUM

HOLIDAY INN

Mercado Ignacio Manuel Altamirano

EFRAÍN AGUILAR

To Chetumal Airport

INTERNET CAFÉS

MUSEO DE LA CIUDAD

HOTEL LOS COCOS

HÉROES DE CHAPULTEPEC

CALZ TAMPICO

AV INDEPENDENCIA

AV BENITO JUAREZ

BANORTE

LÁZARO CÁRDENAS

FARMACIA SIMILARES

POST OFFICE

PLUTARCO ELIAS

AV DE LOS HEROS

AV 5 DE MAYO

AV MIGUEL HIDALGO

AV REFORMA

CALZ VERACRUZ

AV COZUMEL

To Belize and Campeche

I ZARAGOZA

RESTAURANTE EL FENICIO

HOTEL PALMA REAL

ALVARO OBREGON

HEROICA ESCUELA NAVAL

SERGIO'S PIZZA

HOTEL CARIBE PRINCESS

OTHON P BLANCO

AV 18 DE SEPTIEMBRE

HSBC

CITY TOURIST OFFICE

CARMEN OCHOA DE MERINO

22 DE ENERO

PALACIO DE GOBIERNO

IMMIGRATION OFFICE

Plaza la Bandera

TOURIST INFORMATION

BLVD BAHIA

ESMERELDA

Bahía de Chetumal

0   200 yds

0   200 m

© AVALON TRAVEL PUBLISHING, INC.

past the ticket booth usually has good temporary art shows too.

On your way into the museum, check out the **Monumento al Mestizo,** a striking sculpture symbolizing the joining of the Spanish shipwrecked sailor Gonzalo Guerrero and a Maya woman—the birth of the mestizos.

Museo de la Ciudad

The city museum (Calle Héroes de Chapultepec between Avs. Juárez and de los Héroes, tel. 983/832-1350, 9 A.M.–7 P.M. Tues.–Sun., US$1) is a small, well-organized museum describing the political, economic, and cultural history of Chetumal; it spans the period from its founding in 1898 to its naming as capital of Quintana Roo in 1915, to present day. There's a small art exhibit at the end too. Signage in Spanish only.

Boulevard Bahía

This breezy bayside promenade lacks beaches but makes for a fine bay front stroll. Along it you'll find cafés, sculptures, monuments, a lighthouse, and, hopefully, a cooling breeze. The backstreets harbor pastel-colored, clapboard buildings with a classic Caribbean look.

Kohunlich Archaeological Zone

The archaeological site of Kohunlich is outside Chetumal. Neither as grand as Calakmul nor as glorious as Uxmal, it is still worth a trip if only to visit the compelling **Temple of the Masks.** Dedicated to the Maya sun god, this stone pyramid features haunting stucco masks with star-incised eyes, mustaches, and nose plugs. Standing two meters (6.6 feet) tall, these masks are rarities, to say the least. Be sure to wander

© AVALON TRAVEL PUBLISHING, INC.

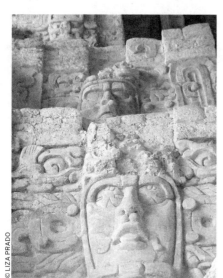

© LIZA PRADO

Kohunlich's intricate Temple of the Masks is worth a day trip from Chetumal.

through the jungle site; you'll be rewarded with more than 200 structures, stelae, and uncovered mounds that date to late Preclassic (A.D. 100–200) through the Classic (A.D. 600–900) periods. Open 8 A.M.–5 P.M. daily, US$3.

Dzibanché and Kinichná Archaeological Zones

If you want to explore a couple of semi-excavated sites, consider heading to Dzibanché and it's smaller neighbor, Kinichná. Located two kilometers (1.2 miles) apart, they date to A.D. 300–800 and are thought to have been part of a Maya city extending 40 square kilometers (25 square miles). Although Dzibanché is known for the extraordinary wood lintels found there, the main reason visitors come is to wander among the ruins' towering structures, most waiting to be uncovered. Both are open from 8 A.M.–5 P.M. daily; admission is US$3 and good for both archaeological zones.

ENTERTAINMENT AND EVENTS

Every Sunday at 6 P.M., locals gather at the **Plaza la Bandera** (Av. de los Héroes at water-front) to enjoy city-sponsored events, typically performances by the municipal band or local musicians and singers. The events are free and family-friendly, with vendors selling drinks and street food.

SHOPPING

There is a fine **bookstore and gift shop** (tel. 983/832-2270, 9 A.M.–7 P.M. Tue.–Sat., 9 A.M.–2 P.M. Sun.) near the entrance of Museo de la Cultura Maya, carrying a small selection of maps, posters, T-shirts, and Spanish-language books and magazines.

Across from the museum, **Mercado Ignacio Manuel Altamirano** (Efraín Aguilar between Avs. Belice and de los Héroes, 8 A.M.–4 P.M. daily) sells everyday items geared at locals, from clothing to kitchenware. For travelers, it's a good place to buy a pair of flip-flops or a travel clock, if the need arises.

The **Corozal Duty Free Zone** is an area jam-packed with stores selling products from around the world. Located in Belize, visitors can enter and leave the area without paying taxes on their purchases, mostly household and personal items. Lots of people complain of second-rate quality, but it's worth a visit if you're in the region for more than a couple weeks and want to stock up on specialty foods or liquor.

ACCOMMODATIONS

Although Chetumal is by no means a resort town, its status as the state capital and its location on the Belize border make it a busy town. Arrive as early in the day as possible to have your choice of hotel rooms. Better yet, call ahead for a reservation.

Under US$50

The basic but very clean **Hotel Ucum** (Av. Mahatma Gandhi between Avs. 5 de Mayo and 16 de Septiembre, tel. 983/832-0711, US$18.50 s/d with fan, US$22 s/d with fan and cable TV, US$32.50 s/d with a/c and cable TV) is the best budget option in town. Just one block from the Museo de la Cultura Maya, rooms are decent size, beds are comfortable, and there's a great pool with a separate wading area for small

TULUM AND QUINTANA ROO

children. The parking lot also is secure. Ask for a room on the top floor for the best breeze.

With tile floors, wood furniture, and flower bedspreads, rooms at the **Hotel Caribe Princess** (Av. Alvaro Obregón between Avs. 5 de Mayo and 16 de Septiembre, tel. 983/832-0900, caribe_princess@hotmail.com, US$36 s with a/c, US$43 d with a/c) are a good value. They're on the small side, but all have air-conditioning, cable TV, and complimentary coffee in the morning. Ask for a room facing the interior of the building—the avenue in front is a busy one.

Hotel Palma Real (Av. Alvaro Obregón at Av. de los Héroes, tel. 983/833-0964, htldene gocios@yahoo.com.mx, US$34–39 s/d with a/c) is another bright spot on the hotel scene. Rooms are spacious, clean, and have appealing decor. Some also have balconies that face the main drag—a somewhat loud but interesting bird's-eye view of the hubbub downtown.

US$50-100

◖ Hotel Los Cocos (Av. de los Héroes at Calle Héroes de Chapultepec, tel. 983/835-0430, toll-free Mex. tel. 800/719-5840, www .hotelloscocos.com.mx, US$70 s/d standard, US$83 s/d premiere, US$95 s/d villas) is a stylish surprise in this small town. Renovated rooms—premiere and villas only—are absolutely worth the price: sleek furniture, gleaming tile floors, and the newest in amenities. Older rooms—standards—are overpriced: outdated white furniture, bathrooms that are begging for new tiles, and air-conditioning units that could use a tune-up. Regardless where guests stay, however, all have access to the lush garden and inviting pool area. There's also a good open-air restaurant on-site.

If Los Cocos is full, try the **Holiday Inn** (Av. de los Héroes near Av. Mahatma Gandhi, tel. 983/835-0400, toll-free U.S. tel. 888/465-4329, www.holiday-inn.com/chetumalmex, US$95). Rooms are comfortable and utilitarian with air-conditioning, cable TV, in-room telephone, and Internet access. The hotel also boasts perks like a pool, Jacuzzi, gym, and business center.

Outside of Chetumal

On the road to Kohunlich is the luxurious **◖ Explorean Kohunlich** (tel. 555/201-8350, toll-free Mex. 800/366-6666, U.S. 877/397-5672, www.theexplorean.com, US$231 s, 360 d, includes meals, open bar, and one excursion/day). This Fiesta Americana all-inclusive resort boasts 40 deluxe suites set in 30 hectares (74 acres) of jungle property. Each has gleaming stone floors, high *palapa* ceilings, elegant furnishings, and private stone-walled yards for sunbathing. Breakfast is served in a private outdoor living room or—if you prefer—in the indoor sitting area. At the main building, a fine restaurant serves delicious regional fare (7:30–10:30 A.M., 1:30–4 P.M., 7:30–10:30 P.M. daily, US$10–20, open to nonguests), a full-service spa is at the ready, and a sleek lap pool overlooks the jungle below (you can even see the ruins at Kohunlich from here). One excursion per day—including rappelling in the jungles of Campeche, kayaking through a crocodile reserve, or mountain biking through forgotten forests—also is included in the rate. Add in all your meals, drinks, and taxes and this is great deal on a great place.

FOOD

◖ Restaurante El Fenicio (Av. de los Héroes at Calle Zaragoza, tel. 983/832-0026, 24 hours daily, US$4–10) is our favorite restaurant in Chetumal, not only because it's open late but also because of its tasty, reliable meals. Be sure to try the "make your own taco" dish, a platter stacked with chicken, chorizo, beef, and melted cheese, and served with tortillas and all the fixings.

Set in a dark wood, dimly lit, faux–Tiffany lamp dining room, **Sergio's Pizza** (Av. 5 de Mayo at Av. Alvaro Obregón, tel. 983/832-0491, 7 A.M.–midnight daily, US$4–16) serves much more than pizza—the extensive menu covers the gamut of Italian and Mexican dishes—from meat lasagna to *molletes rancheros*. Meals are tasty and service is excellent. Popular with families.

Bodegón III (Calle Cristóbal Colon between

TULUM AND QUINTANA ROO

Avs. Belice and de los Héroes, 5 A.M.–9 P.M. Mon.–Sat., 5 A.M.–3 P.M. Sun.) is a large grocery store with a decent selection of canned and dry foods and a huge display of fruits and veggies in front. Nos. I and II are nearby.

INFORMATION
Tourist Information
Near the waterfront, the city tourist office (Av. 5 de Mayo at Carmen Ochoa de Merino, 983/835-0500, 9 A.M.–4 P.M. Mon.–Fri.) has a decent selection of brochures and maps. It also maintains a kiosk on the waterfront at Avenida Hidalgo.

Hospitals
About two kilometers (1.2 miles) from the center of town, **Hospital General de Chetumal** (Avs. Andrés Quintana Roo at Juan José Isiordia, tel. 983/832-8194, 24 hours daily) is the city's main hospital.

Pharmacies
Farmacia Similares (Av. de los Héroes at Calle Plutarco Elias, 8 A.M.–9 P.M. Mon.–Sat., 8 A.M.– 8 P.M. Sun.) also has a sister store behind the Maya museum (Calle Cristóbal Colón between Avs. Belice and de los Héroes) that is open 24 hours daily.

SERVICES
Money
HSBC (Othon P. Blanco between Av. 5 de Mayo and Av. de los Héroes, 8 A.M.–7 P.M. Mon.–Sat.) and **Banorte** (Av. de los Héroes between Lázaro Cárdenas and Plutarco Elias, 9 A.M.–4 P.M. Mon.–Fri.) both have ATMs. There also is an ATM at the bus station.

Internet and Telephone
A string of Internet cafés are conveniently lined up across from the **Mercado Ignacio Manuel Altamirano** (Efraín Aguilar between Avs. Belice and de los Héroes). Charging around US$1 an hour, most are open 7 A.M.–2 A.M. Monday–Saturday and 8 A.M.–midnight on Sunday. Many also have cheap international telephone service.

Post Office
The post office (Av. Plutarco Elias Calles between Avs. 5 de Mayo and 16 de Septiembre, 8 A.M.–6 P.M. Mon.–Fri., 9 A.M.–1 P.M. Sat.) is just a block from the main drag.

Immigration
The immigration office (Calzada del Centenario 582, tel. 983/832-6353) is open 9 A.M.–1 P.M. Monday–Friday.

For information on the Belizean and Guatemalan consulates, see the *Foreign Consulates* sidebar in the *Essentials* chapter.

Storage
Conveniently located in the bus station, **Revistas and Novedades Laudy** stores bags for US$0.50 per hour.

GETTING THERE
Air
The small **Chetumal Airport** (CTM, tel. 983/832-0898) receives only a few flights each day. Airlines serving it include: **Aviacsa** (toll-free Mex. tel. 800/006-2200, www.aviacsa.com), **Click Mexicana** (toll-free Mex. tel. 800/112-5425, www.clickmx.com), and **Mexicana** (toll-free Mex. tel. 800/502-2000, www.mexicana.com).

Bus
Most first- and second-class buses leave from the main bus terminal (Av. Insurgentes at Av. de los Héroes, tel. 983/832-5110, ext. 2404). You can buy tickets there or at a ticket office (Avs. Belice and Cristóbal Colón, tel. 983/832-0639) just west of the Maya museum. Two other terminals—the Minibus terminal (Av. Primo de Verdad at Av. Miguel Hidalgo, no phone) and Mercado Nuevo (Av. de los Héroes and Circuito Segundo, no phone)— have service to Bacalar, the Zona Libre, and to Belize.

Car
The highways in this area have improved immensely in recent years. The roads from Chetumal to Mahahual, Tulum, and Xpujil have

TULUM AND QUINTANA ROO

CHETUMAL BUS SCHEDULES

Departures from Chetumal's **main bus terminal** (Av. Insurgentes at Av. de los Héroes, tel. 983/832-5110, ext. 2404) include:

DESTINATION	PRICE	DURATION	SCHEDULE
Campeche	US$23	7 hrs	noon
Cancún	US$17-20*	5.5-7 hrs	every 30 min. 8:30 A.M.-5 P.M., plus 6:30 A.M. and every 1-2 hrs 6 P.M.-midnight.
Flores, Guatemala	US$16 plus border fees	7-8 hrs	6 A.M.
Mahahual	US$7.50	3 hrs	5 A.M., 2:30 P.M., 7:30 P.M.
Mérida	US$22	6 hrs	7:30 A.M., 1:30 P.M., 5 P.M., and 11:30 P.M.
Palenque	US$27	7 hrs	7:55 P.M., 9:25 P.M., and 11:25 P.M.
Xpujil	US$5-7	1.5-2 hrs	every 1-2 hrs 11:30 A.M.-11:45 P.M.

*Denotes first class service; not available for all departures.

Buses to **Bacalar** (US$1.50, 20 min.) leave from a **minibus terminal** (Av. Primo de Verdad at Av. Miguel Hidalgo, no phone) every hour 9 A.M.-6 P.M.

Buses for **Corozal** (US$1.50, one hour), **Orangewalk** (US$4, two hours), and **Belize City** (US$7, three hours) leave the **Mercado Nuevo** (Av. de los Héroes and Circuito Segundo, no phone) six times daily 5 A.M.-4:45 P.M. Some pass the main ADO terminal en route.

Buses to the **Zona Libre** (US$1, 30 min.) leave every 15 min. 6:30 A.M.-8 P.M.

transformed from isolated adventure roads to modern highways with very few potholes.

GETTING AROUND

Chetumal is a relatively large city, but the parts most travelers will be interested in are all within easy walking distance—mostly along Avenida de los Héroes. The exception is the main bus terminal and Mercado Nuevo (where you catch buses to Belize), both of which are 10–12 grubby blocks from the center. A cab to either terminal, or anywhere around town, costs US$1.50.

There is no public transportation to either archaeological zone. Highway 186, however, leads to both turnoffs. The bumpy turnoff to **Dzibanché** is about 50 kilometers (31 miles) east of Chetumal and runs north for 24 kilometers (14.9 miles) before hitting the site. The turnoff to **Kohunlich** is three kilometers (1.9 miles) farther west on Highway 186; it's another 8.5 kilometers (5.3 miles) south on a paved road to the site.

INLAND ARCHAEOLOGICAL ZONES

If you can drag yourself from the beaches at Cancún or Tulum, or the diving on Isla Cozumel, a short trip inland will bring you to three of the Yucatán Peninsula's most intriguing ancient ruins—Chichén Itzá, Ek' Balam, and Cobá. Each is quite different from the other, and together they form an excellent introduction to Maya archaeology and architecture.

Chichén Itzá (200 km/124 mi from Cancún) is one of the most famous ruins in the Maya world, with a massive four-sided pyramid and the largest Maya ball court ever built. Just two hours from Cancún, it's inundated with tour groups; get there early to beat the crowds.

Even closer, but far less visited, is the small ruin of Ek' Balam (175 km/109 mi from Cancún), boasting a beautiful stucco frieze partway up a massive pyramid. The frieze has winged priests

and a gaping monster mouth that are so well preserved they look like modern-day plaster art.

Less than an hour from Tulum is the ancient city of Cobá (42 km/26 mi from Tulum), home of the second-tallest known Maya pyramid. Unlike many other ruins, Cobá is ensconced in a thick tropical forest that teems with birdlife, including parrots and toucans.

PLANNING YOUR TIME

Chichén Itzá, Ek' Balam, and Cobá can each be reached as a day trip from Cancún or Tulum. You can visit all three in two or three days, staying overnight at hotels near the sites, or in Valladolid, an attractive and centrally located colonial town.

All the sites can be reached by bus or taxi, especially Chichén Itzá and Cobá. But if you plan on visiting more than one site, a rental car

© LIZA PRADO

HIGHLIGHTS

◖ Chichén Itzá Archaeological Zone: The Yucatán's most well-known ancient ruin is also the most heavily visited. Arrive early to enjoy the site's awesome scale and superlative design, including the largest ball court in the Maya world (page 233).

◖ Ek' Balam Archaeological Zone: A well-preserved frieze with angel-like figures and a huge "monster mouth" is the highlight of this small, serene sight near Valladolid (page 243).

◖ Iglesia y Ex-Convento San Bernardino de Siena: Located in a quiet corner of Valladolid, this elegant church has a spacious esplanade and beautiful interior, plus a natural cenote inside the convent walls (page 247).

◖ Cobá Archaeological Zone: Less than an hour from Tulum, Cobá boasts the peninsula's second-highest pyramid and is surrounded by a forest teeming with birds instead of tourists (page 253).

LOOK FOR ◖ TO FIND RECOMMENDED SIGHTS, ACTIVITIES, DINING, AND LODGING.

may make your trip easier and more rewarding. You won't be tied to a bus schedule, and you'll be able to beat the crowds by getting to the sites bright and early. There also are numerous organized tours to Chichén Itzá from Cancún (though fewer to Cobá and Ek' Balam). While certainly convenient, many travelers find the large groups off-putting.

Chichén Itzá and Pisté

Chichén Itzá is one of the finest archaeological sites in the northern part of the peninsula, and in all of Mesoamerica. It is also one of the most visited. Located just two hours from Cancún (and two from Mérida), the site is inundated by tour groups, many of them bikini-clad day-trippers on loan from the pool at their all-inclusive. That fact should not dissuade in-dependent travelers from visiting—crowded or not, Chichén Itzá is a truly magnificent ruin and a must-see on any archaeology tour of the Yucatán. Just be sure to arrive early, and you can see the big stuff first and be exploring the outer areas by the time the tour buses roll in.

Pisté is a one-road town that is strangely underdeveloped considering it is just two ki-

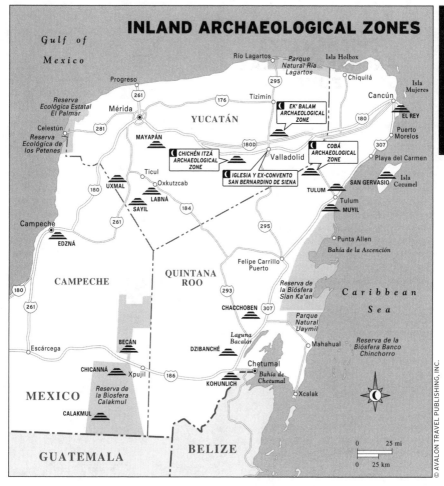

Gulf of Mexico

INLAND ARCHAEOLOGICAL ZONES

Progreso

Río Lagartos — Parque Natural Ría Lagartos   Isla Holbox

Chiquilá

Mérida   Tizimín   295   EK' BALAM ARCHAEOLOGICAL ZONE   Cancún   Isla Mujeres

176

261   YUCATÁN   180   EL REY

Celestún   281   Puerto Morelos

Reserva Ecológica Estatal El Palmar   MAYAPÁN   CHICHÉN ITZÁ ARCHAEOLOGICAL ZONE   COBÁ ARCHAEOLOGICAL ZONE   307   Playa del Carmen

Reserva Ecológica de los Petenes   180D   Valladolid   IGLESIA Y EX-CONVENTO SAN BERNARDINO DE SIENA   SAN GERVASIO   Isla Cozumel

Ticul   Oxkutzcab   TULUM   Tulum   MUYIL

UXMAL   LABNÁ   184

180   SAYIL

Campeche   261

EDZNÁ   295   Punta Allen

Bahía de la Ascención

Felipe Carrillo Puerto

CAMPECHE   QUINTANA ROO   293   Reserva de la Biósfera Sian Ka'an   Caribbean Sea

180   CHACCHOBEN   307   Parque Natural Uaymil

261   Laguna Bacalar   Reserva de la Biósfera Banco Chinchorro

Escárcega   BECÁN   DZIBANCHÉ   Mahahual

CHICANNÁ   Xpujil   186   Chetumal   Bahía de Chetumal

MEXICO   Reserva de la Biosfera Calakmul   KOHUNLICH   Xcalak

CALAKMUL

GUATEMALA   BELIZE

0   25 mi
0   25 km

© AVALON TRAVEL PUBLISHING, INC.

lometers (1.2 miles) from such an important and heavily touristed site. The hotels and restaurants here are unremarkable and there's not much to do or see beyond the ruins.

CHICHÉN ITZÁ ARCHAEOLOGICAL ZONE

Chichén Itzá is a monumental archaeological site, remarkable for both its size and scope. The ruins include impressive palaces, temples, and altars, as well as the largest-known ball court

in the Maya world. One of the most widely recognized (and heavily visited) ruins in the world, it was declared a World Heritage site by UNESCO in 1988.

History

What we call Chichén Itzá surely had another name when it was founded. The name means "Mouth of the Well of the Itzá" but the Itzá, an illiterate and semi-nomadic group of uncertain origin, didn't arrive here until the 12th century.

CHICHÉN ITZÁ ARCHAEOLOGICAL ZONE

Sacred Cenote

SACBE

TEMPLE OF THE BEARDED MAN

TZOMPANTLI

GREAT BALL COURT

PLATFORM OF EAGLES AND JAGUARS

PLATFORM OF VENUS

TEMPLE OF THE JAGUARS

TEMPLE OF TABLES

TEMPLE OF WARRIORS

To Pisté and Hwy 180

MAIN PLAZA

EL CASTILLO/ TEMPLE OF KUKULCÁN

MAIN ENTRANCE/ MUSEUM/ATM

GROUP OF A THOUSAND COLUMNS

EL OSARIO

HOUSE OF THE DEER

RED HOUSE

Xtoloc Cenote

MARKET

ZONA HOTELERA ENTRANCE

EL CARACOL

HOTEL AND BUNGALOWS MAYALAND

TEMPLE OF RELIEFS

NUNNERY

HACIENDA CHICHÉN RESORT

AKAB DZIB

CLUB MED VILLAS CHICHÉN ITZÁ

0   100 yds
0   100 m

To Hwy 180

© AVALON TRAVEL PUBLISHING, INC.

FRIAR DIEGO DE LANDA

Just north of Oxkutzcab, the town of Mani has a quiet, peaceful atmosphere that belies a wrenching history. It was here, in 1562, that Friar Diego de Landa conducted his infamous *auto-da-fé*, in which he burned an untold number of irreplaceable Maya codices, pottery, and other records because he deemed them works of the devil. He accused numerous Maya religious leaders and laypeople of idolatry, and ordered them tortured, publicly humiliated, and imprisoned. The act was outrageous, even by Spanish colonial standards, and Landa was shipped back to Spain to face the Council of the Indies, the colonial authority. He was eventually absolved – a panel of inspectors found he had broken no laws – but during the ordeal Landa evidently came to regret his act. Confined to a convent awaiting judgment, he set about writing down all he could remember about the Maya.

It was no minor document: Landa spoke Maya fluently, and had lived, traveled, and preached in the Yucatán for 13 years before his expulsion. In all, Landa spent close to a decade completing *An Account of the Things of Yucatán*. He eventually returned to Mérida, where he died in 1579, and the work was forgotten until being rediscovered in 1863. Among other things, the manuscript contains a crude alphabet, which proved invaluable to the modern-day decoding of the Maya hieroglyphics. Ironically, it was the very man who destroyed so much of the Maya's written history, who provided the key for future researchers to unlock what remained.

found at Tula, the ancient Toltec capital, in the present state of Hidalgo. Before the Toltecs, the area was populated by Maya, evidenced by the Puuc- and Chenes-style design of the earliest structures here, such as the Nunnery and Casa Colorada.

The three major influences—Maya, Toltec, and Itzá—are indisputable, but the exact chronology and circumstances of those groups' interaction (or lack thereof) is one of the most hotly contested issues in Maya archaeology. Part of the difficulty in understanding Chichén Itzá more fully is that its occupants created very few stelae, and left few Long Count dates on their monuments. In this way Chichén Itzá is very different from virtually every other ancient city in the Yucatán. It's ironic, actually, that Chichén Itzá is the most widely recognized "Maya" ruin considering it was so deeply influenced by non-Maya cultures, and its history and architecture are so atypical of the region.

Chichén Itzá's influence ebbed and flowed over its many centuries of existence and occupation. It first peaked in the mid-9th century, or Late Classic period, when it eclipsed Cobá as the dominant power in the region. The effects of a widespread collapse of Maya cities to the south (like Calakmul, Tikal, and Palenque) reached Chichén Itza in the late 900's. The city rose again under Toltec and later Itzá influence, but went into its final decline after an internal dispute led to the rise of Mayapán, which would come to control much of the Yucatán peninsula. Chichén Itzá was all but abandoned by the early 1200s, though it remained an important pilgrimage site long after the arrival of the Spanish.

El Castillo/Temple of Kukulcán

The most dramatic structure in Chichén Itzá is El Castillo (the Castle), also known as the Temple of Kukulcán. At 24 meters (79 feet) it's the tallest structure on the site, and certainly the most recognizable. Dating to around A.D. 850, the Castillo was built according to strict astronomical guidelines. There are nine levels, which, divided by the central staircase, make

Before the Itzá, the area was controlled—or at least greatly influenced—by Toltec migrants who arrived from central Mexico around A.D. 1000. Most of Chichén's most notable structures, including its famous four-sided pyramid, and images like the reclining *chac-mool,* bear a striking resemblance to structures and images

THE MAYA COLLAPSE

Something went terribly wrong for the Mayas between the years A.D. 800 and A.D. 900. Hundreds of Classic Maya cities were abandoned, monarchies disappeared, and the population fell by the million, mainly by death and plummeting birth rates. The collapse was widespread but was most dramatic in the Southern Lowlands, a swath of tropical forest stretching from the Gulf of Mexico to Honduras and including once-glorious cities such as Palenque, Tikal, and Copán. (Archaeologists first suspected a collapse after noticing a sudden drop-off in inscriptions; it has been confirmed through excavations of peasant dwellings from before and after that period.)

There are many theories for the collapse, varying from climate change and epidemic diseases to foreign invasion and peasant revolt. In his carefully argued book *The Fall of the Ancient Maya* (Thames and Hudson, 2002), archaeologist and professor of anthropology at Pennsylvania State University David Webster suggests it was a series of events, not any single event, that led to the collapse. Webster argues that a population boom just before the collapse left agricultural lands depleted just as demand was at its highest. Maya farmers probably did not have large stores of corn and other food, as their farming methods – and especially the lack of draft animals – kept productivity relatively low. Even if they could generate large surpluses, storage was difficult in the lowlands' humid climate. And with so many rival states – whose populations were also increasing – there was little undepleted land to cultivate. When "too many farmers grew too many crops on too much of the landscape," as Webster puts it, the population would have suffered malnutrition, disease, lower birthrates, increased infighting, and it would have been especially vulnerable to a large-scale catastrophe such as drought or epidemic disease. Whatever blend of social stress existed – and they surely varied somewhat from kingdom to kingdom – it seems clear that in the 9th century ordinary Mayas finally lost all faith in their leaders who, after all, legitimized their rule by being able to please or appease the gods. When the elites abandoned their positions, large-scale collapse was not far behind.

for 18 platforms, the number of months in the Maya calendar. Each of the four sides has 91 steps; together with the platform on top, there are 365 steps, or one for each day of the year. There are 52 inset panels on each face, equal to the number of years in each cycle of the Calendar Round.

On the spring and autumn equinoxes (March 21 and September 22), the afternoon sun lights up a bright zigzag strip on the outside wall of the north staircase and the giant serpent heads at the base, giving the appearance of a serpent slithering down the steps. Chichén Itzá is mobbed during those periods, especially by spiritual-minded folks seeking communion with the ancient Mayas. The effect also occurs in the days just before and after the equinox, and there are many fewer people blocking the view.

Climbing the Castillo used to be a given for any visit to Chichén Itzá, and the views from its top level are breathtaking. However, an elderly tourist died in 2005, after tumbling from near the top of the pyramid to the ground. The accident, combined with longtime warnings from archaeologists that the structure was being irreparably eroded by the hundreds of thousands of visitors who climbed it yearly, prompted officials to close it off. Pyramids at other sites have been restricted as well, and it's looking more and more like a permanent policy.

Deep inside the Castillo, accessed by way of a steep, narrow staircase, are several chambers. Inside one archaeologists discovered a red-painted, jade-studded figure of a jaguar.

Great Ball Court

Chichén Itzá's famous Great Ball Court is the largest ball court in Mesoamerica, by a wide margin. The playing field is 135 meters (443 feet) by 65 meters (213 feet), with two parallel walls eight meters high (26 feet), with scoring rings in impossibly high perches in the center. The players would've had to hit a 12-pound rubber ball through the rings using only their elbows, wrists, and hips. They wore heavy padding and the game likely lasted for hours. At the game's end, the captain of one team—or even the whole team—was apparently sacrificed, possibly by decapitation. There's disagreement about *which* team got the axe, however. Some say it was the losers—otherwise the game's best players would constantly be wiped out. Some argue that it was the winners, and that being sacrificed would have been the ultimate honor. Of course, it's likely the game varied from city to city, and evolved over the many centuries it was played. Along the walls, reliefs depict the ball game and sacrifices.

On the outside of the ball court, the **Lower Temple of the Jaguars** has incredibly fine relief carvings depicting the Maya creation myth. An upper temple is off-limits to visitors, but is decorated with a variety of carvings and remnants of what were likely colorful murals.

The Platforms

As you make your way from the Ball Court to the Temple of the Warriors, you'll pass the gruesome **Tzompantli** (Wall of Skulls). A low T-shaped platform, it is decorated on all sides with row upon row of carved skulls, most with eyes staring out of the large sockets. Among the skulls are images of warriors holding the heads of decapitated victims, skeletons intertwined with snakes, and eagles eating human hearts (a common image in Toltec design, further evidence of their presence here). It is presumed that ceremonies performed on this platform culminated in a sacrificial death for the victim, the head then left on display, perhaps with others already in place. It's estimated that the platform was built A.D. 1050–1200. Nearby, the **Platform of Venus** and **Platform of Eagles and Jaguars** are smaller square structures, each with low stairways on all four sides, and were likely used for ritual music and dancing.

Sacred Cenote

This natural well is 300 meters (984 feet) north of the main structures, along the remains of a *sacbé* (raised stone road) constructed during the Classic period. Almost 60 meters (197 feet) in diameter and 30 meters (98.4 feet) down to the surface of the water, it was a place for sacrifices, mostly to Chac, the God of Rain, who was believed to live in its depths. The remains of scores of victims, mostly children and young adults, were dredged from the cenote, as well as innumerable jade and stone artifacts. On the edge of the cenote is a ruined sweat bath, probably used for purification rituals before sacrificial ceremonies. The name Chichén Itzá (Mouth of the Well of the Itzá) is surely derived from this deeply sacred cenote, and it remained an important Maya pilgrimage site well into the Spanish conquest.

Temple of Warriors and Group of a Thousand Columns

The Temple of Warriors is where some of the distinctive, reclining *chac-mool* figures are found. However, its name comes from the rectangular monoliths in front, which are carved on all sides with images of warriors. (Some are also prisoners, their hands tied behind their backs.) This temple is also closed to entry, and it can be hard to appreciate the fading images from the rope perimeter. You can get a much closer look around back, on the temple's south side, where you can easily make out the figures' expressions and dress. There you can also check out the temple's impressive south-facing facade. A series of well-preserved human and animal figures adorn the lower portion, while above, human faces emerge from serpents' mouths, framed by eagle profiles, with masks of Chac, the hook-nosed God of Rain, on the corners.

The aptly named Group of a Thousand Columns is adjacent to the Temple of Warriors. Its perfectly aligned cylindrical columns likely held up a grand roof structure.

Across the plaza, the **Palacio de las Columnas Esculpidas** (Palace of Sculptured Columns) also has cylindrical columns,

© LIZA PRADO

Chichén Itzá's El Castillo is one of the most visited structures in the Maya world.

but with intricate carvings, suggesting this was the ceremonial center of this portion of the complex. Continuing through the trees, you'll reach **el Mercado** (the Market). The name is purely speculative, though it's easy to imagine a breezy bustling market here, protected from the sun under a wood and *palapa* roof built atop the structure's remarkably high columns.

Osario, Caracol, and the Nunnery

From the market, bear left (away from the Castillo, just visible through the trees) until you meet the path leading to the site's southern entrance. You'll pass the **Osario** (Ossuary) also known as the Tomb of the High Priest. Like a miniature version of Castillo, the pyramid at one time had four stairways on each side and a temple at the crest. From the top platform, a vertical passageway leads into a cave where seven tombs were discovered, along with numerous copper and jade artifacts indicating the deceased were of special importance (and hence the temple's name). Continuing on,

you'll pass two more large structures, **Casa del Venado** (House of the Deer) and **Casa Colorada** (Red House).

But the highlight of this portion of Chichén Itza is **El Caracol** (The Shell), also known as the Observatory and perhaps the most graceful structure at Chichén Itzá. A two-tiered circular structure is set atop a broad rectangular platform, with window slits facing south and west, and another aligned according to the path of the moon during the spring equinoxes. Ancient astronomers used structures like this one to track celestial events and patterns—the orbits of the Moon and Venus, and the coming of solar and lunar eclipses, for example—with uncanny accuracy.

Beyond the Caracol is the **Nunnery,** so-named by Spanish explorers who thought it looked like convents back home. Judging from its size, location, and many rooms, the Nunnery was probably an administrative palace. Its exuberant facades show strong Chenes influence, another example of the blending of styles in Chichén Itzá.

Museum

In the visitor services area, Chichén Itzá's museum (8 A.M.–5 P.M. daily) is curiously small for a site as important and oft-visited as this one, but it's worth visiting nonetheless. An air-conditioned auditorium nearby shows films (circa 1971, apparently) on Chichén Itzá and other sites.

Light Show

The site puts on a nightly high-tech sound and light show at 7 P.M. (winter hours) and 8 P.M. (summer hours). The fee to enter is included in the general admission, although if you'd like to see the show the night before you visit the ruins, you can pay for the light show portion of the ticket (US$4.50) in advance. Just be sure to let the salesperson know that you would like to buy a half ticket and save the stub so that you're not double-charged the next day. The show is presented in Spanish. For an additional US$2.25 you can rent earphones with translations in English, French, and German.

Practicalities

The grounds are open daily 8 A.M.–5 P.M. Admission is US$9 per person, plus US$3 to bring a video camera. The fee includes entrance to the ruins, plus the sound and light show, presented nightly at 7 P.M. in the winter (October–April) and at 8 P.M. in the summer (May–September); hold onto your ticket. There is no discount if you don't wish to go to the sound and light show, but there is a show-only price (US$3). You can go to show the night before you visit the ruins, but be sure to buy a US$5 partial entrance—not the US$3 show-only ticket—and keep your stub for credit the next morning. Just tell the ticket seller your plan, and he'll sell you the right ticket.

Guides can be hired at the entrance according to fixed and clearly marked prices: US$35 for a 1.5- or two-hour tour in Spanish, US$42 in English, French, Italian, or German. Prices are per group, which can include up to eight people. Tips are customary and not included in the price. The visitor center also has restrooms, ATM, luggage storage, a café, bookstore, gift shop, and information center.

OTHER SIGHTS
Balankanche Caves

Six kilometers (3.7 miles) east of Chichén Itzá, the **Grutas de Balankanche** (9 A.M.–5 P.M., US$4.65, children under 13 free) are a disappointment. The 1959 excavation of the caves by the National Geographic archaeologist Dr. E. Wyllys Andrews uncovered numerous artifacts and ceremonial sites giving researchers a better understanding of ancient Maya cosmology, especially related to the notion of *xibalbá* (the underworld). Nowadays, the caves are basically a tourist trap—a wide path meandering 500 meters (0.3 mile) down a tunnel with urns and other artifacts supposedly set up in their original locations. Wires and electric lights illuminate the path, but the recorded narration does nothing of the sort—you can hardly understand it, no matter what language it's in.

Entry times are fixed according to language: Spanish at 9 A.M., noon, 2 P.M., and 4 P.M.; English at 11 A.M., 1 P.M., and 3 P.M.; and French at 10 A.M. A minimum of six visitors are needed for the tour to depart.

Parque Ecoarqueológico Ik Kil

Three kilometers (1.9 miles) east of Pisté, the centerpiece of the Parque Ecoarqueológico Ik Kil (Carretera Mérida-Cancún Km. 122, tel. 985/858-1525, 8 A.M.–6 P.M. daily, US$5.50 adults, US$2.75 children) is the immense, perfectly round **Cenote Sagrado Azul** with a partial stone roof. Although real, the alterations to the cenote's natural state—supported walls, a set of stairs leading you in, a waterfall—make it feel pretty artificial. While not representative of the typical cenote experience, this is a good option if you are traveling with small children and need a spot to cool off. The cenote and on-site restaurant get packed with tour groups 12:30–2:30 P.M.; try visiting outside those times for a mellower visit. Better yet, stay at one of the on-site bungalows.

ACCOMMODATIONS

A handful of upscale hotels make up the small *Zona Hotelera* (Hotel Zone) on the east side of Chichén Itzá, complete with its own entrance to the ruins. Nearby, in the town of Pisté, there are a handful of budget and mid-range options. Be sure to reserve early during the spring and fall equinoxes.

Under US$25

At the eastern end of Pisté, **Pirámide Inn** (Calle 15 No. 30, tel. 985/851-0115, www.chichen.com, US$4 pp camping) has a grassy garden for camping and several open-air *palapas* with concrete floors where you can hang hammocks. Shared bathrooms are clean, and you can use the swimming pool. The hotel rents hammocks for another US$4 a night, if you need one.

Posada Olalde (Calle 6 s/n at Calles 17, tel. 985/851-0086, US$23.25 s/d, US$26 s/d bungalow) is the best budget option in town. Rooms are no frills but they are brightly painted, have a shared porch, and face a leafy courtyard. The hotel also has four bungalows, which sound nice (and cost more) but are inferior to the rooms, with saggy beds, bad light, and a dank feel about them. The posada is a little hard to find—coming from Mérida, turn right on a narrow dirt alley across from El Pollo Mexicano restaurant. From there it's two blocks down on the right.

Posada Flamboyanes (Calle 15 s/n, no phone, US$18.50 s/d with fan, US$21 with a/c) has only three small simple rooms, and the low price and welcoming pink exterior means they are often taken. Moreover, the caretaker is often running errands, leaving no one to attend the rooms. If you do manage to get one, it should be relatively clean and will open onto an airy covered corridor. Coming from Mérida, look for it on your right, just beyond the Hotel Chichén Itzá.

US$25-50

The **(Hotel Dolores Alba Chichén** (Carretera Mérida-Cancún Km. 122, tel. 985/858-1555, www.doloresalba.com, US$42 s/d with a/c) is one of the best deals in the area especially given its choice location three kilometers (1.9 miles) east of the ruins, one kilometer (0.6 miles) from the Balankanche Caves, and across the street from the Parque Ecoarqueológico Ik Kil. Rooms are spotless and smallish, with good beds and simple tile work on the walls to spiff up the decor. The hotel has a pleasant outdoor restaurant (7 A.M.–10 P.M. daily, US$4–10) and two large swimming pools—the one in back has a mostly natural stone bottom, with holes and channels reminiscent of an ocean reef, which is perfect for kids with active imaginations. The hotel also provides free shuttle service to the ruins.

On the eastern end of Pisté, **Pirámide Inn** (Calle 15 No. 30, tel. 985/851-0115, www.chichen.com, US$4 pp camping, US$38 s/d) is a low sprawling hotel with large rooms that are clean though a bit dark. The decor is distinctly 1970s den, with some rooms sporting bubblegum paint jobs and lacquered brick walls. The air-conditioning units appear to be from the same era, and can be loud. On the upside, there's a pool in back, facing a pleasant garden, and a restaurant serving reliable breakfasts and dinners. The bus station is nearby, and the ruins are just a kilometer (0.6 miles) down the road.

US$50-100

Set in a lush, green forest **(Parque Ecoarqueológico Ik Kil** (Carretera Mérida-Cancún Km. 122, tel. 985/858-1525, US$93 s/d with a/c) offers 12 modern and ultra-comfortable bungalows. All are spacious and have Jacuzzi tubs, comfortable beds, and pullout sofas. Silent air-conditioning and a private porch make it all the better. Unlimited use of the popular cenote on-site is included too. A fantastic value, especially if traveling with kids.

Club Med Villas Chichén Itzá (Zona Hotelera, Carr. Mérida-Valladolid Km. 120, tel. 985/856-6000, scottsdale.mexicores@clubmed.com, www.clubmed.com, US$81 s/d with a/c, US$135 suite with a/c) is a pleasant two-story hotel with a mellow ambiance. Boxy, though nice, rooms are set around a lush courtyard with an inviting L-shaped pool in the center. A library/TV room with comfy couches and a variety of books—from romance novels to archaeology books—also faces the courtyard. A decent restaurant and a tennis court are on-site too.

US$100-150

In a former life, the **Hotel Chichén Itzá** (Calle 15 s/n, tel. 985/851-0022, US$74–111 s/d with a/c) was the Hotel Misión Chichén, before being bought and renovated by the hotel/tour conglomerate Mayaland. When we passed through it was in the midst of being remodeled (again) and acquired (again), this time by the Best Western chain hotel. Regardless of who owns it when you're in town, it is definitely the nicest hotel in Pisté proper. All rooms have simple Mexican decor, comfortable furnishings, and large modern bathrooms; the least expensive rooms face the street and can be noisy, while the top ones are larger and overlook the hotel's attractive garden and pool area. There's also a cavernous restaurant (7 A.M.–10 P.M. daily) that's often packed with tour groups.

ARCHAEOLOGICAL ZONES

Over US$150

Once the headquarters for the Carnegie Institute's Chichén Itzá expedition, the **Hacienda Chichén Resort** (Zona Hotelera, Carr. Mérida-Valladolid Km. 120, tel. 999/920-8407, toll-free U.S. tel. 877/631-4006, www.haciendachichen.com, US$160 s/d with a/c, US$170–225 suite) now is a tranquil hotel set in a lush tropical garden. A beautiful setting, most of the rooms are in the original cottages used by the archaeologists—very cool to stay where they once lived but not-so-cool to have to look at cinder block walls and to deal with the musty smell that pervades some of the older units. The decor is simple—tile floors, exposed beam ceilings, wood furnishings—but the rooms are quite comfortable. Be sure to wander the grounds with an eye for the narrow-gauge railroad tracks that were used to transport artifacts from Chichén Itzá and the original hacienda chapel. A pool, full-service spa (9 A.M.–2 P.M., 5–10 P.M. daily), and a fine dining room also are nice finds.

The **Hotel and Bungalows Mayaland** (Zona Hotelera, Carr. Mérida-Valladolid Km. 120, tel. 985/851-0100, www.mayaland.com, US$150–370 s/d) is literally at the entrance to Chichén Itzá—guests and non-guests alike must pass through the resort and by two of its gift shops to get to the ticket booth. The grounds are gorgeous: 100 acres of tamed tropical jungle filled with birds, plus three restaurants and four pools. Tour groups stop here for meals and shopping, and their sudden loud presence can be a turnoff for paying guests; however, you can avoid the crush by asking the reception desk what time the buses will arrive. Definitely take advantage of being so close to the ruins by getting there right at opening time. Rooms and bungalows are pleasant if somewhat dated, including stained-glass windows, hardwood furniture, and terraces. Suites have whirlpool tubs and, in some, a view of Chichén Itzá's Observatory. If you really want to splurge, ask about the Pavarotti Suite, a luxurious suite that was expressly built for the corpulent tenor when he sang in concert at Chichén Itzá. The restaurants here are pricey

and so-so at best; better to take your appetite to Hacienda Chichén, a five-minute walk away.

FOOD

Eating options are pretty limited in Pisté but improve somewhat if you have a car and can get to and from the large hotels.

The newly remodeled **(€ Restaurante Las Mestizas** (Calle 15 s/n, tel. 985/851-0069, 7:30 A.M.–10:30 P.M. daily, US$2.50–8) is without a doubt the best place to eat in Pisté, with an airy, colonial-style interior and tasty, good-sized portions. The food is classic Yucatecan fare, from *panuchos* to *pollo pibil*. Service is exceptional.

True to its name, **Restaurante y Pizzería Mr. Pizzas** (Calle 15 s/n, tel. 985/851-0079, 2–11 P.M. Tue.–Sun., US$6–11) serves mostly pizza, plus hamburgers and other items. The dining room is appealing—not fancy but clean—and the service is good.

Set in a 16th-century hacienda, the **(€ Hacienda Chichén Resort's restaurant** (Zona Hotelera, tel. 999/920-8407, 7 A.M.–10 P.M. daily, US$10–16) is a relaxing place to eat after a long day at the ruins. The menu is varied—Yucatecan specialties, pastas, sandwiches, and on the occasional evening, a trio plays regional music.

Although often inundated by day-trippers from Club Med Cancún, the restaurant at the **Club Med Villas Chichén Itzá** (Zona Hotelera, Carr. Mérida-Valladolid Km. 120, tel. 985/856-6000, 7:30 A.M.–10 P.M. daily, US$6–16) is a good option. With an international menu, indoor and outdoor seating, and a lunch buffet, there's something for everyone.

If you can stand the tour groups, the lunch buffet at **Hotel and Bungalows Mayaland** (Zona Hotelera, Carr. Mérida-Valladolid Km. 120, tel. 985/851-0100, noon–3 P.M. daily, US$14.50) is a good choice. With its variety of hot and cold dishes, you definitely will find something to fill you up. Live music, ballet folklórico shows, and outdoor seating are nice touches.

For groceries, **Abarrotes Alba** (Calle 15 s/n, 50 m/164 ft east of the plaza, 6 A.M.–10 P.M.

daily) has a decent selection of fresh fruit, canned goods, drinks, and toiletries.

INFORMATION AND SERVICES

There is no tourist office in Pisté; if you have questions about the region or the ruins, ask at the front desk of your hotel.

Hospitals

Clínica La Promesa (Calle 14 between Calle 13 and 15, tel. 985/851-0005, open 24 hours) is the only clinic in town. For anything serious, you're better off going to Valladolid.

Pharmacies

Farmacia Lidia (Calle 15 s/n, no phone, 7 A.M.–10 P.M. daily) is on the west end of town, 25 meters (82 feet) from Abarrotes Alba.

Police

The police have an office (but no phone) in the Palacio Municipal (City Hall), facing the church. An officer is on duty 24 hours a day.

Money

Pisté doesn't have a bank, but there are reliable ATMs in Chichén Itzá's visitor complex.

Internet and Telephone

Across from the bus terminal, **Tienda San Antonio** (tel. 985/851-0089, 9 A.M.–9 P.M. Mon.–Fri., 10 A.M.–9 P.M. Sat., 10 A.M.–6 P.M. Sun.) is a quiet shop with Internet service (US$1.50/hr) and international calling to the United States and Canada for US$0.50 a minute and to Europe for US$1 a minute.

A handful of small Internet shops near the central park charge the same and are open late, but cater to local kids and can be crowded and noisy.

Launderette

Lavandería Guadalupe (Calle 10 near Calle 13, 8 A.M.–6 P.M. Mon.–Sat.) charges US$0.90 per kilogram (2.2 pounds) to wash and dry clothes; same-day service if you drop your load off first thing in the morning. Located two blocks north of the main drag—turn north at the Posada Kari sign, east of Abarrotes Alba.

GETTING THERE AND AROUND

Buses from all directions converge on Chichén Itzá and Pisté; those from Mérida and Cancún often will drop off passengers at the main entrance to the ruins, which is about 1.5 kilometers (0.9 mile) west of town. If you are in Pisté, passing bus drivers may be willing to drop you at the entrance for around US$0.50, or just walk.

Bus

Most bus service here is on Oriente, ADO's second-class line, but there are a few first-class buses as well, and are worth the extra cost. Pisté's small bus terminal (tel. 985/851-0052, 7 A.M.–6 P.M. daily, cash only) is at the far east end of town, next to the Pirámide Inn. There is also a ticket office in the gift shop at the ruins (tel. 985/851-0377, 10 A.M.–5 P.M.). All buses stop at the terminal, and at the ruins if it's between 8 A.M. and 5:30 P.M. Departure times listed here are for the terminal—those from the ruins will be slightly earlier or later depending on the direction you're headed. The visitor center has **luggage storage,** which is handy if you plan to catch an onward bus after visiting the ruins.

To Mérida, first-class buses (US$7.50, two hours) leave Pisté at 2:10 P.M. and 5 P.M., plus 3:50 P.M. on Sat., while second-class buses (US$5, 2.5 hours) leave every 30–60 minutes 7 A.M.–5:30 P.M.

To Cancún, one daily first-class bus (US$10.50, 2.5 hours) leaves at 4:15 P.M. Second-class buses (US$8.50, 4.5 hours) depart every 30–60 minutes 8:30 A.M.–6:30 P.M.

To Valladolid, first-class buses (US$3.25, 45 minutes) depart at 8:10 A.M., 11:10 A.M., 2:20 P.M., and 4:15 P.M., while second-class service (US$2, one hour) is available every 30–60 minutes, 7:30 A.M.–4:30 P.M.

To Tulum, first-class buses (US$10, 2.5 hours) leave Pisté at 8:10 A.M., 2:20 P.M., and 4:15 P.M., and there's one second-class departure at 7:30 A.M. (US$6, three hours).

For Playa del Carmen, take the first-class Tulum bus at 2:20 P.M. or 4:15 P.M. (US$13.25, 3.5 hours) or the 7:30 A.M. second-class bus (US$7.50, five hours).

To Cobá town and archaeological site, take the second-class Tulum/Playa del Carmen bus (US$4.25, 2.5 hours). The first-class buses do not stop there.

Car

Chichén Itzá lies adjacent to Highway 180, 40 kilometers (25 miles) west of Valladolid, 120 kilometers (75 miles) east of Mérida, and 200 kilometers (124 miles) west of Cancún. An eight-lane highway known as the *cuota* (toll road) connects Cancún and Mérida; exit at Pisté. Tolls from Mérida are US$6, but a whopping US$28 from Cancún. You can save a little by getting off at the Valladolid exit (US$18) and taking the *libre* (free road) for the remaining 45 kilometers (27 miles). Or take the *libre* the whole way; it's slower but in good condition, passing through numerous villages and past simple farms. Watch for *topes* (speed bumps) around villages—in all, there are nearly 100 between Mérida and Cancún, and hitting one at anything faster than a crawl can jar you—and your rental—to the bones.

Air

Aeropuerto Internacional Chichén Itzá (tel. 985/851-0408) is 16 kilometers (9.9 miles) east of Pisté, between the towns of Xcalacot and Kaua. Inaugurated in April 2000, it is one of the most modern airports in the country, with an 1,800-meter (5,900-foot) runway capable of receiving 747 jets. Although initially receiving dozens of regular and charter flights, its license was suspended in 2001. Today it stands virtually empty, receiving only a smattering of charters, mostly from Cancún, Cozumel, and Chetumal.

Ek' Balam

Ek' Balam (8 A.M.–5 P.M., US$3) is a unique and fascinating site that has only recently been appreciated by researchers and tourists. Maya for "Black Jaguar," serious restoration didn't begin here until the mid-1990s. It was during that time that a remarkable and incredibly well-preserved stucco mural was uncovered partway up the site's largest pyramid. The discovery revealed a great deal about this commercially important city, which thrived A.D. 700–1100, though much remains unknown. Although it's located just 30 kilometers (19 miles) north of Valladolid, and in close proximity to Cancún and Mérida, Ek' Balam has not attracted the bus loads of tourists that other sites have. That may change: already a huge parking lot has been completed, a new visitor center is under way, and there are plans to widen the access roads.

A **village** by the same name is two kilometers (1.2 miles) away and provides basic accommodations and food; for more options and other traveler services, head to Valladolid.

◖ EK' BALAM ARCHAEOLOGICAL ZONE

Entering Ek' Balam, you'll pass through a low thick wall and an elegant corbel arch. Walls are rare in Maya cities, and were most commonly used for defense, as in the cases of Becán and Tulum. Ek' Balam's low thick walls would not have slowed marauding rivals, however, and so they most likely served to enforce social divisions, with some areas off-limits (but not out of view!) to all but the elite. They may also have been decorative—the city possessed great aesthetic flair, as the arch at the entrance and the site's famous stucco frieze demonstrate.

Acrópolis and El Trono

The highlight of Ek' Balam is, without question, an artful and remarkably pristine stucco frieze known as El Trono (The Throne). It is located under a protective *palapa* roof, about two thirds the way up the Acrópolis, a massive pyramid at the north end of the site, and Ek'

Balam's largest structure. In fact, at 32 meters (105 feet) high and 158 meters (514.8 feet) wide, it is among the largest Maya pyramids ever built. A steep stairway leads up the center of the pyramid, and a platform to the left of the stairs provides visitors a close-up view of El Trono.

About 85 percent of El Trono is the original stucco. Often structures like this would have been painted blue or red, but not so here. In fact, shortly after it was built, El Trono was sealed behind a stone wall 50–60 centimeters (19–24 inches) thick. It remained there untouched until the 1990s, when restoration workers accidentally dislodged one of the protective stones while removing a tree growing above it.

The tall, winged figures immediately catch your eye, as they appear so much like angels. In fact, they are high priests. Notice that one is deformed—his left arm is longer than the right, and has only four fingers. The Maya considered birth defects to be a sign of divinity, and the priest depicted here may have risen to his position precisely because of his deformation.

EK' BALAM ARCHAEOLOGICAL ZONE

OUTER WALL

INNER WALL

THE ACROPOLIS

STRUCTURE II

STRUCTURE III

BALL COURT

STRUCTURE X

OUTER WALL

STRUCTURE XVII

OVAL PALACE

INNER WALL

OUTER WALL

ENTRANCE

SACBE

SACBE

© AVALON TRAVEL PUBLISHING, INC.

SCALE NOT AVAILABLE

© LIZA PRADO

the view from Ek' Balam's impressive Acrópolis

Directly over the door is a seated figure (unfortunately, the head is missing). This represents Ukit Kan Le'k Tok,' one of Ek' Balam's former rulers, described in inscriptions as the "king of kings," and the person for whom El Trono was built and dedicated. A tomb was discovered in the chamber behind the frieze that contained thousands of jade, gold, obsidian, and ceramic artifacts, left as offerings to this powerful leader. The small face at the king-figure's navel represents a rival whom he defeated in war.

Viewed as a whole, the frieze is unmistakably a Chenes-style "monster mouth": a huge stylized mask in which the doorway represents the gaping mouth of a high god. The pointed upper and lower teeth are easy to spot, as are the spiral eyes. Monster mouths are never mundane, but this one is especially elaborate: notice how two beautifully crafted figures straddle the lower eyelids, while hoisting the upper lids with their shoulders. At least five more figures, plus lattice patterns and other designs, adorn the rest of the mask.

Before heading down, climb the rest of the way to the top of the Acrópolis to take in the view. With the exception of the odd telephone and radio tower, and the site's large new visitor's center, the view of the broad flat Yucatecan landscape is probably not all that different than the one Maya priests and kings enjoyed from this very same vantage point, more than a thousand years ago.

South Plaza

Chances are you bee-lined straight from the entrance to the Acrópolis and the frieze—who can blame you? Descending the pyramid, you can see that Ek' Balam is a small site, with buildings somewhat crowded together. It has two plazas (north and south) with the ball court in the middle.

On the south side of the south plaza—opposite the Acrópolis—stands **La Rodonda,** or the Oval Palace. A squat midsize structure, La Rodonda has an eclectic array of overlapping lines and curves, stairs and terraces. It underwent numerous iterations, as did virtually all

Maya temples, but the result here was especially eclectic. Archaeologists suspect La Rodonda was used for astronomical observations, and the discovery of several richly adorned tombs suggest it had a ceremonial purpose as well.

Flanking La Redonda are **Las Gemelas** (The Twins), known as Structure 17. As the plaque indicates, these identical structures are perhaps the best example of Ek' Balam's particular architectural style. Having perfected the use of stucco, Ek' Balam's builders did not concern themselves with precise masonry, as the stones would be covered in a thick stucco cap. However, stucco proved much less resilient to erosion, and centuries later the structures here appear shabbier than even much older ones, like in the Río Bec region, where stucco was less common and stone blocks were more carefully cut and fitted.

Guides usually can be hired at the entrance to the ruins, or arranged via Genesis Ek' Balam (see *Accommodations*).

ACCOMMODATIONS AND FOOD

In the Maya village near the ruins, **Genesis Ek' Balam** (tel. 985/101-0277, www.genesis retreat.com, US$50–62 d, family unit US$75–100) has nine rooms and cabañas, set on a leafy enclosed property with a natural bio-filtered pool in the middle. Six units share a large clean bathroom, three have private bathrooms, one has air-conditioning, and all are different in style and decor. One of the favorites, the Birdhouse, has screen windows on all sides and a small balcony overlooking the pool and garden. A full breakfast is included, and lunch is open to non-guests as well (1–3 P.M. only, US$8–12). The mostly vegetarian dishes make ample use of *chaya,* a rich spinach-like plant

used by the Maya since before the conquest (and still today), and grown right in the Genesis garden. The hardworking Canadian owner offers tours of the village and local artisan workshops (US$7 pp, minimum four people) and can arrange guided excursions to the ruins, plus nearby cenotes, haciendas, and more. Be aware that a number of friendly pooches lounge about the property—fine if you like dogs, but not everyone's thing.

Much more rustic accommodations are available at **Uh Najil Ek' Balam** (US$32.50 cabin), a community-run complex a short distance from Genesis Ek' Balam. Eleven wood bungalows have very basic furnishings; a few have private baths, others share equally basic common bathrooms and showers. The concept is great—a cooperative of more than 20 local people share in the camp's operation and profit—but the place could use a little better upkeep. Guests can use the kitchen here. The best feature may be the new **observation tower** (US$2.50) that affords a terrific view of the village and surroundings.

GETTING THERE AND AROUND

If you're driving from Valladolid, head north on Highway 295 toward Tizimín. After about 17 kilometers (10.6 miles), turn right (east) onto the well-marked turnoff toward Ek' Balam. From there, it's another 11 kilometers (6.8 miles) to a fork: One direction leads to the village and accommodations, the other to the archaeological site.

A taxi from Valladolid to the village costs US$15–20 for up to four people. If you're just visiting the ruins, you can negotiate for a driver to take you there and wait 1–2 hours and bring you back for around US$25.

Valladolid

Valladolid is gaining attention from tourists because of its colonial atmosphere and its central location: 30 minutes from the archaeological zones of Chichén Itzá and Ek' Balam, an hour from the ruins at Cobá and the flamingo reserve in Río Lagartos, and two hours from Mérida, Cancún, and Tulum. It's an easy bus or car ride to any of these destinations, restaurants and hotels are reasonably priced, and you have the advantage of staying in a colonial Mexican town. If you're en route to one of the regional sites or simply want to have a small-town experience, consider spending a night here—you're sure to be happily surprised.

HISTORY

The site of several Maya revolts against the Spanish, Valladolid was conquered in 1543 by Francisco de Montejo, cousin of the like-named Spaniard who founded Mérida. It was once the Maya city of Zací; Montejo brutalized its inhabitants and crushed their temples, building large churches and homes in their place. It is perhaps not surprising, then, that the Caste War started in Valladolid, and that the city played an important role in the beginning of the Mexican Revolution. Today, Valladolid is a charming colonial town with a rich history and strong Maya presence.

ORIENTATION

Valladolid is easy to get around. It's laid out in a grid pattern with even-numbered streets running north to south, odd-numbered streets running east to west. The central plaza at the center of the city, is bordered by Calles 39, 40, 41, and 42.

SIGHTS
☾ Iglesia y Ex-Convento San Bernardino de Siena

In a well-kempt colonial neighborhood several blocks southwest of the *parque central,* the Iglesia y Ex-convento San Bernardino de Siena (Calle 41-A, tel. 985/856-2160, 8 A.M.–noon

and 5–7 P.M. Tue.–Sat., until noon Sun.) is one of Valladolid's most attractive structures. Built by Franciscan missionaries between 1552 and 1560, the church entrance is through a series of arches, and the facade, covered in a checkerboard-like stucco pattern, rises into a squat tower complete with turrets. Annexed to it, the ex-convent has rooms radiating from a center courtyard, which features, uniquely, a cenote. Called *Sis-Há,* (Cold Water), the cenote helped the monks to be self-reliant. In 2004, an exploration of the cenote resulted in the discovery of 164 rifles and one canon—neither the age nor the nationality of the arms have been disclosed. Mass is held in the church at 7 P.M. Tuesday to Saturday, and at 7 A.M., 9 A.M., 11 A.M., 6 P.M., and 7 P.M. on Sunday. Special permission is required to visit the ex-convent; call ahead or ask in the church office.

Museo San Roque

A long high-ceilinged room—this used to be a church—the Museo San Roque (Calle 41 between Calles 38 and 40, 9 A.M.–8 P.M. daily, free) is a worthwhile stop, with fascinating displays on Valladolid's history, with a focus on the Caste War and the beginning of the Mexican Revolution. Interestingly, both conflicts, so important to Mexican history, grew out of incidents in and around Valladolid. Displays of local handicrafts also are notable. Signage, unfortunately, in Spanish only.

Palacio Municipal

On the 2nd floor of the city hall (7 A.M.–7 P.M. daily, free) is a large balcony overlooking the plaza, with four large paintings by local talent Manuel Lizama. The paintings depict events in Valladolid's history: pre-Hispanic communities, the city's founding, the Caste War, and the Mexican Revolution. Not spectacular, exactly, but something to see.

Cenote Zaci

Cenote Zaci (Calle 36 between Calles 37 and

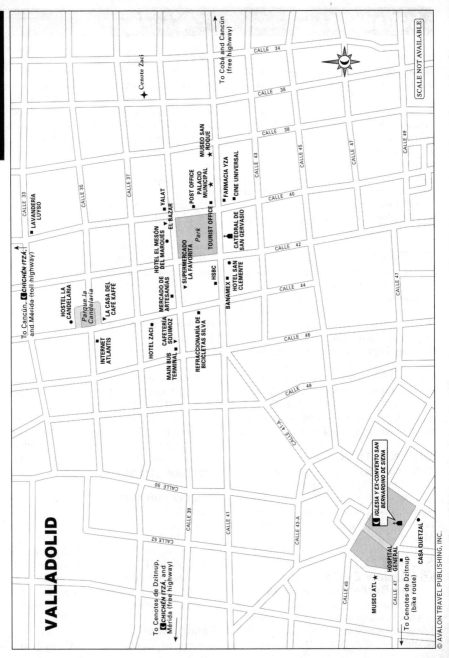

VALLADOLID

SCALE NOT AVAILABLE

To Cobá and Cancún (free highway)

To Cancún, CHICHÉN ITZA, and Mérida (toll highway)

Cenote Zaci

CALLE 33
CALLE 34
CALLE 35
CALLE 36
CALLE 37
CALLE 38
CALLE 40
CALLE 42
CALLE 43
CALLE 44
CALLE 45
CALLE 46
CALLE 47
CALLE 48
CALLE 49
CALLE 39
CALLE 41
CALLE 41-A
CALLE 43-A
CALLE 45
CALLE 47
CALLE 50
CALLE 62

LAVANDERÍA LUYSO
HOSTEL LA CANDELARIA
Parque la Candelaria
LA CASA DEL CAFÉ KAFFÉ
INTERNET ATLANTIS
HOTEL ZACI
MAIN BUS TERMINAL
CAFETERÍA SQUIMOZ
REFRACCIONARIA DE BICICLETAS SILVA
MERCADO DE ARTESANÍAS
HOTEL EL MESÓN DEL MARQUÉS
SUPERMERCADO LA FAVORITA
HSBC
BANAMEX
HOTEL SAN CLEMENTE
YALAT
EL BAZAR
POST OFFICE
PALACIO MUNICIPAL
Park
TOURIST OFFICE
CATEDRAL DE SAN GERVASIO
MUSEO SAN ROQUE
FARMACIA YZA
CINE UNIVERSAL

IGLESIA Y EX-CONVENTO SAN BERNARDINO DE SIENA
HOSPITAL GENERAL
CASA QUETZAL
MUSEO ATL

To Cenotes de Dzitnup, CHICHÉN ITZA, and Mérida (free highway)

To Cenotes de Dzitnup (bike route)

© AVALON TRAVEL PUBLISHING, INC.

ARCHAEOLOGICAL ZONES

39, 8 A.M.–7:30 P.M. daily, US$1.50, under 13 US$1) is in the middle of town and often pooh-poohed in comparison to the cenotes at Dzitnup. But it's a peaceful, attractive spot, especially if you have it to yourself. (You can scope out the scene before going in by looking over the wall halfway down Calle 37, around the corner from the entrance.) A dark natural pool lies in a huge cavern with a bank of trees on one side and a path looping down from the entrance. You may find leaves and pollen floating on the water's surface, but it's still refreshing. There's also a small—and sad—zoo and a simple eatery.

Cenotes de Dzitnup

Four kilometers (2.5 miles) west of Valladolid on Highway 180 is the small community of Dzitnup, home to two appealing underground cenotes. Both make for a unique and refreshing swim—in fact, on warm days both can be somewhat crowded. At both cenotes, there are parking lots and many small *artesanía* stands at the entrance, and you'll be aggressively pursued by children offering to watch your car or sell you a postcard.

Although the two are across the street from each other, **Cenote X'keken** (8 A.M.–6 P.M. daily, US$2.50 adults, US$1.50 under 17, video cameras US$2.75) has been open longer and is better known; many postcards and travel guides show it as "Cenote Dzitnup." After a reasonably easy descent underground (in a few places you must bend over because of a low ceiling; there's a hanging rope to help), you'll come to a circular pond of clear, cool water. It's a pretty, albeit damp, place, with a high dome ceiling that has one small opening at the top letting in a ray of sun and dangling green vines. Often an errant bird can be seen swooping low over the water before heading to the sun and sky through the tiny opening. Stalactites and at least one large stalagmite adorn the ceiling and cenote floor.

At **Cenote Samula** (7 A.M.–5 P.M. daily, US$2.50 adults, US$1.50 under 17, video cameras US$2.75) tree roots dangle impressively from the ground-level roof all the way down

to the water. Enter through a narrow tunnel, which opens onto a set of stairs that zigzag down to the water. Fearless kids jump from the first or even second switchback, into the clear turquoise water below.

Many people ride their bikes here—a bike path runs parallel to the highway, making it a pleasant trip. A cab to the cenotes runs about US$5.

ENTERTAINMENT AND EVENTS

Cine Universal (Calle 40 between Calles 41 and 43, tel. 985/856-2040, US$3.75) shows mostly Hollywood films on its two screens. Ticket prices cover the nightly double feature, which begin at 7 P.M. and 9 P.M. If you're only interested in seeing one movie, there are no discounts.

SHOPPING

Although you're likely to be followed around the shop by vigilant salespeople, **Yalat** (Calle 39 at Calle 40, tel. 985/856-1969, 9 A.M.–8 P.M. daily) is worth a stop if you're interested in purchasing high-end Mexican handicrafts and art. Definitely pricey—almost astronomical—the quality of the items sold is excellent.

Mercado de Artesanías (Calle 39 at Calle 44; 8 A.M.–8 P.M. Mon.–Sat., 8 A.M.–2 P.M. Sun.) has a decent variety of *guayaberas,* embroidered *huilpiles,* hammocks, and other popular handicrafts. The selection isn't very large—there are only about a dozen shops here—so be sure to bargain.

ACCOMMODATIONS

Valladolid offers a good selection of simple and mid-range hotels. All are convenient to the central plaza.

Under US$50

Hostel La Candelaria (Parque La Candelaria, Calle 35 between Calles 42 and 44, tel. 985/856-2267, candelaria_hostel@hotmail .com, www.hostellingmexico.com, US$8.25 dorm, US$19.50 s with shared bath, US$26 d with shared bath) offers clean though somewhat worn rooms—many beds needed to be replaced and a coat of paint would do wonders. Still, it's a good choice, given the outstanding common areas: an outdoor kitchen that is amazingly equipped with loads of kitchenware, spices, and even tea; a laundry area (hand wash only) with soap provided; a comfy indoor lounge decorated with Mexican art and instruments; and a lush garden with hammocks, tables, and chairs. There's lots of information about the region, plus a great book exchange. Continental breakfast is included in the rate as are sheets and private lockers.

With spotless rooms set along a grassy, flower-lined courtyard, **Hotel Zaci** (Calle 44 between Calles 37 and 39, tel. 985/856-2167, US$23 s, US$31.50, US$32.50 d with a/c, US$36 d with a/c) is a good option. Rooms are kept up nicely and have details such as stenciling on the walls and ironwork furnishings. The top floor rooms are a bit cheaper—the decor and amenities are a bit dated—so if you're counting your pennies, ask for one of those. A small, clean pool is a nice plus.

Across from the cathedral, **Hotel San Clemente** (Calle 42 between Calles 41 and 43, tel. 985/856-2208, www.hotelsanclemente .com.mx, US$32 s/d with fan, US$37 s/d with a/c) has 64 rooms surrounding a pleasant courtyard and pool. The rooms are spacious and clean with simple decor. Some units have a musty smell, unfortunately; ask for one on the top floor, which have the benefit of a good breeze.

US$50-100

Originally a 16th-century home, **(Hotel El Mesón del Marqués** (central plaza, Calle 39 between Calles 40 and 42, tel. 985/856-2073, www.mesondelmarques.com, US$53–65 s/d with a/c, US$99 junior suite with a/c) is a favorite among travelers—a traditionally Mexican hotel with lush courtyards, a gurgling fountain, arches upon arches, and personalized service. Rooms are divided into three categories: standard, superior, and junior suite. The first two are decorated similarly with heavy wood furniture, iron headboards, and brightly colored woven bedspreads—the difference is that the superior is bigger and more expensive. Junior suites are brand new rooms, with modern decor and amenities, and even more space than the others. All of the rooms lead to an egg-shaped pool in a verdant garden—a perfect place to relax after a day of sightseeing. Be sure to enjoy at least one meal at the hotel restaurant, considered one of the best in town.

Located just a half-block from pretty San Bernardino de Siena church, **Casa Quetzal** (Calle 51 No. 218, tel. 985/856-4796, www .casa-quetzal.com, US$55.50 s/d, including breakfast) is Valladolid's first true B&B. Five large high-ceilinged rooms surround a pretty garden and swimming pool, while a community kitchen and lovely reading room—with excellent Mexican artwork, especially from Oaxaca and Jalisco—lend a homey feel. The plain ceramic floors and somewhat flimsy furniture clash with the hacienda-esque style intended here, but it's a charming place nonetheless and a model that is sure to be replicated and refined in this increasingly popular colonial city. All rooms have air-conditioning and wireless Internet, and four additional suites were in the works. The hotel is a bit removed from the central plaza—which can be a good thing—but you can easily walk into town or catch a taxi (US$1).

FOOD

(La Casa del Café Kaffé (Parque La Candelaria, Calle 35 at Calle 44, tel. 985/856-2879, 9 A.M.–1 P.M., 6:30 P.M.–midnight daily, US$1.25–4.25) is a fantastic place to get breakfast or a late-night snack. Owned and run by a welcoming Chilean couple, the menu features empanadas, quesadillas, sandwiches, fruit shakes, and a nice variety of coffee drinks. If you don't see what you crave on the menu, be sure to ask for it—meals often are made to order. With tables on the lovely Parque Candelaria, tasty food, and great service, you can't go wrong.

Located next to the bus station, **(Cafetería Squimoz** (Calle 39 near Calle 46, tel. 985/856-4156, 7 A.M.–9:30 P.M. Mon.–Sat., 8 A.M.–

VALLADOLID BUS SCHEDULES

Departures from Valladolid's **bus station** (Calle 39 at Calle 46, tel. 985/856-3448) include:

DESTINATION	PRICE	DURATION	SCHEDULE
Campeche	US$20	4 hrs	1:45 P.M.
Cancún	US$6.50-10*	3 hrs	every 30-60 min., 6 A.M.-10:30 P.M.
Chetumal	US$12	5 hrs	5:30 A.M., 7:30 A.M., and 2:30 P.M.
Chichén Itzá	US$2-3	45 min.	every 30-60 min., 7:15 A.M.-5:30 P.M.
Chiquilá	US$6	3 hrs	2:45 A.M.
Cobá	US$2	1 hr	9:30 A.M., 2:45 P.M., and 5:15 P.M.
Izamal	US$3.75	1.5 hrs	12:45 P.M. and 3:50 P.M.
Mérida	US$6.75-10.25*	3 hrs	every 30-60 min., 5 A.M.-10:30 P.M.
Playa del Carmen	US$7-13*	3 hrs	8:30 A.M., 9:30 A.M., 2:45 P.M., and 5:15 P.M., plus 6:30 A.M. (Mon., Tue., Sat. only)
Tizimín	US$1.75	1 hr	every 30-75 min., 5:30 A.M.-8 P.M.
Tulum	US$4-6.50*	2 hrs	eight departures daily 8:30 A.M.-5:20 P.M.

*Denotes first-class service; not available for all departures.

3 P.M. Sun., US$2.50–6) is well worth a stop even if you're not on your way out of town. Big breakfasts and sandwiches made to order are the specialties, though the coffee drinks and to-die-for milkshakes can't be overlooked. If you've got a sweet tooth, be sure to try the homemade flan.

On the central plaza, the restaurant at the ⓒ **Hotel El Mesón del Marqués** (Calle 39 between Calles 40 and 42, tel. 985/856-2073, 7 A.M.–10:30 P.M. daily, US$4–12) is considered the best eatery in town. The setting is classic Mexican—an interior courtyard with a colonial-style fountain and masses of fuchsia-colored bougainvillea draped over the balconies—and the menu is ambitiously Yucatecan and international. For breakfast try the scrambled eggs with *chaya* (a local green similar to spinach), for lunch, order the marinated chicken breast salad, and for dinner, start with the *sopa de lima* before moving on to the *poc chuc*. A fine experience any time of day.

El Bazar (central plaza, Calle 39 at Calle 40, 7 A.M.–11 P.M. daily, US$2.50–6) is a local food court, with a dozen or so inexpensive eateries, mostly selling pre-made Yucatecan specialties. Food is hit or miss—take a look at the offerings and decide which looks the freshest. Better yet, order something off the menu that hasn't been sitting around like scrambled eggs or salbutes. Avoid the rubbery tamales.

For groceries, **La Favorita** (Calle 39 between Calles 42 and 44; tel. 985/856-2036, 9 A.M.–3 P.M., 6–9:30 P.M. Mon.–Sat., 9 A.M.–3 P.M. Sun.) has a decent selection of fresh and canned foods.

INFORMATION
Tourist Information

Try your best at prying some useful information from Valladolid's tourist office (Palacio Municipal, Calle 40 at Calle 41, tel. 985/856-2063, ext. 115, 9 A.M.–9 P.M. Mon.–Fri., 9 A.M.–7 P.M. Sat., 9 A.M.–1 P.M. Sun.). At the very least, you should be able to get a map or two.

Hospitals

For medical assistance, head to the **Hospital General** (Parque de Sisal, Calle 49 s/n, tel. 985/856-2883, 24 hours).

Pharmacies

Just off the central plaza, **Farmacia Yza** (Calle 41 near Calle 40, tel. 985/856-4018) is open 24 hours.

Police

The police (Parque Bacalar, Calle 41 s/n, 24 hours) can be reached at tel. 985/856-2100.

SERVICES
Money

Half a block from the central plaza, **HSBC** (Calle 41 between Calles 42 and 44, 8 A.M.–7 P.M. Mon.–Sat.) and **Banamex** (Calle 41 between Calles 42 and 44, 9 A.M.–4 P.M. Mon.–Fri.) both have ATMs.

Internet and Telephone

Internet Atlantis (Calle 35 near Calle 44, 10 A.M.–11 P.M. daily) charges US$1 per hour.

Post Office

This tiny post office (central plaza, Calle 40 between Calles 39 and 41) is open 9 A.M.–3 P.M. Monday–Friday.

Launderette

The busy **Lavandería Luyso** (Calle 40 at Calle 33, tel. 985/856-3542, 8 A.M.–8 P.M. Mon.–Sat., 8 A.M.–2 P.M. Sun., US$0.75 per 1 kg/2.2 lbs) offers next-day service only.

GETTING THERE AND AROUND

Bus: Valladolid's bus station (Calle 39 at Calle 46, tel. 985/856-3448) is an easy walk from the central plaza, or if you have a lot of bags, a cheap taxi ride. With the exception of a few first-class departures, most of the service here is second-class.

Taxi: Taxis are relatively easy to flag down, especially around the central plaza. If you need to call one, try **Catedral** (tel. 985/856-2090).

Bicycle Rental: Rent bikes at **Refraccionaría de Bicicletas Silva** (Calle 44 between Calles 39 and 41, tel. 985/856-3667, 9 A.M.–8 P.M. daily) for US$0.65 an hour or US$3.75 a day.

Cobá

The Maya ruins of Cobá (7:30 A.M.–5 P.M. daily, US$3) make an excellent complement—or even alternative—to the beautiful but vastly overcrowded ruins at Tulum. Cobá doesn't have Tulum's stunning Caribbean view and beach, but it's surrounded by lakes and thick forest, making it a great place to see birds, butterflies, and tropical flora. In fact, some people come here more for the bird-watching than the ruins. Which is not to say the ruins are unimpressive. To the contrary: Cobá boasts the second-tallest pyramid on the Peninsula—and this one you can climb!—and other intriguing, if badly decayed, structures and temples.

The Cobá ruins are 42 kilometers (26 miles) of well-paved but speed bump–infested road from Tulum to Cobá—drive slow and pray you'll still have your muffler when you get there.

Just five minutes on foot from the Cobá ruins, a **village** by the same name offers a few dining and lodging options.

◖ COBÁ ARCHAEOLOGICAL ZONE

Cobá is especially notable for the complex system of *sacbeob* (raised stone causeways) that connected it to other cities, near and far. Dozens of such roads crisscross the Yucatán Peninsula, but Cobá has more than any other city, underscoring its status as a commercial, political, and military hub. One road extends in an almost perfectly straight line from the base of Cobá's principal pyramid to the town of Yaxuna, more than 100 kilometers (62 miles) away. No small feat considering it was 1–2 meters (3.3–6.6 feet) high and about 4.5 meters (15 feet) wide, and covered in white mortar. (The term *sacbeob*—whose singular form is *sacbé*—means "white road.") In Cobá, some roads were even bigger—10 meters across (32.8 feet)—and archaeologists have uncovered a massive stone cylinder believed to have been used to flatten the broad roadbeds.

TROPICAL MONKEYS

The jungles of Mexico are home to three species of monkeys: spider, howler, and black howler. Intelligent and endearing, these creatures are prime targets for the pet trade. The have been so hunted, in fact, that today all three are in danger of extinction. Experts estimate that for every monkey sold, three die during transportation and distribution. In an effort to protect these creatures, the Mexican government has prohibited their capture or trade. As you wander through the ruins of Cobá or the Punta Laguna Reserve, keep your ears perked and your eyes peeled. You're sure to see – or, at least, hear – a few tropical monkeys. A tip: spider and howler monkeys are most active at sunrise and sundown; if possible, consider waking early or staying late to increase your chances of spotting a few.

History

The Yucatán Peninsula has virtually no rivers, lakes, or other aboveground water. The same was true in ancient times, so a collection of small lakes, teeming with fish and fowl, some 40 kilometers (45 miles) from the coast would have been no small wonder. And it was no accident that a great city would rise up around this fortuitous geographic feature. Cobá was settled as early as 300 B.C. and over the next 500 years became an important center of trade, especially with the Petén region in present-day Guatemala. Petén influence is obvious in Cobá's temples, which resemble the high-steeped structures constructed in cities like Tikal. Cobá reached its zenith A.D. 600–800, when it controlled most of the northeastern portion of the peninsula. By then Cobá had a population of more than 40,000, making it among the largest urban centers in the northern lowlands; archaeologists

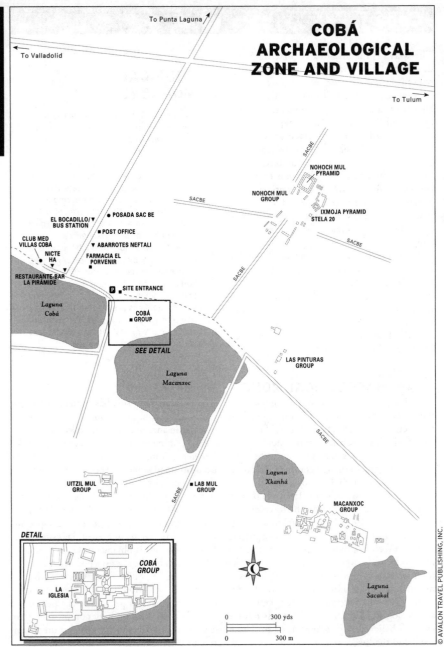

COBÁ ARCHAEOLOGICAL ZONE AND VILLAGE

To Punta Laguna

To Valladolid

To Tulum

SACBE

NOHOCH MUL PYRAMID

NOHOCH MUL GROUP

SACBE

IXMOJA PYRAMID
STELA 20

EL BOCADILLO/
BUS STATION
● POSADA SAC BE

■ POST OFFICE

CLUB MED
VILLAS COBÁ
▼ ABARROTES NEFTALI

NICTE
● HA
FARMACIA EL
PORVENIR
■

RESTAURANTE-BAR
LA PIRÁMIDE

P ■ SITE ENTRANCE

SACBE

SACBE

Laguna
Cobá

COBÁ
■ GROUP

SEE DETAIL

Laguna
Macanxoc

LAS PINTURAS
GROUP

SACBE

UITZIL MUL
GROUP

SACBE

■ LAB MUL
GROUP

Laguna
Xkanhá

MACANXOC
GROUP

DETAIL

COBÁ
GROUP

LA
IGLESIA

Laguna
Sacakal

0   300 yds

0   300 m

© AVALON TRAVEL PUBLISHING, INC.

have mapped more than 6,000 structures pertaining to the city, spread over some 50 square kilometers (31 square miles). Cobá fought a protracted war against the Itzá at Chichén Itzá, and was beaten decisively in the middle of the 9th century. A widespread Maya collapse—of which the fall of Cobá was not the cause, though perhaps an early warning sign—occurred over the next century. Cobá was briefly re-inhabited in the 13th or 14th century, and a few structures added, but was again abandoned to the forest by the time of the Spanish conquest.

La Iglesia

The first group of ruins you come to after entering the site is known as the Cobá Group. La Iglesia (The Church) is the group's primary structure; in fact, at 22.5 meters (74 feet) it's the second-highest pyramid at the site. Rising steeply from a low platform, the structure clearly follows the style of Tikal and other Petén cities, and could hardly be more different from the long palaces and elaborate facades common in the nearby Puuc and Chenes regions. Visitors are no longer allowed to climb the Iglesia pyramid, due to the poor state of its stairs. Next to the Iglesia pyramid is a Ball Court that's been nicely restored—perhaps too nicely, in fact, as the reproduction scoring rings stand out like sore thumbs against the original weathered stones.

Nohoch Mul

Leaving the Cobá Group, the path skirts the edge of Laguna Macanxoc for about 500 meters (0.3 mile). Along the way you'll pass the Xaibé, or Crossroads temple, so-called because it marked the intersection of several *sacbeob*. For the same reason, archaeologists believe it may have served as a watchtower, though its peculiar shape suggests a more important, but as-yet-unknown, function. Bearing left when the path forks, its another kilometer (0.5 mile) to the Nohoch Mul Group. The namesake pyramid, Nohoch Mul (aka Ixmoja) rises 42 meters (138 feet) above the forest floor, the equivalent of 12 stories. It was long touted as the highest structure in the Yucatán, until the main pyramid at Calakmul in Campeche was

© AMBER PIRKER

At about twelve stories, Nohoch Mul is the second highest Maya pyramid in the world.

found to be higher—and by a good 12 meters (39.4 feet). The view from the top of Nohoch Mul is impressive—a broad flat expanse draped in thick forest. A small temple at the top bears a fairly well-preserved carving of the Descending God, and a rope running down the stairs makes going up and down easier.

Las Pinturas Group

At the intersection is the **Grupo de las Pinturas** (Paintings Group), a collection of five platforms encircling a plaza. Their name comes from paintings that once lined the walls; minute traces of the images, in layers of red and blue, are still visible in the largest structure, but you can't really get close enough to see them. The temples here, among the last to be constructed in Cobá, are well preserved and picturesque with green moss growing up the gray limestone walls.

Macanxoc Group

Back on the main path, and taking the second fork this time, walk about a kilometer (0.6 mile) to the Macanxoc Group. Numerous stelae have been found here, indicating it was a place of great ceremonial significance. The most famous of these monuments is Stela 1, aka the Macanxoc Stela. It depicts a scene from the Maya creation myth—"the hearth stone appears"—along with a Long Count date referring to a cycle ending the equivalent of 41.9 billion, billion, billion years in the future. It is the most distant Long Count date known to have been conceived and recorded by the ancient Maya.

Flora and Fauna

The name Cobá (Water Stirred by the Wind) is surely a reference to the group of shallow lagoons here (Cobá, Macanxoc, Xkanha, and Sacakal). The archaeological site and the surrounding wetlands and forest are rich with birdlife—herons, egrets, motmot, parrots, and the occasional toucan are not uncommon. Arrive early to see the most birds—at the very least you'll get an earful of their varied songs and cries. Later, as the temperature climbs, you'll start to see myriad color-

Keep your eyes peeled and your camera poised – lizards are typically spotted at Maya ruins.

© LIZA PRADO

ful butterflies, including the large, deep-blue *morphidae* and the bright yellow-orange barred sulphur.

If you look on the ground, you'll almost certainly see long lines of leaf-cutter ants. One column carries freshly cut leaves to the burrow and the other marches in the opposite direction, empty-jawed, returning for more. The vegetation decays in their nests, and the fungus that grows on the compost is an important staple of the ants' diet—a few scientists even claim this makes leaf-cutter ants the world's second species of agriculturists. Only particular types of leaves will do, and the columns can be up to one kilometer (0.6 mile) long.

Practicalities

It takes several kilometers of walking to see the whole site, or you can rent a bike or hire a bicycle taxi near the entrance. Whether you walk or ride, don't forget a water bottle, comfortable shoes, bug repellent, sunscreen, and a hat. Watch for signs and stay on the designated trails. Guide service is available—prices are not fixed, but typically are US$35 per group (two hours, up to six people).

OTHER SIGHTS

About 17 kilometers (10.6 miles) north of Cobá, **Punta Laguna** (6 A.M.–6 P.M. daily, US$4) is a forested area where spider and howler monkeys can be spotted and heard. The largest number of monkeys can be seen in the early morning and at dusk; there also are several small unexcavated Maya ruins along the path. While the admission fee grants access to the forest trails, your best chance of spotting monkeys is by hiring one of the guides near the entrance (US$26 per group, 10 people maximum); guides typically speak basic English. Whether you hire a guide or not, be sure to wear good walking shoes and bring plenty of bug repellant. Traveling by car, look for the cutoff road from Cobá toward Nuevo Xcan—that'll lead you straight to the entrance.

In Cobá village, the main activity is watching **alligators being fed** off the pier near the ruins. Local kids usually charge US$1 per person for the show.

ACCOMMODATIONS

There aren't many hotel options in this tiny town—three to be exact and only two worth considering. Be sure to call ahead to reserve a room; no worries if all the rooms are booked—Tulum, with its surplus of hotels, is just 40 minutes away.

The modest **Posada Sac Be** (Calle Principal s/n, tel. 984/206-7067, US$23.25 d with fan, US$32.50 d with a/c) has spotless rooms with one or two beds, television, and a small desk. All have private bathrooms and nice yellow tile floors. If no one is around to show you a room, go two doors down to the no-name *artesanía* shop that doubles as the post office. Someone inside will be able to assist you. Very friendly service.

Club Med Villas Cobá (facing Laguna Cobá, tel. 984/206-7000, scottsdale.mexicores@clubmed.com, www.clubmed.com, US$81 s/d with a/c, US$135 suite with a/c) is one of three identical Club Med mini-resorts at Maya archaeological sites (the others are at Chichén Itzá and Uxmal). Boxy but attractive rooms surround a courtyard with a well-tended pool. The hotel also has a restaurant that serves good, somewhat overpriced meals, a reading room with a good selection of books on the Maya, and a tennis court. The hotel faces Laguna Cobá—a pretty view but be sure not to jump in since crocodiles make it unsafe for swimmers.

FOOD

With a large raised patio overlooking the lagoon, **Restaurante-Bar La Pirámide** (Calle Principal at Laguna Cobá, tel. 984/858-1450, 7:30 A.M.–9 P.M. daily, US$5–12) is a nice place for lunch après-ruins or beer and snacks in the evening. The restaurant receives a number of tour groups, and it often has a buffet set up (US$9.50); otherwise, the menu has grilled fish, chicken, and meat dishes as well as typical Mexican fare.

A few doors down and just before the entrance to Club Med Villa Cobá, **Nicte Ha** (facing

Laguna Cobá, tel. 984/206-7025, 8 A.M.–7 P.M. daily, US$1.50–4) is a small place serving tacos, enchiladas, and various pork dishes. The name Nicte Ha (Flower of the Water) may refer to the eyes of a hungry resident crocodile the restaurant owner feeds occasionally—raw chicken is his favorite, apparently.

The restaurant at **Club Med Villas Cobá** (tel. 984/206-7000, 7:30 A.M.–10 P.M. daily, US$4.50–12) is comfortable and has the best selection of dishes in town, including pasta, seafood, and Yucatecan dishes. The prices are a bit high; depending mostly on your mood, eating here is a worthwhile splurge or an unnecessary expense.

Across the street from a peach-colored church, **Abarrotes Neftalí** (Calle Principal s/n, 7 A.M.–11 P.M. daily) is a mini-mart that sells canned goods, bread, and some fresh produce.

INFORMATION AND SERVICES

Cobá has neither an official tourist office nor a health clinic. There also are no banks or ATMs—the nearest banking and medical services are in Tulum and Valladolid.

Pharmacies: Facing the lagoon, **Farmacia El Porvenir** (Calle Principal s/n, 9 A.M.–1 P.M. and 2 A.M.–9 P.M. Mon.–Sat.) is a small shop selling basic medicines, toiletries, and film.

Police: Impossible to miss, the police station is halfway down the main drag, before you hit the lagoon.

GETTING THERE AND AROUND

You can easily walk to any of the listed hotels, restaurants, and services in town; the archaeological site is just a five-minute walk down the main road along the lagoon.

Bus: A tiny bus station operates out of El Bocadillo restaurant (Calle Principal s/n). There's only one first-class bus, which departs Cobá at 3:30 P.M. for Tulum (US$2.75, one hour), Playa del Carmen (US$6, 2.5 hours), and Cancún (US$9.50, 3.5 hours). Second-class buses also serve those destinations, as well as Valladolid and Chichén Itzá, though departures are limited.

Car: Getting to Cobá is easiest by car. The roads are smooth and fast, if a bit narrow in places, cutting though pretty farmland and small towns; watch for *topes* (speed bumps). Just outside of Cobá is a large roundabout: head south a few hundred meters to town and the ruins; head west via Chemex to get to Valladolid, Chichén Itzá, and Mérida; head north for Punta Laguna and Cancún; head east to Tulum. For Playa del Carmen, go via Tulum.

BACKGROUND

The Land

The history of the Yucatán Peninsula is deeply intertwined with its unique geology and ecology. From the ancient Maya to modern-day tourism, the land and its resources have shaped the course of Yucatecan events. And the Yucatán, in turn, has helped shape the course of Mexican history, from being the stage upon which the early Spanish conquest was conducted to helping rescue a moribund Mexican economy in the 1980s. An understanding of the Yucatán Peninsula's land, ecology, culture, and politics is vital to understanding the region today.

The Yucatán Peninsula spans some 113,000 square kilometers (70,215 square miles) in southeastern Mexico, and is made up of three states: Yucatán, Campeche, and Quintana Roo. It has more than 1,600 kilometers (994 miles) of shoreline, with the Caribbean Sea to the east and the Gulf of Mexico to the north and west. To the southwest are the Mexican states of Tabasco and Chiapas, and directly south are the countries of Belize and Guatemala.

Geologically, the Yucatán Peninsula is a flat shelf of limestone, a porous rock that acts like a huge sponge. Rainfall is absorbed into the ground and delivered to natural stone-lined sinks and underground rivers. The result is that the Yucatán has virtually no surface water, neither rivers nor lakes. (It also has very few hills.) The geology changes as you move south, and

© GARY CHANDLER

CHICXULUB CRATER

Sixty-five million years ago, a meteorite more than 10 kilometers wide (6.2 miles) collided with the Earth. It was traveling at 20 kilometers per second (12.4 miles per second) and at the time of impact, its temperature was 18,000°C (32,432°F) – three times that of the sun's surface. The massive meteor created a colossal crater – more than 2.5 kilometers (1.6 miles) deep and about 200 kilometers (124.3 miles) in diameter – the largest and best-preserved crater on Earth. It caused volcanoes to erupt, the planet to tremble, and tidal waves more than 500 meters (0.3 miles) high. This monumental movement, in turn, sent millions of tons of pulverized rock into Earth's atmosphere, plunging it into darkness. The lack of sun eventually led to the demise of more than 70 percent of all living things on the planet, including the dinosaurs.

All very interesting, but why mention it in a guidebook to the Yucatán? Because this is where the meteor hit – in what is today the coastal town of Chicxulub, just east of Progreso. In 1981, scientists from PEMEX (Mexico's national petroleum company) were drilling in the Yucatán Peninsula when they discovered gravitational anomalies near the town of Chicxulub. The scientists took core samples and soon concluded that the meteor that had changed the face of the planet crashed in the Yucatán. It provided an explanation as to why the limestone-covered peninsula had eroded so dramatically, creating a ring of caves and cenotes in numbers found nowhere else on Earth. In 1991, UNAM (the National Autonomous University of Mexico) in cooperation with NASA confirmed the theory.

The Yucatán Peninsula is well known as one of the richest parts of the world; what many do not know, however, is that life as we know it began here.

---

the first sizable river—the Río Hondo—forms a natural boundary between Belize and Mexico.

GEOGRAPHY
The Coast

The northern and western coasts are bordered by the emerald waters of the Gulf of Mexico. Just inland, the land is dotted with lagoons, sandbars, and swamps. The east coast is edged by the turquoise Caribbean and the glorious islands of Isla Cozumel, Isla Mujeres, and Isla Contoy lie just offshore. Along the coast runs the Mesoamerican Reef, the second-longest coral reef in the world.

Cenotes

Over the course of millennia, water that seeped below the Yucatán's porous limestone shelf eroded a vast network of underground rivers and caves. When a cave's ceiling wears thin, it may eventually cave in, exposing the water below. The Maya called such sinkholes *dzo'not*, which Spanish explorers recorded as *cenotes*. Most cenotes are extremely deep, and interconnected by way of underground channels. A cenote's surface may be near ground level, but more often it is much farther down, as much as 90 meters (295 feet) below. In those cases, the Maya gathered water by carving stairs into the slick limestone walls or by hanging long ladders into abysmal hollows that lead to underground lakes.

CLIMATE

The weather in the Yucatán falls into a rainy season (May–October) and a dry season (November–April). Travelers to the Yucatán Peninsula in the dry season will experience warm days, occasional brief cold storms called *nortes,* and plenty of tourists. In the rainy season, expect spectacular storms and hot, muggy days. The region is infamous for its heat and humidity in May and June, which hovers around 90°F *and* 90 percent humidity.

Hurricane season runs July–November with most activity occurring mid-August–mid-October. Though tropical storms are common this time of year, full-fledged hurricanes are relatively rare. If one is bearing down, don't try to tough it out. Head inland immediately.

Flora

Quintana Roo's forests are home to mangroves, bamboo, and swamp cypresses. Ferns, vines, and flowers creep from tree to tree and create a dense growth. The southern part of the Yucatán Peninsula, with its classic tropical rainforest, hosts tall mahoganies, *campeche zapote,* and *kapok*—all covered with wild jungle vines. On topmost limbs, orchids and air ferns reach for the sun.

TREES
Palms
A wide variety of palm trees and their relatives grow on the peninsula—tall, short, fruited, and even oil-producing varieties. Though similar, various palms have distinct characteristics:

- Royal palms are tall with smooth trunks.

- Queen palms are often used for landscaping and bear a sweet fruit.

- Thatch palms are called *chit* by Mayas, who use the fronds extensively for roof thatch.

- Coconut palms—the ones often seen on the beach—produce oil, food, drink, and shelter and are valued by locals as a nutritious food source and cash crop.

- Henequen is a cousin to the palm tree; from its fiber come twine, rope, matting, and other products. Because of its abundance, new uses for it are constantly sought.

Fruit Trees
Quintana Roo grows sweet and sour oranges, limes, and grapefruit. Avocado is abundant and the papaya tree is practically a weed. The mamey tree grows full and tall (15–20 meters/49–65 feet), providing not only welcome shade but also an avocado-shaped fruit, brown on the outside with a vivid, salmon-pink flesh that tastes like a sweet yam. The *guaya* is another unusual fruit tree and a member of the litchi nut family. This rangy evergreen thrives on sea air and is commonly seen along the coast. Its small, green, leathery pods grow in clumps like grapes and contain a sweet, yellowish, jellylike flesh—tasty! The calabash tree provides gourds used for containers by Mayas.

Other Trees
The ceiba (also called *kapok*) is a sacred tree for the Mayas. Considered the link between the underworld, the material world, and the heavens, this huge tree is revered and left undisturbed—even if it sprouts in the middle of a fertile cornfield.

When visiting in the summer, you can't miss the beautiful *framboyanes* (royal poinciana). When in bloom, its wide-spreading branches become covered in clusters of brilliant orange-red flowers. These trees often line sidewalks and plazas and when clustered together present a dazzling show.

FLOWERS
While wandering through jungle regions, you'll see numerous plants that have vexed amateur botanists the world over. Here in their natural environment, these plants thrive in a way unknown to windowsills at home: Crotons exhibit wild colors, *pothos* grow 30-centimeter (11.8-inch) leaves, the philodendron splits every leaf in gargantuan glory, and common morning glory creeps and climbs for miles over bushes and trees. You'll also be introduced to many delicate strangers in this tropical world: the exotic white and red ginger, plumeria (sometimes called frangipani) with its wonderful fragrance and myriad colors, and hibiscus and bougainvillea, which bloom in an array of bright hues. In fact, keeping jungle growth away from the roads, utility poles, and wires is a constant job for local authorities because the warm, humid air and ample rainfall encourage a lush green wonderland.

Orchids
Orchids can be found on the highest limbs of the tallest trees, especially in the state of Quintana Roo. Of the 71 species reported on the Yucatán Peninsula, 80 percent are epiphytic, attached to host trees and deriving

© LIZA PRADO

Seventy-one species of orchids are found in the Yucatán Peninsula.

moisture and nutrients from the air and rain. Orchids grow in myriad sizes and shapes: tiny buttons spanning the length of a half-meter-long (two-foot) branch, large-petaled blossoms with ruffled edges, or intense, tiger-striped miniatures.

Fauna

Many animals found nowhere else in Mexico inhabit the Yucatán Peninsula's expansive flatlands and thick jungles. Spotting them can be difficult, though with patience and a skilled guide, not impossible.

LAND MAMMALS
Nine-Banded Armadillos
The size of a small dog and sporting a thick coat of armor, this peculiar creature gets its name from the nine bands (or external "joints") that circle the midsection and give the little tank some flexibility. The armadillo's keen sense of smell can detect insects and grubs—its primary food source—up to 15 centimeters (6 inches) underground, and its sharp claws make digging for them a cinch. An armadillo also digs underground burrows, into which it may carry a full bushel of grass to make its nest, where it will sleep through the hot day and emerge at night. Unlike armadillos that roll up into a tight ball when threatened, this species will race to its burrow, arch its back, and wedge in so that it cannot be pulled out. The tip of the Yucatán Peninsula is a favored habitat for its scant rainfall; too much rain floods the burrow and can drown young armadillos.

Giant Anteaters
A cousin of the armadillo, this extraordinary animal measures two meters (6.6 feet) from the tip of its tubular snout to the end of its bushy

tail. Its coarse coat is colored shades of brown-gray; the hindquarters are darker in tone, while a contrasting wedge-shaped pattern of black and white decorates the throat and shoulders. Characterized by an elongated head, long tubular mouth, and extended tongue (but no teeth), it can weigh up to 39 kilograms (86 pounds). The anteater walks on the knuckles of its paws, allowing its claws to remain tucked under while it looks for food.

Giant anteaters are found in forests and swampy areas in Mexico and through Central and South America. It is mainly diurnal in areas where there are few people but nocturnal in densely populated places. Its razor-sharp claws allow it to rip open the leathery mud walls of termite and ant nests, the contents of which are a main food source. After opening the nest, the anteater rapidly flicks its viscous tongue in and out of its small mouth opening. Few ants escape.

Tapirs

South American tapirs are found from the southern part of Mexico to southern Brazil. A stout-bodied animal, it has short legs and a tail, small eyes, and rounded ears. The nose and upper lip extend into a short but very mobile proboscis. Tapirs usually live near streams or river, which they use for daily bathing and as an escape from predators, especially jaguars and humans. Shy and placid, these nocturnal animals have a definite home range, wearing a path between the jungle and their feeding area. If attacked, the tapir lowers its head and blindly crashes off through the forest; they've been known to collide with trees and knock themselves out in their chaotic attempt to flee.

Peccaries

Next to deer, peccaries are the most widely hunted game on the Yucatán Peninsula. Two species of peccaries are found here: the collared javelina peccary and the white-lipped peccary. The feisty collared javelina stands 50 centimeters (20 inches) at the shoulder and can be one meter (3.3 feet) long, weighing as much as 30 kilograms (66 pounds). It is black and white with a narrow, semicircular collar of white hair on the shoulders. The name *javelina* (which means "spear" in Spanish) comes from the two tusks that protrude from its mouth. This more familiar peccary is found in the desert, woodlands, and rainforests, and it travels in groups of 5–15. The white-lipped peccary is reddish brown to black and has an area of white around its mouth. Larger than the javelina, it can grow to 105 centimeters (41 inches) long, and is found deep in tropical rainforests living in herds of 100 or more. Peccaries often are compared to the wild pigs found in Europe, but in fact they belong to entirely different families.

Felines

Seven species of cats are found in North America, four in the tropics. One of them—the jaguar—is heavy chested with sturdy, muscled forelegs. It has small, rounded ears and its tail is relatively short. Its color varies from tan and white to pure black. The male can weigh 65–115 kilograms (143–254 pounds), females 45–85 kilograms (99–187 pounds). The largest of the cats on the peninsula, the jaguar is about the same size as a leopard. Other cats found here are the ocelot and puma. In tropical forests of the past, the large cats were the only predators capable of controlling the populations of hoofed game such as deer, peccaries, and tapirs. If hunting is poor and times are tough, the jaguar will go into rivers and scoop up fish with its large paws. The river also is one of the jaguar's favorite spots for hunting tapirs, when the latter comes to drink.

SEALIFE
Coral Reefs

The spectacular coral reefs that grace the peninsula's east coast are made up of millions of tiny carnivorous organisms called polyps. Individual polyps can be less than a centimeter (0.4 inch) long or up to 15 centimeters (6 inches) in diameter. Related to the jellyfish and sea anemone, coral polyps capture prey with tiny tentacles that deliver a deadly sting.

Reef-building polyps have limestone exoskeletons, which they create by extracting calcium from the seawater. Reefs are formed as generation after generation of polyps attach themselves to and atop each other. Different species attach in different ways, resulting in the many shapes and sizes of ocean reefs: delicate lace, trees with reaching branches, pleated mushrooms, stovepipes, petaled flowers, fans, domes, heads of cabbage, and stalks of broccoli. Though made up of individual polyps, coral structures function like a single organism, sharing nutrients through a central gastro-vascular system. Even in ideal conditions, most coral grows no more than five centimeters (2 inches) per year.

Reefs are divided into three types: barrier, atoll, and fringing. A barrier reef runs parallel to the coast, with long stretches separated by narrow channels. The Mesoamerican Reef extends 250 kilometers (155 miles) from the tip of Isla Mujeres to Sapodilla Cay in the Gulf of Honduras—only the Great Barrier Reef in Australia is longer. An atoll typically formed around the crater of a submerged volcano. The polyps begin building their colonies along the lip of the crater, forming a circular coral island with a lagoon in the center. The Chinchorro Bank, off the southern coast of Quintana Roo, is the largest coral atoll in the northern hemisphere, measuring 48 kilometers long and 14 kilometers wide (30 miles by 9 miles) long. A fringing reef is coral living on a shallow shelf that extends outward from shore into the sea.

Fish

The Yucatán's barrier reef is home to myriad fish species, including parrot fish, candy bass, moray eels, spotted scorpion fish, turquoise angelfish, fairy basslets, flame fish, and gargantuan manta rays. Several species of shark also thrive in the waters off Quintana Roo, though they're not considered a serious threat to swimmers and divers. Sport fish—sailfish, marlin, and blue fin tuna—also inhabit the outer Caribbean waters.

Inland, anglers will find hard-fighting bonefish and pompano in the area's lagoons, and those snorkelers and divers looking to float through caves will find several species of blind fish in the crystal-clear waters of cenotes. These fish live out their existence in dark underground rivers and lakes and have no use for eyes.

Sea Turtles

Tens of thousands of sea turtles of various species once nested on the coastal beaches of Quintana Roo. As the coast became populated, turtles were severely over-hunted for their eggs, meat, and shell, and their numbers began to fall. Hotel and resort developments have hastened the decline, as there are fewer and fewer patches of untrammeled sand for turtles to dig nests and lay their eggs. The Mexican government and various ecological organizations are trying hard to save the dwindling turtle population. Turtle eggs are dug up and reburied in sand on safe beaches; when the hatchlings break through their shells, they are brought to a beach and allowed to rush toward the sea in hopes of imprinting a sense of belonging there so that they will later return to the spot. In some cases the hatchlings are scooped up and placed in tanks to grow larger before being released into the open sea. The government also is enforcing tough penalties for people who take turtle eggs or capture, kill, sell, or imprison these animals.

Manatees

The manatee—or the sea cow, as it is often called—is a creature of immense proportions with gentle manners and the curiosity of a kitten. Large numbers of this enormous animal once roamed the shallow inlets, bays, and estuaries of the Caribbean. Images of them are frequently seen in the art of the ancient Mayas, who hunted them for their flesh. In modern times, the population has been reduced by the encroachment of people in the manatees' habitats along the river ways and shorelines. Ever-growing numbers of motorboats also inflict deadly gashes on the inquisitive, surface-

Once prevalent on Mexico's Caribbean coast, manatees are now rarely seen outside of reserves or eco-parks.

feeding creatures. Nowadays it is very rare to spot one; Punta Allen and Bahía de la Acensión have the most sightings.

At birth the manatee weighs 30–35 kilograms (66–77 pounds); it can grow up to four meters (13.1 feet) long and weigh more than a ton. Gray with a pinkish cast and shaped like an Idaho potato, it has a spatulate tail, two forelimbs with toenails, pebbled coarse skin, tiny sunken eyes, and numerous fine-bristled hairs scattered sparsely over its body. The head of the mammal seems small for its gargantuan body, and its preproboscidean lineage includes dugongs (in Australia), hyrax, and elephants. The manatee's truncated snout and prehensile lips help push food into its mouth. The only aquatic mammal that survives entirely on plants, the manatee grazes on bottom-growing grasses and other aquatic vegetation. It eats as much as 225 kilograms (496 pounds) per day, cleaning rivers of oxygen-choking growth. It also is unique among mammals in that it constantly grows new teeth—to replace worn ones, which fall out

regularly. Posing no threat to any other living thing, it has been hunted for its oil, skin, and flesh.

BIRDS

Since a major part of the Yucatán Peninsula is still undeveloped and covered with trees and brush, it isn't surprising to find exotic, rarely seen birds all across the landscape. The Mexican government is beginning to realize the great value in this treasure of nature and is making efforts to protect nesting grounds. In addition to the growing number of nature reserves, some of the best bird-watching locales are the archaeological zones. At dawn and dusk, when most of the visitors are absent, the trees that surround the ancient structures come alive with birdsong. Of all the ruins, Cobá—with its marshy-rimmed lakes, nearby cornfields, and relatively tall, humid forest—is a particularly good site for birders. One of the more impressive birds to look for here is the keel-billed toucan, often seen perched high on a bare limb in the early hours of the morning. Others include *chachalacas* (held in reverence by the Mayas), screeching parrots, and, occasionally, the ocellated turkey.

Flamingos

At the northern end of the peninsula, the reserve at Río Lagartos plays host to thousands of long-necked, long-legged flamingos during the nesting season (June–August). They begin arriving around the end of May, when the rains begin. This homecoming is a breathtaking sight: a profusion of pink/salmon colors clustered together on the white sand, or sailing across a blue sky, long, curved necks straight in flight, the flapping movement exposing contrasting black and pink on the undersides of their wings. The estimated flamingo population on the Yucatán Peninsula is 30,000. This wildlife refuge, called El Cuyo, protects the largest colony of nesting American flamingos in the world.

Many of these flamingos winter in Celestún, a small fishing village on the northwest coast a few kilometers north of the Campeche-Yucatán state border. Celestún lies between the Gulf of Mexico and a long tidal estuary known as La Ciénega. Since the disruption of Hurricane Gilbert, a flock of flamingos has found a new feeding ground near Chicxulub.

Quetzals

Though the ancient Mayas made abundant use of the dazzling quetzal feathers for ceremonial costumes and headdresses, they hunted other fowl for food; nevertheless, the quetzal is the only known bird from the pre-Columbian era and is now almost extinct. Today, they are still found (though rarely) in the high cloud forests of Chiapas and Central America, where they thrive on the constant moisture.

Estuary Havens

Estuaries play host to hundreds of bird species. A boat ride into one of them will give you an opportunity to see a variety of wintering ducks from North America, blue-winged teals, northern shovelers, and lesser scaups. You'll also see a variety of wading birds feeding in the shallow waters, including numerous types of heron, snowy egret, and, in the summer, white ibis. There are 14 species of birds endemic to the Yucatán Peninsula, including the ocellated turkey, Yucatán whippoorwill, Yucatán flycatcher, orange oriole, black catbird, and the yellow-lored parrot.

REPTILES

Although reptiles thrive in Yucatán's warm, sunny environment, humans are their worst enemy. In the past, some species were greatly reduced in number because they were hunted for their unusual skin. Although hunting them is now illegal in most countries, a few black marketers still take their toll on the species.

Caymans

Similar in appearance to the crocodile, the cayman is a part of the crocodilian order. Its habits and appearance are similar to those of crocodiles with the main difference being in its underskin. The cayman's skin is reinforced with bony plates on the belly, making it useless for the leather market. (Alligators and crocodiles, with smooth belly skin and sides, have been hunted almost to extinction in some parts of the world.)

Several species of cayman frequent the brackish inlet waters near the estuaries of Río Lagartos (whose name means "River of Lizards"). They are broad-snouted and often look as though they sport a pair of spectacles. A large cayman can be 2.5 meters (8.2 feet) long and very dark gray-green with eyelids that look swollen and wrinkled. Some species have eyelids that look like a pair of blunt horns. They are quicker than alligators and have longer, sharper teeth. Skilled hunters, cayman are quick in water and on land, and will attack a person if cornered. The best advice you can heed is to give the cayman a wide berth when you spot one.

Iguanas

This group of American lizards—family Iguanidae—includes various large plant-eaters seen frequently in Quintana Roo. Iguanas grow to be one meter (3.3 feet) long and have a blunt head and long flat tail. Bands of black and gray circle its body, and a serrated column reaches down the middle of its back almost to the tail. The young iguana is bright emerald green and often supplements its diet by eating insects and larvae.

The lizard's forelimbs hold the front half of its body up off the ground while its two back limbs are kept relaxed and splayed alongside its hindquarters. When the iguana is frightened, however, its hind legs do everything they're supposed to, and the iguana crashes quickly (though clumsily) into the brush searching for its burrow and safety. This reptile is not aggressive—it mostly enjoys basking in the bright sunshine along the Caribbean—but if cornered it will bite and use its tail in self-defense.

From centuries past, recorded references attest to the iguana's medicinal value, which partly explains the active trade of live iguana in the marketplaces. Iguana stew is believed to cure or relieve various human ailments such as impotence.

Other Lizards

You'll see a great variety of other lizards in the peninsula; some are brightly striped in various shades of green and yellow, others are earth-toned and blend in with the gray and beige limestone that dots the landscape. Skinny as wisps of thread running on hind legs, or chunky and waddling with armorlike skin, the range is endless and fascinating.

Be sure to look for the black anole, which changes colors to match its environment, either when danger is imminent or as subterfuge to fool the insects that it preys on. At mating time, the male anole puffs out its bright-red throat-fan so that all female lizards will see it.

Coral Snakes

Two species of coral snakes, which are related to the cobra, are found in the southern part of the Yucatán Peninsula. They have prominent rings around their bodies in the same sequence of red, black, yellow, or white and grow to 1–1.5 meters (3.3–4.9 feet). Their bodies are slender, with no pronounced distinction between the head and neck.

Coral snakes spend the day in mossy clumps under rocks or logs, emerging only at night. Though a coral snake bite can kill within 24 hours, chances of the average tourist being bitten by a coral (or any other) snake are slim.

Tropical Rattlesnakes

The tropical rattlesnake (*cascabel* in Spanish) is the deadliest and most treacherous species of the rattler. It differs slightly from other species by having vividly contrasting neckbands. It grows 2–2.5 meters (6.6–8.2 feet) long and is found mainly in the higher and drier areas of the tropics. Contrary to popular myth, this serpent doesn't always rattle a warning of its impending strike.

INSECTS AND ARACHNIDS

Air-breathing invertebrates are unavoidable in any tropical locale. Some are annoying (gnats and no-see-ums), some are dangerous (black widows, bird spiders, and scorpions), and others can cause pain when they bite (red ants); but many are beautiful (butterflies and moths), and *all* are fascinating.

Butterflies and Moths

The Yucatán has an abundance of beautiful moths and butterflies. Of the 90,000 types of butterflies in the world, a large percentage is seen in Quintana Roo. You'll see, among others, the magnificent blue morpho, orange-barred sulphur, copperhead, cloudless sulphur, malachite, admiral, calico, ruddy dagger-wing, tropical buckeye, and emperor. The famous monarch also is a visitor during its annual migration from Florida. It usually makes a stopover on Quintana Roo's east coast on its way south to the Central American mountains where it spends the winter.

Environmental Issues

SIAN KA'AN BIOSPHERE RESERVE

With the growing number of visitors to Quintana Roo and the continual development of its natural wonders, there's a real danger of decimating the wildlife and destroying the resources that are vital to the Maya inhabitants. In 1981, authorities and scientists collaborated on a plan to stem that threat. The plan, which takes into account land titles, logging, hunting, agriculture, cattle ranching, and tourist development—and which local people feel comfortable with—culminated in the October 1986 establishment of the Reserva de la Biósfera Sian Ka'an, part of UNESCO's World Network of Biosphere Reserves. Inside, visitors will find hundreds of species of birds including the ocellated turkey, great currasow, parrots, toucans, roseate spoonbill, jabiru stork, and 15 species of herons, egrets, and bitterns. Land mammals also are in abundance: jaguars, pumas, ocelots, margays, jaguarundis, spider and howler monkeys, tapirs, as well as white-lipped and collared peccaries. In the lagoons and ocean you're also sure to see crocodiles, a myriad of turtles (green, loggerhead, hawksbill, and leatherbacks), and maybe even a manatee or two. Needless to say, this is an environmentally rich part of the region and one worth visiting.

CONSERVATION

Among the top concerns of environmentalists in Mexico is deforestation, which has accelerated with Mexico's burgeoning population. Slash-and-burn farming is still widely practiced in remote areas, with or without regulation. In an effort to protect the land, environmentalists are searching for alternative sources of income for locals. One is to train them to become guides by teaching them about the flora and fauna of the region as well as English. While not solving the problem, it does place an economic value on the forest itself and provides an incentive for preserving it.

Another focus is the plight of the palm tree. The palm is an important part of the cultural and practical lifestyle of the indigenous people of Quintana Roo—it is used for thatch roofing and to construct lobster traps. However, the palms used—*Thrinax radiata* and *Coccothrinax readii*—are becoming increasingly rare. Amigos de Sian Ka'an together with the World Wildlife Fund are studying the palms' growth patterns and rates; they are anticipating a management plan that will encourage future growth. Other environmental projects include limiting commercial fishing, halting tourist development where it endangers the ecology, and studying the lobster industry and its future. A number of other worthwhile projects are still waiting in line.

History

ACROSS THE BERING LAND BRIDGE

People and animals from Asia crossed the Bering land bridge into North America in the Pleistocene epoch about 50,000 years ago, when sea levels were much lower. As early as 10,000 B.C., Ice Age humans hunted woolly mammoth and other large animals roaming the cool, moist landscape of Central Mexico. The earliest traces of humans in the Yucatán

Peninsula are obsidian spear points and stone tools dating to 9,000 B.C. The Loltún caves in the state of Yucatán contained a cache of extinct mammoth bones, which were probably dragged there by a roving band of hunters. As the region dried out and large game disappeared in the next millennia, tools of a more settled way of life appeared, such as grinding stones for preparing seeds and plant fibers. The epic human trek south continued until only

STEPHENS AND CATHERWOOD

The Maya ruins of the Yucatán Peninsula were all but unknown in the United States and Europe until well into the 19th century. Although Spanish explorers and colonizers had occupied the peninsula for more than two centuries, conflicts with local Mayas and Catholic antipathy for all things "pagan" probably account for the Spaniards' lack of research or even apparent interest. To be fair, the immensity of the task was surely daunting – by the time the Spanish reached the Yucatán in the early 1500s, the majority of sites had been abandoned for at least 300 years, and in some cases double or triple that. Many were piles of rubble, and those still standing were mostly covered in vegetation. Just getting to the sites was a task in itself.

Between 1839 and 1841, an American explorer and diplomat named John Lloyd Stephens and an English artist and architect named Fredrick Catherwood conducted two major explorations of the Maya region, including present-day Yucatán, Chiapas, and Central America. Stephens, an amateur archaeologist, kept a detailed account of their travels and the ruins they visited, while Catherwood made incredibly precise drawings of numerous structures, monuments, hieroglyphs, and scenes of peasant life. They published their work in two volumes, made a sensation in the United States and Europe, and awakened outside interest in ancient Maya civilization. Their books now are condensed into a single, very readable volume, *Incidents of Travel in Yucatan* (Panorama Editorial, 1988), available in English and in many bookstores in the Yucatán. It makes for fascinating reading, not only for the historic value but also as a backdrop for your own travels through the Yucatán.

3,000 years ago, however, when, anthropologists say, people first reached Tierra del Fuego, at the tip of South America.

ANCIENT CIVILIZATION

Between 7,000 and 2,000 B.C., society evolved from hunting and gathering to farming; corn, squash, and beans were independently cultivated in widely separated areas in Mexico. Archaeologists believe that the earliest people we can call Mayas, or proto-Mayas, lived on the Pacific coast of Chiapas and Guatemala. These tribes lived in villages that might have held more than 1,000 inhabitants and made beautiful painted and incised ceramic jars for food storage. After 1,000 B.C. this way of life spread south to the highlands site of Kaminaljuyú (now part of Guatemala City) and, through the next millennium, to the rest of the Maya world. Meanwhile, in what are now the Mexican states of Veracruz and Tabasco, another culture, the Olmecs, was developing what is now considered Mesoamerica's first civilization. Its influence was felt throughout Mexico and Central America. Archaeologists believe that before the Olmecs disappeared around 300 B.C., they contributed two crucial cultural advances to the Mayas: the Long Count calendar and the hieroglyphic writing system.

LATE PRECLASSIC PERIOD

During the Late Preclassic era (300 B.C.– A.D. 250), the Pacific coastal plain saw the rise of a Maya culture in Izapa near Tapachula, Chiapas. The Izapans worshipped gods that were precursors of the Classic Maya pantheon and commemorated religious and historical events in bas-relief carvings that emphasized costume and finery.

During the same period, the northern Guatemalan highlands were booming with construction; this was the heyday of Kaminaljuyú, which grew to enormous size, with more than 120 temple-mounds and numerous stele. The earliest calendar inscription that researchers are able to read comes from a monument found at El Baúl to the southwest of Kaminaljuyú; it has been translated as A.D. 36.

EARLY CIVILIZATIONS AND MAYA TIMELINE

PERIOD	YEAR
Paleoindian	before 7000 B.C.
Archaic	7000-2500 B.C.
Early Preclassic	2500-1000 B.C.
Middle Preclassic	1000-300 B.C.
Late Preclassic	300 B.C.-A.D. 250
Early Classic	A.D. 250-600
Late Classic	A.D. 600-925
Early Postclassic	A.D. 925-1200
Late Postclassic	A.D. 1200-1530

In the Petén jungle region just north of the highlands, the dominant culture was the Chicanel, whose hallmarks are elaborate temple-pyramids lined with enormous stucco god-masks (as in Kohunlich). The recently excavated Petén sites of Nakbé and El Mirador are the most spectacular Chicanel cities yet found. El Mirador contains a 70-meter (230-foot) tall temple-pyramid complex that is the tallest ancient structure in Mesoamerica. Despite the obvious prosperity of this region, there is almost no evidence of Long Count dates or writing systems in either the Petén jungle or the Yucatán Peninsula just to the north.

EARLY CLASSIC PERIOD

The great efflorescence of the southern Maya world stops at the end of the Early Classic period (A.D. 250–600). Kaminaljuyú and other cities were abandoned; researchers believe that the area was invaded by Teotihuacano warriors extending the reach of their Valley of Mexico–based empire. On the Yucatán Peninsula, there is evidence of Teotihuacano occupation at the Río Bec site of Becán and at Acanceh near Mérida. You can see Teotihuacano-style costumes and gods in carvings at the great Petén city of Tikal and at Copán in Honduras. By A.D. 600, the Teotihuacano empire had collapsed, and the stage was set for the Classic Maya eras.

LATE CLASSIC PERIOD

The Maya heartland of the Late Classic period (A.D. 600–900) extended from Copán in Honduras through Tikal in Guatemala and ended at Palenque in Chiapas. The development of these city-states, which also included Yaxchilán and Bonampak, almost always followed the same pattern. Early in this era, a new and vigorous breed of rulers founded a series of dynasties bent on deifying themselves and their ancestors. All the arts and sciences of the Maya world, from architecture to astronomy, were focused on this goal. The Long Count calendar and the hieroglyphic writing system were the most crucial tools in this effort, as the rulers needed to recount the stories of their dynasties and of their own glorious careers.

During the Late Classic era, painting, sculpture, and carving reached their climax; objects such as Lord Pakal's sarcophagus lid from Palenque are now recognized as among the finest pieces of world art. Royal monuments stood at the center of large and bustling cities. Cobá and Dzibilchaltún each probably contained 50,000 inhabitants, and there was vigorous intercity trade. Each Classic city-state reached its apogee at a different time; the southern cities peaked first, with the northern Puuc region cities following close behind.

By A.D. 925 nearly all of the city-states had collapsed and were left in a state of near-abandonment. The Classic Maya decline is one of the great enigmas of Mesoamerican archaeology. There are a myriad of theories—disease, invasion, peasant revolt—but many researchers now believe the collapse was caused by a combination of factors, including overpopulation, environmental degradation, and a series of devastating droughts. With the abandonment of

© LIZA PRADO

Among their many talents, the Maya were master artists.

the cities, the cultural advances disappeared as well. The last Long Count date was recorded in A.D. 909 and many religious customs and beliefs were never seen again.

EARLY POSTCLASSIC PERIOD

After the Puuc region was abandoned—almost certainly because of a foreign invasion—the center of Maya power moved east to Chichén. During this Early Postclassic era (A.D. 925–1200), the Toltec influence took hold, marking the end of the most artistic era and the birth of a new militaristic society built around a blend of ceremonialism, civic and social organization, and conquest. Chichén was the great power of northern Yucatán. Competing city-states either bowed before its warriors or, like the Puuc cities and Cobá, were destroyed.

LATE POSTCLASSIC PERIOD

After Chichén's fall in 1224—probably due to an invasion—a heretofore lowly tribe calling themselves the Itzá became the Late Postclassic

(A.D. 1200–1530) masters of Yucatecan power politics. Kukulcán II of Chichén founded Mayapán A.D. 1263–1283. After his death and the abandonment of Chichén, an aggressive Itzá lineage named the Cocom seized power and used Mayapán as a base to subjugate northern Yucatán. They succeeded through wars using Tabascan mercenaries and intermarrying with other powerful lineages. Foreign lineage heads were forced to live in Mayapán where they could easily be controlled. At its height, the city covered 6.5 square kilometers (four square miles) within a defensive wall that contained more than 15,000 inhabitants. Architecturally, Mayapán leaves much to be desired; the city plan was haphazard, and its greatest monument was a sloppy, smaller copy of Chichén's Pyramid of Kukulcán.

The Cocom ruled for 250 years until A.D. 1441–1461, when an upstart Uxmal-based lineage named the Xiu rebelled and slaughtered the Cocom. Mayapán was abandoned and Yucatán's city-states weakened themselves in a series of bloody intramural wars that left them hopelessly divided when it came time to face the conquistadors. By the time of that conquest, culture was once again being imported from outside the Maya world. Putún Maya seafaring traders brought new styles of art and religious beliefs back from their trips to Central Mexico. Their influence can be seen in the Mixtec-style frescoes at Tulum on the Quintana Roo coast.

SPANISH ARRIVAL AND CONQUEST

After Columbus's arrival in the New World, other adventurers traveling the same seas soon found the Yucatán Peninsula. In 1519, 34-year-old Hernán Cortés sailed from Cuba against the wishes of the Spanish governor. With 11 ships, 120 sailors, and 550 soldiers he set out to search for slaves, a lucrative business with or without the government's blessing. His search began on the Yucatán coast and would eventually encompass most of Mexico. However, he hadn't counted on the ferocious resistance and cunning of the Maya Indians. It

Monuments of the conquistadors are reminders of the region's brutal past.

took many decades and many lives for Spanish conquistadors to quell Maya resistance, despite a huge advantage in military technology, including horses, gunpowder, and metal sword and armor. Francisco de Montejo, who took part in Cortés's earlier expedition into central Mexico, spent 1528–1535 trying to conquer the Yucatán, first from the east at Tulum and later from the west near Campeche and Tabasco, but was driven out each time. Montejo's son, also named Francisco de Montejo "El Mozo" (The Younger), took up the effort and eventually founded the city of Campeche in 1546 and Mérida in 1542. From those beachheads, the Spanish conquest slowly spread across the peninsula.

Economic and religious oppression were central to the conquest too, of course. The Xiu indigenous group proved an important ally to the Spanish after its leader converted to Christianity. And in 1562, a friar named Diego de Landa, upon learning his converts still practiced certain Maya ceremonies, became enraged and ordered the torture and

imprisonment of numerous Maya spiritual leaders. He also gathered all the religious artifacts and Maya texts—which he said contained "superstitions and the devil's lies"—and had them burned. It was a staggering loss—at least 27 codices—one that Landa later seemed to regret and attempted to reconcile by writing a detailed record of Maya customs, mathematics, and writing.

The Caste War

By the 1840s, the brutalized and subjugated Mayas organized a revolt against Euro-Mexican colonizers. Called the Caste War, this savage war saw Mayas taking revenge on every white man, woman, and child by means of murder and rape. European survivors made their way to the last Spanish strongholds of Mérida and Campeche. The governments of the two cities appealed for help to Spain, France, and the United States. No one answered the call. It was soon apparent that the remaining two cities would be wiped out. But just as the governor of Mérida was about to begin evacuating the city, the Mayas picked up their weapons and walked away.

Attuned to the signals of the land, the Mayas knew that the appearance of the flying ant was the first sign of rain and signaled the time to plant corn. When, on the brink of the Mayas' destroying the enemy, the winged ant made an unusually early appearance, the Indians turned their backs on certain victory and returned to their villages to plant corn.

Help came immediately from Cuba, Mexico City, and 1,000 U.S. mercenary troops. Vengeance was merciless. Mayas were killed indiscriminately. Some were taken prisoner and sold to Cuba as slaves; others left their villages and hid in the jungles—in some cases, for decades. Between 1846 and 1850, the population of the Yucatán Peninsula was reduced from 500,000 to 300,000. Quintana Roo along the Caribbean coast was considered a dangerous no-man's land for almost another 100 years.

Growing Maya Power

Many Maya Indians escaped slaughter during the Caste War by fleeing to the isolated coastal forests of present-day Quintana Roo. A large number regrouped under the cult of the "Talking Cross"—an actual wooden cross that, with the help of a priest and a ventriloquist, spoke to the beleaguered indigenous fighters, urging them to continue fighting. Followers called themselves Cruzob (People of the Cross) and made a stronghold in the town of Noj Kaj Santa Cruz, today Carrillo Puerto. Research (and common sense) suggest the Mayas knew full well that a human voice was responsible for the "talking," but that many believed it was inspired by God.

Close to the border with British Honduras (now Belize), the leaders of Noj Kaj Santa Cruz began selling timber to the British and were given arms in return. At the same time (roughly 1855–1857), internal strife weakened the relations between Campeche and Mérida, and their mutual defense as well. Maya leaders took advantage of the conflict and attacked Fort Bacalar, eventually gaining control of the entire southern Caribbean coast.

Up until that time, indigenous soldiers simply killed the people they captured, but starting in 1858 they took lessons from the colonials and began to keep whites for slave labor. Women were put to work doing household chores and some became concubines, men were forced to work the fields and even build churches. (The church in Carrillo Puerto was built largely by white slaves.)

For the next 40 years, the Maya people and soldiers based in and around Noj Kaj Santa Cruz kept the east coast of the Yucatán for themselves, and a shaky truce with the Mexican government endured. The native people were economically independent, self-governing, and, with no roads in or out of the region, almost totally isolated. They were not at war as long as everyone left them alone.

The Last Stand

Only when President Porfirio Díaz took power in 1877 did the Mexican federal government begin to think seriously about the Yucatán Peninsula. Through the years, Quintana Roo's isolation and the strength of the Mayas in their treacherous jungle had foiled repeated efforts by Mexican soldiers to capture the Indians. The army's expeditions were infrequent, but it rankled Díaz that a relatively small and modestly armed Maya force had been able to keep the Mexican federal army at bay for so long. An assault in 1901, under the command of General Ignacio Bravo, broke the government's losing streak. The general captured a village, laid railroad tracks, and built a walled fort. Supplies arriving by rail kept the fort stocked, but the indigenous defenders responded by holding the fort under siege for an entire year. Reinforcements finally came from the capital, the Mayas were forced to retreat, first from the fort and then from many of their villages and strongholds. A period of brutal Mexican occupation followed, lasting until 1915, yet Maya partisans still didn't give up. They conducted guerrilla raids from the tangled coastal forest until the Mexican army, frustrated and demoralized, pulled out and returned Quintana Roo to the Mayas.

But beginning in 1917 and lasting to 1920, influenza and smallpox swept through the Maya-held territories, killing hundreds of thousands of Indians. In 1920, with the last of their army severely diminished and foreign gum-tappers creeping into former Maya territories, indigenous leaders entered into a negotiated settlement with the Mexican federal government. The final treaties were signed in 1935, erasing the last vestiges of Maya national sovereignty.

LAND REFORMS

Beginning in 1875, international demand for twine and rope made from henequen, a type of agave cactus that thrives in northern Yucatán, brought prosperity to Mérida, the state capital. Beautiful mansions were built by entrepreneurs who led the gracious life, sending their children to school in Europe, cruising with their wives to New Orleans in search of new luxuries and entertainment. Port towns were developed on the gulf coast, and a two-kilometer (1.2-mile) wharf named Progreso was built to accommodate the large ships that came for sisal (hemp from the henequen plant).

The only thing that didn't change was the lifestyle of indigenous people, who provided most of the labor on colonial haciendas. Henequen plants have incredibly hard, sharp spines and at certain times emit a horrendous stench. Maya workers labored long, hard hours, living in constant debt to the hacienda store.

Prosperity helped bring the Yucatán to the attention of the world. But in 1908, an American journalist named John Kenneth Turner stirred things up when he documented the difficult lives of the Indian plantation workers and the accompanying opulence enjoyed by the owners. The report set a series of reforms into motion. Felipe Carrillo Puerto, the first socialist governor of Mérida, helped native workers set up a labor union, educational center, and political club that served to organize and focus resistance to the powerful hacienda system. Carrillo made numerous agrarian reforms, including decreeing that abandoned haciendas could be appropriated by the govern-

ment. With his power and popularity growing, conservatives saw only one way to stop him. In 1923, Felipe Carrillo Puerto was assassinated.

By then, though, the Mexican Revolution had been won and reforms were being made throughout the country, including redistribution of land and mandatory education. Mexico entered its golden years, a 40-year period of sustained and substantial growth dubbed "The Mexican Miracle," all the more miraculous because it took place in defiance of the worldwide great Depression. In the late 1930s, President Lázaro Cárdenas undertook a massive nationalization program, claiming the major electricity, oil, and other companies for the state, and created state-run companies like PEMEX, the oil conglomerate still in existence today. In the Yucatán, Cárdenas usurped large parts of hacienda lands—as much as half of the Yucatan's total arable land, by some accounts, most dedicated to the growing of henequen—and redistributed it to poor farmers.

The economic prosperity allowed the ruling Institutional Revolutionary Party, or PRI, to consolidate power, and before long it held every major office in the federal government, and most state governments as well. The Mexican Miracle had not ameliorated all social inequalities—and had exacerbated some—but the PRI grew increasingly intolerant of dissent. Deeply corrupt, the party—and by extension the state—resorted to brutal and increasingly blatant repression to silence detractors. The most notorious example was the gunning down of scores of student demonstrators—some say up to 250—by security forces in 1968 in Mexico City's Tlatelolco plaza. The massacre took place at night, and by morning the plaza was cleared of bodies and scrubbed of blood, and the PRI-led government simply denied that it ever happened.

The oil crisis that struck the United States in the early 1970s was at first a boon for Mexico, whose coffers were filled with money from pricey oil exports. But a failure to diversify the economy left Mexico vulnerable; as oil prices stabilized, the peso began to devalue. It had fallen as much as 500 percent by 1982, prompting then-president López Portillo to nationalize Mexico's banks. Foreign investment quickly dried up and the 1980s were dubbed *la década perdida* (the lost decade) for Mexico and much of Latin America, a time of severe economic stagnation and crisis. In September 1985, a magnitude 8.1 earthquake struck Mexico City, killing 9,000 people and leaving 100,000 more homeless. It seemed Mexico had hit its nadir.

Yet it was during this same period that Cancún began to take off as a major vacation destination, drawing tourism and much-needed foreign dollars into the Mexican economy. The crises were not over—the implementation of the North American Free Trade agreement (NAFTA) in 1994 was met simultaneously by a massive devaluation of the peso and an armed uprising by a peasant army called the Zapatistas in the state Chiapas—but Mexico's economy regained some of its footing. A series of electoral reforms implemented in the late 1980s and through the 1990s paved the way for the historic 2000 presidential election, in which an opposition candidate—former Coca Cola executive Vicente Fox of the right-of-center PAN—defeated the PRI, ending the latter's 70-year reign of power. Fox was succeeded in 2006 by another PAN member, Felipe Calderón Hinojosa, in an election in which the PRI finished a distant third. However, the election was marred by allegations of fraud and weeks of post-election demonstrations. President Calderón's priority list for the early part of his term include expanding the job market, encouraging foreign investment (including for new tourism projects in the Yucatán and elsewhere), and combating the country's persistent drug and gang problem.

Government

Mexico enjoys a constitutional democracy modeled after that of the United States, including a president (who serves one six-year term), a two-house legislature, and a judiciary branch. For 66 years (until the year 2000) Mexico was controlled by one party, the so-called moderate Partido Revolucionario Institutional, or Institutional Revolution Party (PRI). A few cities and states elected candidates from the main opposition parties—the conservative Partido de Acción Nacional (PAN) and leftist Partido de la Revolución Democrática (PRD)—but the presidency and most of the important government positions were passed from one hand-picked PRI candidate to the next, amid rampant electoral fraud.

Indeed, fraud and corruption have been ugly mainstays of Mexican government for generations. In the 1988 presidential election, PRI candidate Carlos Salinas Gortari officially garnered 51 percent of the vote, a dubious result judging from polls leading up to the election and rendered laughable after a mysterious "breakdown" in the election tallying system delayed the results for several days.

Salinas Gortari ended his term under the same heavy clouds of corruption and fraud that ushered him in—he is in hiding somewhere in Europe, accused of having stolen millions of dollars from the federal government during his term. That said, Salinas pushed through changes such as increasing the number of Senate seats and reorganizing the federal electoral commission that helped usher in freer and fairer elections. He also oversaw the adoption of NAFTA in 1993, which has sped up Mexico's manufacturing industry but seriously damaged other sectors, especially small farmers, many of whom are indigenous.

The 1994 presidential election was marred by the assassination in Tijuana of the PRI candidate Luis Donaldo Colosio, the country's first major political assassination since 1928. Colosio's campaign manager, technocrat Ernesto Zedillo, was nominated to fill the candidacy and eventually elected. Zedillo continued with reforms, and in 2000, for the first time in almost seven decades, the opposition candidate officially won. PAN candidate Vicente Fox, a

© LIZA PRADO

Government offices in the region's cities are often architecturally distinct.

businessman and former Coca-Cola executive from Guanajuato, took the reigns promising continued electoral reforms, a stronger private sector, and closer relations with the United States. He knew U.S. President-elect George W. Bush personally, having worked with him on border issues during Bush's term as governor of Texas. Progress was being made until the terrorist attacks of September 11, 2001, pushed Mexico far down on the U.S. administration's priority list. With Mexico serving a term on the U.N. Security Council, Fox came under intense pressure from the United States to support an invasion of Iraq. He ultimately refused—Mexican people were overwhelmingly opposed to the idea—but it cost Fox dearly in his relationship with Bush. The reforms he once seemed so ideally poised to achieve were largely incomplete by the time Fox's term ended.

The presidential elections of 2006 were bitterly contested, and created—or exposed—a deep schism in the country. The eventual winner was PAN candidate Felipe Calderón Hinojosa, a former Secretary of Energy under Fox. His main opponent, Andrés Manuel López Obrador, is a former mayor of Mexico City and member of the left-leaning PRD. Though fraught with accusations and low blows, the campaign also was a classic clash of ideals, with Calderón advocating increased foreign investment and free trade, and López Obrador assailing the neo-liberal model and calling for government action to reduce poverty and strengthen social services. Both men claimed victory after election day; when Calderón was declared the winner, López Obrador alleged widespread fraud and called for a total recount; his supporters blocked major thoroughfares throughout the country for weeks. The Mexican Electoral Commission did a selective recount and affirmed a Calderón victory; the official figures set the margin at under 244,000 votes out of 41 million casts, a difference of just one-half percent. Calderón's inauguration was further marred by legislators fist-fighting in the chamber, and the new president shouting his oath over jeers and general ruckus.

Calderón was confronted with a number of thorny problems upon inauguration, including a protest in Oaxaca that had turned violent, and spiraling corn prices which in turn drove up the cost of tortillas, the most basic of Mexican foods. While addressing those issues, he pressed forward with promised law and order reforms, raising police officers' wages and dispatching the Mexican military to staunch rampant gang and drug-related crime in cities like Tijuana and Monterrey. He also launched a First Employment program, giving incentives to companies who hire first-time job seekers, including students and women who have never worked outside of the home.

Economy

OIL

The leading industry on the Yucatán Peninsula is oil. Produced by the nationally owned PEMEX, the oil industry is booming along the Gulf Coast from Campeche south into the state of Tabasco. Most of the oil is shipped at OPEC prices to Canada, Israel, France, Japan, and the United States. Rich in natural gas, Mexico sends the United States 10 percent of its total output. Two-thirds of Mexico's export revenue comes from fossil fuels. As a result, peninsula cities are beginning to show signs of financial health.

FISHING

Yucatecan fisheries also are abundant along the Gulf Coast. At one time fishing was not much more than a family business, but today fleets of large purse seiners with their adjacent processing plants can be seen on the Gulf of Mexico. With the renewed interest in preserving fishing grounds for the future, the industry could continue to thrive for many years.

TOURISM

Until the 1970s, Quintana Roo's economy amounted to very little. For a few years the chicle boom brought a flurry of activity up and down the state—it was shipped from the harbor of Isla Cozumel. Native and hardwood trees have always been in demand; coconuts and fishing were the only other natural resources that added to the economy—but neither on a large scale.

With the development of an offshore sandbar—Cancún—into a multimillion-dollar resort, tourism became the region's number-one moneymaker. The development of the Riviera Maya (extending from Cancún to Tulum)—and now, the Costa Maya (south of Sian Ka'an)—only guaranteed the continued success of the economy. New roads now give access to previously unknown beaches and Maya structures. Extra attention is going to archaeological zones ignored for hundreds of years. All but the smallest have restrooms, ticket offices, gift shops, and food shops.

People and Culture

PAPEL PICADO

Mexicans are famous for their celebrations – whether it's to honor a patron saint or to celebrate a neighbor's birthday, partying is part of the culture. Typically, fiestas feature great music, loads of food, fireworks, and brightly colored decorations, often including *papel picado* (literally, diced paper).

Dancing at the slightest breeze, *papel picado* is tissue paper cut or stamped with a design that is appropriate for the occasion: a manger scene at Christmas, church bells and doves for a wedding, skeletons in swooping hats for Day of the Dead. Once cut, row upon row of *papel picado* is strung across city streets, in front of churches, or in people's backyards.

After the celebration, few are inclined to take down the decorations. Eventually, all that's left are bits of colored paper blowing in the wind, the cord that it was hung on, and the memories of the fine fiesta.

DEMOGRAPHY

Today, 75–80 percent of the Mexican population is estimated to be mestizo (a combination of the indigenous and Spanish-Caucasian races). Only 10–15 percent are considered to be indigenous peoples. For comparison, as recently as 1870, the indigenous made up more than 50 percent of the population. While there are important native communities throughout Mexico, the majority of the country's indigenous peoples live in the Yucatán Peninsula, Oaxaca, and Chiapas.

RELIGION

The vast majority of Mexicans are Roman Catholic, especially in the generally conservative Yucatán Peninsula. However, a vigorous evangelical movement gains more and more converts every year.

LANGUAGE

The farther you go from a city, the less Spanish you'll hear and the more dialects of indigenous languages you'll encounter. The government estimates that of the 10 million indigenous people in the country, about 25 percent do not speak Spanish. Of the original 125 native languages, 70 are still spoken, 20 of which are classified as Maya languages, including Tzeltal, Tzotzil, Chol, and Yucatec.

Although education was made compulsory for children in 1917, this law was not enforced in the Yucatán Peninsula until recently. Today, schools throughout the peninsula use Spanish-language books, even though many children do not speak the language. In some of the rural schools, bilingual teachers are recruited to help children make the transition.

ART

Mexico has an incredibly rich colonial and folk-art tradition. While not art for the people who make and use it, traditional indigenous clothing is beautiful and travelers and collectors are increasingly able to buy it in local shops and markets. Prices for these items can be high, for the simple fact that they are hand-woven and can literally take months to complete. Mérida has shops filled with pottery, carving, and textiles from around Yucatán state.

HOLIDAYS AND FESTIVALS

People in Mexico take their holidays seriously—of their country, their saints, and their families. You'll be hard-pressed to find a two-week period when something or someone isn't being celebrated. On major holidays—Christmas, New Year's Day, and Easter—be prepared for crowds on the beaches and ruins. Be sure to book your hotel and buy your bus tickets well in advance; during holidays, the travel industry is saturated with Mexican travelers.

In addition to officially recognized holidays, villages and cities hold numerous festivals and celebrations: patron saints, birthdays of offi-

REGIONAL HOLIDAYS AND CELEBRATIONS

Jan. 1: **New Year's Day**

Jan. 6: **Día de los Reyes Magos** (Three Kings Day – Christmas gifts exchanged)

Feb. 2: **Virgen de la Candelaria** (religious candlelight processions light up several towns)

Feb. 5: **Flag Day**

Feb./March: **Carnaval** (seven-day celebration before Ash Wednesday)

March 21: **Birthday of Benito Juárez** (President of Mexico for five terms; born in 1806)

March 21: **Vernal Equinox in Chichén Itzá** (a phenomenon of light and shadow displays a serpent slithering down the steps of El Castillo)

May 1: **Labor Day**

May 3: **Day of the Holy Cross** (Dance of the Pigs' Head performed in Celestún, Carrillo Puerto, and Hopelchén)

May 5: **Battle of Puebla** (aka **Cinco de Mayo**; celebration of the 1862 defeat of the French)

May 20-30: **Jipi Festival** (Becal's celebration of the jipijapa plant, used in making *jipi* hats)

Early July: **Founding of Ticul**

Sept. 16: **Independence Day** (celebrated on the night of the 15th)

Sept. 27-Oct. 14: **El Señor de las Ampollas** (religious celebration in Mérida)

Oct. 4: **Feast Day of San Francisco de Asisi** (religious celebrations in Conkal and Telchac Puerto)

Oct. 12: **Columbus Day**

Oct. 18-28: **El Cristo de Sitilpech** (religious celebration in Izamal – the height is on the 25th)

Nov. 1-2: **All Souls' Day and Day of the Dead** (church ceremonies and graveside parties in honor of the deceased)

Nov. 20: **Día de la Revolución** (celebration of the beginning of the Mexican Revolution in 1910)

Dec. 8: **Feast of the Immaculate Conception** (religious celebrations in Izamal and Celestún)

Dec. 12: **Virgen de Guadalupe** (religious celebration in honor of Mexico's patron saint)

Dec. 25: **Christmas** (celebrated on the night of the 24th)

cials, a good crop, a birth of a child. You name it, and it's probably been celebrated. Festivals typically take place in and around the central plaza of a town with dancing, live music, colorful decorations, and fireworks. Temporary food booths are set up around the plaza and typically sell tamales (both sweet and meat), *buñuelos* (sweet rolls), tacos, *churros* (fried dough dusted with sugar), *carne asada* (barbecued meat), and plenty of beer.

ESSENTIALS

Getting There

For centuries, getting to the Yucatán Peninsula required a major sea voyage to one of the few ports on the Gulf of Mexico, only to be followed by harrowing and uncertain land treks limited to mule trains and narrow paths through the tangled jungle. Today, the peninsula is easily accessible. Visitors arrive every day via modern airports, a network of good highways, excellent bus service, or by cruise ship. From just about anywhere in the world, the Yucatán is only hours away.

AIR

The main international airports on the Yucatán Peninsula are in **Cancún** and **Mérida;** another is reportedly being built in Tulum. Most travelers use the Cancún airport—it's well located for those vacationing in the Caribbean as well as for those traveling inland. Fares typically are cheaper here than to any other airport in the region.

Travelers who are planning to spend their entire time inland, often choose to fly to Mérida instead—the city itself is an important destination and it's close to many of the area's key sights and archaeological ruins.

Similarly, many travelers who only will be visiting **Isla Cozumel,** fly directly there—it's often more expensive than landing in Cancún but avoids the time and hassle of traveling from

© LIZA PRADO

the mainland to the island (more time to dive and to enjoy the island!).

There also are airports in **Chetumal, Villahermosa, Tuxtla Gutiérrez,** and **Tapachula,** which are typically used for domestic travel. However, for travelers planning to spend most of their time in Campeche, Tabasco, or Chiapas, they may be most convenient.

Departure Tax
There is a US$36 departure tax to fly out of Mexico—most airlines incorporate the tax into their tickets, but it's worth setting aside some cash just in case.

BUS
The Yucatán's main interstate bus hubs are Mérida and Cancún, with service to and from Mexico City, Veracruz, Oaxaca, and other major destinations in the country. There also are buses between Chetumal and cities in Belize and Guatemala. Travel agencies and tour operators in San Cristóbal and Palenque offer van service to various cities in Guatemala, including Flores, Quetzaltenango, Panajachel, Antigua, and Guatemala City.

CAR
Foreigners driving into Mexico are required to show a valid driver's license, and title, registration, and proof of insurance for their vehicle. Mexican authorities do not recognize foreign-issued insurance; Mexican vehicle insurance is available at most border towns 24 hours a day and several companies also sell policies over the Internet. Do not cross the border with your car until you have obtained the proper papers.

CRUISE SHIP
Increasing numbers of cruise ships stop along Mexico's Caribbean coast every year, some carrying as many as 5,000 people. Many sail out of Miami and Fort Lauderdale, stopping at Key West before continuing to Punta Venado (Riviera Maya), Isla Cozumel, and Mahahual.

Prices are competitive and ships vary in services, amenities, activities, and entertainment. Pools, restaurants, nightclubs, and cinemas are commonplace. Fitness centers and shops also make ship life convenient. To hone in on the type of cruise you'd like to go on, research options on the Internet, in the travel section of your local newspaper, and by contacting your travel agent.

If your budget is tight, consider traveling standby. Ships want to sail full and are willing to cut their prices—sometimes up to 50 percent—to do so. Airfare usually is not included. Note: Once you're on the standby list, you likely will have no choice of cabin location or size.

NEIGHBORING COUNTRIES
Cancún is an important international hub, not only for tourists from North America and Europe but for regional flights to Central America and the Caribbean. In southern Quintana Roo, Chetumal is the gateway to Belize and there's a direct bus to Flores, Guatemala. Most travel to Guatemala, however, is through Chiapas, from the towns of San Cristóbal and Palenque.

Travel agencies can book tours to Belize, Guatemala, and Cuba, though it's relatively easy to arrange a trip yourself. Most travelers do not need prearranged visas to enter either Belize or Guatemala, but they may have to pay an entrance fee at the airport or border. Call the respective consulates for additional information.

Note: The U.S. government prohibits most ordinary travel to Cuba by U.S. citizens—technically, Americans without permits are not allowed to spend money in Cuba, and hefty fines against Americans traveling there are being levied. Nevertheless, tens of thousands of Americans travel to Cuba every year, a large share of them via Cancún. Most Cancún travel agencies sell plane tickets to Cuba; Americans are issued a separate paper visa that Cuban officials stamp instead of their passport. Needless to say, most American travelers manage to lose that visa before getting onto a plane back to the United States. Remember you won't be able to use any U.S.-based credit cards, debit cards, or travelers checks in Cuba—take plenty of cash as Cuba can be shockingly expensive. Don't count on any help from the U.S. State Department if you have problems.

Getting Around

AIR

Although budget airlines like Click Mexicana are starting to appear on the Mexican airline scene, flying domestically is still relatively expensive. The Yucatán is no exception. Once you factor in the check-in process, security, and baggage claim, there are very few flights within the region that make sense travel-wise, unless your time is incredibly tight. And if that is the case, you may as well see what you can do by car or bus and start planning a return trip.

BUS

Mexico's bus and public transportation system is one of the best in Latin America, if not the Western Hemisphere, and the Yucatán Peninsula bus system is no exception. ADO and its affiliate bus lines practically have a monopoly, but that has not made bus travel any less efficient or less affordable. Dozens of buses cover every major route many times per day, and even smaller towns have frequent and reliable service.

Buses come in three main categories. **First-class**—known as *primera clase* or sometimes *ejecutivo*—is the most common and the one travelers use most often. Buses have reclining seats and TVs where movies are played on long trips. First-class buses make some intermediate stops but only in large towns. The main first-class lines in the Yucatán are ADO and OCC (primarily serving Chiapas).

Deluxe class—usually called *lujo* (luxury)—is a step up; they often are slightly faster since they're typically nonstop. The main deluxe line is ADO-GL, which costs 10–25 percent more than regular ADO. ADO-GL buses have nicer seats and better televisions (even more recent movies!). Sometimes there are even free bottles of water in a cooler at the back. Even nicer are UNO buses, which often charge twice as much as

Ferries and catamarans stand side-by-side at Isla Mujeres's small dock.

© LIZA PRADO

regular ADO. UNO offers cushy, extra-wide seats (only three across instead of four), headphones, and usually a light meal like a sandwich and soda.

Second-class—*segunda clase*—are significantly slower and less comfortable than first-class buses, and they're not all that much cheaper. Whenever possible, pay the dollar or two extra for first-class. Second-class buses are handy in that you can flag them down anywhere on the roadside, but that also is precisely the reason they're so slow. In smaller towns, second-class may be the only service available, and it's fine for shorter trips. The main second-class lines in the Yucatán are Mayab, Oriente, Noreste, and ATS.

For overnight trips, definitely take first-class or deluxe. Not only will you be much more comfortable, second-class buses are sometimes targeted by roadside thieves since they drive on secondary roads and stop frequently.

Wherever bus service is thin, you can count on there being frequent *colectivos* or *combis*—vans or minibuses—that cover local routes.

They can be flagged down anywhere along the road.

FERRY

Ferries are used to get to and from the region's most visited islands, including Isla Mujeres (reached from Cancún), Isla Cozumel (reached from Playa del Carmen), and Isla Holbox (reached from Chiquilá). Service is safe, reliable, frequent, and affordable.

CAR

As great as Mexico's bus system is, a car is the best way to tour the Yucatán Peninsula. Most of the sights—ruins, deserted beaches, haciendas, caves, cenotes, wildlife—are well outside of the region's cities, down long access roads, or on the way from one town to the next. Having a car also saves you the time and effort of walking or the cost of cabbing to all those "missing links"; it allows you to enjoy the sights for as long or as little as you choose.

If you're here for a short time—a week or less—definitely get a car for the simple reason

© LIZA PRADO

Busy but orderly city streets are typical in the region.

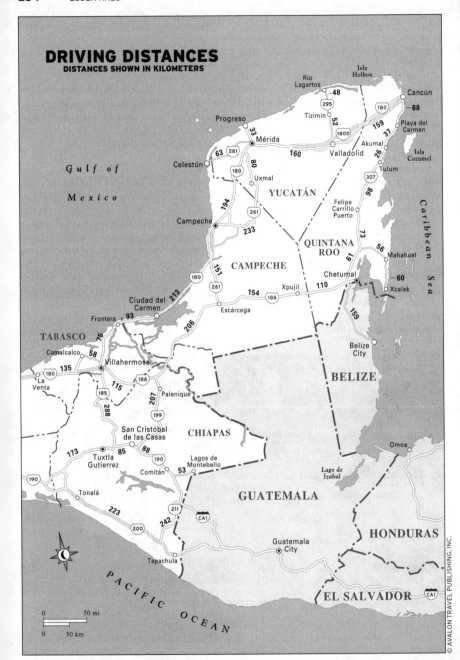

DRIVING DISTANCES
DISTANCES SHOWN IN KILOMETERS

Gulf of Mexico

Isla Holbox

Río Lagartos — **48**
Cancún — **68**

295
Progreso
Tizimín
52
180D
Playa del Carmen
33
159
37
Mérida
180
63 **281**
Valladolid
Akumal
160
26
Celestún
80
Isla Cozumel
Uxmal
Tulum
194
YUCATÁN
307

261
Felipe Carrillo Puerto
86

Campeche
233
QUINTANA ROO
73

CAMPECHE
151
61
56
Mahahual
Chetumal — **60**
180
Xpujil
110
Xcalak

261
154 **186**

Ciudad del Carmen
213
Escárcega
159

Frontera — **93**
206
Belize City

TABASCO
75
BELIZE

Comalcalco
58

135
Villahermosa
180
La Venta
115
186

195
207
Palenque
199

288
San Cristóbal de las Casas
Omoa

173
Tuxtla Gutiérrez
85
88
CHIAPAS
Lago de Izabal

190
Lagos de Montebello
53

190
Comitán
GUATEMALA
HONDURAS

Tonalá
211
CA1

223
242

200
Guatemala City
EL SALVADOR
CA1

Tapachula

Caribbean Sea

PACIFIC OCEAN

0   50 mi

0   50 km

© AVALON TRAVEL PUBLISHING, INC.

that you'll have the option of seeing and doing twice as much. If renting for your entire vacation isn't feasible money-wise, consider renting in choice locations: a couple of days in Mérida to see the Puuc Route, a few in Campeche to see the Río Bec archaeological zones, and a couple of days to explore the less-accessible parts of Quintana Roo. You also may want a car for a day in Cozumel to check out the island. Cars aren't necessary to visit Cancún, Isla Mujeres, Mérida, or San Cristóbal de las Casas.

Car Rental

International rental chains like Hertz, Budget, and Avis sometimes have good online specials but otherwise they tend to be much more expensive than local shops. Mexican car rental agencies may have an older fleet; it is rare, however, that travelers are tricked or mistreated.

Regardless of where you rent, be sure to ask about the insurance policy: Is it partial or full? How much is the deductible? Does it offer a zero-deductible plan? Note: you will be asked to leave a blank credit card imprint, ostensibly to cover the deductible if there is any damage. Be sure that this is returned to you when you bring back the car.

Before renting, be sure to have the attendant review the car for existing damage—definitely accompany him on this part and don't be shy about pointing out every nick, scratch, and ding. Other things to confirm before driving off include:

- There is a spare tire and a working jack.

- All doors lock and unlock, including trunk.

- All windows roll up and down properly.

- The proper—and current—car registration is in the car.

- The amount of gas—you'll have to return it with the same amount.

- There is a 24-hour telephone number for the car rental agency in case of an emergency.

Highways and Road Conditions

Driving in Mexico isn't as nerve-racking as you might think. The highways are in excellent condition and even secondary roads are well maintained. There are a few dirt and sand roads—mostly along the Costa Maya, in the Sian Ka'an Biosphere Reserve, and to some of the lesser-visited archaeological sites in Campeche.

The main **highways** in the region are Highway 307, which runs the length of Mexico's Caribbean coast; Highway 180, the thoroughfare that links Cancún, Mérida, and Campeche City; Highway 186, which crosses the southern portion of the Yucatán Peninsula and leads travelers to Campeche's Río Bec region and Villahermosa; and Highways 195, 190, and 200 which criss-cross the state of Chiapas.

In the entire region, there are only two **toll roads,** both sections of Highway 180: Between Mérida and Cancún (US$28) and between Campeche City and the town of Champotón (US$4.25). They're not cheap, but they can shave off a bit of travel time. Good if you're in a rush, otherwise you're better off taking secondary roads, which pass through picturesque countryside and by indigenous villages.

Off the highways, the biggest hazard are *topes*—speed bumps. They are common on all roads and highways, save the toll roads. They vary in size, but many are big and burly and hitting them at even a slow speed can do a number on you, your passengers, and your car. As soon as you see a sign announcing an upcoming town or village, be ready to slow down. By the same token, few roads have much of a shoulder—watch for people and animals on the roads, especially around villages but even in places you don't expect.

If you break down or run out of gas on a main road during daylight hours, stay with your car. *Los Ángeles Verdes* (The Green Angels, toll-free Mex. tel. 078 or 800/903-9200), a government-sponsored tow truck and repair service, cruise these roads on the lookout for drivers in trouble. They carry a CB radio, gas, and small parts and are prepared to fix tires. If you have a cellular phone—or happen to be near a pay phone—call your car rental agency; the Green Angels are a great backup. If you

FOREIGN CONSULATES

Foreign consulates and consular agencies in the region include:

BELGIUM

* Cancún: Plaza Protical, Av. Tulum 192, Local 59, S.M. 4, tel. 998/892-2512, 10 A.M.-2 P.M. Monday-Friday.

BELIZE

* Cancún: Av. Nader 34, S.M. 2-A, tel. 998/887-8417, 9 A.M.-1 P.M. Monday-Friday.

* Chetumal: Av. Armada de México 91, tel. 983/832-1803, 9 A.M.-1 P.M. Monday-Friday.

* Mérida: Calle 53 between Calles 56 and 58, tel. 999/928-6152, 9 A.M.-1 P.M. Monday-Friday.

CANADA

* Cancún: Plaza Caracol, Blvd. Kukulcán Km. 8.5, Local 330, tel. 998/883-3360, 9 A.M.-5 P.M. Monday-Friday. In case of an emergency, call the embassy in Mexico City at toll-free Mex. tel. 800/706-2900.

CUBA

* Cancún: Pecari 17, S.M. 20, tel. 998/884-3423, 9 A.M.-1 P.M. Monday-Friday.

* Mérida: Calle 42 between Calles 1-D and 1-E, tel. 999/944-4216, 8:30 A.M.-1:30 P.M. Monday-Friday.

FRANCE

* Cancún: France no longer has a consulate in Cancún.

* Mérida: Calle 33-D between Calles 62-A and 72, tel. 999/925-2886. (Appointment only.)

GERMANY

* Cancún: Punta Conoco 36, S.M. 24, tel. 998/884-1898, 9 A.M.-noon (by telephone until 1:30 P.M.) Monday-Friday.

GREAT BRITAIN

* Cancún: Royal Sands Resort, Blvd. Kukulcán Km. 13.5, tel. 998/881-0100, 9 A.M.-5 P.M. Monday-Friday.

GUATEMALA

* Chetumal: Av. Héroes de Chapultepec 356, tel. 983/832-3045, 9 A.M.-5 P.M. Monday-Friday.

---

are on a remote road and don't have a phone, you're better off walking or hitching a ride to the nearest town.

Driving Scams

Most travelers have heard horror stories about Mexican police and worry about being taken for all their money or being trundled off to jail without reason. While it is true that there is corruption among the police, they don't target tourists; foreigners are, after all, the economic life blood of the region—the police don't want to scare them away.

As long as you are a careful and defensive driver, it is very unlikely you'll have any interaction with the police. Most travelers who

are pulled over actually have done something wrong—speeding, running a stop sign, turning on red. In those situations, remain calm and polite. If you have an explanation, definitely give it; it is not uncommon to discuss a given situation with an officer. Who knows, you may even convince him you're right—it's happened to us!

Of real concern are gas station attendants. Full service is the norm here—you pull up, tell the person how much you want, and he or she does the rest. A common scam is for one attendant to distract you with questions about wiper fluid or gas additives while another starts the pump at 50 or 100 pesos. Before you answer any questions, be sure the attendant "zeroes" the pump before starting.

- Comitán: Calle 1 Sur Poniente at Av. 2 Poniente Sur, tel. 963/632-2669, 9 A.M.–5 P.M. Monday–Friday.

- Tapachula: Calle 2 Oriente 33, tel. 962/626-1252, 9 A.M.–5 P.M. Monday–Friday.

ITALY

- Cancún: Parque Las Palapas, Alcatraces 39, Retorno 5, S.M. 22, tel. 998/884-1261, 9 A.M.–2 P.M. Monday–Friday.

NETHERLANDS

- Cancún: Cancún International Airport, 2nd floor, tel. 998/886-0070, 9 A.M.–2 P.M. Monday–Friday.

- Mérida: Calle 64 between Calles 47 and 49, tel. 999/924-3122, 9 A.M.–5 P.M. Monday–Friday. (Appointment only.)

SPAIN

- Cancún: Oasis Cooperativo, Blvd. Kukulcán Km. 6.5, tel. 998/848-9900, 10 A.M.–1 P.M. Monday–Friday. MAY MOVE

- Mérida: Calle 8 between Calles 5 and 7, tel.

999/984-0181, 9:30 A.M.–1 P.M. Monday–Friday.

SWITZERLAND

- Cancún: above Rolandi's restaurant, Av. Cobá 12, Local 214, tel. 998/884-8446, 8 A.M.–3 P.M. Monday–Friday.

UNITED STATES

- Cancún: Plaza Caracol, Blvd. Kukulcán Km. 8.5, Local 323, tel. 998/883-0272, 9 A.M.–2 P.M. Monday–Friday. The after-hours contact number is 044-998/845-4364, but should be used *only* for serious emergencies involving an American citizen, e.g., death, arrest, or a major crime such as kidnapping, assault, rape, or murder. Officials look extremely unkindly on any nonemergency calls made to this phone number.

- Isla Cozumel: Main plaza, Villa Mar shopping center, 2nd floor, tel. 987/872-4574, after-hours emergency tel. 044-987/876-0624, noon–2 P.M. Mon.–Fri.)

- Mérida: Paseo de Montejo at Av. Colón, tel. 999/925-5011, 8:30 A.M.–5:30 P.M. Monday–Friday.

HITCHHIKING

Hitchhiking is not recommended for either men or women. That said, it sometimes can be hard to know what is a private vehicle and what is a *colectivo* (shared van). If there's no bus terminal nearby, your best bet is to look for locals who are waiting for public transportation and see which vans they take.

TOURS

Regional travel agents and tour operators offer a vast range of organized trips. You pay extra, of course, but all arrangements and reservations are made for you: from guides and transportation to hotels and meals. Special-interest trips also are common—archaeological tours, hacienda and convent routes, bird-watching and dive trips. Ask around, surf the Internet, and you'll find a world of organized adventure.

Visas and Officialdom

PASSPORTS

Gone are the days you can zip down to Mexico with just your driver's license and birth certificate. Since January 2007, all **U.S. citizens** returning from Mexico (and elsewhere) by air are required to have a passport. The same will apply to those re-entering by land or sea starting in 2008. **Canadians** may travel to Mexico without a passport; they simply need an official photo I.D. and proof of citizenship, such as an original birth certificate. All **other nationalities** must have a valid passport.

VISAS AND TOURIST CARDS

Citizens of most countries, including the United States and Canada and members of the E.U. do not need to obtain a visa to enter Mexico. Foreigners, however, are issued a white tourist card when they enter, with the number of days that they are permitted to stay in the county written at the bottom, typically 30–60 days. If you plan to stay for more than a month, politely ask the official to give you the amount of time you need; the maximum stay is 180 days.

Hold onto your tourist card! It must be returned to immigration officials when you leave Mexico. If you lose it, you'll be fined and may not be permitted to leave the country (much less the immigration office) until you pay.

To extend your stay up to 180 days, head to the nearest immigration office a week *before* your tourist card expires. Be sure to bring it along with your passport. There, you'll pick up several forms and fill them out, go to a bank to pay the US$22 processing fee, make photocopies of all the paperwork (including your passport, entry stamp, tourist card, and credit card), and then return to the office to get the extension. For every extra 30 days requested, foreigners must prove that they have US$1,000

available, either in cash, travelers checks, or simply by showing a current credit card. The process can take anywhere from a couple hours to a week, depending on the office.

CUSTOMS

Plants and fresh foods are not allowed into Mexico and there are special limits on alcohol, tobacco, and electronic products. Archaeological artifacts, certain antiques, and colonial art cannot be exported from Mexico without special permission.

Above all, do not attempt to bring marijuana or any other narcotic in or out of Mexico. Jail is one place your trusty guidebook won't come in handy.

Returning home, you will be required to declare all items you bought in Mexico. Citizens of the United States are allowed to re-enter with US$800 worth of purchases duty-free; the figure varies by country.

CONSULATES

The consulates in Cancún, Mérida, and Chetumal handle passport issues (replacing a lost one, adding pages, etc.) and can help their citizens if they are in a serious or emergency situation, including hospitalization, assault, arrest, lawsuits, or death. They usually do not help resolve common disputes—with tour operators or hotels, for example.

UNDERAGE TRAVELERS

In the United States, anyone under 18 traveling internationally without *both* parents or legal guardians must present a signed, notarized letter from the parent(s) staying at home granting permission to leave the country. This requirement is aimed at preventing international abductions, but it causes frequent and major disruptions for vacationers.

Conduct and Customs

THE BEACH

Topless and nude sunbathing are not customary on Mexican beaches, and are rarely practiced in Cancún and other areas frequented by Americans and Canadians. However, on beaches popular with Europeans, especially Playa del Carmen and Tulum, it is more commonplace. Wherever you are, take a look around to help decide whether baring some or all is appropriate.

PHOTOGRAPHING LOCALS

No one enjoys having a stranger take his or her picture for no good reason. Indigenous people are no different. The best policy simply is not to take these photographs unless you've asked the person's permission—and they've agreed—first.

Food

Considered among the most distinct cuisines of the country, Yucatecan food reflects the influences of its Maya, European, and Caribbean heritage. Some of the most popular menu items follow:

Cochinita Pibil: pork that has been marinated in achiote, Seville orange juice, peppercorn, garlic, cumin, salt, and pepper, wrapped in banana leaves, and baked. Typically served on weekends only.

CHILE PEPPERS

It's almost a given that at some point you'll bite into a seemingly innocent quesadilla, or dip a chip into a cute little bowl of salsa, and end up with a raging fire in your mouth. A wide variety of chile is used to spice food in the Yucatán, and throughout Mexico. Some are quite mild, even sweet, while others can make you sweat just sniffing them. (In all chiles, the seeds are the hottest part.) Many waiters are kind enough to warn you if a sauce or dish is *pica mucho* (stings a lot). Here are some of the chiles you may encounter on your trip:

- **Pimiento** (bell pepper): benign

- **Chile dulce** (sweet pepper – small, pumpkin-shaped, and light green): benign

- **Güero** (light-skinned – long, light green): mildly hot

- **Chile seco** (dried pepper – comes in *pasilla* and *Ancho* varieties: mildly hot

- **Poblano** (medium-size, dark green): ranges from mild to very hot

- **Serrano** (small torpedo-shaped peppers, typically green or red): medium hot

- **Puya** (small, thin, red peppers): hot

- **Jalapeño** (small to medium-size, hard and green, often pickled): hot

- **Chipotle** (medium and rust-colored, often dried): hot

- **Morita** (smoked and red): very hot

- **Piquín** (tiny, red, torpedo-shaped): extremely hot

- **De árbol** (literally, "from a tree" – long, red, thin): extremely hot

- **Habanero** (bulbous, small, typically green, orange, or yellow): five-alarm fire.

If you take a wrong bite, you'll find some quick relief in a glass of milk, a bite of banana, a pinch of salt, or a glass of beer. *Buen provecho!*

Seafood is king of the menu in this part of Mexico.

Dzoto-bichay: tamales made of *chaya* (a leafy vegetable similar to spinach) and eggs. It comes smothered in tomato sauce.

Empanizado: slices of pork or chicken that has been breaded and fried. This is often served with salad, rice, and beans.

Panucho: handmade tortilla stuffed with refried beans and covered with shredded turkey, pickled onion, and slices of avocado. Like a *salbute* plus!

Papadzules: hard-boiled eggs chopped and rolled into a corn tortilla. It comes smothered in a creamy pumpkin-seed sauce.

Poc-Chuc: slices of pork that have been marinated in Seville orange juice and coated with a tangy sauce. Pickled onions are added on the side.

Salbute: handmade tortilla covered with shredded turkey, pickled onion, and slices of avocado. Served hot and fast.

Sopa de Lima: turkey-stock soup prepared with shredded turkey or chicken, fried tortilla strips, and lemon juice.

Tips for Travelers

OPPORTUNITIES FOR STUDY AND EMPLOYMENT

While it may never approach neighboring Guatemala for the sheer number of Spanish schools, the Yucatán Peninsula has a variety of options for travelers who want to learn the language. Cancún, Isla Mujeres, Playa del Carmen, Mérida, and San Cristóbal all have schools or private instruction available. All also are well positioned to maximize travelers' enjoyment of the area's richness, whether its beaches, Maya ruins, colonial cities, or indigenous villages.

WOMEN TRAVELING ALONE

Solo women should expect a certain amount of unwanted attention, mostly in the form of whistles and catcalls. It typically happens as they walk down the street and sometimes comes from the most unlikely sources—we saw a man dressed as Bozo the clown turn mid–balloon animal to whistle at a woman walking by. Two or more women walking together attract much less unwanted attention, and a woman and man walking together will get none at all (at least of this sort—street vendors are a different story). While annoying and often unnerving, this sort of attention is almost always completely benign, and ignoring it is definitely the best response. Making eye contact or snapping a smart retort only will inspire more attention. Occasionally men will hustle alongside a woman trying to strike up a conversation—if you don't want to engage, a brief *hasta luego* or *no gracias* should make that clear. If it really gets on your nerves, carrying a notebook—or creating the appearance of working—reduces the amount of unwanted attention greatly.

GAY AND LESBIAN TRAVELERS

While openly gay women are still rare in Mexico, gay men are increasingly visible in large cities and certain tourist areas. Mérida has a fairly large gay community, of which a number of expat hotel and guesthouse owners are a prominent part. Cancún and Playa del Carmen both have a visible gay presence and a number of gay-friendly venues. Nevertheless, many locals—even in large cities—are not accustomed to open displays of homosexuality and may react openly and negatively. Many hotel attendants also simply don't understand that two travel companions of the same gender may prefer one bed—in some cases they will outright refuse to grant the request. Some couples find it easier to book a room with two queen-size beds and just sleep in one.

TRAVELERS WITH DISABILITIES

Mexico has made many improvements for the blind and people in wheelchairs—many large stores and tourist centers have ramps or elevators. A growing number of hotels have rooms designed for guests with disabilities, and there are two museums in the region—the Museo de las Estelas (Campeche City) and the Museo Regional de Antropología Carlos Pellicer Cámara (Villahermosa)—that have high-quality replicas of Maya artifacts that visually impaired travelers can hold and touch. That said, Mexico is still a hard place to navigate if you have a disability. Smaller towns are the most problematic, as their sidewalks can be narrow and even some main streets are not paved. Definitely ask for help—for what Mexico lacks in infrastructure, its people make up for in graciousness and charity.

SENIOR TRAVELERS

Seniors should feel very welcome and safe visiting the Yucatán. Mexico is a country that affords great respect to its *personas de la tercer edad*, literally "people of the third age," and especially in the tradition-minded Yucatán Peninsula. But as anywhere, older travelers should take certain precautions. The Yucatán, especially Mérida and the surrounding area, is known to be extremely hot and humid, especially May–July. Seniors should take extra care to stay cool and hydrated. Exploring the Maya ruins can also be hot, not to mention exhausting. Bring water and snacks, especially to smaller sites where they may not be commonly sold. Travelers with balance or mobility concerns should think twice about climbing any of the pyramids or other structures. They can be deceptively treacherous, with steps that are steep, uneven, and slick.

Cancún, Playa del Carmen, and Mérida all have state-of-the-art hospitals, staffed by skilled doctors, nurses, and technicians, many of whom speak English. Most prescriptions medications are available in Mexico, often at discount prices. However, pharmacists are woefully under trained and you should always double-check the active ingredients and dosage of any pills you buy here.

TRAVELING WITH CHILDREN

The Yucatán Peninsula is a great place to take kids, whether youngsters or teenagers. The variety of activities and relative ease of transportation help keep everyone happy and engaged. Cancún and the Riviera Maya are especially family-friendly, with several different eco- and water parks, miles of beaches, and (if all else fails!) plenty of malls with movie theaters, arcades, bowling, minigolf, aquariums, and more. Perhaps best of all, Mexico is a country where family is paramount.

TRAVELING WITH IMPORTANT DOCUMENTS

Make several copies of your passport, tourist card, and airline tickets. Whether you're traveling solo or with others, leave a copy with someone you trust at home. Store one copy in a separate bag and if you have a travel companion, give a copy to him. Be sure to carry a copy of your passport and tourist card in your purse or wallet instead of the originals, which can be left in the hotel safe or locked in your bag; they're a lot more likely to be lost or stolen on the street than taken by hotel staff. When you move from place to place, carry your passport and important documents in a travel pouch, always under your clothing. Write down your credit card and ATM numbers and the 24-hour service numbers and keep those in a safe place.

Health and Safety

SUNBURN

Common sense is the most important factor in avoiding sunburn. Use waterproof and sweatproof sunscreen with a high SPF. Reapply regularly—even the most heavy-duty waterproof sunscreen washes off faster than it claims to on the bottle (or gets rubbed off when you use your towel to dry off). Be extra careful to protect parts of your body that aren't normally exposed to the sun and give your skin a break from direct sun every few hours. Remember that redness from a sunburn takes several hours to appear—that is, you can be sunburned long before you *look* sunburned.

If you get sunburned, treat it like any other burn by running cool water over it as long and as often as you can. Do not expose your skin to more sun. Re-burning the skin can result in painful blisters that can easily become infected. There are a number of products designed to relieve sunburns, most with aloe extracts. Finally, be sure to drink plenty of water to keep your skin hydrated.

HEAT EXHAUSTION AND HEAT STROKE

The symptoms of **heat exhaustion** are cool moist skin, profuse sweating, headache, fatigue, and drowsiness. It is associated with dehydration and commonly happens during or after a strenuous day in the sun, such as visiting ruins. You should get out of the sun, remove any tight or restrictive clothing, and sip a sports drink such as Gatorade. Cool compresses and raising your feet and legs helps too.

Heat exhaustion is not the same as **heat**

stroke, which is distinguished by a high body temperature, a rapid pulse, and sometimes delirium or even unconsciousness. It is an extremely serious, potentially fatal condition and victims should be taken to the hospital immediately. In the meantime, wrap the victim in wet sheets, massage his arms and legs to increase circulation, and do not administer large amounts of liquids. Do not give liquids if the victim is unconscious.

DIARRHEA

Diarrhea is not an illness itself, but your body's attempt to get rid of something bad in a hurry; that something can be any one of a number of strains of bacteria, parasites, or amoebae that are often passed from contaminated water. No fun, it is usually accompanied by cramping, dehydration, fever, and of course, frequent trips to the bathroom.

If you get diarrhea, it should pass in a day or two. Anti-diarrheals such as Lomotil and Imodium A-D will plug you up but don't cure you—use them only if you can't be near a bathroom. The malaise you feel from diarrhea typically is from dehydration, not the actual infection, so be sure to drink plenty of fluids—a sports drink such as Gatorade is best. If it's especially bad, ask at your hotel for the nearest *laboratorio* (laboratory or clinic) where the staff can analyze a stool sample for around US$5 and tell you if you have a parasitic infection or a virus. If it's a common infection, the lab technician will tell you what medicine to take. Be aware that medicines for stomach infection are seriously potent, killing not only the bad stuff but the good stuff as well; they cure you but leave you vulnerable to another infection. Avoid alcohol and spicy foods for several days afterward.

A few tips for avoiding any stomach problems include:

Only drink bottled water. Avoid using tap water even for brushing your teeth.

Avoid raw fruits or vegetables that you haven't disinfected and cut yourself. Lettuce is particularly dangerous since water is easily trapped in the leaves. Also, as tasty as they look, avoid the bags of sliced fruit sold from street carts.

Order your meat dishes well done, even if it's an upscale restaurant. If you've been to a market, you'll see that meat is handled very differently here.

INSECTS

Insects are not of particular concern in the Yucatán, certainly not as they are in other parts of the tropics. Mosquitoes are common, but are not known to carry malaria. Dengue fever, also transmitted by mosquitoes, is somewhat more common, but still rare. Some remote beaches, like Isla Holbox and the Costa Maya, may have sand flies or horseflies, but they have been all but eliminated in the more touristed areas. Certain destinations are more likely to be buggy, like forested archaeological zones and coastal bird-watching areas, and travelers definitely should bring and use insect repellent there, if only for extra comfort.

CRIME

The Yucatán Peninsula is generally quite safe, and few travelers report problems with crime of any kind. Cancún is the one area where particular care should be taken, however. You may find illicit drugs relatively easy to obtain, but bear in mind that drug crimes are prosecuted vigorously in Mexico (especially ones involving foreigners), and your country's embassy can do very little to get you off. Sexual assault and rape have been reported by women who attend nightclubs, sometimes after having been slipped a "date rape" drug. While the clubs are raucous and sexually charged by definition, women should be especially alert to the people around them, and wary of accepting drinks from strangers. In all areas, common-sense precautions are always recommended, such as taking a taxi at night (especially if you've been drinking) and avoiding flashing your money and valuables, or leaving them unattended on the beach or elsewhere. Utilize the safety deposit box in your hotel room, if one is available; if you rent a car, get one with a trunk so your bags will not be visible through the window.

Information and Services

MONEY
Currency
Mexico's official currency is the *peso,* divided into 100 *centavos.*

Exchange Rates
At the time of research, US$1 was equal to MP$10.8, while the Canadian dollar exchanged at MP$9.5, and the Euro at MP$14.0.

ATMs
Almost every town in the Yucatán Peninsula has an ATM and they are without question the easiest, fastest, and best way to manage your money. The ATM may charge a small transaction fee (US$1–2.50 typically) and your home bank may as well, but you don't lose any more than you would by buying travelers checks and then exchanging them for a fee or at a bad rate.

Travelers Checks
With the spread of ATMs, travelers checks have stopped being convenient for most travel, especially in a country as developed as Mexico. If you do bring them, you will have to exchange them at banks or a *casa de cambio* (exchange booth).

Credit Cards
Visa and MasterCard are accepted at all large hotels and many medium and small ones, upscale restaurants, main bus terminals, travel agencies, and many shops throughout Mexico. American Express is accepted much less frequently. Some merchants tack on a 5–10 percent surcharge for any credit card purchase—ask before you pay.

Cash
It's a good idea to bring a small amount of U.S. cash, on the off-chance your ATM or credit cards suddenly stop working; US$200 is more than enough for a two-week visit. Stow it away with your other important documents, to be used only if necessary.

Tax
A 12 percent value-added tax (*IVA* in Spanish) applies to hotel rates, restaurant and bar tabs, and gift purchases. When checking in or making reservations at a hotel, ask if tax has already been added. In some cases, the tax is 17 percent.

Bargaining
Bargaining is common and expected in street and artisans' markets, but try not to be too aggressive. Some tourists derive immense and almost irrational pride from haggling over every last cent, and then turn around and spend several times that amount on beer or snacks. The fact is, most bargaining comes down to the difference of a few dollars or even less, and earning those extra dollars is a much bigger deal for the artisan than spending them is to most tourists.

Tipping
While tipping is always a choice, it is a key supplement to many workers' paychecks. In fact, for some, the tip is the *only* pay they receive. And while dollars and euros are appreciated, pesos are preferred. (Note: Foreign coins are useless in Mexico since moneychangers—whether banks or exchange houses—will not accept them.) Average gratuities in the region include:

- Archaeological zone guides: 10–15 percent if you're satisfied with the service; for informal guides (typically boys who show you around the site) US$0.50–1 is customary.

- Gas station attendants: around US$0.50 if your windshield has been cleaned, tires have been filled, or the oil and water have been checked; no tip is expected for simply pumping gas.

- Grocery store baggers: US$0.30–0.50.

- Housekeepers: US$1–2 per day; either left daily or as a lump sum at the end of your stay.

- Porters: about US$1 per bag.
- Taxi drivers: Tipping is not customary.
- Tour guides: 10–15 percent; and don't forget the driver—US$1–2 is typical.
- Waiters: 10–15 percent; make sure the gratuity is not included in the bill.

MAPS AND TOURIST INFORMATION
Maps
An excellent source of maps of Cancún, Isla Cozumel, and other places on the Riviera Maya and beyond is www.cancunmap.com. Providing detailed city and area maps, virtually every building and business is identified, most with a short review, plus useful information like taxi rates, driving distances, ferry schedules, and more. Maps cost around US$8–10.

Otherwise, maps can be hard to come by in the Yucatán Peninsula. The tourist office is always a good place to start, where maps are distributed to tourists free of charge. Car-rental agencies often have maps and many hotels create maps for their guests of nearby restaurants and sights.

Tourist Offices
Most cities in the Yucatán have a tourist office, and some have more. Some tourist offices are staffed with friendly and knowledgeable people and have a good sense of what tourists are looking for—the city tourism office in Mérida is one of the best. At others, you'll seriously wonder how the people there were hired. It is certainly worth stopping in if you have a question—you may well get it answered, but don't be surprised if you don't.

Film, Photography, and Video
It's easy to find 35mm film in Mexico, but you can probably buy it for less at home. If you do bring your own film, do not send it through the X-ray machine at the airport or in your checked luggage (most of which is also X-rayed). Instead, ask the security officers to hand-inspect your film, both exposed and unexposed rolls. The modern machines are not supposed to hurt 400-plus-speed film or lower, but it's better to be safe than to risk coming home with 10 rolls of faded or grainy shots.

Digital cameras are as popular in Mexico as they are everywhere else, but memory sticks and other paraphernalia are still prohibitively expensive. Bring what you think you'll need, including a few blank CDs and a USB cable to download photos—most Internet cafés allow you to download and burn photos, but may not have the CD or cable.

Video is another great way to capture the color and movement of the Yucatán. Be aware that all archaeological sites charge an additional US$3 to bring in a video camera; tripods are often prohibited.

COMMUNICATIONS AND MEDIA
Postal Service
Mailing letters and postcards from Mexico is neither cheap nor necessarily reliable. Delivery times vary greatly, and letters get "lost" somewhat more than postcards. Letters (under 20 grams) and postcards cost US$1 to the United States and Canada; US$1.20 to South America; and US$1.35 to the rest of the world.

Telephone
Ladatel—Mexico's national phone company—maintains good public phones all over the peninsula and country. Plastic phone cards with little chips in them are sold at most mini-marts and supermarkets in 30-, 50-, 100-, and 200-peso denominations. Ask for a *tarjeta Ladatel*—they are the size and stiffness of a credit card, as opposed to the thin cards used for cell phones. Insert the card into the phone, and the amount on the card is displayed on the screen. Rates and dialing instructions are inside the phone cabin. At the time of research, rates were US$0.10 a minute for local calls, US$0.40 a minute for national calls, and US$0.50 a minute for calls to the United States and Canada.

To dial a cellular phone, you must dial 044 and the area code, then the number. Note that calling a cell phone, even a local one, costs the

USEFUL TELEPHONE NUMBERS

TRAVELER ASSISTANCE

* Emergencies: 060 or 066

* Green Angels: 078 or 800/903-9200

* Directory Assistance: 044

LONG-DISTANCE DIRECT DIALING

* Domestic long-distance: 01 + area code + number

* International long-distance (United States only): 001 + area code + number

* International long-distance (rest of the world): 001 + country code + area code + number

LONG DISTANCE COLLECT CALLS

* Domestic long-distance operator: 02

* International long-distance operator (English-speaking): 09

same as a domestic long-distance telephone call (US$0.40/min.).

A number of Internet cafés offer inexpensive Web-based phone service, especially in the larger cities where broadband connections make this sort of calling possible. Rates tend to be slightly lower than those of Ladatel, and you don't have to worry about your card running out.

Beware of phones offering "free" collect or credit card calls; far from being free, their rates are outrageous.

Internet Access

Internet cafés can be found in virtually every town in the Yucatán Peninsula. Prices vary— the cheapest we saw was US$0.45 per hour,

the most expensive was US$7 per hour. The vast majority, however, charge US$0.85–1 per hour. Most places also will burn digital photos onto a CD—they typically sell the blank CD, but travelers should bring their own USB cable. Expect to pay US$2–3 a burn, plus the computer time. Many Internet shops also offer telephone and fax service.

Newspapers

The main daily newspapers in the Yucatán Peninsula are *El Diario de Yucatán, Novedades Quintana Roo,* and *Voz del Caribe.* The main national newspapers are also readily available, including *Reforma, La Prensa,* and *La Jornada.* For news in English, you'll find the *Miami Herald Cancún Edition* in Cancún and occasionally in Playa del Carmen, Isla Cozumel, and Mérida.

Radio and Television

Most large hotels and a number of midsize and small ones have cable or satellite TV, which usually includes CNN (though sometimes in Spanish only), MTV, and other U.S. channels. AM and FM radio options are surprisingly bland—you're more likely to find a good *rock en español* station in California than you are in the Yucatán.

WEIGHTS AND MEASURES
Measurements

Mexico uses the metric system, so distances are in kilometers, weights are in kilograms, gasoline is sold by the liter, and temperatures are given in Celsius. See the chart at the back of this book for conversions from the Imperial system.

Time Zone

The Yucatán Peninsula, Tabasco, and Chiapas are in the same time zone—U.S. Central Standard Time. Daylight Savings Time is recognized April–October.

Electricity

Mexico uses the 60-cycle, 110-volt AC current common in the United States. Bring a surge protector if you plan to plug in a laptop.

RESOURCES

Maya Glossary

MAYA GODS AND CEREMONIES

Acanum protective deity of hunters

Ahau Can serpent lord and highest priest

Ahau Chamehes deity of medicine

Ah Cantzicnal aquatic deity

Ah Chuy Kak god of violent death and sacrifice

Ahcit Dzamalcum protective god of fishermen

Ah Cup Cacap god of the underworld who denies air

Ah Itzám the water witch

Ah kines priests that consult the oracles and preside over ceremonies and sacrifices

Ahpua god of fishing

Ah Puch god of death

Ak'Al sacred marsh where water abounds

Bacaboob supporters of the sky and guardians of the cardinal points, who form a single god, Ah Cantzicnal Becabs

Bolontiku the nine lords of the night

Chac god of rain and agriculture

Chac Bolay Can butcher serpent living in the underworld

Chaces priests' assistants in agricultural and other ceremonies

Cihuateteo women who become goddesses through death in childbirth

Cit Chac Coh god of war

Hetzmek ceremony when the child is first carried astride the hip

Hobnil Bacab bee god, protector of beekeepers

Holcanes warriors charged with obtaining slaves for sacrifice

Hunab Ku giver of life, builder of the universe, and father of Itzámna

Ik god of the wind

Itzámna lord of the skies, creator of the beginning, god of time

Ixchel goddess of birth, fertility, and medicine; credited with inventing spinning

Ixtab goddess of the cord and of suicide by hanging

Kinich face of the sun

Kukulcán quetzal-serpent, plumed serpent

Metnal the underworld, place of the dead

Nacom warrior chief

Noh Ek Venus

Pakat god of violent death

Zec spirit lords of beehives

FOOD AND DRINK

alche inebriating drink, sweetened with honey and used for ceremonies and offerings

ic chili

itz sweet potato

kabaxbuul heaviest meal of the day, eaten at dusk and containing cooked black beans

kah pinole flour

kayem ground maize

macal a root

muxubbak tamale

on avocado

op plum

p'ac tomatoes

put papaya

tzamna black bean

uah tortillas

za maize drink

ANIMALS

acehpek dog used for deer hunting
ah maax cal prattling monkey
ah maycuy chestnut deer
ah sac dziu white thrush
ah xixteel ul rugged land conch
bil hairless dog reared for food
cutz wild turkey
cutzha duck
hoh crow
icim owl
jaleb hairless dog
keh deer
kitam wild boar
muan evil bird related to death
que parrot
thul rabbit
tzo domestic turkey
utiu coyote

MUSIC AND FESTIVALS

ah paxboob musicians
bexelac turtle shell used as percussion instrument
chohom dance performed in ceremonies related to fishing
chul flute
hom trumpet
kayab percussion instrument fashioned from turtle shell
Oc na festival where old idols of a temple are broken and replaced with new ones
okot uil dance performed during the Pocan ceremony
Pacum chac festival in honor of the war gods
tunkul drum
zacatan drum made from a hollowed tree trunk, one opening is covered with hide

ELEMENTS OF TIME

baktun 144,000-day Maya calendar
chumuc akab midnight
chumuc kin midday
chunkin midday
haab solar calendar of 360 days plus five extra days of misfortune, which complete the final month
emelkin sunset

kaz akab dusk
kin the sun, the day, the unity of time
potakab time before dawn
yalhalcab dawn

NUMBERS

hun one
ca two
ox three
can four
ho five
uac six
uuc seven
uacax eight
bolon nine
iahun 10
buluc 11
iahca 12
oxlahum 13
canlahum 14
holahun 15
uaclahun 16
uuclahun 17
uacaclahun 18
bolontahun 19
hunkal 20

PLANTS AND TREES

ha cacao seed
kan ak plant that produces a yellow dye
ki sisal
kiixpaxhkum chayote
kikche tree trunk that is used to make canoes
kuche red cedar tree
k'uxub annatto tree
piim fiber of the cotton tree
taman cotton plant
tauch black zapote tree
tazon te moss

MISCELLANEOUS WORDS

ah kay kin bak meat-seller
chaltun water cistern
cha te black vegetable dye
chi te eugenia, plant for dyeing
ch'oh indigo
ek dye
hadzab wooden swords

halach uinic leader
mayacimil smallpox epidemic
palapa traditional Maya structure constructed without nails or tools
pic underskirt
ploms rich people

suyen square blanket
xanab sandals
xicul sleeveless jacket decorated with feathers
xul stake with a pointed, fire-hardened tip
yuntun slings

Spanish Glossary

Many of the following words have a socio-historical meaning; others you will not find in the usual English-Spanish dictionary.

abarrotería grocery store
alcalde mayor or municipal judge
alfarería pottery
alfarero, alfarera potter
andando walkway or strolling path
antojitos native Mexican snacks, such as tamales, *chiles rellenos*, tacos, and enchiladas
artesanías handicrafts, as distinguished from *artesano, artesana* a person who makes handicrafts
audiencia one of the royal executive-judicial panels sent to rule Mexico during the 16th century
ayuntamiento either the town council or the building where it meets
bienes raíces literally "good roots," but popularly, real estate
birria pit-barbequed goat, pork, or lamb – especially typical of Jalisco
boleto ticket, boarding pass
caballero literally, "horseman," but popularly, gentleman
cabercera head town of a municipal district, or headquarters in general
cabrón literally a cuckold, but more commonly, bastard, rat, or S.O.B.; sometimes used affectionately
cacique chief or boss
calandria early 1800s-style horse-drawn carriage, common in Guadalajara
camionera central central bus station
campesino country person; farm worker
canasta basket of woven reeds, with handle

casa de huéspedes guesthouse, often operated in a family home
caudillo dictator or political chief
charro, charra gentleman cowboy or cowgirl
chingar literally, "to rape," but is also the universal Spanish "f- word," the equivalent of "screw" in English
churrigueresque Spanish baroque architectural style incorporated into many Mexican colonial churches, named after José Churriguera (1665-1725)
científicos literally, scientists, but applied to President Porfirio Díaz's technocratic advisers
cofradía Catholic fraternal service association, either male or female, mainly in charge of financing and organizing religious festivals
colectivo a shared public taxi or minibus that picks up and deposits passengers along a designated route
colegio preparatory school or junior college
colonia suburban subdivision/satellite of a larger city
Conasupo government store that sells basic foods at subsidized prices
correo post office
criollo person of all-Spanish descent born in the New World
cuadra Huichol yarn painting, usually rectangular
Cuaresma Lent
curandero, curandera indigenous medicine man or woman
damas ladies, as in "ladies room"
Domingo de Ramos Palm Sunday
ejido a constitutional, government-sponsored form of community, with shared land ownership and cooperative decision making

encomienda colonial award of tribute from a designated indigenous district

estación ferrocarril railroad station

farmacia pharmacy or drugstore

finca farm

fonda food stall or small restaurant, often in a traditional market complex

fraccionamiento city sector or subdivision

fuero the former right of clergy to be tried in separate ecclesiastical courts

gachupín "one who wear spurs"; a derogatory term for a Spanish-born colonial

gasolinera gasoline station

gente de razón "people of reason"; whites and mestizos in colonial Mexico

gringo once-derogatory but now commonly used term for North American whites

grito impassioned cry, as in Hidalgo's *Grito de Dolores*

hacienda large landed estate; also the government treasury

hidalgo nobleman; called honorifically by "Don" or "DoÑa"

indígena indigenous or aboriginal inhabitant of all-native descent who speaks his or her native tongue; commonly, but incorrectly, an Indian *(indio)*

jardín literally garden, but often denoting a town's central plaza

jejenes "no-see-um" biting gnats, especially around San Blas, Nayarit

judiciales the federal or state "judicial," or investigative police, best known to motorists for their highway checkpoint inspections

jugería stall or small restaurant providing a large array of squeezed vegetable and fruit *jugos* (juices)

juzgado the "hoosegow," or jail

larga distancia long-distance telephone service, or the *caseta* (booth) where it's provided

licenciado academic degree (abbr. Lic.) approximately equivalent to a bachelor's degree

lonchería small lunch counter, usually serving juices, sandwiches, and *antojitos* (Mexican snacks)

machismo; macho exaggerated sense of maleness; person who holds such a sense of himself

mescal alcoholic beverage distilled from the fermented hearts of maguey (century plant)

mestizo person of mixed European/indigenous descent

milpa native farm plot, usually of corn, squash, and beans

mordida slang for bribe; literally, "little bite"

palapa thatched-roof structure, often open and shading a restaurant

panga outboard launch *(lancha)*

Pemex acronym for Petróleos Mexicanos, Mexico's national oil corporation

peninsulares the Spanish-born ruling colonial elite

peón a poor wage-earner, usually a country native

petate a mat, traditionally woven of palm leaf

plan political manifesto, usually by a leader or group consolidating or seeking power

Porfiriato the 34-year (1876-1910) ruling period of president-dictator Porfirio Díaz

pozole popular stew, of hominy in broth, usually topped by shredded pork, cabbage, and diced onion

presidencia municipal the headquarters, like a U.S. city or county hall, of a Mexican *municipio*, county-like local governmental unit

preventiva municipal police

pronunciamiento declaration of rebellion by an insurgent leader

pueblo town or people

puta derogatory term for women, as in whore, bitch, or slut

quinta a villa or country house

quinto the royal "one-fifth" tax on treasure and precious metals

retorno cul-de-sac

rurales former federal country police force created to fight *bandidos*

Semana Santa pre-Easter holy week

Tapatío, Tapatía a label, referring to anyone or anything from Guadalajara or Jalisco

taxi especial private taxi, as distinguished from *taxi colectivo*, or shared taxi

telégrafo telegraph office, lately converting to high-tech

telecomunicaciones, or **telecom,** offering telegraph, telephone, and public fax services

tenate soft, pliable basket, without handle, woven of palm leaf
vaquero cowboy
vecinidad neighborhood
vinchuca "kissing" or "assassin" bug
yanqui Yankee
zócalo town plaza or central square

Abbreviations

Av. *avenida* (avenue)

Blv. *bulevar* (boulevard)
Calz. *calzada* (thoroughfare, main road)
Fco. Francisco (proper name, as in "Fco. Villa")
Fracc. *Fraccionamiento* (subdivision)
Nte. *norte* (north)
Ote. *oriente* (east)
Pte. *poniente* (west)
s/n *sin número* (no street number)

Spanish Phrasebook

Whether you speak a little or a lot, using your Spanish will surely make your vacation a lot more fun. You'll soon see that Mexicans truly appreciate your efforts and your willingness to speak their language.

PRONUNCIATION

Spanish commonly uses 30 letters–the familiar English 26, plus four straightforward additions: ch, ll, ñ, and rr, which are explained in "Consonants," below.

Once you learn them, Spanish pronunciation rules–in contrast to English–don't change. Spanish vowels generally sound softer than in English. (Note: The capitalized syllables below receive stronger accents.)

Vowels

a *like ah, as in "hah": agua AH-gooah (water), pan PAHN (bread), and casa CAH-sah (house)*
e *like eh, as in "hem:" mesa MEH-sah (table), tela TEH-lah (cloth), and de DEH (of, from)*
i *like ee, as in "need": diez dee-EHZ (ten), comida ko-MEE-dah (meal), and fin FEEN (end)*
o *like oh, as in "go": peso PEH-soh (weight), ocho OH-choh (eight), and poco POH-koh (a bit)*
u *like oo, as in "cool": uno OO-noh (one), cuarto KOOAHR-toh (room), and usted oos-TEHD (you); when it follows a "q" the u is silent; when it follows an "h" or has an umlaut, it's pronounced like "w"*

Consonants

b, d, f, k, l, m, n, p, q, s, t, v, w, x, y, z, and *ch* pronounced almost as in English; *h* occurs, but is silent.

c *like k as in "keep": cuarto KOOAR-toh (room), Tepic the-PEEK (capital of Nayarit state); when it precedes "e" or "i," pronounce c like s, as in "sit": cerveza sehr-VEH-sah (beer), encima ehn-SEE-mah (atop).*
g *like g as in "gift" when it precedes "a," "o," "u," or a consonant: gato GAH-toh (cat), hago AH-goh (I do, make); otherwise, pronounce g like h as in "hat": giro HEE-roh (money order), gente HEN-teh (people)*
j *like h, as in "has": Jueves HOOEH-vehs (Thursday), mejor meh-HOR (better)*
ll *like y, as in "yes": toalla toh-AH-yah (towel), ellos EH-yohs (they, them)*
ñ *like ny, as in "canyon": año AH-nyo (year), señor SEH-nyor (Mr., sir)*
r *is lightly trilled, with your tongue at the roof of your mouth like a very light English d, as in "ready": pero PEH-roh (but), tres TREHS (three), cuatro KOOAH-troh (four).*
rr *like a Spanish r, but with much more emphasis and trill. Let your tongue flap. Practice with burro (donkey), carretera (highway), and Carrillo (proper name), then really let go with ferrocarril (railroad).*
Note: The single exception to the above is the pronunciation of y when it's being used as the Spanish word for "and," as in "Eva y Leo."

In such case, pronounce it like the English ee, as in "keep": Eva "ee" Leo (Eva and Leo).

Accent

The rule for accent, the relative stress given to syllables within a given word, is straightforward. If a word ends in a vowel, an n or an s, accent the next-to-last syllable; if not, accent the last syllable.

Pronounce *gracias* GRAH-seeahs (thank you), *orden* OHR-dehn (order), and *carretera* kah-reh-TEH-rah (highway) with the stress on the next-to-last syllable.

Otherwise, accent the last syllable: *venir* veh-NEER (to come), *ferrocarril* feh-roh-cah-REEL (railroad), and *edad* eh-DAHD (age).

Exceptions to the accent rule are always marked with an accent sign: (á, é, í, ó, or ú), such as *teléfono* teh-LEH-foh-noh (telephone), *jabón* hah-BON (soap), and *rápido* RAH-pee-doh (rapid).

BASIC AND COURTEOUS EXPRESSIONS

Most Spanish-speaking people consider formalities important. Whenever approaching anyone, do not forget the appropriate salutation–good morning, good evening, etc. Standing alone, the greeting *hola* (hello) can sound brusque.

Hello. *Hola.*
Good morning. *Buenos días.*
Good afternoon. *Buenas tardes.*
Good evening. *Buenas noches.*
How are you? *¿Cómo está Usted?*
Very well, thank you. *Muy bien, gracias.*
Okay; good. *Bien.*
Not okay; bad. *No muy bien; mal.*
So-so. *Más o menos.*
And you? *¿Y usted?*
Thank you. *Gracias.*
Thank you very much. *Muchas gracias.*
You're very kind. *Muy amable.*
You're welcome. *De nada.*
Good-bye. *Adios.*
See you later. *Hasta luego.*
please *por favor*
yes *sí*
no *no*
I don't know. *No sé.*

Just a moment, please. *Un momentito, por favor.*
Excuse me, please (when you're trying to get attention). *Disculpe or Con permiso.*
Excuse me (when you've made a mistake). *Lo siento.*
Pleased to meet you. *Mucho gusto.*
How do you say...in Spanish? *¿Cómo se dice...en español?*
What is your name? *¿Cómo se llama Usted?*
Do you speak English? *¿Habla Usted inglés?*
Is English spoken here? *¿Se habla inglés?*
I don't speak Spanish well. *No hablo bien el español.*
I don't understand. *No entiendo.*
My name is . . . *Me llamo...*
Would you like . . . *¿Quisiera Usted...*
Let's go to . . . *Vamos a...*

TERMS OF ADDRESS

When in doubt, use the formal *Usted* (you) as a form of address.

I *yo*
you (formal) *Usted*
you (familiar) *tu*
he/him *él*
she/her *ella*
we/us *nosotros*
you (plural) *ustedes*
they/them *ellos* (all males or mixed gender); *ellas* (all females)
Mr., sir *señor*
Mrs., ma'am *señora*
miss, young lady *señorita*
wife *esposa*
husband *esposo*
friend *amigo* (male); *amiga* (female)
boyfriend; girlfriend *novio; novia*
son; daughter *hijo; hija*
brother; sister *hermano; hermana*
father; mother *padre; madre*
grandfather; grandmother *abuelo; abuela*

TRANSPORTATION

Where is...? *¿Dónde está...?*
How far is it to...? *¿A cuánto está...?*
from...to . . . *de...a...*
How many blocks? *¿Cuántas cuadras?*

Where (Which) is the way to...? *¿Dónde está el camino a...?*
the bus station *la terminal de autobuses*
the bus stop *la parada de autobuses*
Where is this bus going? *¿Adónde va este autobús?*
the taxi stand *la parada de taxis*
the train station *la estación de ferrocarril*
the boat *el barco or la lancha*
the airport *el aeropuerto*
I'd like a ticket to . . . *Quisiera un boleto a...*
first (second) class *primera (segunda) clase*
round-trip *ida y vuelta*
reservation *reservación*
baggage *equipaje*
Stop here, please. *Pare aquí, por favor.*
the entrance *la entrada*
the exit *la salida*
the ticket office *la taquilla*
(very) near; far *(muy) cerca; lejos*
to; toward *a*
by; through *por*
from *de*
the right *la derecha*
the left *la izquierda*
straight ahead *derecho; directo*
in front *en frente*
beside *al lado*
behind *atrás*
the corner *la esquina*
the stoplight *el semáforo*
a turn *una vuelta*
here *aquí*
somewhere around here *por aqui*
right there *allí*
somewhere around there *por allá*
street; boulevard *calle; bulevar*
highway *carretera*
bridge *Puente*
toll *cuota*
address *dirección*
north; south *norte; sur*
east; west *oriente (este); poniente (oeste)*

ACCOMMODATIONS

hotel *hotel*
Is there a room? *¿Hay cuarto?*

May I (may we) see it? *¿Podría (podríamos) verlo?*
What is the rate? *¿Cuál es la tarifa?*
Is that your best rate? *¿Es su mejor precio?*
Is there something cheaper? *¿Hay algo más económico?*
a single room *un cuarto sencillo*
a double room *un cuarto doble*
double bed *cama matrimonial*
twin bed *cama individual*
with private bath *con baño privado*
hot water *agua caliente*
shower *ducha*
towels *toallas*
soap *jabón*
toilet paper *papel higiénico*
blanket *cobija*
sheets *sábanas*
air-conditioned *aire acondicionado*
fan *abanico; ventilador*
key *llave*
manager *gerente*

FOOD

I'm hungry *Tengo hambre.*
I'm thirsty. *Tengo sed.*
menu *carta; menú*
order *orden*
glass *vaso*
fork *tenedor*
knife *cuchillo*
spoon *cuchara*
napkin *servilleta*
soft drink *refresco*
coffee *café*
tea *té*
drinking water *agua pura; agua potable*
carbonated water *agua mineral*
bottled uncarbonated water *agua sin gas*
beer *cerveza*
wine *vino*
milk *leche*
juice *jugo*
cream *crema*
sugar *azúcar*
cheese *queso*
snack *antojito; botana*

breakfast *desayuno*
lunch *almuerzo or comida*
daily lunch special *comida corrida*
dinner *cena*
the check *la cuenta*
eggs *huevos*
bread *pan*
salad *ensalada*
fruit *fruta*
mango *mango*
watermelon *sandía*
papaya *papaya*
banana *plátano*
apple *manzana*
orange *naranja*
lime *limón*
fish *pescado*
shellfish *mariscos*
shrimp *camarones*
meat (without) *(sin) carne*
chicken *pollo*
pork *puerco*
beef; steak *res; bistec*
bacon; ham *tocino; jamón*
fried *frito*
roasted *asada*
barbecue; barbecued *barbacoa; al carbón*

SHOPPING

money *dinero*
money-exchange bureau *casa de cambio*
I would like to exchange traveler's checks. *Quisiera cambiar cheques de viajero.*
What is the exchange rate? *¿Cuál es el tipo de cambio?*
How much is the commission? *¿Cuánto cuesta la comisión?*
Do you accept credit cards? *¿Aceptan tarjetas de crédito?*
money order *giro*
How much does it cost? *¿Cuánto cuesta?*
What is your final price? *¿Cuál es su último precio?*
expensive *caro*
cheap *barato; económico*
more *más*
less *menos*

a little *un poco*
too much *demasiado*

HEALTH

Help me please. *Ayúdeme por favor.*
I am ill. *Estoy enfermo.*
Call a doctor. *Llame un doctor.*
Take me to . . . *Lléveme a...*
hospital *hospital; clinica medica*
drugstore *farmacia*
pain *dolor*
fever *fiebre*
headache *dolor de cabeza*
stomachache *dolor de estómago*
burn *quemadura*
cramp *calambre*
nausea *náusea*
vomiting *vomitar*
medicine *medicina*
antibiotic *antibiótico*
pill; tablet *pastilla*
aspirin *aspirina*
ointment; cream *pomada; crema*
bandage *venda*
cotton *algodón*
sanitary napkins *Kotex*
birth control pills *pastillas anticonceptivas*
contraceptive foam *espuma anticonceptiva*
condoms *preservativos; condones*
toothbrush *cepillo de dientes*
dental floss *hilo dental*
toothpaste *pasta de dientes*
dentist *dentista*
toothache *dolor de dientes*

POST OFFICE AND COMMUNICATIONS

long-distance telephone *teléfono de larga distancia*
I would like to call . . . *Quisiera llamar a...*
collect *por cobrar*
person to person *persona a persona*
credit card *tarjeta de crédito*
post office *correo*
letter *carta*
stamp *estampilla, timbre*
postcard *tarjeta postal*
air mail *correo aereo*

registered *registrado*
money order *giro*
package; box *paquete; caja*
string; tape *cuerda; cinta*

AT THE BORDER

border *frontera*
customs *aduana*
immigration *migración*
tourist card *tarjeta de turista*
inspection *inspección; revisión*
passport *pasaporte*
profession *profesión*
marital status *estado civil*
single *soltero*
married; divorced *casado; divorciado*
widowed *viudado* (male); *vuidada* (female)
insurance *seguro*
title *título*
driver's license *licencia de manejar*

AT THE GAS STATION

gas station *gasolinera*
gasoline *gasolina*
unleaded *sin plomo*
fill it up, please *lleno, por favor*
tire *llanta*
tire repair shop *vulcanizadora*
air *aire*
water *agua*
oil; oil change *aceite; cambio de aceite*
grease *grasa*
My...doesn't work. *Mi...no sirve.*
battery *batería*
radiator *radiador*
alternator *alternador*
generator *generador*
tow truck *grúa*
repair shop *taller mecánico*
tune-up *afinación*
auto parts store *refaccionería*

VERBS

Verbs are the key to getting along in Spanish. They employ mostly predictable forms and come in three classes, which end in *ar*, *er*, and *ir*. Note that the first-person *(yo)* verb form is often irregular.

to buy *comprar*
I buy, you (he, she, it) buys *compro, compra*
we buy, you (they) buy *compramos, compran*
to eat *comer*
I eat, you (he, she, it) eats *como, come*
we eat, you (they) eat *comemos, comen*
to climb *subir*
I climb, you (he, she, it) climbs *subo, sube*
we climb, you (they) climb *subimos, suben*

to do or make *hacer*
I do or make, you (he she, it) does or makes *hago, hace*
we do or make, you (they) do or make *hacemos, hacen*
to go *ir*
I go, you (he, she, it) goes *voy, va*
we go, you (they) go *vamos, van*
to go (walk) *andar*
to love *amar*
to work *trabajar*
to want *desear, querer*
to need *necesitar*
to read *leer*
to write *escribir*
to repair *reparar*
to stop *parar*
to get off (the bus) *bajar*
to arrive *llegar*
to stay (remain) *quedar*
to stay (lodge) *hospedar*
to leave *salir* (regular except for *salgo*, I leave)
to look at *mirar*
to look for *buscar*
to give *dar* (regular except for *doy*, I give)
to carry *llevar*
to have *tener* (irregular but important: *tengo, tiene, tenemos, tienen*)
to come *venir* (similarly irregular: *vengo, viene, venimos, vienen*)

Spanish has two forms of "to be." Use *estar* when speaking of location or a temporary state of being: "I am at home." "*Estoy en casa.*" "I'm sick." "*Estoy enfermo.*" Use *ser* for a permanent state of being: "I am a doctor." "*Soy doctora.*"

Estar is regular except for *estoy,* I am. *Ser* is irregular:

to be *ser*
I am, you (he, she, it) is *soy, es*
we are, you (they) are *somos, son*

NUMBERS

zero *cero*
one *uno*
two *dos*
three *tres*
four *cuatro*
five *cinco*
six *seis*
seven *siete*
eight *ocho*
nine *nueve*
10 *diez*
11 *once*
12 *doce*
13 *trece*
14 *catorce*
15 *quince*
16 *dieciseis*
17 *diecisiete*
18 *dieciocho*
19 *diecinueve*
20 *veinte*
21 *veintiuno*
30 *treinta*
40 *cuarenta*
50 *cincuenta*
60 *sesenta*
70 *setenta*
80 *ochenta*
90 *noventa*
100 *cien*
101 *cientiuno*
200 *doscientos*
500 *quinientos*
1,000 *mil*
10,000 *diez mil*
100,000 *cien mil*
1,000,000 *millón*
one half *medio*
one third *un tercio*
one fourth *un cuarto*

TIME

What time is it? *¿Qué hora es?*
It's one o'clock. *Es la una.*
It's three in the afternoon. *Son las tres de la tarde.*
It's 4 A.M. *Son las cuatro de la mañana.*
six-thirty *seis y media*
a quarter till eleven *un cuarto para las once*
a quarter past five *las cinco y cuarto*
an hour *una hora*

DAYS AND MONTHS

Monday *lunes*
Tuesday *martes*
Wednesday *miércoles*
Thursday *jueves*
Friday *viernes*
Saturday *sábado*
Sunday *domingo*
today *hoy*
tomorrow *mañana*
yesterday *ayer*
January *enero*
February *febrero*
March *marzo*
April *abril*
May *mayo*
June *junio*
July *julio*
August *agosto*
September *septiembre*
October *octubre*
November *noviembre*
December *diciembre*
a week *una semana*
a month *un mes*
after *después*
before *antes*

Adapted from Bruce Whipperman's *Moon Pacific Mexico.*

Suggested Reading

The following titles provide insight into the Yucatán Peninsula and the Maya people. A few of these books are more easily obtained in Mexico, but all of them will cost less in the United States. Most are nonfiction, though several are fiction and great to pop into your carry-on for a good read on the plane, or for when you're in a Yucatecan mood. Happy reading.

Beletsky, Les. *Travellers' Wildlife Guides: Southern Mexico* Northampton: Interlink Books, 2007. A perfect companion guide if you plan on bird-watching, diving/snorkeling, hiking, or canoeing your way through your vacation. Excellent illustrations.

Coe, Andrew. *Archaeological Mexico: A Traveler's Guide to Ancient Cities and Sacred Sites.* Emeryville: Avalon Travel Publishing, 2001.

Coe, Michael D. *The Maya.* New York: Thames and Hudson, 1993. A well-illustrated, easy-to-read volume on the Maya people.

Coe, Michael D. *Breaking the Maya Code.* New York: Thames and Hudson, 1992, 1999. A fascinating account of how epigraphers, linguists, and archaeologists succeeded in deciphering Maya hieroglyphics.

Cortés, Hernán. *Five Letters.* Gordon Press, 1977. Cortés' letters to the king of Spain, telling of his accomplishments and justifying his actions in the New World.

Davies, Nigel. *The Ancient Kingdoms of Mexico.* New York: Penguin Books. An excellent study of the preconquest of the indigenous peoples of Mexico.

De Landa, Bishop Diego. *Yucatán Before and After the Conquest.* New York: Dover Publications, 1978. This book, translated by William Gates from the original 1566 volume, has served as the basis for all the research that has taken place since.

Díaz del Castillo, Bernal. *The Conquest of New Spain.* New York: Penguin Books, 1963. History straight from the adventurer's reminiscences, translated by J. M. Cohen.

Fehrenbach, T. R. *Fire and Blood: A History of Mexico.* New York: Collier Books, 1973. Over 3,000 years of Mexican history, related in a way that will keep you reading.

Ferguson, William M. *Maya Ruins of Mexico in Color.* Norman: University of Oklahoma Press, 1977. Good reading before you go, but too bulky to carry along. Oversized with excellent drawings and illustrations of the archaeological structures of the Maya.

Franz, Carl. *The People's Guide to Mexico.* Emeryville: Avalon Travel Publishing, 2002. A humorous guide filled with witty anecdotes and helpful general information for visitors to Mexico. Don't expect any specific city information, just nuts-and-bolts hints for traveling south of the border.

Greene, Graham. *The Power and the Glory.* New York: Penguin Books, 1977. A novel that takes place in the 1920s about a priest and the anti-church movement that gripped the country.

Heffern, Richard. *Secrets of the Mind-Altering Plants of Mexico.* New York: Pyramid Books. A fascinating study of many substances, from ancient ritual hallucinogens to today's medicines that are found in Mexico.

Laughlin, Robert M. *The People of the Bat.* Smithsonian Institution Press, 1988. Maya tales and dreams as told by the Zinacantán Indians in Chiapas.

Maya: Divine Kings of the Rain Forest. Könemann, 2006. A beautifully compiled book of essays, photographs, and sketches relating to the Maya, past and present. Too heavy to take on the road but an excellent read.

McNay Brumfield, James. *A Tourist in the Yucatan*. Tres Picos Press, 2004. A decent thriller that takes place in the Yucatán Peninsula; good for the beach or a long bus ride.

Meyer, Michael and William Sherman. *The Course of Mexican History*. Oxford University Press. A concise, one-volume history of Mexico.

Nelson, Ralph. *Popul Vuh: The Great Mythological Book of the Ancient Maya*. Boston: Houghton Mifflin, 1974. An easy-to-read translation of myths handed down orally by the Quiche Maya, family to family, until written down after the Spanish conquest.

Riding, Alan. *Distant Neighbors*. Vintage Books. A modern look at today's Mexico.

The Rise and Fall of the Maya Civilization. Norman: University of Oklahoma Press, 1954. One man's story of the Maya. Excellent reading.

Sodi, Demetrio M. (in collaboration with Adela Fernández). *The Mayas*. Mexico: Panama Editorial S.A. This small pocketbook presents a fictionalized account of life among the Mayas before the conquest. Easy reading for anyone who enjoys fantasizing about what life *might* have been like before recorded history in the Yucatán.

Stephens, John L. *Incidents of Travel in Central America, Chiapas, and Yucatán*. 2 vols. New York: Dover Publications, 1969. Good companions to refer to when traveling in the area. Stephens and illustrator Frederick Catherwood rediscovered many of the Maya ruins on their treks that took place in the mid-1800s. Easy reading.

Thompson, J. Eric. *Maya Archaeologist*. Norman: University of Oklahoma Press, 1963. Thompson, a noted Maya scholar, traveled and worked at most of the Maya ruins in the 1930s.

Webster, David. *The Fall of the Ancient Maya*. New York: Thames and Hudson, 2002. A careful and thorough examination of the possible causes of one of archaeology's great unsolved mysteries—the collapse of the Classic Maya in the 8th century.

Werner, David. *Where There Is No Doctor*. Palo Alto, California: The Hesperian Foundation, 1992. This is an invaluable medical aid to anyone traveling not only to isolated parts of Mexico but to any place in the world where there's not a doctor.

Wolf, Eric. *Sons of the Shaking Earth*. University of Chicago Press, 1962. An anthropological study of the indigenous and mestizo people of Mexico and Guatemala.

Wright, Ronald. *Time Among the Maya*. New York: Weidenfeld and Nicolson, 1989. A narrative that takes the reader through the Maya country of today with historical comments that help put the puzzle together.

Internet Resources

www.campeche.gob.mx
Official website of the Campeche state tourism authority.

www.cancunmap.com
An excellent source of detailed maps of the Riviera Maya.

www.cancuntips.com.mx
The online version of Cancún's main tourist magazine, with tons of listings, travel tips, and tourist resources.

www.la5ta.com
The online version of a hip Playa del Carmen

magazine, with nightlife, restaurants, art, and culture listings.

www.locogringo.com

Privately operated website with extensive business listings for Playa del Carmen and other areas on the Riviera Maya.

www.mayayucatan.com

Official website of the Yucatán state tourism authority.

www.mesoweb.com

Detailed website relating to Mesoamerican cultures, including detailed reports and photos of past and current archaeological digs.

www.sedetur.qroo.gob.mx

Official website of the Quintana Roo state tourism authority.

www.turismochiapas.gob.mx

Official website of the Chiapas state tourism authority.

www.visitetabasco.com

Official website of the Tabasco state tourism authority.

www.yucatantoday.com

Website of the helpful monthly tourist magazine of the same name. Based in Mérida but contains coverage of all of Yucatán state.

Index

Acknowledgments

**To Eva Quetzal Chandler,
the love of our lives.**

Thank you first and foremost to the many, many residents of the Riviera Maya and Yucatán Peninsula, most of whose names we never learned, who helped us in the course of updating this book. From friendly bus drivers to helpful shop owners to patient hotel receptionists, they made this project possible and have our sincere gratitude.

Particular people we met along the way deserve special mention and thanks. We are indebted to Bob Rodríguez of Casa Colonial in Isla Cozumel, Curtis and Ashley at Villa La Bella in Isla Mujeres, and Rosy Besomi of La Bambina II in Isla Holbox. Along the Costa Maya, our many thanks to Carol and Alan at Hotel Balamkú, Carolien and Jan at Hotel Maya Luna, and Margo and Robert at Sin Duda.

We are fortunate to have—and extremely grateful to receive—such excellent editorial and production support from everyone at Avalon Travel Publishing. Thanks to Grace Fujimoto for sending us off on the right foot, Kevin McLain for his gentle and able shepherding during the research and writing, and Naomi Adler Dancis for her sharp editing. Thank you to Kevin Anglin and the cartography department for their excellent work on the maps, and Stefano Boni and others in the production department for making this book look so great. Thank you to Sarah Juckniess for navigating us through Avalon's administrative waters, and to Hannah Cox for arranging all those book talks and radio interviews, and for generally making us feel famous.

We'd like to extend, once again, a special acknowledgment to Chicki Mallan, who, with husband and photographer Oz Mallan, wrote the first six editions of this book—a remarkable achievement. Her dedication, experience, and enduring love for the Yucatán region are a model for any would-be travel writer.

Finally, and above all, thank you to our families and friends for their unwavering love and support: Mom and Dad Prado, Mom and Dad Chandler, Ellen, Elyse, Joey and Sue and the little one, Katy and Kyle and their little one, Brian and Becky and their little *two*—it's been a productive couple of years!—Dave, Javier, Debbie, Owen, Sammy, Tío Miguel, Kelly, Dan, Kaitlyn, TJ, Beatriz, Rich, Scott, Lulu, and Rukaiyah.

www.moon.com

For helpful advice on planning a trip, visit www.moon.com for the **TRAVEL PLANNER** and get access to useful travel strategies and valuable information about great places to visit. When you travel with Moon, expect an experience that is uncommon and truly unique.

HANDBOOKS | METRO | OUTDOORS | LIVING ABROAD

MAP SYMBOLS

▦ Expressway	⟨ Highlight	✗ Airfield	⚲ Golf Course
▦ Primary Road	○ City/Town	✈ Airport	℗ Parking Area
▦ Secondary Road	◉ State Capital	▲ Mountain	⬟ Archaeological Site
▦ Unpaved Road	⊛ National Capital	✦ Unique Natural Feature	⛪ Church
▦ Trail	★ Point of Interest		
▦ Ferry	• Accommodation	≋ Waterfall	⛽ Gas Station
⊢⊢⊢ Railroad	▼ Restaurant/Bar	▲ Park	⬡ Glacier
▦ Pedestrian Walkway	■ Other Location	⊟ Trailhead	▦ Mangrove
▦ Stairs	⋀ Campground	�skiing Skiing Area	▦ Reef
			▦ Swamp

CONVERSION TABLES

°C = (°F - 32) / 1.8
°F = (°C x 1.8) + 32
1 inch = 2.54 centimeters (cm)
1 foot = 0.304 meters (m)
1 yard = 0.914 meters
1 mile = 1.6093 kilometers (km)
1 km = 0.6214 miles
1 fathom = 1.8288 m
1 chain = 20.1168 m
1 furlong = 201.168 m
1 acre = 0.4047 hectares
1 sq km = 100 hectares
1 sq mile = 2.59 square km
1 ounce = 28.35 grams
1 pound = 0.4536 kilograms
1 short ton = 0.90718 metric ton
1 short ton = 2,000 pounds
1 long ton = 1.016 metric tons
1 long ton = 2,240 pounds
1 metric ton = 1,000 kilograms
1 quart = 0.94635 liters
1 US gallon = 3.7854 liters
1 Imperial gallon = 4.5459 liters
1 nautical mile = 1.852 km

MOON CANCÚN & COZUMEL

Avalon Travel Publishing
a member of the Perseus Books Group
1400 65th Street, Suite 250
Emeryville, CA 94608, USA
www.moon.com

Editors: Naomi Adler Dancis, Grace Fujimoto
Series Manager: Kathryn Ettinger
Copy Editor: Mary Miller
Graphics Coordinator: Stefano Boni
Production Coordinator: Darren Alessi
Cover Designer: Stefano Boni
Map Editor: Kevin Anglin
Cartographers: Chris Markiewicz, Kat Bennett,
    Suzanne Service
Cartography Director: Mike Morgenfeld
Indexer: Rachel Kuhn

ISBN-10: 1-56691-780-8
ISBN-13: 978-1-56691-780-3
ISSN: 1556-5122

Printing History
1st Edition – 1990
8th Edition – October 2007
5 4 3 2 1

Text © 2007 by Chicki Mallan and
    Avalon Travel Publishing, Inc.
Maps © 2007 by Avalon Travel Publishing, Inc.
All rights reserved.

Some photos and illustrations are used by permission
and are the property of the original copyright
owners.

Front cover photo: © Liza Prado
Title page photo: © Liza Prado
Front matter photos: Pages 8–13, 21, 24, 26, 27, 29–32
© Liza Prado

Printed in the United States by Worzalla

Moon Handbooks and the Moon logo are the property
of Avalon Travel Publishing. All other marks and
logos depicted are the property of the original
owners. All rights reserved. No part of this book may
be translated or reproduced in any form, except brief
extracts by a reviewer for the purpose of a review,
without written permission of the copyright owner.

Although every effort was made to ensure that
the information was correct at the time of going
to press, the author and publisher do not assume
and hereby disclaim any liability to any party for any
loss or damage caused by errors, omissions, or any
potential travel disruption due to labor or financial
difficulty, whether such errors or omissions result
from negligence, accident, or any other cause.

KEEPING CURRENT

If you have a favorite gem you'd like to see included in the next edition, or see anything that needs updating, clarification, or correction, please drop us a line. Send your comments via email to feedback@moon.com, or use the address above.